WITHDRAWN

CAMBRIDGE STUDIES
IN ENGLISH LEGAL HISTORY

Edited by
S. J. BAILEY
*Fellow of St. John's College, Cambridge,
and Rouse Ball Professor of English Law;
Barrister-at-Law, Inner Temple*

ENGLISH LAW IN IRELAND
1290-1324

BY

G. J. HAND

Of King's Inns, Dublin, Barrister-at-Law;
Lecturer in Legal and Constitutional History
at University College, Dublin

CAMBRIDGE
AT THE UNIVERSITY PRESS
1967

Published by the Syndics of the Cambridge University Press
Bentley House, 200 Euston Road, London, N.W.1
American Branch: 32 East 57th Street, New York, N.Y. 10022

© Cambridge University Press 1967

Library of Congress Catalogue Card Number: 67-13804

Printed in Great Britain
at the University Printing House, Cambridge
(Brooke Crutchley, University Printer)

CONTENTS

Preface		*page* vii
List of Abbreviations		ix
I	Introduction: The First Century of English Law in Ireland	1
II	Governors of a Troubled Lordship	21
III	The Justiciar's Court	40
IV	The Dublin Bench and the Exchequer	89
V	The General Eyre and other Commissions	104
VI	Liberties and Franchises	113
VII	The Irish Jurisdiction of English Courts	135
VIII	Statutes	159
IX	The Custom of the Land of Ireland	172
X	The Status of the Native Irish at English Law	187
XI	*Una et eadem Lex:* The Place of Law in the History of the Lordship	214

Appendices

I	The Justices Itinerant, 1248 to 1269	219
II	Examples of the writ *procedendo ad judicium*, with clause *si difficultas*	223
III	List of Justiciary Rolls, Edward I–II	226
IV	Sessions of the Justiciar's Court during the Lieutenancy of Roger Mortimer, 1317–18	230
V	Analyses of Justiciary Rolls	233

CONTENTS

VI List of Rolls of the Dublin Bench, Edward I–II *page* 241

VII Analyses of Rolls of the Bench 244

VIII List of Itinerant Justices' Rolls, Henry III–Edward I 247

IX Analysis of Pleas of the Crown and Gaol Delivery, Eyre of Kildare, 1297–8 249

Bibliography 251

Table of Statutes 262

Index 265

MAPS

1 Places mentioned in the text *facing page* 1

2 Sessions of the Justiciar's Court, September 1312–August 1313 59

PREFACE

MUCH of this book represents work done in the preparation of a thesis for the degree of Doctor of Philosophy of the University of Oxford. The years 1290 and 1324 were initially adopted as limits in the light of what was then thought concerning the evolution of the principal Irish court, that of the justiciar. In fact, 1290 proved to be less appropriate in this particular context than had been anticipated, though there is no question that 1324 marks an important step in the development of the justiciar's personal court towards an independent Irish king's bench. But other justifications for these limits soon appeared, even apart from the familiar division of the reign of Edward I at about 1290. Almost all the justiciary rolls to survive to modern times came from between these years, while the earliest original roll of the Dublin bench now surviving and the first eyre rolls of Edward I for which we have substantial texts come from 1290. 1290 witnessed, in the appointment of William de Vescy as justiciar, and 1324, in that of John Darcy, important occasions in the history of the chief governorship of Ireland. The years between deserve to be called, more fittingly than any other period, 'the climax of medieval Ireland'.

In its earliest stages, my work was supervised by Professor V. H. Galbraith, and one of my chief debts is to him, for characteristically critical, stimulating—and entertaining—encouragement. Mr G. D. G. Hall, to whom the task of supervision was transferred, provided patient and painstaking guidance into unfamiliar areas of medieval English law. Miss M. C. Griffith, Deputy-Keeper of the Public Records of Ireland, not only helped with her deep knowledge of the records under her care but also generously allowed me to make use of a transcript she had prepared of the sole surviving justiciary roll.

Dr A. G. Donaldson, Dr R. A. Griffiths, and Dr J. F. Lydon facilitated my consultation of their unpublished theses. A like kindness was done by one who unfortunately has not lived to read this expression of thanks. To some it may be surprising to learn that the late Professor Arthur Redford, whose later distinction was in so different a field of historical study, was the author of a remarkable Manchester B.A. thesis (1915), 'The Climax of Medieval Ireland'. The value, as an introduction, of this able survey from the major printed sources, which Professor Redford went to considerable inconvenience to make available to me, proved to be great, but of its nature such assistance cannot be made sufficiently apparent in the text and foot-notes of the present book, and it is therefore particularly acknowledged here. In passing, one must lament that, though Professor Redford's thesis was lent to Edmund Curtis when he was preparing the first edition of *Medieval Ireland* (1923), he made astonishingly little use of it. Had Curtis done otherwise, some criticisms of his work by later scholars would have been less necessary.

There are other acknowledgments that can no longer be made as I should wish. The late H. E. Bell prolonged his duties as moral tutor into a most helpful concern for the revision of the work for publication. My late father, J. A. Hand, read early drafts, which often profited by his critical insistence on clarity and legal precision.

One expression of gratitude is imperative above all others upon a student of the medieval lordship of Ireland. Mr H. G. Richardson and Professor G. O. Sayles have taught us nearly all we know of the institutions and administration of the lordship. Much of what I have written is barely more than an exploration of territory which they have already mapped in outline. But, in addition to this common indebtedness, I have incurred personal obligations, for their assistance and advice has been courteous and unfailing.

I must thank the President and Council of the Royal Irish Academy for permission to incorporate in chapter III material published in the Academy's *Proceedings*, vol. LXII (1962); and my colleagues on the Board of *The Irish Jurist*, for a similar permission in the case of the greater part of chapter X. My thanks are also due to Mr Douglas Grainger, who drew the maps.

May 1967 G. J. H.

LIST OF ABBREVIATIONS

I. REFERENCES TO RECORDS IN THE PUBLIC RECORD OFFICE OF IRELAND (P.R.O.I.)

Transcripts and translations of copyright records in the Public Record Office of Ireland appear by permission of the Deputy-Keeper.

It should be noted that, with the exception of the references RC. 7 and RC. 8, the abbreviations which follow are not office class references.

C.P.   Common pleas (Dublin Bench).
J.I.   Justices Itinerant.
J.R.   Justiciary Roll. Followed by a membrane reference, this may variously refer to an original or to English calendars in manuscript: see Appendix III.
Mem.   Memoranda Roll.
RC. 7   Irish Record Commission papers, Calendar of Plea Rolls. For details of the method followed in citing this class, and RC. 8, see p. 90, n. 3, below.
RC. 8   Irish Record Commission papers, Calendar of Memoranda Rolls.

II. REFERENCES TO RECORDS IN THE PUBLIC RECORD OFFICE, LONDON (P.R.O.)

Transcripts and translations of Crown copyright records in the following classes in the Public Record Office, London, appear by permission of the Controller of H.M. Stationery Office.

C. 47   Miscellanea of the Chancery
C. 49   Parliamentary and Council Proceedings (Chancery)
C. 54   Close rolls
C. 62   *Liberate* rolls (Chancery)
C. 66   Patent rolls
C. 81   Warrants for the Great Seal, series I
E. 13   Exchequer of Pleas, Plea rolls
E. 101   Exchequer, K.R., Various accounts
E. 163   Exchequer, K.R., Miscellanea of the Exchequer
E. 372   Pipe rolls
Just. Itin. 1   Eyre rolls, Assize rolls, etc.
K.B. 26   *Curia regis* rolls
K.B. 27   *Coram rege* rolls

x LIST OF ABBREVIATIONS

S.C. 1 Ancient Correspondence
S.C. 8 Ancient Petitions
S.C. 9 Parliament rolls (Exchequer series)

III. OTHER ABBREVIATIONS

Abbreviated references to the modern series of record publications are not included in the following list, as it is thought that they are sufficiently self-explanatory.

Anal. hib. — *Analecta hibernica* (Irish MSS. Comm.).
Arch. hib. — *Archivium hibernicum.*
Cal. rot. pat. Hib. — *Rotulorum patentium et clausorum cancellariae Hiberniae calendarium.* Ir. rec. comm. 1828.
C.J.R. — *Calendar of justiciary rolls.* In progress. Dublin, 1905–
Cole, Documents — *Documents illustrative of English history in the thirteenth and fourteenth centuries.* Ed. H. Cole. Rec. comm. 1844.
Curtis, Medieval Ireland — E. Curtis, *Medieval Ireland.* References throughout, unless otherwise stated, are to the second edition (London, 1938).
E.H.R. — *English Historical review.*
Hist. & mun. doc. Ir. — *Historical and municipal documents of Ireland.* Ed. J. T. Gilbert. Rolls ser. 1870.
Holdsworth — Sir William Holdsworth, *History of English law* (edition as specified in each case).
I.H.S. — *Irish historical studies.*
I.R. — *Irish Reports.*
Irish arch. soc. — Irish archaeological society.
Irish MSS Comm. — Irish manuscripts commission.
Ir. rec. comm. rep. — *Reports of the commissioners appointed to execute the measures recommended respecting the public records of Ireland.* 3 vols. London, 1815–25.
M. — Michaelmas (term).
N.I.L.Q. — *Northern Ireland legal quarterly.*
Orpen — G. H. Orpen, *Ireland under the Normans.* 4 vols. Oxford, 1911–20.
P. — Easter (term).
Pollock and Maitland — F. Pollock and F. W. Maitland, *A history of English law.* 2nd ed.; Cambridge, 1898.
P.R.I. rep. D.K. 1 [etc.] — *First* [etc.] *report of the deputy keeper of the public records of Ireland.* In progress. Dublin, 1869–

LIST OF ABBREVIATIONS

R.I.A. Proc.   *Proceedings of the Royal Irish Academy.*
Richardson and Sayles, *The Irish Parliament*   H. G. Richardson and G. O. Sayles, *The Irish parliament in the middle ages.* Philadelphia, 1952.
Richardson and Sayles, *Administration*   H. G. Richardson and G. O. Sayles, *The administration of medieval Ireland.* Irish MSS. Comm. 1963.
R.S.A.I. Jn.   *Journal of the Royal Society of Antiquaries of Ireland.*
S.S.   Selden Society.
T.   Trinity (term).
Y.B.   Year Book.

NOTE: All references to the *Calendar of documents relating to Ireland* (*Cal. doc. Ire.*) are by item number, except where page ('p.') is expressly indicated.

MAP I. PLACES MENTIONED

CHAPTER I

INTRODUCTION: THE FIRST CENTURY OF ENGLISH LAW IN IRELAND

IRELAND was the scene of the first of those extensions which have helped to make the common law one of the principal legal traditions of the world. The men who from 1169 crossed the Irish Sea brought with them their customary law, as they brought their accustomed speech. The author of the *chanson de geste* which commemorates their coming does not tell us that, when

> Esteit herberge la tere
> E de chastels e de cites,
> De dunguns e de fermetes.
> Ki ben est aracinez
> Les gentils vassals aloses,[1]

a pattern of seignorial courts was likewise established; yet it must have been so. Those years of territorial expansion of English law were in addition years in which it was developing in ways which, under royal guidance, tended to make it truly a law common to all the realm. A conscious, efficient and uniform introduction to Ireland of English law, thus developed and developing, had to wait upon the establishment of an adequate organization to govern the lordship which Henry II gave to his son John in 1177. Before the end of the twelfth century, indeed, the authority of the lord of Ireland found expression in the rudiments of later Irish administration.[2] But the placing of English law and legal institutions upon a firm basis in Ireland is attributed to King John after his accession had united the lordship to the English crown.

As early as 1204 John authorized his justiciar in Ireland to issue five of the most needed original writs—right, mort d'ancestor, novel disseisin, *de fugitivis et nativis* and *de divisis faciendis*—and

[1] 'The country was planted with castles and with cities, with keeps and with strongholds; thus the noble renowned vassals were well-rooted': *Song of Dermot and the Earl*, ed. G. H. Orpen (Oxford, 1892), ll. 3203-7.
[2] H. G. Richardson, 'Norman Ireland in 1212', *I.H.S.* III (1942), 144-58, at p. 149.

set the limitations to be observed.[1] On his visit in 1210, according to the chronicler Roger of Wendover, John *fecit quoque ibidem constituere leges et consuetudines Anglicanas*.[2] A council was held at Dublin at which the magnates of the lordship and, probably, some native rulers swore to English law and this formal acknowledgment was followed by the issue of a charter, no text of which survives.[3] Those who governed in the minority of Henry III continued his father's policy in these matters. The Great Charter, as issued on 12 November 1216, was sent to Ireland in the following year.[4] In 1222, procedure on the writ *de divisis faciendis* and the limitation of mort d'ancestor were brought into line with English practice.[5]

The second justiciarship of Geoffrey Marsh (1226-8) was especially marked by measures to strengthen English law in Ireland. Within days of his appointment, Geoffrey was ordered, on 29 June 1226, to keep and cause to be kept the laws and customs of England, as enjoined by King John.[6] On 8 July, he was instructed to see that certain assizes were held in the manner customary since John came *ad leges et consuetudines Anglicanas assidendas*.[7] In December of the same year the application of the curtesy of England to Ireland was stressed and a month later English practice with regard to contumacious excommunicated persons enjoined.[8] In November 1227 perhaps the most important practical step towards uniformity of law was taken: a register of

[1] *Rot. litt. pat.* p. 47; *Rot. liberate*, pp. 105–6. The two writs last named are apparently *de nativo habendo* and *de rationabilibus divisis*.
[2] *Flores historiarum* (Rolls ser.), II, 56.
[3] The principal official allusions are found in letters of Henry III in 1226, 1228 and 1233 (*Patent rolls, 1225–32*, p. 96; *Close rolls, 1227–31*, p. 45; *Cal. pat. rolls, 1232–47*, p. 31); they are discussed by H. G. Richardson and G. O. Sayles, *The Irish parliament in the middle ages* (Philadelphia, 1952), p. 12, n. 11.
[4] *Patent rolls, 1216–25*, p. 31. Ireland and the Great Charter is a vexed question with an extensive historiography. A. G. Donaldson has an excellent discussion in an unfortunately unpublished thesis (Ph.D., Q.U.B. 1952), 'The application in Ireland of English and British legislation made before 1801', pp. 48–59. The leading case in modern Irish law is *Little* v. *Cooper* [1937] I.R. 1. Cf. also H. G. Richardson, 'Magna Carta Hiberniae', *I.H.S.* III (1942), 31–3.
[5] *Rot. litt. claus. 1204–24*, p. 497 (but cf. *ibid.* p. 532 and pp. 173–4, below); *Patent rolls, 1216–25*, p. 336.
[6] *Patent rolls, 1216–25*, p. 48.
[7] *Rot. litt. claus. 1224–7*, p. 128.
[8] *Ibid.* p. 166; *Patent rolls, 1225–32*, p. 96.

writs was dispatched for use in Ireland.[1] Some months after Geoffrey left office his successor, Richard de Burgh, was ordered (8 May 1228) to summon the magnates and tenants of Ireland and read to them King John's charter of 1210 concerning the law of England.[2] In March 1229 a particular case was made the occasion of enjoining the rule, necessary in justification of the *casus regis*, that a younger son inherits before the son of his deceased elder brother.[3]

Early in the justiciarship of Maurice fitz Gerald (1232–45) English practice was ordered to be followed in regard to the writ of bounds and pleas of advowson.[4] The years 1236 to 1238 are especially notable in the extension of English law. The statute of Merton was sent to Ireland, the doing of homage by co-parceners regulated, and the writ of escheat through bastardy transmitted.[5] The maintenance of conformity in the law and practice of the lordship was again particularly stressed under the justiciar John fitz Geoffrey (1245–56). He had not been many weeks in Ireland when the principle was reiterated (9 September 1246) in letters patent which stated that the king

vult quod omnia brevia de communi jure que currunt in Anglia similiter currant in Hibernia.[6]

This may well bear out the suggestion of the late G. J. Turner that when John fitz Geoffrey became justiciar a formulary of writs and pleadings was provided for his use, which may have become the basis of the collection known as *Brevia placitata*.[7] It is noteworthy that at a later time some Irish prelates blamed John fitz Geoffrey for having taken away what they claimed to be ancient liberties of the church—meaning, no doubt, that he

---

[1] F. W. Maitland, 'The introduction of English law into Ireland', *E.H.R.* IV (1889), 516–17 (*Collected papers*, ed. H. A. L. Fisher [Cambridge, 1911], II, 81–3); 'History of the register of original writs', 3 *Harvard Law Rev.* pp. 97–115, 167–79, 212–25 (*Select essays in Anglo-American legal history* [Boston, 1907–9], II, 549–96, and *Collected papers*, II, 110–73).
[2] *Close rolls, 1227–31*, p. 45.
[3] *Ibid.* p. 236.
[4] *Cal. pat. rolls, 1232–47*, p. 31; *Close rolls, 1234–7*, p. 157.
[5] *Close rolls, 1234–7*, pp. 353–5 (cf. p. 501 and *Cal. pat. rolls, 1232–47*, pp. 176–7), 376–7 and *1237–42*, p. 123.
[6] *Foedera* (Rec. comm. ed.), I, 1, 266. A new seal was evidently sent to Ireland for his use.
[7] *Brevia placitata*, ed. G. J. Turner (S.S. LXVI), pp. xxvi–ix.

sought to conform Irish to English practice in such matters.[1] The need to standardize writs was again emphasized in letters of 1254 and 1257, arising out of particular cases:

volumus quod brevia nostra que placitari debent in Hibernia sint in eadem forma concepta et confecta qua et [sic] brevia nostra que [?] placitantur in Anglia.[2]

In the latter part of the century uniformity of law became a question of applying the great new statutes to Ireland, rather than of reiterating the traditional rules of common law, by then adequately inculcated in the lordship. The application of these statutes to Ireland raises one of the most contested topics of Irish legal and constitutional controversy over the centuries—was any form of ratification in Ireland required before English statutes bound the lordship?[3] An authoritative recent view is that 'English legislation was, in principle, applicable to Ireland'.[4] Alone of the great thirteenth-century statutes, however, the Statute of Merchants (1285) contained an express provision applying it to Ireland. The preamble to the Statute of Westminster II (1285) declared that the king's *populus Anglicanus et Hibernicus* had profited by the remedies contained in the Statute of Gloucester (1278). Amongst the earliest surviving legislation of an Irish parliament (1278) there is a clause which implies some deliberation upon the question of English statutes, though the text is now disappointingly defective:

En dreit de les estatuz de Engletere à tenir en ceste tere n'en est mie ... par ... hauz hommes.[5]

[1] Lambeth Library MS 619, f. 206r (printed by M. P. Sheehy, 'English law in medieval Ireland', *Archiv. Hib.* XXIII (1960), pp. 167–75, at p. 175).

[2] *Close rolls, 1253–4*, p. 114 (P.R.O., C. 54, no. 67, m. 13d), and *1256–9*, p. 120.

[3] Rival seventeenth-century pamphlets of importance are: Anon. [attributed to R. Bolton and also to P. Darcy], 'A declaration setting forth how, and by what means, the laws and statutes of England came to be of force in Ireland', and S. Mayart, 'The answer of Sir Samuel Mayart ... to a book entitled, *A declaration* ... [*as before*]', both in W. Harris, *Hibernica* (Dublin, 1770), part 2, pp. 9–231. There are useful comments in ch. II ('Irish patriotism and British imperialism') of R. L. Schuyler, *Parliament and the British Empire* (New York, 1929), pp. 40–101. The best modern discussion—unhappily unpublished—is in Donaldson, 'Application of English legislation', pp. 318–75; some of the points made are accessible in his *Some comparative aspects of Irish law* (Durham, N.C. 1957) and in *Statutes revised: Northern Ireland*, I, p. lxxxix.

[4] Richardson and Sayles, *The Irish parliament*, p. 92.

[5] *Ibid.* p. 292.

INTRODUCTION

At all events, the statutes of Westminster I, Gloucester, Merchants and Westminster II were given to a clerk of the then justiciar on 14 September 1285 *in Hiberniam deferenda et ibidem proclamanda et observanda*.[1] Here there is adaptation of the ordinary procedure of communication of statutes to suit the administrative special case of Ireland, but there is no suggestion of any need for ratification in that country.[2] Similarly, the so-called Statute of Money of 1284 was ordered to be enforced in Ireland in 1289.[3] Curiously, although both the statute of Rhuddlan (1284) and that of Mortmain (1279) were entered in the Red Book of the Irish exchequer, probably begun under Edward I, neither was mentioned in the list sent over in 1285.[4] By its nature as exchequer provisions the Statute of Rhuddlan hardly called for the type of publication which was then employed, but the application of the statute of Mortmain to Ireland is a more difficult problem, which will be discussed in a later chapter. The application of the statute of Marlborough (1267) to Ireland in this period has been questioned.[5] But, although there is no evidence of express extension, there is sufficient evidence of user to dispel the doubt. The writ of entry in the *post* given by the statute (c. 29) was used in the Dublin bench in 1278, and in 1286, in the course of proceedings upon such a writ, reference was made to the publication of the statute in Ireland.[6] In general, however, the paucity of the surviving evidence makes detailed study of the application of English statutes in Ireland impossible until after 1290. The most that can be said is that formal extension and publication, as in 1285, was one means of application, which may also have occurred in cases of which no record of the circumstances survives, and that user without formal transmission took place to an extent that cannot be accurately assessed.

[1] *Stat. Ire., John–Hen. V*, p. 46.
[2] On the publication of statutes in general, H. G. Richardson and G. O. Sayles, 'The early statutes', 50 *L.Q.R.* (1934), pp. 201–23, 540–71, at pp. 545–6.
[3] H. G. Richardson, *The English Jewry under Angevin kings* (Jewish Hist. Soc. 1960), p. 221.
[4] *Stat. Ire., John–Hen. V*, pp. 36–45.
[5] By J. Mills in his introduction to *C.J.R. 1305–7*, p. iii.
[6] C.P., 6 Edw. I, in P.R.O.I., RC. 8/1, *Cal. mem. rolls*, I, 26, 58, 63; P.R.O., K.B. 27/124, m. 8 (*Cal. doc. Ire. 1285–92*, 666). In 1295, c. 23 (*monstravit de compoto*) was employed in the Dublin bench: C.P., M. 23–4 Edw. I, in P.R.O.I., *Cal. plea rolls*, III, 380. This evidence is in addition to arguments adduced to the same effect by Donaldson: 'Application of English legislation', pp. 75–6.

We may now turn to the early history of the principal courts which administered English law in Ireland. First in importance among them was that which grew around the person of the representative of the lord of Ireland. The justiciar Meiler fitz Henry (?1198–1200 and 1200–8) had evidently enjoyed a jurisdiction in civil pleas before general powers to hold pleas of the crown were conferred on him in 1207.[1] The oath to be administered to Maurice fitz Gerald when he took office in 1232 included

quod justiciam faciet cuilibet de regno secundum legale posse suum et legalem scientiam suam, secundum consuetudines regni.[2]

It is clear that, as well as exercising original jurisdiction, both civil and criminal, the justiciar was capable of hearing cases brought in various ways before him from other courts, but the failure of any justiciary rolls of earlier date than 1295 to survive to modern times makes it impossible to say much more of the nature of his judicial business before then. The *curia regis Hibernie*, mentioned in 1199, was apparently before the justiciar.[3] There is one reference, in 1230, to proceedings as *coram rege in curia sua apud Dublin'*.[4] But this is an isolated instance of a style that was not regularly adopted until the presence of Richard II had, for a brief time, made it literally accurate.[5] From 1233 '*coram* [the justiciar of the day]' becomes the usual description of proceedings, though the earliest full heading of pleas to survive comes from nearly half-a-century later:

Placita corone coram Roberto de Dofford capitali justiciario apud Dublin' in octabis sancti Martini anno regni regis Edwardi sexto.[6]

As we shall see, a permanent judicial assistant to the justiciar was appointed towards the end of the century and the justiciar's court then emerges with a distinct personnel.[7]

[1] *Rot. chart.* p. 98; *Rot. litt. pat.* p. 76 and cf. p. 80.
[2] *Close rolls, 1231–4*, p. 103.
[3] *Rot. oblatis*, p. 36; cf. *Rot. litt. pat.* pp. 45, 56.
[4] *Close rolls, 1227–31*, p. 453.
[5] *Ire. rec. comm. rep. 1816–20*, pp. 101–3 (headings of rolls now destroyed).
[6] *Close rolls, 1231–4*, p. 293, and *1242–7*, pp. 253–4; *Chartularies of St Mary's abbey, Dublin* (Rolls ser.), I, 1.
[7] Chapter III, below; for the special case of Roger Huscarl in 1222–3, H. G. Richardson and G. O. Sayles, *The administration of medieval Ireland* (Irish MSS. Comm. 1963), pp. 33–4.

INTRODUCTION 7

For the greater part of the thirteenth century the itinerant justices at work in Ireland formed a judiciary only later differentiated into separate courts. There are references to these justices under John.[1] In March 1221, as there was only one regular justice itinerant, and consequently only one, uncontrolled, roll, two more justices, a knight and a clerk, were appointed to sit with him, each to have his roll.[2] In the eyre of Waterford at Easter 1228 the justiciar presided, with two itinerant justices, and the activity of these justices is amply attested in the succeeding years.[3]

The emergence of a common bench sedentary at Dublin seems to have occurred about the middle of the century through differentiation of function in the itinerant court rather than, initially, of personnel.[4] From 1236, phrases such as *coram justic' nostris in curia Dublin'* occur, which may or may not refer to such a court.[5] The first seemingly unambiguous reference comes in 1248: *coram justic' regis in banco Dublin'*.[6] Similar references are found in 1251 and 1255.[7] The pipe roll of 45 Henry III refers to estreats of the bench of the forty-third and forty-fifth years.[8] The first reference to an individual justice as *in banco* is in an *inspeximus* of 1262, but no other is found until 1273.[9] The first reference to

[1] *Rot. litt. pat.* p. 76; *Irish pipe roll, 14 John* (supplement to *Ulster Jn. of archaeology*, 3rd ser. IV), p. 18; *Chartae, privilegia et immunitates* (Ir. rec. comm.), p. 14.

[2] *Rot. litt. claus. 1204–24*, p. 451. Richardson and Sayles, *Administration*, p. 30, take the view that what happened in 1221 was merely a prohibition of justices sitting alone, rather than an addition to the judiciary; but it seems likely that both elements were present in some degree.

[3] *Close rolls, 1227–31*, pp. 60–1; many references will be found in *Cal. doc. Ire. 1171–1251*, after this date.

[4] Cf. Richardson and Sayles, *Administration*, pp. 32–3, where the emergence is put by 1240, but the early evidence is not wholly compelling.

[5] *Close rolls, 1234–7*, p. 393; *1237–42*, p. 113 (*justic' Hibernie*); *1247–51*, p. 102 (*justic' Dublin'*). Care must be taken with the printed text of the close rolls as the editors seem invariably to have expanded *justic'* as *justiciarii* even where [*capitalis*] *justiciarius* is a more probable meaning: e.g. *Close rolls, 1234–7*, pp. 435, 535. All the references in this and the succeeding note have been verified against the originals and the meaning and correct expansion concluded from the context.

[6] *Close rolls, 1247–51*, p. 116.

[7] *Ibid. 1251–3*, p. 179; 'Rôle Gascon de lettres closes, 1254–5' (ed. C. Bémont, in *Bulletin philologique et historique*, *1915*), no. 13.

[8] R.I.A., MS 12 D 9, ff. 38 (Kildare county, *de banco*), 30 (Dublin county, *justic' de banco*); but cf. also f. 10 (*justic' de banco apud Drochd'*).

[9] *Calendar of archbishop Alen's register*, ed. C. McNeill (R.S.A.I. 1950), p. 96; *Cal. pat. rolls, 1272–81*, p. 3 (*Cal. doc. Ire. 1252–84*, 947). In the context *in banco* is plainly equivalent to *de banco*, meaning 'of the bench', rather than 'in court'.

a chief justice of the bench is in the pipe roll of 46 Henry III.[1] On the other hand, mention was made in 1255 of proceedings as *in curia nostra coram justic' nostris itinerantibus apud Dublin'*.[2] A list of justices, chiefly drawn from final concords, for the years 1248 to 1269 is revealing. They are invariably described as *justiciarii itinerantes*. They are almost always mentioned in the same order and the composition of the court is strikingly constant. The same three justices were at Limerick in Trinity term, 1251, as at Dublin in the following Easter term, and pairs of them differently combined appear again at Limerick in Trinity 1252 (for crown as well as common pleas) and Michaelmas 1253.[3] An eyre of Cork *ad omnia placita* in 1260 shows two regular justices at work with two others, one of whom appears regularly at a somewhat later time. At Limerick in 1261 and 1267 the courts were almost identical with those found at Dublin about the same time. The court evidently settled more and more at Dublin, however, so that itineration came to hold a secondary place among the activities of the justices. Between 1252 and 1269 no final concord survives made at Dublin in any term from which there is one made elsewhere. Probably sessions were suspended at Dublin when most of the justices itinerated, as was the practice in the English bench somewhat earlier in rather similar circumstances.[4] But it is to be observed that the same justice might be at Dublin for part of a term and itinerate in another part.[5]

In 1274 Robert Bagod was appointed chief justice of the bench in terms which make it clear that he was to go on *iter* as well as presiding in the court at Dublin:

[1] *P.R.I. rep. D.K. 35*, p. 43 (Tipperary county). Presumably Walrand of Wellesley is meant: cf. Appendix I, below. But the roll has now been destroyed and the English calendar may represent a misunderstanding of *capitalis justiciarius*, meaning the justiciar. Cf. 'Sheriff's account of the honor of Dungarvan... 1261-3' (*ed.* E. Curtis, *R.I.A. Proc.* XXXIX, 1-17), p. 9 (Waterford county, 46 Hen. III), and 'Sheriff's account for county Tipperary, 1275-6', (*ed.* Curtis, *ibid.* XLII, 65-95), p. 85 (Limerick).

[2] *Close rolls, 1254-6*, p. 374; of course, an eyre *ad omnia placita* is possibly in question.

[3] The evidence will be found tabulated in Appendix I, 'The Justices Itinerant, 1248 to 1269'.

[4] C. A. F. Meekings, *Crown pleas of the Wiltshire Eyre, 1249* (Devizes, 1961), p. 2.

[5] A fine was made before Alexander of Nottingham in the quinzaine of Michaelmas 1267, at Dublin, but the morrow of All Souls found him at Cashel; *Reg. St Thomas, Dublin* (Rolls ser.), p. 100; P.R.O., K.B. 27/92, m. 7 (*Cal. doc. Ire. 1285-92*, 58).

INTRODUCTION 9

sciatis quod constituimus . . . Robertum Bagod capitalem justiciarium nostrum ad placita nostra in banco nostro Dublin' tenenda et ad itinerandum ad communia placita in terra nostra predicta . . .[1]

He remained in office for over twenty years. A heading of pleas in the bench (*coram Roberto Bagod et sociis suis justiciariis de banco D[ublinie]*) survives from 1276.[2] It appears that by the eighties itinerant activities were coming to an end and the English pattern was being more precisely followed, so that the justices of the bench remained permanently at Dublin. In 1284 Robert Bagod personally was relieved of the obligation to itinerate,[3] while in 1288 a writ recited *cum itinera justiciariorum in partibus Hibernie ob certas causas in presenti se non habeant ut solebant*.[4] The earliest of the rolls of the bench that survived until the virtual destruction of the Public Record Office of Ireland and its contents in 1922 came from 1278 and 1280–2.[5] They do not suggest that the justices were engaged on itinerant activities of the kind encountered earlier. Attendance on the justiciar remained a claim on their services, however. About 1280, there is reference to *aukun des justices del Baunk ki la chef justice acumpaignont a luy a cele assise prendre*.[6] In 1284 or 1285 the sending of some records summoned to England was delayed by the absence of Robert Bagod in Munster with the justiciar, and in 1287 similar circumstances led to other difficulties.[7]

At all events, by 1290 the bench consisted of Robert Bagod, at a fee of forty pounds a year, and several puisne judges at fees ranging between twenty pounds and fifty marks. The earliest

[1] *Foedera* (Rec. comm. ed.), I, II, 518. *Communia placita* need not exclude pleas of the crown: cf. C. A. F. Meekings, *List of rolls and writs of the court coram rege* (MS. in P.R.O. literary search-room), p. 19; Sayles, *Select cases in K.B.* IV, p. xxxii. *Placita nostra* presents a difficulty. In this context, it can scarely mean either *placita corone* or *proprie cause regis*: cf. Sayles, *ibid*.

[2] C.P., P. 18 Edw. I, m. 9.

[3] *Cal. pat. rolls, 1281–92*, p. 119.

[4] Cole, *Documents*, p. 84.

[5] Appendix VI, below. Ten of the twenty-one membranes calendared as C.P., 6 Edw. I, in P.R.O.I., RC. 8/1, *Cal. mem. rolls*, I, 1–101, are in fact a record of quite a different kind, being pleas of the crown of, possibly, an eyre of Dublin (or even portion of a justiciary roll): cf. Richardson and Sayles, *The Irish parliament*, pp. 294–7.

[6] P.R.O., S.C. 1/30, no. 166.

[7] P.R.O., S.C. 1/23, no. 146; *Select cases in K.B.*, II, 49. Bagod may perhaps have been frequently away: e.g., for part of Easter term, 1290 (C.P., 18 Edw. I, mm. 10, 10*d*).

plea roll known in modern times, that of 6 Edw. I, reveals the court engaged in hearing the standard actions of thirteenth-century common law: right of land, mort d'ancestor, novel disseisin, and litigation concerning dower provided the bulk of the business. Put another way, of the one hundred and forty or so cases known to have appeared on the roll, there were over seventy pleas relating to land, twenty-six involved questions of marriage, dower, and minors, ten were appeals and trespasses, and eight concerned such matters as advowsons, debts and chattels.[1]

Some at least of the sessions in which justices of the bench took part outside Dublin were eyres *ad omnia placita*. Five rolls of such business survived from the reign of Henry III until 1922. Pleas of the crown are known to have been recorded on three of them.[2] Later, in successive eyres in 1278–9 Richard of Exeter was the principal justice and it is possible that this was a recognized office.[3] A little is known of the constitution of the eyre of Tipperary which began on 14 January 1289, when the personnel of the Dublin bench and the itinerant court seem to have become quite distinct. There was no justiciar, strictly speaking, at the time, but the chief governor, the *custos*, Archbishop John of Sandford, attended on the first day and instructed the justices. The chancellor and escheator were also present for part of the eyre. Of the six justices, five are found on eyre at Limerick in the next year.[4] The destruction of the rolls of the Irish chancery in 1304[5] reduces our knowledge of special commissions, however, to a few under the English seal.[6] Such activities as those of justices of gaol delivery are known only from incidental references.[7]

---

[1] C.P., 6 Edw. I, in P.R.O.I. RC. 8/1, *Cal. mem. rolls*, I, 23–65.

[2] Appendix VIII; the crown pleas are found on the rolls for 36 Hen. III, 44 Hen. III and 45 Hen. III (Limerick).

[3] Richardson and Sayles, *Administration*, p. 140; cf. p. 41 below.

[4] *Ibid.* pp. 142–3 and references. J.I., 18 Edw. I (no. 13), in P.R.O., RC. 7/2, *Cal. plea rolls*, II, 139, adds the information that John of Houghton was also on the Limerick eyre.

[5] *Facsimiles of the national manuscripts of Ireland*, pt. III, pl. III, from destroyed close roll, 2 Edw. II: 'Chronicle of Pembridge', in *Chartul. St Mary's, Dublin*, II. 332; *Annals of Friar Clyn*, ed. R. Butler (Irish arch. soc. 1849), p. 10.

[6] E.g. *Close rolls, 1251–4*, p. 499; *Cal. pat. rolls, 1281–93*, p. 141 (*Cal. doc. Ire. 1252–84*, 2208).

[7] E.g. *Cal. close rolls, 1279–88*, p. 214.

Although the exchequer was the oldest department of the administration of the lordship,[1] its legal side is very obscure in the thirteenth century. In theory, only matters affecting the king or the ministers of the exchequer might be brought to it, and in 1285 a petitioner complained that he had been impleaded there by someone who 'is neither a baron of the exchequer nor one of the king's servants'.[2] One of a number of complaints about the exchequer, $c.$1285, was that pleas which ought to have been held in the bench or the county court were admitted there.[3] This dispute over jurisdiction was to continue in later years.

Ireland, like the other lands of the kings of England, had its great liberties; as was said in 1292 on behalf of John Hastings, one of the claimants to the Scottish throne: 'there are many lordships and honours of the ... members of England, which have [administration of] peace and justice, such as ... many of the earldoms and baronies in Ireland'.[4] The characteristic Irish reservation from liberty jurisdiction of four pleas of the crown—rape, arson, forestalling, and treasure-trove—seems to have begun with the re-grant of Leinster to William I Marshal in 1208.[5] By 1290 it applied everywhere except in east Meath. The Marshal liberty would no doubt have been the most important, had it not fallen to be divided among the representatives of the five daughters of the elder Earl William in 1245; in 1247-9 the franchises were renewed in each purparty.[6] Since Leinster was already administratively divided into the four counties of Wexford, Kilkenny, Kildare and Carlow, four of the five purparties had both a county court and a chief court of the liberty.[7] If record was summoned from the chief liberty court by four knights, as from a county court, instead of by written record of the justices of the liberty,

[1] Richardson and Sayles, *Administration*, p. 21.
[2] Prynne, *Records*, II, 435-6, 1273-4 (two petitions, one now P.R.O., S.C. 1/24, no. 32, the other not traced; P.R.O., C. 47/35/14, no. 44, must have been attached). Whether the matter was testamentary, involving the ecclesiastical jurisdiction, was also at issue in this case.
[3] *Cal. doc. Ire. 1285-92*, p. 2.
[4] W. Rishanger, *Chronica et annales* (Rolls ser.), p. 327.
[5] J. Otway-Ruthven, 'The medieval county of Kildare', *I.H.S.* XI (1959), 181-99, at pp. 189-90; S. Painter, *William Marshal* (Baltimore, 1933), pp. 159-60.
[6] G. H. Orpen, *Ireland under the Normans* (Oxford, 1911-20), III, 75; *Close rolls, 1242-7*, pp. 526, 529; *1247-51*, pp. 115, 159; *Cal. pat. rolls, 1247-58*, pp. 21, 38.
[7] Otway-Ruthven, *I.H.S.* XI, 185.

it was early held to be a ground of error, because the lord of a Leinster liberty

habet in terra nostra Hybernie vicecomites et justiciarios suos in terris suis in Hybernia excercentes jurisdicciones suas secundum leges et consuetudines regni nostri Anglie.[1]

In 1280 the English king's bench accepted that the 'greater pleas' belonging to the liberty court (as distinct from those of the county court), for which there were two 'assizes' a year, must be held by the steward in person, and not by deputy; it was found that in fact this rule was obeyed only in the de Clare liberty of Kilkenny.[2] Oddly enough, that liberty otherwise scarcely appears in the records, while the others had somewhat varied histories after 1249. The Bigod liberty of Carlow was involved in difficulties with the Dublin administration in 1282–5 and for some time was actually in the king's hand.[3] The de Valence liberty of Wexford may have enjoyed a measure of protection from Dublin interference through difficulty of access and the lord's near kinship to the king. The liberty of Kildare had a chequered history, partly because of its division between four co-parceners. All these liberties were 'intendant' to the sheriff of Dublin, who was entitled to act in default of the liberty administration. In them, as in all Irish liberties, certain church lands, the 'cross-lands', were exempt from the lord's jurisdiction and were juridically part of a convenient royal county; so, in 1280, William de Valence, lord of Wexford, is found securing a pardon for the trespass of his steward in granting pardons for a homicide in the lands of the bishop of Ferns.[4]

The other great liberties were Ulster and Meath. The earldom of Ulster, established in 1205, lapsed from 1243 to 1264, but little is known of its administration at any time and it remained, largely for reasons of physical geography, independent and aloof.[5] The de Lacy liberty of Meath dated from the days of Henry II, but most of the franchises were resumed by the crown early in the

[1] *Close rolls, 1253–4*, p. 113 (Kilkenny), *1254–6*, pp. 212–13 (Carlow).
[2] P.R.O., K.B. 27/53, m. 28 d (*Cal. doc. Ire. 1252–84*, 1647); cf. *Close rolls, 1254–6*, p. 229, and Richardson and Sayles, *The Irish parliament*, pp. 294–6.
[3] *Cal. doc. Ire. 1252–84*, 1919; *Cal. close rolls, 1279–88*, p. 330.
[4] *Cal. pat. rolls, 1272–81*, p. 383; these points are discussed at greater length in chapter VI, below.
[5] Orpen, III, 264–80; IV, 130–9.

INTRODUCTION 13

reign of Henry III.[1] On the death of Walter de Lacy in 1241, his claims went to his granddaughters, the wives of Geoffrey de Joinville and John de Verdun, who respectively received the lordships of Trim in the east and Loxeudy in the west. Geoffrey and his wife succeeded in recovering the original franchises.[2] They retained them for many years, despite friction with the administration at Dublin.[3] The only thirteenth-century Irish list of the articles of a sheriff's tourn comes from the Joinville liberty.[4] It is a reminder of the constant activity, both in the royal counties and in the liberties, of local courts and officials, an aspect of Irish administration which, fortunately and exceptionally, has been authoritatively examined in print.[5] The de Verdun lords of Loxeudy never had any greater privilege than that of acting as sheriffs of their lands and an attempt to recover the right to try pleas of the crown failed in 1267.[6] Even what franchise there was was lost in 1280.[7]

Above both the royal and liberty courts of Ireland was the king and his court in England. Whatever the situation may have been before the justiciar's jurisdiction was confirmed and extended in 1207, no Irish case appears in English records in the later years of John.[8] There is one example early in the reign of Henry III. The tenant had produced a charter of John and vouched the king to warranty; despite this, judgment was given against him (his opponent was the justiciar's wife), but the decision was

[1] 'The muniments of Edmund de Mortimer, third earl of March, concerning his liberty of Trim', ed. H. Wood, *R.I.A. Proc.* XL, 312–55, at p. 313.
[2] *Calendar of the Gormanston register*, ed. J. Mills and M. J. McEnery (R.S.A.I. 1916), p. 178; *Close rolls, 1251–3*, pp. 363, 396, and *1253–4*, p. 28; *Rôles gascons*, I, 511.
[3] 'Muniments of Edmund de Mortimer', ed. Wood, *R.I.A. Proc.* XL, 313–16, 319–20; P.R.O., S.C. 1/5, no. 88 (*Cal. doc. Ire. 1252–84*, 634); *Royal letters, 1236–72*, pp. 135–6; *Cal. close rolls, 1272–9*, p. 548.
[4] *Register of the priory of the blessed virgin Mary of Tristernagh*, ed. M. V. Clarke (Irish MSS. Comm.), pp. 32–3.
[5] J. Otway-Ruthven, 'Anglo-Irish shire government in the thirteenth century', *I.H.S.* V (1946), 1–28. I have therefore excluded a detailed consideration of the subject from the present study.
[6] *Cal. misc. inq. 1219–1307*, 339; *Cal. doc. Ire. 1252–84*, 810, 1666.
[7] P.R.O., S.C. 8/77, no. 3825, and 145, no. 7236; *Cal. close rolls, 1279–88*, pp. 55–6; *Cal. doc. Ire. 1252–84*, 1670; *Cal. fine rolls, 1272–1307*, p. 129.
[8] Richardson and Sayles, *The Irish parliament*, pp. 22–3, and references. Those given on p. 22, n. 13, hardly afford adequate support to the statement in the text that civil matters might come to England for trial in the early years of John; but *Curia regis rolls, 1205–6*, p. 195, bears it out and may be added to them.

reversed in England.[1] The English proceedings were before the council (*de hiis igitur tractatu habito inter magnates fideles nostros et jurisperitos*), as might be expected during the minority. In 1240 and 1241, cases were summoned *coram rege*—one of them before Henry on his proposed visit to Ireland.[2] In 1243 an Irish entry appears on a roll *coram rege* for the first time since 1206 and there were two more cases before 1272.[3] In the only one of the three of which much is known the tenant in an action before the Dublin bench claimed that he could not answer without the king.[4] It came before the Oxford parliament of June 1258 and it is not surprising that Mr Richardson and Professor Sayles have seen in the consideration of such a matter at so important and busy a parliament a useful illustration of their view of parliamentary origins and development.[5] Apart from the plea rolls there are, however, clear indications of cases being summoned to England in 1250 (from the itinerant court), 1253 (from the embryonic Dublin bench), 1255 (from the liberty court of Kilkenny and the justiciar's court), 1256 (from the court of Richard de la Rochelle, steward of Ireland for the Lord Edward) and 1260 (from the Dublin bench?).[6] This last instance was one in which Walrand of Wellesley, the senior judge, was suspected of using his influence to obstruct justice, since the demandant was his son-in-law; the justiciar was commissioned with three others to certify the king of his findings, so that justice might be done in England. All these cases appear to have been intended for decision by the council. In 1251, when a vouchee to warranty in the emerging bench had no property in Ireland, the warranty alone was to be investigated *coram rege*.[7]

[1] *Rot. litt. claus. 1204–24*, pp. 353, 549.
[2] *Close rolls, 1237–42*, pp. 241, 360.
[3] This statement is based on the references in *Cal. doc. Ire.*, verified against the originals, not on independent search of the rolls; it does not take into account some entries of recognizances relating to Ireland. Although the nineteenth-century class K.B. 26 comprises both bench and *coram rege* rolls of Henry III, Mr C. A. F. Meekings has produced separate lists of the two, accessible in the Public Record Office, literary search room.
[4] *Cal. doc. Ire. 1252–84*, 582; for an extract and some comment, H. G. Richardson and G. O. Sayles, 'The Irish parliaments of Edward I', *R.I.A. Proc.* XXXVIII (1929), 128–47, at p. 134, n. 45; also *The Irish parliament*, p. 62, n. 29.
[5] *Parliaments and great councils in medieval England* (London, 1961), p. 35.
[6] *Close rolls, 1247–51*, p. 367; *1251–3*, p. 460; *1254–6*, pp. 158–9, 206, 411; *1259–61*, p. 455.
[7] *Ibid. 1251–3*, pp. 179–80.

INTRODUCTION

The years 1254 to 1272, from which some of the cases just mentioned come, were those when the lordship of Ireland was held by the Lord Edward, and they have been called 'one of the obscurest periods of Anglo-Irish history'.[1] With Edward's accession to the throne the evidence of Irish cases finding their way across the sea becomes much richer. An examination, in search of the marginal note *Hibernia*, has been made of the king's bench rolls for the first seventeen years of Edward's reign; conveniently, there is almost a clean break in the Irish business of the court at the dividing line Trinity/Michaelmas 1289, for only one Irish case has proceedings recorded on rolls on both sides of that division. The search has revealed some forty-three cases.[2] Irish cases were being regularly directed to the king's bench, rather than the council, which, none the less, intervened on occasion. It is not easy to put these cases into neat categories. As Professor Sayles has written, 'it is impossible to discover any sharply-defined rules'.[3] Yet something can be done to break the list of cases into smaller groups.

Seven cases either make such fleeting appearances on the rolls that it is impossible to classify them in any way or else involved Ireland only because of accidental requirements of process; these we may ignore. There remain a further seven which seemingly originated in the king's bench itself and the main group of twenty-nine which were brought to it from Ireland. Five of the seven which seem to have begun *coram rege* were between members of great baronial families concerned in the partition of Leinster made by the council among the Marshal co-parceners.[4] One of the other two involved merchants of Bruges and, indirectly, the

---

[1] Richardson and Sayles, *The Irish parliament*, p. 57, and cf. also p. 246.

[2] The precise number, forty-three, should not be pressed; it is not always possible to distinguish proceedings in closely related matters. Generally, I have here indicated only the most important references to each case; but full references to all the cases will be found in my thesis, 'English law and its administration in Ireland, c.1290–c.1324' (D.Phil. Oxford, 1960), pp. 18–25. The number of cases making their first appearance on the rolls of each of the seventeen regnal years may be given as follows: 2, 0, 2, 3, 3, 3, 2, 2, 3, 4, 1, 1, 2, 4, 2, 3, 6.

[3] *Select cases in K.B.*, II, p. lxi; pp. lix–lxii are an illuminating survey of Irish material on the rolls of the king's bench, to which the present account owes much, though the classifications used there and here vary.

[4] There are some thirty references to these cases in *Cal. doc. Ire. 1252–84*, between nos. 935 and 1445. An attempt to analyse the material will be found in my thesis, referred to in n. 2, above, p. 20, n. 110.

difficulties that had occurred between the Lord Edward and the countess of Flanders.[1] The last of this group was a dispute between the magnates William de Valence, Thomas de Clare and Roger Mortimer (d.1282) over an Irish wardship granted to Thomas by the king, sold by him to William, and then admitted by the king to belong in part to Roger.[2] In all these instances it is easy to see how the king's interest and authority were specially involved.

Without exception the twenty-nine cases which found their way from Irish courts to the king's bench were civil pleas. More than half of them had begun in the Dublin bench, several in liberty courts, and one each in the exchequer, the eyre, and the borough court of Dublin. Most came to England direct from these inferior Irish courts, while some went at first before the justiciar. Two, perhaps three, were simply matters in which a vouchee to warranty had land in England but none in Ireland.[3] When this happened all that the Irish courts could do was to tell the parties

quod sequantur breve de Anglia ad faciendum venire recordum et processum loquele predicte in Anglia si sibi viderit expedire.[4]

The surviving records make it difficult always to be clear how far the case had proceeded in the Irish court and what kind of writ was employed to bring it to England. Although the distinct writ of error had not yet fully evolved, there was an instance in 1278 of a writ expressly referring to error being used to bring a case direct from the Dublin bench.[5] In four cases an undifferentiated writ of *certiorari* was used in similar circumstances.[6] On the other hand, in two instances cases from the bench first went to the justiciar: in one of these an Irish writ mentioning error was employed.[7] A writ of *certiorari* was used from the bench in a case

[1] *Cal. doc. Ire. 1252–84*, 1312.
[2] *Cal. doc. Ire. 1285–92*, 1039.
[3] *Ibid. 1285–92*, 493, 524 and 504, 527; *ibid.* 10, is doubtful—P.R.O., S.C. 1/22, no. 90 (*ibid.* 1156) is perhaps concerned with it.
[4] P.R.O., K.B. 27/121, m. 6d (*Cal. doc. Ire. 1285–92*, 524).
[5] *Cal. doc. Ire. 1252–84*, 1450; cf. pp. 117–18, below.
[6] (a) *Ibid.* 1648, 1741; (b) *1285–92*, 270, 306, 350, 385, 387, 435, 436, 505, and P.R.O., K.B. 27/110, m. 24d; (c) *Cal. doc. Ire. 1285–92*, 453, 525; (d) *ibid.* 396 (cf. Cole, *Documents*, pp. 75–6). *Cal. doc. Ire. 1252–84*, 1592, tells nothing of the way in which the case there in question was brought from the bench.
[7] *Cal. doc. Ire. 1252–84*, 1862; *1285–92*, 28.

where there had been an adjournment *sine die* till the expiry of a writ of protection for seven years and *certiorari* was also used to bring a case from the liberty of Wexford.[1]

One writ used from time to time to transfer cases at hearing in Ireland is of unusual interest, since no detailed attention seems to have been given to it in studies of other jurisdictions. It was a variety of the writ *procedendo ad judicium*. *Procedendo* itself was closely akin to *mandamus*, of which, indeed, it can be regarded as a variant. The most usual form of *procedendo* was when justices unreasonably delayed justice, but it had other uses as well.[2] In the special form of the writ with which we are here concerned the characteristic feature was that the court to which it was directed was told that, if some difficulty was present wherefore the court could not proceed to give judgment unless the king were consulted (*nobis inconsultis*), the record should be sent *coram rege*.[3] But in fact this form of *procedendo* seems normally to have operated as a command to transfer the case. Four such cases are found. The first was a tangled assize of novel disseisin which had already been before Irish courts when Edward was merely lord of Ireland and had then been committed to the English chancellor for examination of alleged errors.[4] In another, an exception of bastardy pleaded in the Dublin bench necessitated a certificate from an English bishop who could not be distrained in Ireland;[5] a third case was of a broadly similar kind—a royal ward vouched to warranty had negligible property in the Irish jurisdiction.[6] The last turned on the allegation that a certain church and lands within a liberty were *terre incroceate*, cross-lands, and eventually led into the wider question of the lord's right to hold pleas of advowson at all.[7] The sending of a case by an Irish court when difficulty was encountered is illustrated by a letter from the chancellor of the Irish exchequer to Robert Burnell:

[1] *Ibid.* 307, 349, 374, 477; *1252–84*, 1647.
[2] Fitzherbert, *Nouvelle Natura Brevium*, ff. 153–4; Blackstone, *Commentaries* (1st ed.), III, 109–10; Holdsworth (7th ed.), I, 229, n. 6. None of these authorities discuss the particular form of the writ considered above.
[3] Examples are given in Appendix II.
[4] *Cal. doc. Ire. 1252–84*, 1163.
[5] *Ibid. 1285–92*, 351.
[6] *Ibid.* 480, 481 (Dublin bench); cf. Cole, *Documents*, p. 57 (petition of Joan de Boun).
[7] *Cal. doc. Ire. 1285–92*, 452, 526, 599; cf. *Cal. chancery warrants, 1244–1326*, p. 12.

litteras domini regis justiciariis de banco Dublin pro domino Galfrido de Geynvill et Milone de Crus directas exhibuit dictus dominus Galfridus, qui nichil pro eisdem facientes responderunt ambiguum esse in processu pro quo voluerunt recordum et processum domino regi destinare.[1]

In this instance it is not known for certain whether a writ in *si difficultas* form was in question or the justices acted simply on their own initiative.

Of the remaining cases, one came to England as a result of a plaint concerning law merchant administered in the borough court of Dublin.[2] Another might perhaps have been classified, somewhat pedantically, as arising *coram rege*, for there had been no more than administrative action in Ireland and the king's bench acted *ex officio curie*.[3] The transfer of seven cases to England whilst at hearing in Ireland can perhaps best be explained on the grounds that the king's interests were peculiarly involved. Production of a royal charter,[4] the fact that a matter touched a royal ward,[5] the claim of an incumbent whose patron was a bishop that he could not answer without the king, *sede vacante*,[6] the need to refer to the partition of Leinster among the Marshal heirs,[7] and possibly the fact that the parties were important tenants-in-chief,[8] appear to have been relevant features. In two instances, the reasons for transfer to England are altogether obscure.[9] The intervention of the king and council occurred in at least three of the seven cases in which royal interests seem

[1] P.R.O., S.C. 1/23, no. 146. Almost certainly this refers to the proceedings on a writ of entry, which began in Geoffrey's liberty of Trim and went to the Dublin bench, between Nicholas Bacon and Milo de Crus, who vouched Robert son of Richard de Crus. It first appears in the king's bench in Michaelmas term, 1295: *Cal. doc. Ire. 1285–92*, 146, 265, 308, 342, 386, 457, 476, and cf. 821, 961.

[2] *Select cases concerning the law merchant* (S.S. 46) II, pp. xviii–xix, 46–50; cf. *State trials of Edward I*, ed. T. F. Tout and H. Johnstone (R. Hist. Soc., Camden, 3rd ser. IX), pp. 46–8.

[3] This was the remarkable Comyn wardship case: for a full account see chapter IX.

[4] (*a*) *Cal. doc. Ire. 1285–92*, 666; Cole, *Documents*, pp. 57, 68 (petitions of the abbot of Dunbrody). (*b*) *Cal. doc. Ire. 1252–84*, 1662, 1929, 1976; also P.R.O., C. 47/87/2, no. 17.

[5] *Cal. doc. Ire. 1252–84*, 1313, 1635, 1858 (two cases).

[6] *Ibid. 1285–92*, 213, 214.

[7] *Ibid.* 12, 54, 211.

[8] *Ibid.* 29, 56. This is a very tentative suggestion.

[9] *Ibid. 1252–84*, 1164, 1329, 1331, 1334, and *1285–92*, 384.

INTRODUCTION

especially to have been involved: there are notes *loquendum cum rege*[1] and *postea nichil actum est quia placitatum fuit in concilio domini regis coram ipso rege*.[2] There is also record of conciliar concern in five other cases originating in Ireland.

A search for formal statements of theory and policy behind this Irish business of the king's bench is to some degree misguided. The king is the centre and in Ireland his lordship has developed in ways sufficiently gradual to render unnecessary the clarifications which Edward attempted in Wales and in Scotland. The court *coram rege* is a fit place for the consideration of his interests when they are in question and a proper resort for those who wish him to correct errors in the courts of his Irish lordship. It is also a suitable clearing-house when his lower English courts and those of Ireland need each other's assistance. As yet, too, there is little rigidity in the hierarchy of Irish courts. More often than not before 1290 the justiciar is by-passed by a case in its progress from an inferior Irish court to the king's bench.

Admittedly, in 1278 the justiciar, Robert of Ufford, protested against the by-passing of his jurisdiction, and asked that the English chancery should not give writs to Irish litigants unless they showed that they had first applied to him for a remedy.[3] But there is no evidence that his complaint had any effect. It is true that, in the Michaelmas term of 1289 a case before the king's bench was returned to its original court in Ireland—the Dublin borough court—but this was because the citizens claimed as their special privilege that proceedings in their court should be first redressed before the Dublin bench or the justiciar, and there was no question of laying down a general principle.[4]

Quite apart from the actual summoning and transfer of cases to England, there was, during the thirteenth century, a good deal of intervention in proceedings in Ireland. A few examples from the years 1252-5 will illustrate the point. A case at hearing in Ireland is to be expedited,[5] a party is not to suffer because of his inability to get to Ireland in time to prosecute his appeal or plaint,[6] the justiciar should grant attaint of a jury which he has

[1] P.R.O., K.B. 27/62, m. 22d, and 110, m. 9d (*Cal. doc. Ire. 1252-84*, 1826, and *1285-92*, 373). [2] P.R.O., K.B. 27/90, m. 32d (*ibid. 1285-92*, 56).
[3] P.R.O., C. 47/10/13, no. 19 (*Cal. doc. Ire. 1252-84*, 1511).
[4] *Select cases concerning the law merchant*, II, 50.
[5] *Close rolls, 1251-3*, p. 129.
[6] *Ibid.* pp. 436, 438.

already refused,[1] he should stop the Limerick county court from harassing Conchobar Ua Briain, king of Thomond,[2] he should hear cases from inferior courts,[3] his lieutenant should respite a case until the Lord Edward or the justiciar himself arrives.[4] There was always of necessity much appointment of attorneys in each country for proceedings in the other, though perhaps not many litigants were as cautious as William de Valence was in December 1282, when he sought duplicate writs from the English chancery, so that one attorney could cross from Chester and the other from Pembroke, thereby minimizing the risk which the Irish Sea offered to the prosperity of his affairs.[5]

[1] *Close rolls, 1251–3*, p. 470.
[2] *Ibid.* p. 496.
[3] *Ibid.* p. 501, and *1253–4*, p. 116.
[4] *Ibid. 1254–6*, p. 213.
[5] P.R.O., S.C. 1/24, no. 156 (*Cal. doc. Ire. 1252–84*, 2016). His prudence was justifiable: in 1302 a petitioner claimed that he had lost by default in proceedings in Ireland because a storm prevented his attorney from appearing: P.R.O., S.C. 9/25, m. 2.

CHAPTER II

GOVERNORS OF A TROUBLED LORDSHIP

THE administration of the lordship of Ireland naturally took its tone from the chief governor, who, in the reigns of the first two Edwards, was normally known as the justiciar.[1] The men chosen as justiciars by the king fell, broadly speaking, into the two classes of Anglo-Irish magnate and English administrator. A magnate justiciar brought the weight of his personal position to the side of government, but, conversely, he might bring the authority of the lordship into disrepute by using it for his own ends, and his enemies would allege this almost as a matter of course. An administrator demanded more sustained guidance and support from England, but he was a surer instrument of policy. On 12 September 1290 letters patent were dated appointing William de Vescy as justiciar in succession to John of Sandford, archbishop of Dublin, who had been acting as chief governor since July 1288. De Vescy, who arrived on 11 November following, had just become an Irish magnate—lord of Kildare—on the death of his mother, and his three-and-a-half years in control of the lordship, to Easter 1294, were disturbed by sharp quarrels with other lords, especially with John fitz Thomas, baron of Offaly. Until October 1294 the government was carried on by two members of the Irish administration in succession, Walter de la Haye and William fitz Roger. William Dodingeseles, another administrator, was then chosen as justiciar, but his death less than six months later put the land under the care of Thomas fitz Maurice fitz Gerald, lord of Desmond, who governed for most of 1295. By letters of 18 October 1295 he was ordered to deliver his charge to John Wogan, who must occupy in such a study as this a position no other can claim.

John Wogan was a Cambro-Norman knight, lord of Picton in

[1] On the office of chief governor, Richardson and Sayles, *Administration*, pp. 8–14, 73–91; whenever statements as to tenure of office are passed over in silence in footnotes to the present study, this book is the authority. A. J. Otway-Ruthven, 'The chief governors of medieval Ireland', *R.S.A.I. Jn.* XCV (1965), 227–36, is chiefly concerned with later medieval evidence.

Pembrokeshire, a vassal of William de Valence, lord (sometimes styled earl) of Pembroke and of Wexford in Ireland.[1] He was probably the John Wogan who appears in 1275 as attorney for William in an Irish case which was before the king's bench[2] and, almost unquestionably, it was his position as a *familiaris* of William that gave him his early administrative training, his acquaintance with Ireland, and his opportunity to enter the king's service. Wogan later showed his gratitude by making William one of the spiritual beneficiaries of the chantry which he founded in the cathedral of St David's.[3] About 1280 he is found as steward of the Valence liberty of Wexford.[4] If reasonable identifications are accepted, we can add that in 1281 he was appointed to inquire into trespasses against the king in Hereford and in the next dozen years or so was employed on royal business in Wales and placed on various judicial commissions, including an eyre of York.[5] At the same time he remained closely associated with his first patron.[6] In 1285 he paid a visit to Ireland[7] and he had probably acquired interests there during his earlier stay.[8] Outside Pembroke he seems to have held lands in Somerset, Dorset, Devon and Oxfordshire.[9]

The terms of his appointment as justiciar provided Wogan with a fee of five hundred pounds a year, the standard sum throughout this period.[10] Out of it he was to maintain himself and nineteen men-at-arms, but when additional forces were required in time

[1] Perhaps the best account of Wogan hitherto has been that by B. G. Charles in *Dictionary of Welsh biography*; but like the earlier writing on which it draws it is very inadequate—and sometimes in error—in treating of the Irish side of his career.

[2] P.R.O., K.B. 27/13, mm. 10d, 12; calendared without Wogan's name in *Cal. Doc. Ire. 1252–84*, 1087.

[3] Orpen, IV, 39, n. 3, and authorities there cited, to which may be added *Cal. pat. rolls, 1307–13*, p. 563.

[4] P.R.O., S.C. 1/30, no. 166 a.

[5] *Cal. pat. rolls, 1272–81*, p. 428; *1281–92*, pp. 485, 507, 510; *1293–1301*, pp. 17, 49, 50, 109, 114; *Cal. close rolls, 1288–96*, pp. 426, 430, 462; *Cal. chancery warrants, 1244–1326*, p. 35.

[6] *Cal. doc. Ire. 1252–84*, 1995; *Cal. close rolls, 1279–88*, pp. 116, 138; *Cal. pat. rolls, 1281–92*, p. 398; *Rot. parl.*, I, 31, 33; P.R.O., K.B. 27/130, m. 37 (*Cal. doc. Ire. 1285–92*, 1052).

[7] *Cal. pat. rolls, 1281–92*, p. 166.

[8] Ibid. p. 134; C.P., 8–9 Edw. I, in P.R.O.I., RC. 8/1, *Cal. mem. rolls*, I, 126–7; *Cal. doc. Ire. 1252–84*, 1995.

[9] *Cal. close rolls, 1279–88*, p. 185, and *1302–7*, p. 325; *Rot. parl.* I, 77; *Cal. inq. p.m., 20–28 Edw. I*, no. 313, and *1–9 Edw. II*, no. 513.

[10] *Cal. pat. rolls, 1292–1301*, p. 155.

of war further payments were to be made from the Irish exchequer. Although the letters patent of course did not mention it, there can be little doubt that one of the chief tasks assigned to Wogan was that of maintaining supplies of men and provisions for the wars of Edward I elsewhere.[1] He took up office in December 1295 and less than six months later brought Richard de Burgh, earl of Ulster, Theobald Butler, and John fitz Thomas, three of the greatest Anglo-Irish magnates, to serve with the king in Scotland.[2] Apart from brief visits across the Irish sea, he remained as chief governor until after the death of Edward I and for the first year of the succeeding reign.[3]

In 1308, Wogan's authority was challenged by the Irish of Wicklow, who burnt the stronghold of Castle Kevin early in May.[4] Although he was reappointed as justiciar by letters patent of 4 June, Wogan had a higher representative of the king placed over him, in the person of Richard de Burgh, earl of Ulster and lord of Connaught, with the novel title of king's lieutenant, by further letters dated eleven days later.[5] The earl had deputized for Wogan in the past, but his chief qualification for office must have been his pre-eminence among the Irish magnates, together, perhaps, with the special place he held in the esteem of the Gaelic race—*iarla uasalgnímach Ulad, aen roga Gall Erend uli*.[6] His appointment never took effect, for similar letters of the next day's date were made in favour of Piers Gaveston, whose enforced exile was thus mitigated. On 8 June Wogan had been defeated by the Irish, but during the year he spent in Ireland Gaveston restored the military situation.[7] Wogan, still justiciar, went to England in September 1308, leaving a deputy, William de Burgh, behind him. Gaveston, Wogan and, after Wogan's departure, de Burgh, all held sessions of the justiciar's court, but whether the king's

[1] J. F. Lydon, 'Ireland's participation in the military activities of English kings in the thirteenth and early fourteenth centuries' (unpublished Ph.D. thesis, London, 1955), *passim*.
[2] 'Chronicle of Pembridge', in *Chartul. St Mary's, Dublin*, II, 326.
[3] On a visit to England in 1302 he was called upon to assist in Welsh business: *Rot. parl.* I, 150; *Cal. pat. rolls, 1301–7*, pp. 90–1.
[4] 'Chronicle of Pembridge', in *Chartul. St Mary's, Dublin*, II, 336.
[5] *Cal. pat. rolls, 1307–13*, pp. 75, 83.
[6] 'The earl of Ulster, of the noble deeds': *Caithréim Thoirdhealbhaigh*, ed. S. H. O'Grady (Irish Texts Soc.), I, 17; 'the choicest of all the foreigners of Ireland': *Annals of Loch Cé, s.a.* 1326.
[7] 'Chronicle of Pembridge', in *Chartul. St Mary's, Dublin*, II, 335–7.

lieutenant and the justiciar (or his deputy) sat in different places at the same time is obscure, on account of deficiencies in the rolls surviving to modern times.[1] On Gaveston's departure Wogan resumed the government.

In April 1312 an army sent by the justiciar was *miserabiliter confectus* by the Anglo-Irish faction of the junior de Verduns in Louth.[2] In addition the Irish of Wicklow had become troublesome again[3] and clearly, bereft of effective support from England—itself in crisis—behind him, Wogan was losing control. In August he left Ireland to the care of Edmund Butler, although he remained nominally justiciar until the end of April 1313.

Wogan spent the next few years quietly. He appears to have been employed on a certain amount of Welsh business.[4] Though the baronial party had Theobald de Verdun appointed as justiciar, he spent only eight months in Ireland, and otherwise Edmund Butler ruled the country from 1312 to 1317. It was he who faced the storm of the Bruce invasion. Late in 1316 Roger Mortimer of Wigmore was appointed as king's lieutenant and came to Ireland in the following April with Wogan in his train.[5] Butler remained as justiciar and he and Mortimer held pleas in different places at the same time, though they also on occasion joined forces.[6] Wogan was closely associated with Mortimer in Ireland, perhaps as his

[1] For sessions held by Wogan and de Burgh, see the evidence summarized on p. v of the preface to *C.J.R. 1308–14*. For proceedings before Gaveston on 18 September 1308, *ibid.* p. 84, and, on 9 June 1309, *Hist. & mun. doc. Ire.* pp. 230–1.
[2] The phrase is from 'Chronicle of Pembridge', in *Chartul. St Mary's, Dublin*, II, 341. I reject the date 10 July 1312 given there—and in *Jacobi Grace annales* (ed. R. Butler, Irish arch. soc. 1842) *s.a.* 1312—in favour of that of the *Annals of Friar Clyn*, the feast of St Anicetus (17 April). The date 10 July seems impossible, for the justiciary roll (*C.J.R. 1308–14*, pp. 237–8, printed in full in *Chartul. St Mary's, Dublin*, II, 417–19) records Wogan's proceedings against the de Verduns under the heading 'three weeks from Easter'. The date 17 April can be reconciled with this heading (16 April) by supposing that the proceedings began within a couple of days of the event, before the next heading employed (a month from Easter) was appropriate. The date 17 April also accords better with Pembridge's own statement (p. 340) that the *riota Urgalie* began on the vigil of St Peter's Chair (21 February).
[3] 'Chronicle of Pembridge', in *Chartul. St Mary's, Dublin*, II, 339, 341.
[4] *Cal. pat. rolls, 1307–13*, pp. 536, 538, 546–7, 555, 592, 596, and *1313–17*, pp. 186, 223, 229, 312. However, in some of these references and those in succeeding notes, another John Wogan may be in question: see Additional Note 1 at the end of this chapter.
[5] *Cal. pat. rolls, 1313–17*, p. 646.
[6] Chapter III and Appendix IV, below.

principal adviser on local conditions.[1] His long services were rewarded with the grant in fee of lands in Kildare which had earlier been given to him for term of years and then for life.[2] He apparently stayed in Ireland after Mortimer's return to England in May 1318 and during the terms of office of the four chief governors who succeeded each other in the next three years.[3] His standing as the elder statesman of the lordship was high; a letter of 1319 names him first, after the justiciar, in the council and in the same year he was one of four commissioners charged with inquiry into Bruce's Irish supporters.[4] Wogan died in 1321[5] and so he did not live to see the opening of a new era with the appointment in 1324 of the justiciar who most invites comparison to him—even in the detail of being a protégé of the house of Valence—Sir John Darcy.[6]

John Wogan was justiciar of Ireland for almost eighteen years and Irish historians as different in outlook as Goddard Orpen and Edmund Curtis have set their estimates of his importance high. In part this is the result of a common enough defect of the historical vision, for his justiciarship was exceptionally well covered in the primary sources conveniently accessible to them. They were also strongly influenced by ideas of parliamentary history that can no longer be accepted, and tended to regard the parliament of 1297, held by Wogan, as Ireland's 'Model Parlia-

[1] J.R., 11 Edw. II (no. 119), m. 4 (prisoner recommitted by order of Wogan until Mortimer should come); cf. J.R., 11 Edw. II (no. 115) and C.P., H. 11 Edw. II, in P.R.O.I., R.C. 7/12, *Cal. plea rolls*, XII, 148, 376.

[2] P.R.O., C. 47/10/18, no. 8 (writ, inquisition and return concerning his life-estates); *Cal. rot. pat. Hib.*, p. 21; *Cal. pat. rolls, 1301–7*, p. 325, and *1307–13*, pp. 122–3, 588; *Red book of Ormond*, ed. N. B. White (Irish MSS. Comm.), pp. 2, 11–17, 21–2; C.P., T. 33 Edw. I (no. 74 and no. 75), in P.R.O.I., RC. 7/11, *Cal. plea rolls*, XI, 79–80, 90, 136–8, 149–51.

[3] *Cal. pat. rolls, 1317–21*, pp. 189, 222.

[4] *Parl. writs*, II (div. 2), p. 517; *Foedera* (Rec. comm. ed.), II, I, 396. In the summer of 1319 he was named first after the justiciar, chancellor and treasurer: City Hall, Dublin, White book, f. 62v. The reference reads: '... *Joh[an]ne Wogan* [punctuation mark] *Walt[er]o Wogan tenent[e] pl[ac]ita sequent[ia] capit[alem] justic[iarium] Hib[er]n[ie]*. As printed in *Hist. & mun. doc. Ire.* p. 435, however, the expansion of *tenent'* is *tenentibus*, while *Calendar of the ancient records of Dublin*, I, 148, reads 'John Wogan, Walter Wogan, justices of common pleas'. The result has been a ghost entry in F. E. Ball, *The judges in Ireland* (London, 1926), I, 39, 65, of a John Wogan, justice of the justiciar's pleas.

[5] 'Chronicle of Pembridge', in *Chartul. St Mary's, Dublin*, II, 362.

[6] R. F. Darcy, *A life of John Darcy, first baron Darcy of Knayth, 1280–1347* (London, 1933), pp. vi, 6, 30.

ment'.[1] A new appraisal is compelled by the evidence. Wogan was not very successful on the military side of his duties. In 1308 and 1312 it was Gaveston and Butler, respectively, who redressed the balance. In the administrative sphere, a re-arrangement of shrievalties carried out by him in 1297, while it was well designed, had rather slight results in practice.[2] Where John Wogan did succeed was in establishing good relations among the greater Anglo-Irish magnates and between them and himself, in supplying the men and supplies needed for Scotland and elsewhere, and in confirming the sway of English law over (in all probability, though the dearth of records prevents certainty) more of Ireland than knew it at any other time before the seventeenth century. It is striking that his tenure of office never exposed him to criticisms and accusations such as surrounded two of his recent predecessors, Stephen of Fulbourn and William de Vescy.

During the terms of office of Wogan and his successors, the Irish official next in dignity and importance to the justiciar was the chancellor, keeper of the great seal of Ireland, and something needs to be said of the Irish chancery and its relations with that of England.[3]

In the earlier years of John, Irish litigants had to sue their original writs from the English chancery.[4] After, in 1204, the justiciar became entitled to issue certain writs, he must have had some secretariat for the purpose. In 1232 the chancellor of England received in addition the title of chancellor of Ireland: the Irish chancery, at first entrusted to a deputy, obtained a chancellor of its own in 1244.[5] For the greater part of what remained of the thirteenth century, however, the chancellor occupied only the third place in the Irish administration, the treasurer being more important. Scandals and maladministration in the Irish exchequer helped to bring about the reforming ordinances of 1292–4 which, amongst other regulations, ended its independence by obliging the treasurer to account periodically at Westminster.[6] Since

[1] Orpen, IV, 40–1; E. Curtis, *Medieval Ireland* (2nd ed., London, 1938), pp. 171–5, followed in this by M. V. Clarke, *Fourteenth-century studies* (Oxford, 1937), p. 2, n. 5. Cf. Richardson and Sayles, *The Irish parliament*, pp. 6–7.
[2] Otway-Ruthven, in *I.H.S.*, v, 5–6; chapter VI, below.
[3] See also Additional Note II to this chapter.
[4] Richardson and Sayles, *The Irish parliament*, p. 22, n. 11.
[5] In general, Richardson and Sayles, *Administration*, pp. 14–16.
[6] *Ibid.* pp. 55–6; J. F. Lydon, 'The Irish exchequer in the thirteenth century', *Ir. Comm. Hist. Sc. Bull.* no. 81, pp. 1–2.

similar provision was made at the same time for the accounts of Aquitaine, it is plain, however, that more general considerations played their part in this arrangement.[1]

These changes had their effect on the relative standing of the treasurer and, from early in the chancellorship of Thomas Quantock, appointed in 1291, the chancellor had precedence over the treasurer.[2] The latest letters to name the treasurer first were dated in August 1295.[3] Quantock was chancellor until his death, as bishop of Emly, in 1309, and it is likely that this long official career contributed to the strength of the administration under Wogan. For example, Quantock is known to have introduced the ordinary English procedure in proofs of age.[4] Normally the justiciar (whose *teste* was on the writs) was the link between England and the Irish chancery.[5] There were rare instances, at moments of crisis, when the English chancery by-passed the justiciar to issue a direct order to the Irish chancellor.[6] In 1323 the powers of the Irish chancery were considerably constricted, with the intention of controlling the justiciar, but these details of the ordinances of that year need not concern us here.[7]

In 1305 the principle that writs of trespass to be pleaded in Ireland should be purchased in the Irish chancery was insisted upon by the leading magnates—the earl of Ulster, Geoffrey de Joinville, Edmund Butler, John fitz Thomas (the defendant in the case in question), Peter de Bermingham, Eustace Power, and others—and upheld by the king and council in England.[8] Despite

[1] J. le Patourel, 'The Plantagenet dominions', *History*, I (1965), 289–308, at p. 302.   [2] Richardson and Sayles, *The Irish parliament*, p. 28, n. 49.
[3] *Cal. close rolls, 1288–96*, p. 458.
[4] *Cal. inq. p. m.*, III, no. 436. There is in the Library of Lincoln's Inn (MS. Hale 140, ff. 91–106) an incomplete register of writs described (f. 90*v*) as *secundum usum Ricardi de Bereford*. Richard of Barford was Quantock's contemporary as treasurer of Ireland from 1300 to 1308 and was amongst his successors as chancellor (1314–16). It is odd if the description of the register (which, on a cursory inspection, offers no particularly Irish features) refers to him, yet there seems no other suitable *Richard* of Barford. I owe this reference to Mr Neil Ker.
[5] Cf. what is said of notes of warranty in Additional Note II to this chapter.
[6] *Cal. close rolls, 1288–96*, pp. 291–2; *1318–23*, p. 55; *1323–7*, p. 10.
[7] *Foedera* (Rec. comm. ed.), II, I, 538–9; cf. a much earlier list of limitations on the Irish chancery (the precise date and nature of the document is uncertain): P.R.O., C. 47/10/17, no. 22 (*Cal. doc. Ire. 1285–92*, 1178).
[8] *C.J.R., 1305–7*, pp. 75–8; *Cal. chancery warrants, 1244–1326*, pp. 253–4; cf. *Memoranda de parliamento, 1305*, no. 416 (petitioner refused writ of English chancery and told to sue in that of Ireland), and chapter VII, below.

the limitations they imposed in some other respects, the chancery ordinances of 1323 appear to have restated this doctrine in more general terms.[1] To some extent, however, they may have been directed in this respect against the jurisdictional claims of the Irish exchequer, rather than against the English chancery.[2] A minor irritant until well into the reign of Edward III was the device of obtaining an English writ of prohibition to a court christian, for the Irish chancellor was unable to grant consultation in such a case.[3] The English chancery also played a considerable part in proceedings in Irish courts through protections and pardons, as well as letters of attorney. At the end of the thirteenth century proceedings in Ireland were often enough affected by English letters of protection,[4] but in 1305 the English chancellor was forbidden to grant letters of protection in Ireland.[5] It does not appear that this put a stop to the practice, and it may have been a temporary measure only.[6] Pardons for felony were often granted under the great seal of Ireland, but an Irish petitioner could also obtain one under that of England.[7] The disorders of the Bruce wars led to a considerable multiplication of pardons under the Irish seal. In September 1315, John of Hotham, a special agent of the king in Ireland, was empowered to grant pardons, in consultation with the justiciar, Edmund Butler, if the grantees undertook to serve against the Scots.[8] In February 1316 a number of persons were pardoned at Cork on the less exacting condition that they should not assist Bruce.[9] This policy, it was alleged, encouraged crime; in April 1317 Roger Mortimer was ordered to consult the Irish council before pardoning and, where the offences had been against the citizens of Dublin or of Drogheda, to consult the king.[10] Between 1316 and 1319 Thomas fitz John, earl of Kildare, and John (?) de

[1] *Foedera* (Rec. comm. ed.), II, 1, 538.
[2] Cf. chapter IV, below.   [3] *Rot. parl.* II, 214.
[4] E.g. *C.J.R. 1295–1303*, pp. 146, 152. In P.R.O., S.C. 1/28, no. 132 (*Cal. doc. Ire. 1285–92*, 672) (c.1300) the chancellor of Ireland queried the authenticity of a transcript of English letters of protection produced to him for enrolment.
[5] *Memoranda de parliamento, 1305*, 459.
[6] *C.J.R. 1305–7*, pp. 265–6, and the English patent rolls after this date.
[7] P.R.O., S.C. 8/49, no. 2435, and 74, no. 3682; S.C. 9/12, m. 16; there are numerous Irish pardons on the English patent rolls.
[8] *Cal. pat. rolls, 1313–17*, p. 347.   [9] J.R., 8–9 Edw. II, m. 12.
[10] *Cal. close rolls, 1313–18*, p. 405. Numerous pardons, and production of many letters previously granted, are recorded on the justiciary roll at Cork in November 1317: J.R., 11 Edw. II (no. 119), mm. 2–9, *passim*.

GOVERNORS OF A TROUBLED LORDSHIP 29

Bermingham petitioned the king 'for the community of his land of Ireland' that

> nul de ses ministres justices gardeins lieutenantz de sa dite terre ne autri ministres dedenz franchises ne dehors ny eient mes poer a pardoner a nulli la mort denglois felonessement occis eins soit de li fait iugement selonc la ley. Et qe tuicion de paes ne soit mes grantee a tieux felons.[1]

Although the justiciar and chancellor were forbidden in 1319 to pardon those who adhered to the Scots, it was not until late in 1320 that a petition of the *liges gentz de Irlaund* brought the desired prohibition of pardons for deaths of English feloniously slain.[2] In July 1323 the justiciar was again forbidden to grant them and the chancellor ordered to ignore his warrants, but in November it was made clear that this did not apply to offences committed before the mandate, which might still be pardoned in Ireland.[3]

Petitions were sometimes received against the grant of pardons in connection with particular offences.[4] About 1320 the citizens of Dublin complained of the *malveises gentz des marches* who harassed them *en espeyr de leger pardoun avoyr*.[5] The problem of pardons continued for many years; but, apart from the question of authority to grant pardons, it was of course not peculiar to fourteenth-century Ireland and in fact had a much wider extension, both in time and in place.[6] Three centuries after the petition of Thomas fitz John and John de Bermingham it was necessary to require that no pardons should be granted until the party had delivered himself to justice and stood trial.[7]

The varied business of the Irish justiciar and chancellor may almost all be illustrated from the justiciary rolls, with their

[1] P.R.O., S.C. 8/218, no. 10873. I presume the second petitioner, whose first name is illegible, to have been the most likely of his surname—John de Bermingham, created earl of Louth in 1319.
[2] *Cal. close rolls, 1318–23*, p. 55; *Rot. parl.* I, 385–6; *Cal. pat. rolls, 1317–21*, p. 551. On 22 October 1319 a pardon was granted at the instance of 'Morghyth Obryn': *Cal. rot. pat. Hib.* p. 27. If this was Muirchertach mac Tairdelbaigh Ua Briain, the victor of Dysert O' Dea, or even an Ua Broin of Wicklow, there was certainly reason for perturbation.
[3] *Cal. close rolls, 1323–7*, p. 10; *Foedera* (Rec. comm. ed.), II, I, 538; *Cal. pat. rolls, 1321–4*, pp. 354–5.   [4] P.R.O., S.C. 8/68, no. 3398, and 82, no. 4082.
[5] P.R.O., S.C. 8/82, no. 4090.
[6] *Cal. pat. rolls, 1324–7*, p. 301; *Foedera* (Rec. comm. ed.), III, I, 217; *Stat. Ire., John–Hen. V*, pp. 325, 411; cf. the English statutes: 2 Edw. III, c. 2; 14 Edw. III, stat. I, c. 15; 13 Ric. II, stat. II, c. 1.
[7] *His Maiesties directions for the ... courts ... of Ireland* (Dublin, 1622), no. IV.

entries of *brevia de Anglia* on many legal and administrative matters, their notes of justiciar's bills sent to the chancellor,[1] especially for pardons and writs of *liberate*, their records of proceedings in the Irish parliament, of plans of the council for campaigns against the Gaelic Irish, and of such routine inquiries as inquisitions *ad quod damnum* and proofs of age. Although there is a close physical resemblance between the justiciary rolls of Ireland and the rolls of the contemporary king's bench in England, their contents are very different, for the English records do not include such miscellaneous entries.[2] In fact, the Irish rolls are a day-to-day register of the more formal business of the chief governor. At the same time, pleas predominate, and it is this strictly legal business which gives the rolls their form. With the exception of the very earliest, covering 24 January to 26 November 1295, none of the rolls that survived to modern times contained both pleas of the crown and common pleas.[3] The time at which the division into two classes occurred points to Wogan as responsible for it. After it was made, the miscellaneous business of the chief governor was entered on the rolls of common pleas only. These were probably constituted by making the membranes up into three terminal rolls—Easter and Trinity not being distinguished by the court—and then into yearly rolls, though what is known of the rolls accessible until 1922 indicates much variation from this scheme.[4] The membranes of pleas of the crown appears to have been allowed to accumulate arbitrarily—one roll covers the third to the seventh years of Edward II. The varying periods of time represented by the rolls makes any calculation of their average bulk very insecure: the figures for the three rolls of common pleas which most nearly covered a year apiece are seventy-three, sixty-six, and one hundred and four membranes, respectively. Estimating from the length of all rolls of this class of which the text substantially survives, there is a suggestion of sixty or seventy membranes a year in the later years of Edward I rising to over a

[1] Usually, the mere fact that the chancellor had been ordered to make letters was noted, but sometimes the bill itself was enrolled: *C.J.R. 1295–1303*, p. 427.
[2] *C.J.R. 1305–7*, p. v (a description broadly applicable to the still surviving roll, 6–7 Edw. II); Sayles, *Select cases in K.B.*, II, p. xxi.
[3] Appendix III.
[4] *C.J.R. 1305–7*, pp. v–vi; *1308–14*, p. iii, appears to imply that the roll for the year 1–2 Edw. II was made up from four rolls, but this is the result of an involved misunderstanding, which is discussed at length at the end of Appendix III, below.

GOVERNORS OF A TROUBLED LORDSHIP 31

hundred under Edward II. There do not seem to have been more than about twenty membranes of crown pleas a year. In neither case is there any hint that more than one roll was kept.

To-day, only one justiciary roll survives, that of common pleas for 6–7 Edward II.[1] The one mixed roll, the nine of common pleas, and the single roll of pleas of the crown which survived to recent times from the reign of Edward I appeared in an English calendar while the originals were still in being.[2] This very full calendar is normally of sufficient quality to permit the Latin text to be discerned through it, despite some curious locutions employed by the editors: fiscal marginalia and process marks are ignored. Unhappily, work on seven common plea rolls and four crown plea rolls of Edward II had reached a stage of no more than crude and incomplete drafts when the destruction of the originals elevated the calendars into primary authorities. Publication of these drafts is in progress, but their imperfections are many.[3] In some instances, however, the text may be supplemented from the Latin calendars prepared for the Irish record commission, and these also include a calendar of a roll not otherwise accessible.[4]

An analysis of the surviving roll, 6–7 Edward II, will at once display the structure of the rolls and illustrate the peripatetic nature of the court. The roll consists of one hundred and four membranes, and was evidently made up from three separate rolls, Michaelmas (mm. 1–37, also m. 77), Hilary (mm. 38–57, also

[1] My thanks are due to Miss M. C. Griffith, Deputy Keeper of the Public Records of Ireland, for giving me access to her transcript, prepared with a view to publication in *C.J.R.* I cite it as J.R., 6–7 Edw. II, and membrane reference. The original has of course been consulted on any points of doubt or difficulty.

[2] *C.J.R. 1295–1303*, and *1305–7*.

[3] *C.J.R. 1308–14*, appeared in 1956 and two further volumes are planned. It is much to be hoped that they will include the full text of the surviving roll, 6–7 Edward II. The unpublished calendars are here cited by regnal year, record commission number (where necessary to avoid confusion), and membrane reference. The problems they present have been described, and some valuable guidance provided, by Professor G. O. Sayles in his review of *C.J.R. 1308–14* (*E.H.R.* LXXIII, 101–5). However, the abbey *de Magio*, referred to in the very first line of the calendar, is not Mayo, as he, following the index, accepts, but Maigue (An Máig), Monasternenagh, co. Limerick, and the passage on p. 197 concerning a pledge putting out the eyes of his principal is almost certainly *not* a mistranslation, for on p. 215 mainpernors engage verbally that, if necessary, they will 'utterly blind' their principals (cf. pp. 177–8, below).

[4] Appendix III. Since these Latin calendars are proportionately of far greater importance for the study of the Dublin bench, they are discussed in chapter IV, p. 90, below, rather than here.

mm. 76, 78), and Easter–Trinity (mm. 58–104, except mm. 76–8). Each section begins with a membrane or membranes devoted to *attornati, plevine et manucapciones* (mm. 1–2, 38, 58–9). All the proceedings of Michaelmas term were before the keeper and acting justiciar, Edmund Butler, and the membranes are in exact chronological order. On the morrow of Michaelmas he was at Cashel and essoins, juries, assizes and plaints are recorded for his stay there (mm. 3–7).[1] Similar business engaged him at Waterford on the octave (mm. 8–9), and a week later he was at Dublin, where essoins, miscellaneous official business and plaints were recorded (mm. 10–12).[2] At Waterford, on the morrow of All Souls, business similar to that at Dublin, with the addition of juries and assizes, occurred (mm. 12–16 d, except for part of m. 13 d).[3] On Monday after All Saints (6 November) there were juries and assizes at Kilcullihen, just beside Waterford (m. 17 d). Butler was back in Dublin for the quinzaine of Martinmas, under which date the clerks entered the decisions reached at a council of war held at Ross on 17 November[4] and attended by the keeper, chancellor, treasurer, some other councillors, the steward of the liberty of Wexford and the Irish chief Maurice MacMurrough (Muirchertach Mac Murchada), to arrange operations against the Irish in Wicklow: there was little legal business at Dublin (mm. 18–19).[5] Butler then turned northwards to Drogheda, where miscellaneous matters and plaints received attention (mm. 20–21 and part of m. 13 d).[6] Then he went south, to reach Ardmayle in Tipperary on 13 December (m. 22) and six days later Gowran (Ballygaveran) in Kilkenny, the centre of his own barony, where he probably passed Christmas (m. 23). Very little business was transacted at these places, but when he started on his travels again in the new year the keeper went through the full range of his court's jurisdiction at Limerick on the morrow of the Circumcision (mm. 24–30) and Cashel on Saturday after the Epiphany (in this year, 1313, actually the feast of Hilary) (mm. 30–37).[7]

[1] Pleas of the crown also: *C.J.R. 1308–14*, p. 257. The places of sessions discussed above are indicated on Map 2.
[2] Pleas of the crown also: *ibid.* p. 258.
[3] Pleas of the crown also: *ibid.* 259.
[4] Pleas of the crown also: *ibid.* p. 263.
[5] Pleas of the crown also: *ibid.* p. 264.
[6] Pleas of the crown also: *ibid.* p. 265.
[7] Pleas of the crown at both places: *ibid.* pp. 266, 270.

GOVERNORS OF A TROUBLED LORDSHIP 33

The sessions of Hilary term present a similar pattern, and the membranes which record them are also in chronological order. Butler was at Dublin on the quinzaine of Hilary (mm. 39–45)[1] and the octave of the Purification (mm. 46–47, also m. 76*r* and part of m. 76*d*). Tuesday after St Valentine (20 February) found him at Carlow (mm. 48–49, also part of m. 76*d*) and 19 March at Clonleynan (m. 50).[2] The next day he was at Castledermot (part of m. 76*d*) and we know from the parallel record of pleas of the crown that on the following day he was at Tullow.[3] At Cashel on the morrow of the Annunciation the session (mm. 51–57, 78)[4] is for the first time described as, not before the keeper, who was *alibi in remotis agens*—in fact he was campaigning in Wicklow[5]— but before deputies, the chancellor, Walter of Thornbury, and the justice of the justiciar's pleas, William Alexander. This was the last session of Hilary term and the remainder of the roll covers sessions from the quinzaine of Easter (mm. 62, 95, 98 and part of 99) to Friday before Michaelmas (28 September) (part of m. 71*d*). As these references immediately indicate, the membranes of this part of the roll are hopelessly jumbled together, and comparison with other rolls shows that such a confused arrangement was indeed more usual than precise order. Three sessions were before Walter of Thornbury and Alexander (mm. 72–75; 61, 69, 81–86; 79, 80, 87, 104), the rest being before Butler himself. The only place (of seven in all) at which sessions had not also been held in the earlier terms was Cork (mm. 61, 69, 81–86).[6]

The wanderings of the justiciar's court, as recorded in the surviving sources, show striking territorial limitations even though, within those limits, the amount of itineration is itself striking. The liberties of the earl of Ulster and lord of Connaught, and the presence of the surviving Gaelic statelets of the north and west

---

[1] Pleas of the crown also: *ibid.* p. 271.
[2] I have not been able to identify this place; but the modern Ballylynan is a suitable distance from Castledermot, if there was then a crossing of the Barrow intermediate between Athy and Carlow.
[3] *C.J.R. 1308–14*, p. 271.
[4] Pleas of the crown also: *ibid.* p. 272.
[5] 'Chronicle of Pembridge', in *Chartul. St Mary's, Dublin*, II, 341.
[6] Dublin, 29 April; Drogheda, 4–7 May; Dublin, 13 May; Castledermot, 21 May; Carlow, 25 May; Waterford, 7 June; the roll of pleas of the crown (*C.J.R. 1308–14*, p. 283) adds Kilkenny, 12 June; Dublin, 17 June; Dublin, 8–11 July; Cashel, 26 July–2 August; Cork, 6–11 August; Cashel, 20 August; Dublin, 28 August and 28 September.

barred much of the island to sessions of the court. Wogan did hold pleas at Ardee in the northern part of county Louth and at Roscommon, west of the Shannon,[1] but that was as far as the court penetrated in those directions. In the mountainous southwest there was an area closed to the court, bounded by a line drawn up the modern Cork–Limerick road, through Mallow, Buttevant and Charleville, and then veering west to Tralee and Ardfert, where alone Wogan reached the Atlantic.[2] There appears to have been a shrinkage under Edward II, so that Drogheda, Cork and Limerick became the practical limits. In the south-east, Wicklow and north Wexford knew the justiciar as a military commander rather than as a judge.

The temptation to think of law and administration as in a political vacuum is especially misleading in Irish history, and the territorial limitations just described may serve as a reminder that Ireland was divided between two races—one ought perhaps to say two civilizations—with strife-ridden marches between. *Preceptum est vicecomiti* might be recorded on the rolls of the justiciar's court or of the Dublin bench, but the return was often in such phrases as *alia bona ... sunt terre de guerra ubi nullus serviens ausus est ingredi*.[3] The parallel with conditions in the Highlands of late medieval Scotland is evident.[4] The law was often powerless to aid in the recovery of cattle driven off by the Gaelic Irish or by lawless Anglo-Irish, and so the procedure grew common of granting licence to those thus despoiled to treat with felons in recovering their chattels as best they could.[5] It even appears that a person might regularly be employed in such negotiations: in 1305 a jury said that a woman, Grathagh le Deveneys, of the Uí Tuathail,

[1] *C.J.R. 1295–1303*, pp. 285, 456; *1305–7*, p. 180.
[2] *C.J.R. 1305–7*, pp. v–xiv (itinerary).
[3] C.P., P. 27 Edw. I (no. 43), in P.R.O.I., RC. 7/6, *Cal. plea rolls*, VI, 211. Cf. *C.J.R. 1295–1303*, pp. 147, 169; *1305–7*, pp. 167, 194, 195, 269, 319; C.P., T. 1 1–2 Edw. II, m. 5 *d* (*nihil inde actum est* because *inter Hibernicos ubi nullus serviens*, etc.).
[4] Cf. W. C. Dickinson, *Scotland from the earliest times to 1603* (2nd ed.: Edinburgh, 1965), p. 9.
[5] E.g. *C.J.R. 1308–14*, pp. 51, 174; *Foedera* (Rec. comm. ed.), I, II, 759; *Cal. rot. pat. Hib.*, pp. 6 (bishop of Limerick), 15 (William de la Ryvere); a petition of the bishop of Kildare for such a licence is in P.R.O., S.C. 9/25, m. 2 *d*.

GOVERNORS OF A TROUBLED LORDSHIP 35

is accustomed ... at the request of faithful men of peace to go to the ... mountains to ... search for cattle carried off by her race.[1]

The atmosphere of the records in such contexts suggests relations with hostile powers rather than with fellow-subjects of a common lordship. The justiciar might think it prudent to take hostages from Irish chieftains,[2] and in 1317 a plaint of debt was brought to recover the amount stipulated in an agreement between two Anglo-Irish lords as the penalty if either made a separate peace with the Irish.[3] Anglo-Irish lords, indeed, came to think in terms of blood relationship, rather than feudal lordship; in April 1297 John Cogan and John fitz Thomas entered into agreements with each other which included saving clauses that referred to *illis qui sunt de cognomine utriusque parentele* and *consanguinei de cognomine utriusque parentele*.[4]

Disorder of course greatly increased in the years (1315-18) of the Bruce invasion. In 1316 the justices of the Dublin bench were ordered to adjourn cases from Hilary to Easter term *in eodem statu*, for parties *propter viarum discrimina et inimicorum insidias* could not come before the bench *absque vite variis periculis*.[5] In the same year Edward Bruce marked his success by himself holding pleas in Ulster.[6] The breakdown of ordinary processes is illustrated by a grant of emergency powers (8 February 1316) by the justiciar, Butler, to the heads of the Laghles (the later Lawless?) family, who dwelt 'in a narrow part of the country between Newcastle McKynegan and Wicklow', and were being harassed by the Irish. They were empowered to treat with their attackers

[1] *C.J.R. 1305-7*, pp. 480-1.
[2] *C.J.R. 1295-1303*, p. 61, and *1305-7*, pp. 16, 270-1; J.R., 8-9 Edw. II, m. 3.
[3] J.R., 11 Edw. II (no. 115), in P.R.O.I., RC. 7/12, *Cal. plea rolls*, XII, 143-4.
[4] *Red book of Kildare*, pp. 42, 45.
[5] J. T. Gilbert, *History of the viceroys of Ireland* (Dublin, 1865), p. 527, from Irish patent roll, 9 Edw. II, now destroyed. The bench roll for Hilary 1316 contained only fourteen membranes, against forty-three in that for Michaelmas preceding; those of the first three terms of 1316 had only fifty-five in all against one hundred and twenty-one for the same terms in 1312 (*Ir. rec. comm. rep. 1816-20*, pp. 86-7, 523; where more than one roll survived from the same term, the longest has been used in this calculation).
[6] 'Chronicle of Pembridge', in *Chartul. St Mary's, Dublin*, II, 349. There is still no adequate account of the Bruce invasion, though the way has been pioneered by J. F. Lydon, 'The Bruce invasion of Ireland', in *Historical studies IV* (Dublin, 1963), ed. G. A. Hayes-McCoy, pp. 111-25.

3-2

in the manner of the marchers: if any of their [own] name offend against the peace they may take and imprison them, and they are not, by reason of such imprisonment, to be charged in the king's council [*sic*] or hindered in any way.[1]

It is right to say, however, that a somewhat similar licence seems to have been known even at the height of Wogan's administration, when it was pleaded by the defendant to a plaint of false imprisonment.[2] In 1317, the year after the grant to the Laghles family, the justiciar's court heard the story of the abduction from a seignorial prison of an Irish prisoner at the instance of an Anglo-Irish knight, who exchanged him for his own brother, held by Irish of the prisoner's clan.[3] The very defenders of the lordship found it impossible to maintain strict legality in their actions. The mayor and community of Dublin had to be granted indemnity for burning the suburbs at the crisis of the war, for *ea quae urgente necessitate guerre fiunt penis legis communis subesse non debent*.[4] In 1319, when all was over, Walter of Islip, the treasurer, obtained personal letters of indemnity for what he had done amiss in the course of the struggle.[5] On the other hand, later in that year, a commission consisting of Thomas fitz John, earl of Kildare, John de Bermingham, earl of Louth, Arnold Power, and John Wogan, was appointed to inquire into Bruce's accomplices. But their activities were abandoned early in 1320, no doubt on the principle of letting sleeping dogs lie.[6]

The Gaelic sources—let alone the records of the lordship—have left us eloquent descriptions of Edward Bruce's destructive career: *fer millti na hEirenn uli co coitchend eidir Gallaibh ocus Goidhelaibh*,[7] 'that overwhelming wave', the furious surge of which the author of the *Caithréim Thoirdhealbhaigh* pictured in a classical metaphor of memorable force.[8] Contemporary valuations of ecclesiastical

---

[1] J.R., 8–9 Edw. II, m. 11*d*; cf. Dickinson, *Scotland to 1603*, p. 60.
[2] *C.J.R. 1305–7*, p. 252.
[3] J.R., 11 Edw. II (no. 116), m. 24.   [4] *Foedera* (Rec. comm. ed.), II, 1, 350.
[5] *Cal. pat. rolls, 1317–21*, p. 269.
[6] *Foedera* (Rec. comm. ed.), III, 1, 396, 417.
[7] 'The man who destroyed all Ireland in common, both the foreigners and the Gaels': *Annals of Loch Cé*, s.a. 1318.
[8] *Caithréim Thoirdhealbhaigh, ed.* O'Grady, 1, 90. The historical value of the *Caithréim* has recently been vindicated: L. F. McNamara, 'An examination of the medieval Irish text *Caithréim Thoirdhealbhaigh*', *North Munster Antiquarian Journal*, VIII (1961), 182–92.

GOVERNORS OF A TROUBLED LORDSHIP 37

property tell their own, more prosaic, tale.[1] Nevertheless it would be an error to think of this harsh visitation falling upon a land thriving under an idyllic *Pax Normannica*.[2] The courts of the lordship, the structure and jurisdiction of which are now to be considered, were never those of a perfectly conquered country, and here we may fittingly fall back upon the wisdom of the man who ultimately played the leading role in the establishment of English law in all Ireland:

> for though the Prince doth beare the title of *Soveraign Lord* of an entire country ... yet if there bee ... parts of that Countrey wherein he cannot punish Treasons, Murders, or Thefts, unlesse he send an Army to do it; if the Jurisdiction of his ordinary courts of Justice doth not extend into those parts to protect the people from wrong and oppression; ... I cannot justly say, that such a Countrey is wholly conquered.[3]

ADDITIONAL NOTE I TO CHAPTER II:
THE FAMILY OF JOHN WOGAN

THE author of the best account of the Wogans has justifiably written: 'the early pedigree of the Wogans is extremely perplexing'.[4] Two particularly puzzling problems in connection with the great justiciar are his marriage or marriages and the relationship to him of the contemporaries who bore the name of Walter Wogan.

It seems clear that Wogan's wife Margaret, daughter of Robert de Valle, died in 1302 or 1304.[5] *D.N.B.*, relying on late Welsh genealogies, makes the justiciar marry in the first place Joan, heiress of Picton Castle, but this evidence is unconvincing.[6] A John Wogan married to one Isabella appears in 1310.[7] But it seems more probable that the John Wogan found married to one Avicia or Amicia in 1315 and 1318 was the former justiciar.[8] It seems also very likely that the

[1] G. J. Hand, 'The dating of the early fourteenth-century ecclesiastical valuations of Ireland', *Ir. theological quarterly*, XXIV (1957), 271–4.
[2] Cf. Orpen, IV, 262–3.
[3] Sir John Davies, 'A discoverie of the true causes why Ireland was never entirely subdued', in *Works*, ed. A. B. Grosart, II, 10.
[4] F. Green, 'The Wogans of Pembrokeshire', in *West Wales historical records*, VI (1916), 169–232, at p. 169.
[5] *Ibid.* pp. 174–5; 'Chronicle of Pembridge', in *Chartul. St Mary's, Dublin*, II, 330, 332.
[6] Green, art. cit. pp. 170–1.   [7] *Cal. rot. pat. Hib.* p. 15.
[8] *Cal. pat. rolls, 1313–17*, p. 223, and *1317–21*, p. 222.

justiciar had a son of the same name by his first wife. Presumably this son was married to either Isabella or Avicia/Amicia and was the John Wogan whom the inquisition *post mortem* of Aylmer of Valence in 1324 shows in possession of the Pembrokeshire lands.[1] John II, on this view, was the father of 'Thomas Wogan, son and heir of John Wogan', who came of age in 1331.[2]

There seem to have been at least two contemporaries of the justiciar named Walter Wogan. One is definitely known to have been his brother and was prebendary of Maynooth in St Patrick's cathedral, Dublin.[3] He probably was the Walter Wogan who was in Ireland in 1296[4] and is frequently mentioned in the justiciary rolls until 1307. But I think that the Walter Wogan who was steward of Wexford in 1312[5] is likely to have been a son of the justiciar, a knight, and the later (from 1317) justice of the justiciar's pleas. He is probably further to be identified with the Walter who held Wiston in Pembrokeshire in 1324, seemingly having married a co-parcener.[6] It is, I think, more than possible that the Walter Wogan who was constable of Roscommon castle in 1302–3[7] and whom some of the justiciary rolls references prior to 1307 may concern was a distinct person.

William Wogan, marshal of the eyre in Ireland, died about 1305, but his relationship to the justiciar is quite obscure.[8]

[1] *Cal. inq. p.m.* VI, 336.
[2] *Cal. close rolls, 1330–33*, p. 213; cf. *Red book of Kildare*, ed. G. MacNiocaill (Irish MSS. Comm., 1964), p. 117.
[3] Christ Church, Dublin, MS. 'Novum Registrum', I, 346; H. J. Lawlor, *The Fasti of St Patrick's* (Dundalk, 1930), p. 192; *C.J.R. 1305–7*, pp. 252–3.
[4] C.P., T. 24 Edw. I, in P.R.O.I., RC. 7/4, *Cal. plea rolls*, IV, 162; *Cal. pat. rolls, 1292–1301*, p. 198.
[5] J.R., 6–7 Edw. II, m. 18*d*.
[6] *Cal. inq. p.m.* VI, 336.
[7] P.R.O., C. 47/10/16. In general, cf. Green, in *West Wales historical records*, VI, 189–90, where broadly similar conclusions about the Walter Wogans are reached, though much of the evidence here cited is not used.
[8] P.R.O., C. 47/10/17, no. 17; Mem. 31–2 Edw. I, in P.R.O.I., RC. 8/1, *Cal. mem. rolls*, I, 283; *C.J.R., 1305–7*, pp. 148, 193, 196, 262.

ADDITIONAL NOTE II TO CHAPTER II: THE IRISH CHANCERY

There is as yet no adequate account of the medieval Irish chancery and its diplomatic. J. Otway-Ruthven, 'The medieval Irish chancery', in *Album H.M. Cam* (Louvain, 1961), I, 119–38, is chiefly of value for the personnel of the chancery in the late medieval period; useful information is also found in the various writings of H. G. Richardson and G. O. Sayles. Other relevant articles are: H. Jenkinson, 'The great seal of England: deputed or departmental seals', in *Archaeologia*, LXXXV (1936), 293–340, at pp. 314–23; P. F. Chaplais, 'The chancery of Guienne, 1289–1453', in *Studies presented to Sir Hilary Jenkinson* (London, 1957), pp. 61–96, at pp. 63–4.

An examination of surviving writs of the Irish chancery now in P.R.O., C. 47/10/14, 15, 16 and 18, and of those enrolled on the plea rolls, suggests that the following four notes of warranty were customary:

(i) *per ipsum justiciarium*—immediate warrant by the justiciar;

(ii) *per billam ipsius justiciarii*—warrant by justiciar's bill;

(iii) *per breve de Anglia* or *de magno sigillo nostro Anglie*—this may mean no more than that English writs addressed to the justiciar were passed by him to the chancellor as warrants;

(iv) *per breve de Anglia de privato sigillo* or *de privato sigillo Anglie*—similar to the last instance, except that a writ of privy seal was in question.

There is a remarkable account of the possible series of authorities—writ of England to the justiciar, bill of the justiciar to the chancellor, writ of chancery to the escheator—in the restoration of a bishop's temporalities in 1275: P.R.O., S.C. 1/18, no. 10. For an unusual letter of Roger Mortimer to the justices of the Dublin bench (the equivalent, as it were, of an English writ of privy seal?), see C.P., P. 11 Edw. II, in P.R.O.I., RC. 7/12, *Cal. plea rolls*, XII, 481–2.

CHAPTER III

THE JUSTICIAR'S COURT

The office of Justice of the justiciar's pleas

THE constant itineration of the justiciar's court, which the rolls make clear, is one sign that it was still closely associated with the person of the chief governor. This is also shown by the curious situation which arose when a king's lieutenant was inserted between the king and the justiciar (or his deputy). The existence in 1308-9 of two divisions, as it were, of the justiciar's court, under Piers Gaveston as king's lieutenant and Wogan as justiciar (or his deputy), cannot be absolutely proved, though it is probable; but there is no doubt that such a division took place under Roger Mortimer as king's lieutenant and Edmund Butler as justiciar in 1317-18.[1]

No clear-out difference of jurisdiction between the divisions *coram locumtenente* and *coram justiciario* has been found, although Butler's court had greater continuity with the justiciar's court as it existed before Mortimer's coming.[2] One might expect the authority enjoyed by the court of the king's lieutenant to have been greater, but no statement, express or implied, of this has come to light.

Clearly, the Irish court was *coram locumtenente, justiciario* or *custode*, as the case might be, in a much more literal sense than the contemporary English king's bench was *coram rege*. Nevertheless, the justiciar of Ireland's other duties were such as to make professional help necessary. *Britton* names him as one of the exceptions to the rule that justices may not, without the king, appoint substitutes for themselves in matters of record.[3] In fact, from the later thirteenth century, the justiciar had a judicial

[1] Pp. 23-4, above; for a list of known sessions during Mortimer's lieutenancy, see Appendix IV.
[2] Headings for essoins and *communia placita* appear, on the known evidence, only in connection with Butler, with whom Walter Wogan, the justice of the justiciar's pleas, appears to have remained. Two legal assistants to Mortimer were paid, David le Blond and Robert Bagod (Richardson and Sayles, *Administration*, pp. 167-8).
[3] *Ed.* F. M. Nichols (Oxford, 1865), I, 7.

THE JUSTICIAR'S COURT

assistant, the justice of the justiciar's pleas. The plea rolls are so reticent about this important person that it must at once be admitted that it can never be known just how much, and what, business was left to his sole discretion. Indeed, the early history of the office would remain even more obscure than it is, and no list of those who held it at this period could be compiled with any confidence, were there not some surviving Irish exchequer sources on which to draw.[1]

The first justice of the justiciar's pleas was almost certainly Richard of Exeter and a review of his career is a necessary part of any examination of the origins of the office. He first appears as a justice of the itinerant bench in 1258 and he is mentioned in eyre regularly until 1282.[2] His son and namesake, himself a chief justice of the bench, much later called him *justice en eyre*.[3] Yet in 1276 he was ordered to lodge in the treasury at Dublin his own rolls and those of the deceased judge, Walrand of Wellesley,

de toto tempore quo vos et prefatus Waleranus fuistis justiciarii Henrici regis ... et ... nostri de banco in Hibernia.[4]

There is an isolated reference to him as *unus justiciariorum nostrorum de banco* in 1279.[5] In the Easter parliament of 1290 at Westminster a petitioner claimed to have been clerk to Richard and to Nicholas Taff (a justice of the bench from 1278 to 1287) in the *baunc de Divelyn*.[6] But the almost complete Irish exchequer records of payments to justices of the bench from 1276 never mention Richard as one of them, though he was paid his fee of forty pounds a year at least as far back as 1275, sometimes without further explanation, sometimes as a justice itinerant.[7] The evidence suggests that he was a justice when the Dublin and itinerant benches were not wholly distinct, and then became in effect chief justice in eyre, but continued to attend in the bench as a supernumerary when he could.

---

[1] These sources, now in the Public Record Office, London, have been used in Richardson and Sayles, *Administration*, on which I have in general relied.
[2] Appendix I, below.
[3] P.R.O., S.C. 8/318, no. E. 331, and 327, no. E. 823.
[4] P.R.O., C. 66/95, m. 10 (*Cal. doc. Ire. 1285–92*, 584).
[5] P.R.O., C. 62/56, m. 9, quoted by Sayles, *Select cases in K.B.* I, p. cxxxvi, n. 1 (with the reference to the roll misprinted as '86').
[6] Cole, *Documents*, p. 72.
[7] E.g. E. 101/230, no. 12 (justice itinerant), no. 25 (unspecified).

Something of importance may have happened in Richard's career in 1282, for in September of that year he was ordered:

Quia intelleximus quod presencia vestra in banco nostro Dublinie est valde necessaria ad placita in eodem banco tenenda, vobis mandamus ... quod ad placita in dicto banco tenenda de cetero diligenter intendatis ... Et taliter vos habeatis in hac parte quod placita huiusmodi in banco illo tenenda amodo diligencius deducantur quam hactenus deduci consueuerint. Et ad placita itineris vestri in diversis comitatibus terre predicte similiter oportunis locis et temporibus intendatis ...[1]

The implications concerning Richard's activities, both past and future, are bewildering. How was his presence in the Dublin bench *valde necessaria*, considering that it is known that at least four justices were paid for services in that court in each term of the preceding three years? There is no evidence of Richard having become more active in the Dublin bench after September 1282, though his activities on eyre seem to have ended. There is, however, an interpretation that makes sense—provided we can accept the doubtful assumption that *bancum nostrum Dublin'* might mean something other than the bench sedentary there. It is that the order just quoted referred to the justiciar's court or justiciar's bench and was in effect Richard's appointment as in a special way justice of the justiciar's pleas. It is perhaps relevant that the letters follow, on the patent roll, those appointing Stephen of Fulbourn as justiciar.

In any event, from a date three years later (Michaelmas 1285) Richard is recorded as having been paid his fee as *justiciarius assignatus ad placita que sequuntur capitalem justiciarium Hibernie tenenda*.[2] Upon his death in 1286 Walter Lenfant was appointed by the justiciar and council to succeed him. It appears, however, that the treasurer, with the characteristic caution of a finance department, thought that so considerable an appointment, involving a fee equal to that of the chancellor, treasurer, or chief justice of the bench, needed to be ratified by the king in England, and so did not pay him his fees. In itself, this suggests a certain lack of definition about the office and its status. We know of these circumstances from a petition which Walter sent to the king at the Hilary parliament of 1290 to secure the arrears of his fee and

[1] Richardson and Sayles, *Administration*, p. 232.
[2] P.R.O., E. 372/139, m. 9d.

THE JUSTICIAR'S COURT 43

its proper payment for the future.[1] The petition was successful. The English chancery issued letters in Walter's favour as follows:

Rex justiciario suo Hibernie vel eius locum tenenti qui pro tempore fuerit salutem. Cum assignaverimus dilectum et fidelem nostrum Walterum Lenfaunt ad tenendum placita nostra vos sequencia ubicumque locorum vos venire contigerit per partes Hibernie et concesserimus eidem Waltero quadraginta libras percipiendas de thesauro nostro singulis annis quibus de voluntate nostra officio intenderit supradicto; vobis mandamus quod dictas quadraginta libras eidem Waltero per breve nostrum de liberate sub sigillo nostro quo utimur in cancellaria nostra Hibernie singulis annis habere faciatis in forma predicta. In cuius etc.[2]

Upon these letters was mistakenly founded the belief that the office of justice of the justiciar's pleas was instituted in 1290. The importance of that year in the history of the court is, nevertheless, real. It was then that what seems initially to have been an experiment made by the Irish administration in the judicial system was ratified by the king in England. The precise date when the office of justice of the justiciar's pleas first appeared remains somewhat doubtful, however. We can take it that it was before 1285, and 1282 is a date which has a good deal to recommend it.[3]

There is an aspect of Richard of Exeter's career, not yet mentioned, which may be relevant to the emergence of the office of justice of the justiciar's pleas. From at latest March 1270 to at least November 1276 Richard served as justiciar's deputy. By this is not here meant a person ruling Ireland in a temporary absence of the chief governor, but a general assistant to him. Now, at Easter 1290 Walter Lenfant is found in the same role; he and William Dodingeseles, described as deputies of the keeper, Archbishop John of Sandford, were campaigning on the Connaught marches of Meath.[4] Perhaps the legal office of justice of the justiciar's pleas evolved by differentiation from that of justiciar's deputy, which in fact seems to have become less prominent with the appearance of the more specialized one.

[1] Cole, *Documents*, p. 56.
[2] P.R.O., C. 66/109, m. 39 (*Cal. doc. Ire. 1285–92*, 584).
[3] 1282 is advanced by Richardson and Sayles, *Administration*, p. 36, on the basis of an argument somewhat different in emphasis and detail from that above.
[4] *Cal. doc. Ire. 1285–92*, p. 270.

Although inconclusive so far as the suggestion just made is concerned, the diplomatic of the headings of pleas in the justiciary rolls is here of some interest. A heading of 1292, surviving in a cartulary, reads *Placita coram Johanne de Malton tenente locum capitalis justiciarii*;[1] John had succeeded Walter Lenfant as justice in the preceding year. In 1295, Walter de la Haye, justice since 1294, is called *locum tenens*,[2] and there is a vaguer reference to a *locum tenens* in 1299 that also seems to mean the justice of the justiciar's pleas.[3] There was a heading of pleas before the justice as deputy justiciar in 1316, but the circumstances are obscure.[4] Otherwise it may be said that, after 1295:

(i) headings of pleas in the justiciar's court are phrased *coram* the actual governor (or one of the governors) in Ireland at the time;[5]
(ii) the words *locum tenens* refer only to a keeper (*custos*) or to the deputy of a chief governor absent from Ireland;[6]
(iii) incidental references to the justice of the justiciar's pleas are as a rule simply by name, such titles as *justiciarius assignatus ad placita justiciarium Hibernie sequentia tenenda* being rarely found on the justiciary rolls (though they are usual in the Irish exchequer accounts).[7]

[1] *Chartul. St Mary's, Dublin*, I, 137.
[2] *C.J.R., 1295–1303*, p. 73; *ibid.* p. 231, refers to a time when Walter was apparently deputy, in the sense of temporary governor, for William de Vescy.
[3] *Ibid.* p. 227.
[4] J.R., 9–11 Edw. II. The relevant pages of the calendar are missing and so the only authority now surviving is a note made at the beginning.
[5] Exceptions are:
  (*a*) Richard de Burgh, earl of Ulster, held pleas as *locum tenens* in Michaelmas and Hilary terms, 1299–1300 (*C.J.R. 1295–1303*, pp. 119, 287–97), although he is not known to have been paid as chief governor. Wogan may none the less have been absent from Ireland; when he went to Scotland in 1296 he retained his fee, which was not paid to a deputy.
  (*b*) At least once in 1310 the justice of the justiciar's pleas, David le Blond, and a clerk of the court, William de Bourne, were commissioned to act for Wogan, *alibi pro arduis negotiis domini regis agentis*, and were described as *assignati loco* etc. (S. Mayart, 'The answer of Sir Samuel Mayart... to a book entitled, *A Declaration...*', in W. Harris, *Hibernica*, part 2, p. 93).
  (*c*) Several times in 1313 the chancellor, Walter of Thornbury, and the justice of the justiciar's pleas, William Alexander, were similarly commissioned to the place of the *custos*, absent elsewhere in Ireland at the time (*C.J.R. 1308–14*, pp. 272, 286; J.R., 6–7 Edw. II, mm. 51, 61, 69, 79, etc.; p. 56, below).
[6] But cf. what is said of Richard de Burgh in the last note.
[7] The only instances in the printed series are: *C.J.R. 1295–1303*, p. 223; *1305–7*, pp. 162, 201, 497, and *1308–14*, p. 318.

THE JUSTICIAR'S COURT

A second justice appears to have been paid in 1290–1, though it is possible that he was merely taking the place of Walter Lenfant.[1] But in 1324 a second justice of the justiciar's pleas was definitely added, the senior justice becoming known as chief justice.[2] The reasons for this can only be surmised: an increase in business, the model of the Dublin bench and of the English king's bench, perhaps the awkwardness and lack of continuity that followed dependence on a single justice. The last point may have been keenly felt: between May 1317 and September 1324 there were nine terms of office of persons acting as justice of the justiciar's pleas.[3] These frequent changes are perhaps to be blamed on one man, Walter Wogan, who was almost certainly the justiciar's son and was first appointed as justice in 1317.[4] Although his interests in Wales were constantly calling him away, he evidently was anxious to retain a grip on the Irish office, and so a succession of temporary appointments occurred; ultimately Walter stepped down to become second justice.

In all fourteen persons acted as justice of the justiciar's pleas between Walter Lenfant's appointment in 1286 and that of a second justice in 1324, and a little may now be said of their careers and qualifications.[5] Seven were knights (Walter Lenfant, senior, John of Houghton, Walter de la Haye, John of Fressingfield, Walter Lenfant, junior, Walter Wogan, Robert Bagod).[6] At

[1] John of Houghton, described as *alter justiciarius ad eadem placita*: P.R.O., E. 372/139, m. 9 d. An immediately succeeding entry concerning John of Malton makes it clear that he was taking Walter's place; but there is no such statement in the case of John of Houghton.

[2] Roger of Birthorpe had letters patent dated 30 May 1324 appointing him as a second justice of the pleas following the justiciar 'with the usual fee' (P.R.O., C. 66/160, m. 12 [*Cal. pat. rolls, 1321–4,* p. 420]), but there is no reason to believe that this implies the existence of a second justice before payment to Roger in that capacity started in the autumn of 1324 (cf. Richardson and Sayles, *Administration,* p. 168).

[3] I have not taken into account the two legal assistants to Mortimer during his lieutenancy: p. 40, n. 2, above.

[4] On Walter Wogan, chapter II, Additional Note I, above.

[5] Throughout this study dates of tenure are taken from Richardson and Sayles, *Administration,* but rendered approximately. Biographical details are drawn from Ball, *Judges,* I, 52–65, very extensively supplemented from a variety of sources. A couple of entries in the *Administration* list of justices of the justiciar's pleas have been ignored above, since I believe them to concern limited commissions in special circumstances (p. 56, n. 2). Mortimer's legal assistants have been included in the reckoning, since they both served at other times also.

[6] Robert Bagod may have been a clerk who had left his clergy: Lawlor, *Fasti of St Patrick's,* p. 192; cf. p. 95.

least two were clerks (Master David le Blond, Richard Brown). A more significant distinction can be made between those, nine in all, who were primarily general administrators by background, and the five who brought substantial judicial or professional legal experience with them to the justiciar's court. The elder Walter Lenfant (1286–91, 1292–4) and Walter de la Haye (1294–7) were key members of the administration whose experience had not been narrowly legal. Lenfant had been engaged in Irish administration for at least a decade before being chosen to succeed Richard of Exeter.[1] Although Walter de la Haye had had some experience as a justice in eyre his chief importance was as escheator from 1285 to 1308 and as keeper of Ireland in 1294. Richard Brown, an exchequer clerk who acted very briefly in 1318, and Roger of Birthorpe (1318, 1320, 1321–2, 1323) are not known to have had previous legal experience, though both later became justices of the bench. John of Houghton (1290–1) had served to a limited extent on eyre; John of Malton (1291–2), though apparently lacking in previous experience, later became steward of Kildare. Walter Wogan (1317–18, 1318–20, 1323–4) had probably been steward of Wexford.[2] The younger Walter Lenfant, while justice of the justiciar's pleas (1298–1302, 1303–5, 1306–8, 1310–11), presided in four eyres between 1300 and 1306.[3] Thomas Ace (1320–1) is thoroughly obscure.

In the reign of Edward II three judges with extensive judicial experience are found coming to serve in the justiciar's court. William Alexander (1311–15) had been regularly on eyre for at least ten years beforehand. Hugh Canon (1315–17) had been a justice of the bench for seven years. Robert Bagod (1322–3) can hardly be said to have left the Dublin bench, on which he sat for almost all the reign of Edward II, for he merely came to the sister court to tide over a difficulty for a few months. Two pleaders were promoted. John of Fressingfield (1302–3, 1305–6) was an English *narrator* who came to Ireland with John Wogan and

---

[1] He was steward of Kildare about 1269: J.I., 53 Hen. III, in P.R.O.I., RC. 7/1, *Cal. plea rolls*, I, 482–3. That there were two Walter Lenfants, father and son, in Edwardian Ireland is unquestionable, but it is with some hesitation that I have followed the distinction drawn between them in *Administration*.

[2] Chapter II, Additional Note I, above.

[3] In two instances John of Fressingfield took his place and fee, in one Walter continued to take his ordinary fee and took nothing for the eyre, in one the records are defective.

discharged much miscellaneous administrative and legal business, including the office of keeper of the rolls and writs of the bench; he acted as justice only when Walter Lenfant was absent on eyre.[1] One personal characteristic of his has come down across the centuries; he was a connoisseur of white wine.[2] Master David le Blond (1308-10) was accused, in the very year he took his place in the justiciar's court, of having obtained four hundred librates of land in four years by champerty, conspiracy, and fraud.[3]

The lesser personnel of the justiciar's court

Thanks to the care with which they noted the assignment of damages to themselves—even though this was often in the simple form *t' c'* (*totum clericis*)—a list of clerks of the court could easily be constructed.[4] For example, the roll for 33-4 Edward I has the names of William de Bourne, John of Patrick's Church, and Nicholas, who was an assistant to William de Bourne. William on occasion performed minor judicial functions, such as the taking of an assize in a case when the justiciar could not conveniently attend in person.[5] John of Patrick's Church, who first appears as a clerk of the court in 1300, is identified by a solitary reference in 1305 as keeper of the rolls of the court, the first holder of this office known.[6] He was still associated with the court well into the reign of Edward II.[7] The only other light on the office of keeper of the rolls and writs in this period comes from 1323, when the office was committed by letters of the English chancery to Henry of Thrapston.[8] A person of this name had held the same office in the Dublin bench in the later years of Edward I. On this occasion (or perhaps on some other, later in the same decade), the English appointment encountered an attempt to have Thomas of Pinxton, who had served more than once as keeper of the rolls of an eyre and was acting in that office in the justiciar's court, retained in

[1] *Cal. pat. rolls, 1292-1301*, p. 167. There were two men of the name, father and son, and their careers may have been confused above: *Cal. pat. rolls, 1307-13*, p. 324.
[2] *C.J.R. 1305-7*, p. 46.
[3] P.R.O., S.C. 8/164, no. 8180; p. 139, below.
[4] E.g. J.R., 6-7 Edw. II, *passim*.
[5] *C.J.R. 1295-1303*, pp. 258, 260; cf. also p. 44, n. 5 (*b*), above.
[6] *C.J.R. 1295-1303*, p. 349; *1305-7*, p. 95.
[7] I have not searched for references beyond the printed volumes of *C.J.R.* and the surviving roll of 6-7 Edw. II.
[8] *Cal. close rolls, 1323-7*, p. 14.

office; Thomas fitz John, earl of Kildare, interested himself in the matter.[1] Another person who sometimes was assigned part of damages was the marshal of the court.[2] The marshals of the Irish courts were appointed by the descendants of John Marshal, nephew of the elder Earl William, who held the marshalsea of Ireland in fee.[3] For example, in January 1313 one Almaric de Bellofago brought into the justiciar's court letters of William II Marshal of this line (1282–1314) committing the marshalsea to James de Bellofago

quamdiu nobis placuerit, coram capitali justiciario domini regis in Hibernia, thesaurario et baronibus de scaccario Hibernie, et omnibus aliis justiciariis et ministris eiusdem domini regis, in omnibus locis ubi decet et expedit in dicto officio ministrare et exequi. Ita quod de exitibus marescalcie predicte nobis respondeat.[4]

A letter of this James was also produced, appointing one John of Appleby to discharge the office, and the new marshal was duly admitted. After the death of John IV Marshal (1314–16), however, some years elapsed before the husband of his sister and heiress obtained livery of the office; the Irish administration seized it into the king's hand, in which it still was in 1324.[5] The chief duty of the marshal of the justiciar's court was of course the custody of prisoners.[6] The amount of his fees was a matter of complaint and attempts at control were made in 1323, 1342, and 1351.[7]

Nothing much can be said of the crier of the justiciar's court, except that he sometimes was assigned part of damages and is also found as the bearer of writs of summons to parliament.[8]

The history of the king's attorney, serjeants and pleaders in Ireland has been elucidated by Mr Richardson and Professor

[1] P.R.O., S.C. 1/35, no. 180, 180 A. These are two letters addressed to John of Hotham, bishop of Ely, one from Thomas fitz John, the other from a correspondent whose name is illegible. A reference to Thomas de Montpellier as chancellor of the Irish exchequer suggests the date 1323. The senders do not call Hotham chancellor, which he was not at the time, and probably relied on his general influence and his knowledge of Irish affairs.
[2] E.g. J.R., 11 Edw. II (no. 116), mm. 4d, 17, 21d; (no. 117), mm. 5d, 10.
[3] *Complete peerage*, VIII, 525–8.
[4] J.R., 6–7 Edw. II, m. 36.
[5] *Cal. inq. p. m., 10–20 Edw. II*, no. 61; *Cal. fine rolls, 1302–19*, p. 393; *Cal. close rolls, 1323–7*, p. 205; cf. J.R., 11 Edw. II (no. 116), m. 4d.
[6] E.g., *C.J.R. 1295–1303*, pp. 53, 65, 72, 73, 120, etc.
[7] *Stat. Ire. John–Hen. V*, pp. 294, 356, 384–6; *Cal. close rolls, 1349–54*, p. 292.
[8] *C.J.R. 1295–1303*, p. 349; *1305–7*, pp. 357, 413.

Sayles.¹ Until about 1300, when a second was added, only one *narrator* appears to have received a regular fee, and the king's attorney does not appear on the issue rolls until 1313; in each case the fee was five marks a year. (An earlier king's serjeant, Roger Owen, appointed between 1261 and 1266, had complained that the Irish council had not kept promises to reward him fittingly *ubi dictus Rogerus magnum sallarium de magnatibus Hibernie potuit recepisse*).²

Richard le Blond, who is found suing for the king in the justiciary rolls,³ was king's serjeant for a quarter of a century and was eventually rewarded with a seat on the Dublin bench. In fact, however, the person who most frequently sued for the king in the justiciar's court in the early days of Wogan's administration, John de Ponz, is not known to have received a regular annual fee for this; he also served as a justice of assize, and on eyre, and, like Richard le Blond, was ultimately found a seat on the bench.⁴ Richard Manning, the first known king's attorney, appears as an attorney and essoiner in the justiciar's court before his appointment.⁵

There are many entries on the rolls referring to the assignment of damages to *narratores*.⁶ The grant of an annual fee and robe, or of land or a rent for life, to such a pleader as a retainer by an individual or corporation was an accepted practice.⁷ In a plea of trespass in 1305, the court 'gave' two pleaders to act for the two Droghedas, but the attorneys of the towns failed to pay them their fee and they applied to the court for it to be taxed and levied.⁸ It came to six marks between the two, a reminder that the five marks annually of a king's pleader was no more than a formal retainer. In conclusion, although no list of pleaders practising in the justiciar's court at a given time can be regarded as complete, it may be noted that eight are found in the two divisions of the court in 1317–18.⁹

¹ *Administration*, pp. 40–42, 174–81; *Select cases in K.B.* v, p. lvii.
² P.R.O., C. 47/10/13, no. 6; this clause has been accidentally omitted from the text as printed by Richardson and Sayles, *Administration*, p. 230.
³ E.g. *C.J.R. 1305–7*, pp. 10, 101–2.
⁴ *C.J.R. 1295–1303*, pp. 87, 103, 109, 111, etc.
⁵ *C.J.R. 1305–7*, pp. 291, 292, 359; *1308–14*, p. 75.
⁶ E.g. ibid. *1305–7*, pp. 54, 69, 323, 337, etc.
⁷ Ibid. *1305–7*, pp. 54, 306; *Cal. close rolls, 1302–7*, p. 487; and *1307–13*, p. 29; J.R., 6–7 Edw. II, m. 47.   ⁸ *C.J.R. 1305–7*, p. 16.
⁹ Thomas Bagod (later a justice of the bench), William Chaumflour, Nicholas of Cardiff, Henry Forester, John Gervas, William Lessayn, John Plunket, and Simon fitz Richard (later a chief justice of the bench): J.R., 11 Edw. II (no. 116), m. 8, and (no. 117), mm. 12, 14; also (no. 115), in P.R.O.I., RC. 7/12, *Cal. plea rolls*, XII, 139–40.

The justiciar's court and the council

The justiciar's court was necessarily closely connected with the Irish council, *secretum concilium*. That the councillors who might be available should be consulted on difficult points is only to be expected, but it must be said that the number of references on the justiciary rolls to the part of the council in judicial business is surprisingly small—about two dozen in the three volumes of the printed series.[1] There is a heading 'Pleas of the council of the king' on the roll for 34 Edward I, but none of the business beneath it was narrowly judicial.[2] In an instance in which the text of a plaint was enrolled, the address is to 'the justiciar and council of the king',[3] but evidence which would enable us to assess how often this form was used is lacking. Some of the incidental references to the council concern the business of the court as the summit of the Irish judicial hierarchy, rather than as a court of first instance. A lower court might be ordered to send a record and process *coram justiciario et illis de consilio nostro in hac terra*; this phrase is quoted from an Irish writ found on a roll of the Dublin bench, but it may be paralleled by English writs entered on the justiciary rolls, which order the justiciar to examine cases in association with members of the council.[4] There is some indication that amendment of a writ or record of a lower court was a matter for the council; a justice in eyre is ordered to revoke a judicial writ,[5] the estreat rolls of the bench are to be amended, for a writ which would have caused a change in an entry on them reached the justices only after they had sent the rolls to the exchequer,[6] a serjeant counter

---

[1] Here I must respectfully disagree with Richardson and Sayles, *The Irish parliament*, pp. 36–7. Some of the references in note 94 to p. 36 are to business that can only be described as judicial by stretching the term—e.g. *C.J.R. 1305–7*, p. 28 (arrangements for the assignment of lands to John fitz Thomas). However probable on general grounds the part suggested by these authors as played by the council may be, it is not fully documented on the surviving rolls.

[2] *C.J.R. 1305–7*, pp. 242–3.

[3] *C.J.R. 1295–1303*, p. 255. This was a particularly serious case, which may explain the enrolment. Complainant alleged that defendant told the chief justice of the English king's bench that complainant had told him that another justice of that court 'would do nothing without bribe'; for which complainant was imprisoned by the marshal.

[4] C.P., P. 27 Edw. I (no. 47), in P.R.O.I., RC. 7/7, *Cal. plea rolls*, VII, 33; *C.J.R. 1295–1303*, pp. 122, 437, and *1305–7*, p. 294.

[5] *C.J.R. 1295–1303*, p. 215.

[6] *C.J.R. 1305–7*, p. 230.

THE JUSTICIAR'S COURT 51

on behalf of the king alleges that a fine made on eyre is in contravention of the statute of *Quia emptores*.[1]

Similarly, when we turn to the instances in which the court's own original jurisdiction is involved, the council is found authorizing an alteration in the estreats of the justiciar's court after they had gone to the exchequer.[2] Other occasions for conciliar intervention were varied. A sheriff defended himself against a plaint of unjust seizure of cattle by claiming that the complainant had been indicted of robbery by an inquisition before him, but it transpired that the jurors had been adjourned before they had completed their presentations and had not in fact indicted the complainant—the council decided against the sheriff.[3] The chancellor, treasurer, justices of the bench, barons of the exchequer, and others of the council deliberated on the admission of the mayor and community of Drogheda to fine for harbouring felons.[4] Two exceptionally grave matters in which the council was involved were the case which produced a protest from the leading magnates against pleading an English writ of trespass in the justiciar's court and the proceedings against those of the de Verdun family who had attacked an army sent by the justiciar and bearing the king's standard.[5] It is of course likely that many informal consultations took place on which the record is silent.

* * * * * * * *

The remainder of this chaptei will treat, first, of the different types of session held by the justiciar's court and of the preparations for them; and then of its jurisdiction considered in detail: pleas of the crown, juries and assizes, procedure without writ, *communia placita*, and review of proceedings of lower courts (together with other relations with them). Analyses of sample rolls of crown and general pleas will illustrate the points made.

The sessions of the court

The movements of the justiciar's court could not be merely haphazard, but had to be planned somewhat in advance, in order to make arrangements for the accommodation and provisioning

---

[1] *C.J.R. 1295–1303*, pp. 383–5.   [2] *C.J.R. 1308–14*, p. 318.
[3] *C.J.R. 1295–1303*, p. 2.   [4] *C.J.R. 1308–14*, p. 167.
[5] *C.J.R. 1305–7*, p. 78; *1308–14*, p. 239; cf. pp. 24, 27, above, and p. 141, below.

of the justiciar and his entourage, and in order to give prospective litigants adequate notice of his coming. The justiciar's progress must have been a considerable cavalcade. In 1302 the chief governor had to adjourn pleas, because there was a state of war with the Irish of Wicklow, where he was, and his rolls and writs had not come.[1] In 1305 his cloth of state was stolen while in transit.[2] There are various references to provisioning for his stay.[3] As for the actual place of pleas, in Dublin all the royal courts were held in the same place:

le maner le Roi pres du chastel de Dyuelyn dehors les murs ou les playdes de tote la terre soleynt tout temps estre tenuz auxi bien les playdes la chef justice e du Baunk come del Escheker e du meisme la counte e la place de la chauncellerie

until this was burnt in the Bruce wars

par quoy les playdes de cheskune place de la dite terre sont tenuz en divers luyes en la dite ville de Diuelyn issint qe nul ministre poet venir ne conseiler ad autre en divers caas tant busoygne le demaunde sicome il soleyent e avereynt faire . . . .[4]

Outside Dublin, suitable houses might be requisitioned, with compensation to the owners for any injury they might suffer.[5]

During this period, the sessions held by the justiciar came to be of two different types, which may be called the 'full' and the 'casual', with sessions held at Dublin occupying a special position. The earliest justiciary roll (23 Edward I) to have survived to modern times was also the only one to survive from a date earlier than the justiciarship of John Wogan, and it shows the chief governor engaged in sessions of irregular length and varied business. By far the commonest heading is simply *placita*, although

[1] *C.J.R. 1295–1303*, p. 383.   [2] *C.J.R. 1305–7*, p. 468.
[3] *C.J.R. 1295–1303*, pp. 38, 297, 332; *1305–7*, pp. 289, 414–15.
[4] P.R.O., S.C. 8/118, no. 5881. This is a request from *les ministres dIrlaund* that the mayor and community, who had burnt the suburbs as a defensive measure, should be made to pay for the rebuilding of the hall of pleas: cf. p. 36, above. Rent was paid to Robert of Willoughby for the use of his houses by the exchequer: P.R.O., E. 101/237, no. 8. John of Hotham had earlier tried to get the treasurer to move into Dublin Castle for safety: *Cal. close rolls, 1313–18*, p. 293. Incidental references to the king's hall of pleas at Dublin are found on the justiciary rolls: *C.J.R. 1295–1303*, p. 315; *1305–7*, p. 250 (a *barrer*' to be made for it).
[5] *C.J.R. 1305–7*, p. 132 (Castledermot); *1308–14*, p. 198 (Cork); cf. J.R., 8–9 Edw. II, m. 8 (repairs to houses at Cork to make them suitable for the justiciar's use).

THE JUSTICIAR'S COURT

the more precise descriptions *deliberacio gaole, placita de corona, placita querelarum* and *placita de juratis et assisis*, are sometimes used. In addition, certain entries, from different sessions but of the same kind, are gathered together—fines, memoranda (chiefly of a general administrative nature), bails and mainprises, and admissions to the king's peace. The sessions as recorded on the roll may be roughly summarized, apart from the five-and-a-half membranes devoted to the special entries just mentioned, as seven sessions of such length as to require more than a single membrane apiece—these take up thirteen membranes in all—and eighteen shorter sessions, occupying six-and-half membranes between them.[1] All but two of the longer sessions, but only half a dozen of the others, included both common pleas and pleas of the crown.

The very first roll surviving from Wogan's justiciarship shows a marked change, although its first entries are little more than a year later in date than the last on the roll for 23 Edward I.[2] Crown pleas are on a separate roll, the memoranda and other special membranes have disappeared, the general term *placita* is much less often used and the more precise headings more often, and a new heading, *communia placita* (under which henceforth goes much of the old memoranda), has appeared. Sessions are less numerous and more is done at them: twenty-one in nine months, taking forty-seven membranes, in 25 Edward I, against twenty-five in seven months, taking twenty-five membranes, in 23 Edward I.

In the next few years, this tendency towards longer sessions in fewer places, recorded under precise descriptive headings instead of the old vague *placita*, developed, and by the last years of the reign of Edward I there is on the rolls a guide which enables us to classify sessions in a revealing way. This is the writ of warning to the sheriff, announcing the justiciar's coming to hold a full session in the county. It may be called, from its opening clause, the writ *venire facias omnes assisas*.[3] It is first noted on the rolls, in a simple form, in 1302.[4] Its absence from the rolls at an earlier

[1] m. 12, which stands apart as of distinctly earlier date than the others, has not been included in this reckoning, while sessions occurring in the same week at Ardfert and at Tralee have been treated as single sessions for Kerry: *C.J.R. 1295-1303*, pp. 1-3, 13, 19-27, 41-7, 52-5. The printed calendar of this roll is arranged neither chronologically nor according to the sewing of the membranes.
[2] Cf. Appendix III, below.   [3] So in J.R., 11 Edw. II (no. 116), m. 21*d*.
[4] *C.J.R. 1295-1303*, p. 413 (assizes only).

date must not be thought to mean that the court's jurisdiction essentially changed or that writs to a broadly similar effect had not been employed before.[1] What did happen was that the exercise of jurisdiction was better organized, and this was accompanied by greater precision in the records of the court. In the last years of Edward I, it became customary to enrol the purport of the writ at the head of the first membrane of a group recording a full county session. The first such enrolment found on the surviving roll for 6–7 Edward II reads as follows:

> Mandatum fuit vicecomiti quod venire faceret hic etc. ad hunc diem omnes assisas nove disseisine mortis antecessoris certificaciones et attinctas coram quibuscumque justiciariis assignatis arramiatas in comitatu isto cum brevibus originalibus et omnibus aliis adminiculis assisas illas certificaciones et attinctas tangentibus; et quod scire faceret partibus assisarum illarum certificacionum et attinctarum quod essent hic etc. facture et recepture quod etc.; et quod venire faceret hic etc. ad hunc diem omnes prisones comitatus istius et omnes manucaptos ad placita corone domini regis per preceptum justic' etc. cum eorum indictamentis et indictatoribus et omnibus aliis que pro eorum deliberacione essent necessaria; et quod omnes illi qui se conqueri voluerint de ministris domini regis aut aliis quibuscumque essent hic etc. ad hunc diem querelas suas prosecuturi si voluerint et ulterius facturi quod etc.; et quod omnes illi qui diem habent coram justiciario etc. ad proximum adventum suum in comitatum istum ex prefixione vel alio quoquo modo essent hic etc. ad hunc diem facturi et recepturi quod etc.; et quod venire faceret hic etc. ad hunc diem viginti quatuor de probioribus et legalioribus militibus et aliis liberis et legalibus hominibus de comitatu isto qui melius sciant et velint dicere veritatem ad certificandum justiciarium hic etc. super quibusdam articulis pacem huius terre tangentibus ab eis requirendis; et quod vicecomes in propria persona sua esset hic etc. ad hunc diem ad certificandum justiciarium hic etc. qualiter premissa fuerint executa; et vicecomes modo venit et testatur quod execucio huius mandati facta est etc.; et retornavit nomina viginti quatuor etc.[2]

While there is a certain family resemblance between this and the writ of summons to the general eyre in England, the likeness is merely a general one.[3] The Irish writ stands on its own. Although

[1] Cf. *ibid.* p. 286 (tenant in assize does not come, but it is simply postponed, as it is stated that the justiciar's coming was not proclaimed).
[2] J.R., 6–7 Edw. II, m. 3.
[3] Examples of the English form are found in *Rot. litt. claus. 1204–24*, p. 403 *b*; and in *Eyre of Kent, 6 & 7 Edw. II*, ed. W. C. Bolland (S.S. 24), I, 1–5.

its phrasing and the order of its clauses show some variations, an examination of eleven examples in the printed calendar[1] shows that the following elements were standard:

(i) The sheriff was ordered to cause to come before the justiciar all the assizes of novel disseisin and mort d'ancestor arraigned before any justices in the county, with the writs, etc. This and the next clause are found in all eleven examples.

(ii) He was to proclaim that all who wished to complain of the king's ministers or of others should come to prosecute their plaints.

(iii) He was to proclaim that all who had a day before the justiciar at his next coming should be present. This element is present in only the three latest in date of the eleven writs mentioned, but it is also found in a closely related writ of earlier date than any of them and appears to have become customary under Edward II.[2]

(iv) He was to have all prisoners and persons mainprised at pleas of the crown, with their indictments and indictors. All eleven examples include this and the next element.

(v) He was to have twenty-four knights and other free and lawful men to certify the justiciar on articles touching the king's peace.

The writ could be suited to special circumstances by omitting one or more of these five elements. In the two printed volumes which have been the basis of the present analysis, there are examples of a writ which is confined to civil business by omitting the elements numbered (iv) and (v) above,[3] of one which, directed to the steward of a liberty exempt from the justiciar's original civil jurisdiction, is confined to pleas of the crown,[4] and of one which omits both pleas of the crown and assizes.[5]

In its full form, this writ is an epitome of the original jurisdiction of the justiciar's court, which will shortly be discussed in more detail. Unfortunately the form in which the writs are enrolled does not include their date, and so we lack information on the amount

---

[1] *C.J.R. 1305–7*, pp. 90–1, 130, 167–8, 168, 360, 403, 428, 439; *1308–14*, pp. 3, 6–7, 136.
[2] *C.J.R. 1308–14*, pp. 3, 6–7, 136; n. 5, below. I have not systematically examined the writs on later rolls, but they seem generally to include this element.
[3] *C.J.R. 1305–7*, pp. 323–4; it also omits (iii).
[4] *Ibid.* p. 467.
[5] *Ibid.* p. 52; it includes (iii).

of warning afforded by them and the consequent proclamation (presumably made in the county court). What happened if the justiciar was unable to come to the county on the date announced? If there was question of a relatively short delay only, it was possible to proclaim this and the inconvenience to litigants would be slight.[1] But if the justiciar's coming was definitely obstructed other courses were taken. Once in 1310 Wogan appointed the justice of the justiciar's pleas and a senior clerk of the court to take his place, and Edmund Butler did the same, appointing the justice and the chancellor on no less than four occasions in 1313.[2] But these instances are rare in the records—the association of the court with the person of the chief governor must have been felt to weigh against such delegation. A more usual procedure was to let pleas of the crown wait and appoint commissioners to continue (in the technical sense) and adjourn common pleas to the next convenient session. An entry on the roll for 6-7 Edward II illustrates this:

Et quia justiciarius ad diem illum interesse non potuit propter alia ardua negocia domini regis quibus alibi intendebat Almaricius de Bellofago miles et Robertus de Bonevill per litteras domini regis patentes sub sigillo suo quo utitur in hac terra et testimonio Edmundi le Botiller custodis etc. assignati fuerunt ad placita predicta usque a die sancti Martini proxime preterito in XV dies apud Kilmehallok adiornanda. Et quid inde fecerint tunc constare facerent prefato custodi etc. Et quia prefatus custos ad diem illum interesse non potuit propter alia ardua negocia domini regis quibus alibi intendebat iidem Almaricius et Robertus per alias litteras domini regis patentes sub sigillo suo quo utitur in hac terra et testimonio predicto assignati fuerunt ad predicta placita adiornanda hic etc. ad hunc diem. Et quid etc. constare facerent prefato custodi etc. Qui modo venerunt et protulerunt predictas litteras patentes et recordantur quod adiorna-

[1] *C.J.R. 1305-7*, pp. 90-1 (from 19 June to 8 July—the court, when it came, remained until the end of July).
[2] P. 44, n. 5 (*b*) and (*c*). Two of the actual writs to effect this in 1313 are entered on the roll: those for the session at Cashel on 26 March (dated 20 March) and for Cork on 6 August (dated 2 August): J.R. 6-7 Edw. II, mm. 51, 82. In 1311 there is record of an apparently similar commission to Reginald Brun and Nicholas fitz Maurice to take the place of John Wogan: *Cal. rot. pat. Hib.* p. 17. But the entry was very much damaged when calendared, the relevant justiciary roll of common pleas is lacking, and the obscurity of the persons named (Nicholas is known only as a *custos pacis* and Reginald as a justice of gaol delivery: *C.J.R. 1305-7*, p. 518, and *1308-14*, p. 297) suggests that it may have been merely a commission to take an assize in place of the justiciar.

THE JUSTICIAR'S COURT 57

menta predicta facta sunt prout patet predicte littere patentes requirebant.[1]

It was of course at all times possible for the justiciar to delegate the taking of an assize or inquisition when he could not conveniently attend, or to remit an assize to the justices from whom it had come into his court by the general summons.[2]

There was one sheriff to whom the full writ *venire facias omnes assisas* could never be sent, the sheriff of Dublin, for only most exceptionally could an assize come before the justiciar in the county in which the common bench sat.[3] On the other hand, Dublin was the centre of administration and the jurisdiction of the justiciar's court over the lesser courts of the lordship was usually exercised there, together with the usual range of business, assizes excepted. Sessions at Dublin bulk large in the rolls and they can most conveniently be treated as a class to themselves.

The sessions recorded on the roll for 6-7 Edward II, which was analysed from a different viewpoint in the last chapter, may now be considered in the light of what has been said. Five of its one hundred and four membranes were terminal enrolments of attorneys, etc. Twelve sessions distinguished by the writ *venire facias omnes assisas* are found and they take up fifty-seven membranes. There were four at Cashel (for Tipperary), three at Waterford, and one each at Limerick, Carlow, Drogheda (Louth), Casteldermot (Kildare), and Cork. Comparison with the parallel roll of crown pleas shows that crown pleas were held at eight of these sessions: the four exceptions (at Cashel, Waterford, Carlow, and Castledermot) occupy only eleven membranes between them. Nine sessions at Dublin account for twenty-eight membranes. Four of the remaining fourteen membranes are devoted to a session at which juries and assizes were taken, though not plaints or pleas of the crown.[4] The remaining ten membranes are the record of eight sessions that may be called 'casual'. They were at Kilculliheen, Drogheda (twice), Ardmayle, Gowran, Clonleynan, Castledermot, and Carlow. At one an assize in which the jurisdiction of a neighbouring liberty was concerned was taken,[5] and

[1] J.R. 6-7 Edw. II, m. 23; similar commissions are enrolled in *Cal. rot. pat. Hib.* pp. 5 (Walter Lenfant), 29 (Walter Cusak, Stephen Roche).
[2] *C.J.R. 1295-1303*, pp. 9, 260, 268.
[3] Pp. 65-6, below.
[4] Cashel, Monday after the Assumption: mm. 79, 80, 87, 104.
[5] Kilculliheen: m. 17.

at two pleas of plaints only;[1] at one, pleas of the crown, pleas of plaints, and some non-judicial business are entered,[2] and at four no judicial business whatever is recorded.[3] It may be added that four sessions of pleas of the crown solely are recorded in the period covered by the roll.

The foregoing analysis of sessions between September 1312 and September 1313 may be expressed in tabular form:

Type of Session	Number held	Membranes of common pleas	Membranes of pleas of the crown
Full county sessions	8	46	13
Similar, without pleas of the crown	4	11	—
Sessions with juries and assizes, but no plaints or pleas of the crown	1	4	—
Sessions at Dublin, with pleas of the crown	5	22	3
Sessions at Dublin, without pleas of the crown	4	6	—
Casual sessions, with both common pleas and pleas of the crown	1	$2\frac{1}{2}$	1
Casual sessions, with common pleas only	7	$7\frac{1}{2}$	—
Casual sessions, with pleas of the crown only	4	—	2
[*Attornati*, etc.]	—	[5]	—
TOTAL	34	104	19

It is evident that the bulk of the business in the year reviewed occurred at the full county sessions, with sessions at Dublin in second place.

[1] Gowran, Castledermot: mm. 23, 76 d.
[2] Drogheda: mm. 13d, 20, 21; *C.J.R. 1308–14*, p. 265.
[3] Ardmayl, Clonleynan, Carlow, Drogheda: mm. 22, 50, 91–2, 64.

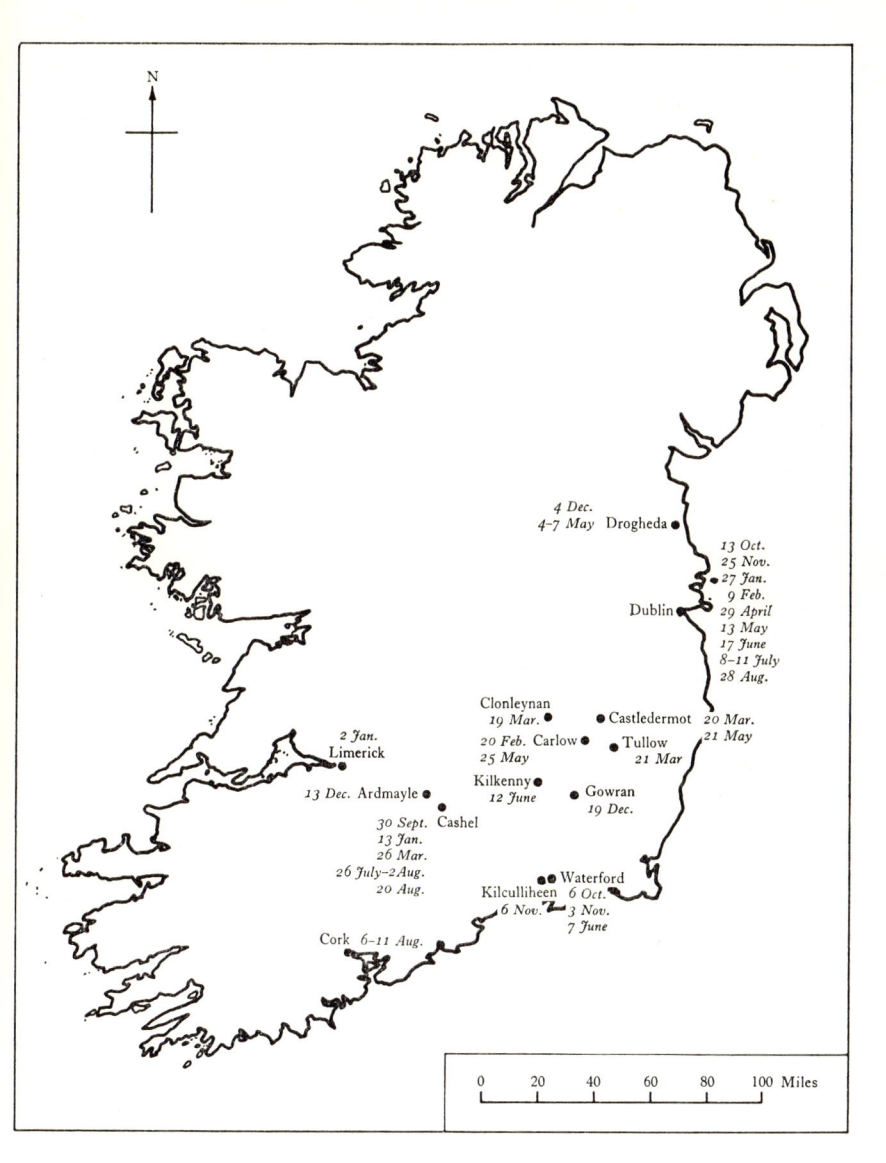

MAP. 2. SESSIONS OF THE JUSTICIAR'S COURT,
SEPTEMBER 1312–AUGUST 1313

(i) *Pleas of the crown*   *Jurisdiction*

The criminal business of the justiciar's court was entered on separate rolls under the headings *placita de corona* and *deliberacio gaole*. At least at the full county sessions, the sheriff with his 'book' and the coroners with their rolls and inquisitions were expected to be present.[1] The nature of the charges which were brought before the justiciar, and what followed on them, can best be shown from examination of a sample roll. This will here be done in some detail, because there will be little occasion to illustrate the court's jurisdiction in pleas of the crown, unlike its civil side, elsewhere in this study, except in connection with the crown plea side of the eyre and with cases reserved from liberty jurisdiction.[2] The selected roll is that portion of the roll for 33-5 Edward I which corresponds to the justiciary roll of common pleas for 34-5 Edward I.[3] The distinction between different types of session, which is illuminating where the common pleas jurisdiction is concerned, is not important for the jurisdiction in pleas of the crown; a division into matters dealt with at different types of session presents no intelligible pattern. There were in all thirteen sessions at which pleas of the crown were recorded in the year reviewed, common pleas also being taken at ten of them.[4] Pleas of the crown occupy much less space in the records than common pleas—ten membranes sufficed for them, against sixty-six.[5]

The roll records some seventy-six cases. Half a dozen are set out as presentments by juries of twelve, though the communities from which the jurors may have come are not specified. Nearly all the rest are in the form of indictments. Offences against the person—eighteen charges of homicide and three of rape—form rather less than a third of the total. In only one case did homicide lead to hanging. Five persons accused of homicide claimed

[1] Writs of summons *venire facias omnes assisas*, pp. 54-5, above; *C.J.R. 1305-7*, pp. 464, 489; J.R., 8-9 Edw. II, m. 7; J.R. 11 Edw. II (no. 119), m. 11.
[2] Chapters V and VI, below.
[3] For the details of analysis, see Appendix V.
[4] See the sessional analysis given in Appendix V.
[5] A curious feature, however, is that more than three membranes of pleas of the crown are devoted to pleas at Naas, on 14 April and 11 June 1306 and on 7 January 1307, whereas the concurrent civil business occupies the equivalent of a single membrane (*C.J.R. 1305-7*, pp. 232-3, 270-1, 328-30, 491-7, 502, 512-14). The explanation may partly lie in the liberties enjoyed by John fitz Thomas, baron of Naas.

THE JUSTICIAR'S COURT

benefit of clergy: his bishop made fine for pardon of one, while the others were all delivered as convicted. In two of these cases of clergy, some difficulty was at first encountered. No ordinary came to claim a clerk who alleged that he had been ordained in Normandy, while in the other instance the bishop's representative had not a warrant satisfactory to the court.[1] In five cases the accused obtained pardon of suit of peace without putting himself on the country and in two he made fine after doing so. In one case the accused was quit because the deceased 'was a common thief'.[2] The remaining cases of homicide conclude in mainprises or in orders to outlaw the accused as a fugitive. Of those accused of rape, one was pardoned, one made fine afterwards, and one was to be outlawed as fugitive.

Rather more than half the offences were against property. One robber found that drunkenness was no excuse.[3] Another of the seven instances of robbery and forestalling led to a pardon, because the accused 'are very useful in fighting . . . the Ototheles'.[4] The other cases of robbery are of less interest. Amongst the twenty-two charges of larceny was one claim of benefit of clergy: the clerk was delivered as convicted.[5] The pardons included one 'for good service . . . against the Irish':[6] another person was mainprised to fight the Irish felons.[7] Some of these cases of larceny reveal strange circumstances. The accused had threatened the owner of a calf, which had eaten hairs of the tail of his horse, into giving him food and drink.[8] A man said that the woman from whom he took a surcoat was his wife; she admitted this, yet he had to make fine by half-a-mark.[9] A prostitute took a box containing some goods, which the jury said were not worth more than twenty pence—they rejected her contention that she had received it in pledge for full payment; she abjured the county and no further action was taken.[10] The prior of Duleek removed from his church

---

[1] *C.J.R. 1305–7*, pp. 493 (John de la Spyne), 511 (Brother James, son of John).
[2] *Ibid.* p. 500 (Richard de Bother).
[3] *Ibid.* p. 498 (Thomas son of William Fwelewryght).
[4] *Ibid*, p. 503 (. . . Hughelot).   [5] *Ibid.* p. 513 (Stephen . . .).
[6] *Ibid.* p. 511 (Philip de Morton).
[7] *Ibid.* p. 500 (William son of Robert son of John).
[8] *Ibid.* p. 496 (Richard de Lyuet).
[9] *Ibid.* pp. 499–500 (William Telyng); cf. Pollock and Maitland (2nd ed.), II, 429.
[10] *C.J.R. 1305–7*, p. 502 (Cristiana la Sadclhackere).

an alms-box, the proceeds of which were accustomed to be shared between the priory and the town of Drogheda-on-the-side-of-Meath.[1] The steward of the town announced that it and the prior were agreed, and the prior gave the king a mark for pardon of the trespass. This is strange matter for presentment, and we may couple with it another curious case, not larceny. One man was charged with carrying off an heir and another with receiving him. The principal put himself upon the country, but the receiver appears to have demanded judgment—surely with reason—whether any action lay to the king in such a case, unless one had been taken by a party.[2] The entry is tantalizingly incomplete, although a jury was had concerning the principal.

There are eighteen indictments for harbouring felons. It is clear that this meant, in many cases, little more than consorting, willingly or not, with hostile Irish in the marches. Pardons are given because the accused 'did good service to the king in the war of Slefblame',[3] 'dwells in a strong march',[4] will serve 'in the company of the justiciar, in fighting said felons, who are all generally against the king'.[5] One unhappy Irishman made fine after a jury found that, although he was guilty, the circumstances were that he moved his dwelling-place to avoid further involvement with one band of 'Irish felons', only to encounter another in the neighbourhood of his new home.[6] There is a high proportion of acquittals for this offence—seven cases out of eighteen end in this way.

We may bring together some miscellaneous indictments and special circumstances. The chief justice of the bench came to the justiciar's court at Dublin to tell how an appellor before his court had been murdered on the way there.[7] A woman appellor was carried off on her way to the justiciar's (?) court in order to prevent her prosecuting her appeal: the fine made for this offence was very heavy—two hundred pounds.[8] A man who had previously abjured the land returned and claimed benefit of clergy, apparently with

[1] *C.J.R. 1305–7*, p. 490.
[2] Ibid. p. 494 (William Quintyn); cf., perhaps, Statute of Merton, c. 6.
[3] Ibid. p. 497 (Richard Taloun).   [4] Ibid. p. 503 (William Lissebon).
[5] Ibid. pp. 506–7 (... Staghlogh).   [6] Ibid. pp. 503–4 (...Oconyl).
[7] Ibid. p. 491.
[8] Ibid. p. 505 (Herbert de Marreys); one hundred marks were later remitted on the usual grounds of fighting the Irish. The text seems to mean she was on her way to the justiciar's court, but is defective.

success.[1] Three men were charged with taking another from sanctuary, but their act was held to have been lawful, for the jury said the alleged sanctuary was not a consecrated church, merely a dedicated oratory.[2] Fine was made for rescuing a felon from the stocks.[3]

The roll also includes twenty other entries: fines, mainprises and amercements in unspecified circumstances, a report from a justice of the bench on his negotiations to restore peace between the MacMahons and the de Verduns,[4] licences to receive back chattels taken by felons.[5]

The value of this record of pleas of the crown for social and political history is probably more conspicuous than for purely legal topics. The disturbed state of the lordship, insisted upon at the end of the last chapter, is reflected in the reasons for which persons are admitted to make fine for their offences and, especially, in the group of indictments for harbouring felons. On the legal side, the curious cases of the prior of Duleek and of ravishment of ward remind us of the absence of a rigid distinction between matters proper for presentment and those suited to actions between the parties themselves. It may be noted that, out of fifty-eight cases in which the record is complete, only four charges (one homicide, one robbery, two larcenies) led to the gallows. Twenty were met with a speedy pardon and fourteen by fine after the accused put themselves upon the country. There were seven claims of benefit of clergy and thirteen acquittals.

Before we leave the subject of the jurisdiction of the justiciar's court in pleas of the crown, the evidence of this roll may be used in the discussion of two special topics. The constitution and relationship of juries of presentment and 'petty' juries is of general interest in the history of English law. The extent to

[1] *Ibid.* p. 513 (Richard de Lyt). This seems to support the view of L. C. Gabel, *Benefit of clergy in England in the later middle ages* (Northampton, Mass., 1929), pp. 106-7, against that of A. Reville, '*L' abjuracio regni*', in *Revue historique*, L (1892), 1-42, at pp. 20-1, 26; cf. also R. F. Hunnisett, *The Medieval Coroner* (Cambridge, 1961), p. 42, n. 7, commenting on *Articuli cleri*, 9 Edw. II, stat. I, c. 15.
[2] *C.J.R. 1305-7*, p. 495 (John Dodyng, etc.).
[3] *Ibid.* p. 497 (Robert le Mareschal).
[4] *Ibid.* pp. 502-3.
[5] *Ibid.* pp. 504 (Adam le Blound), 506 (Reymund Sugagh). The first instance may be merely the restoration of a stolen chattel which had come to the king by conviction for felony, but the second is an example of the type of licence discussed above, p. 34.

which the criminal business of the justiciar's court was taken in the relevant county is an aspect of the court's peripatetic nature. The composition of the jury of presentment is never specified, beyond the number twelve.[1] Most probably, jurors who had presented before the sheriff in his tourn in their cantred (the subdivision of the Irish shire, broadly equivalent to the English hundred)[2] came again before the justiciar. It will be remembered that in the writ *venire facias omnes assisas* the sheriff was commanded to have the indictments and indictors. But had the twenty-four knights and other free and lawful men, ordered to certify the justiciar on articles touching the king's peace, any part to play? The justiciary rolls do not seem to give any returns from them which would indicate the articles on which they were examined. Another problem is the identity of the jury of presentment with the 'petty' jury. Sometimes, they are plainly the same[3] and complete or partial identity of composition was probably very often the case. There are instances of accused being mainprised until the next coming for want of jurors, but these seem to have been due to the need for jurors from a liberty.[4] It looks from one entry as if Wogan may have been prepared to allow an accused to challenge his indictors, though the wording may refer merely to individual challenges of the jurors, one by one, on other grounds:

And because Robert removed by exceptions the indictors, and there were not other fit persons in court, therefore he is committed to gaol until, etc.[5]

Contemporary English practice on the point was not clear-cut.[6] That 'no other fit persons' were present in court strongly suggests that the jurors of the jury of presentment were accustomed to play a dual role. But, on the other hand, no difficulty seems to have been encountered in a case in 1313 when it became necessary to empanel a second jury because one member of the first would not agree with his fellows.[7]

[1] E.g. ibid. pp. 490, 494, 496, 497, etc.
[2] On the cantred, Otway-Ruthven, *I.H.S.* v, 8–9.
[3] E.g. *C.J.R. 1305–7*, p. 484 (Maurice de Alta Ripa).
[4] Ibid. pp. 467–8 (William Serle; prior of Athmakart; vill of Athmakart): the text is very defective.
[5] Ibid. p. 465 (Robert Wodeloc).
[6] Pollock and Maitland (2nd ed.), II, 649; Meekings, *Crown pleas of the Wiltshire eyre, 1249*, p. 52.
[7] *C.J.R. 1308–14*, p. 273.

Indictments came before the justiciar in the relevant county. That Meath indictments might be dealt with at Dublin is probably an exception in appearance only, for the sheriff of Dublin was usually sheriff of Meath as well.[1] Although there are occasional entries outside the appropriate county in the form 'A.B. charged that...', they are usually followed by a note of a fine made for pardon, and it seems likely that that course was intended when the matter was raised.[2] On occasion, when a pardon was sought at a session outside the county, full certification from the authorities there might be ordered.[3] There are a few instances of an accused at a gaol delivery outside his county going to a jury.[4]

(ii) *Juries and assizes*

The civil side of the justiciar's court may conveniently be treated in relation to the first three elements in the writ of summons. Assizes of mort d'ancestor and novel disseisin were entered under the heading *placita de juratis et assisis*. The taking of assizes was of course not a jurisdiction in any way peculiar to the court, for it might be attended to with equal ease by the bench, the eyre, or justices with general or special commissions. The justiciary roll of common pleas for 6–7 Edward II has the characteristic assize heading at all the major sessions held outside Dublin, one session there, and one casual session. Similarly, the roll for 35 Edward I records almost one hundred assizes. But the Easter–Trinity section of the roll for 1 Edward II has only ten assizes and the roll for 34–5 Edward I only once includes a writ of summons *venire facias omnes assisas*[5] and uses the heading *placita de juratis et assisis* twice only, in each case for a single assize.[6] Part of the explanation for these variations in the amount of assize business lies in one of the relatively few aspects in which

[1] E.g. *C.J.R. 1305–7*, pp. 490–1; Otway-Ruthven, *I.H.S.* v, 5–6.
[2] E.g., *C.J.R. 1308–14*, pp. 163, 163–4 (Kildare at Dublin), 270 (Waterford at Dublin). These examples are from sessions at which *deliberacio gaole* is not in the heading used. Examples where it is are: *C.J.R. 1305–7*, p. 483 (Kildare at Dublin), *1308–14*, pp. 144–5 (Waterford at Cashel, co. Tipperary), 215 (Waterford at Limerick).
[3] *C.J.R. 1305–7*, pp. 513–14 (Adam son of David: the sheriff and coroners of Kerry to certify).
[4] All concern Kildare matters: *C.J.R. 1308–14*, pp. 175 (at Carlow), 210 (at Drogheda), 218, 218–19 (at Dublin).
[5] *C.J.R. 1305–7*, pp. 323–4 (pleas of the crown are omitted).
[6] *Ibid.* pp. 311–12, 323–4; cf. Appendix v.

the Irish justiciar's court precisely corresponded to the English king's bench. Just as the court *coram rege* could take assizes in any county in which it might be, other than Middlesex, for there the Westminster bench sat,[1] so the assize jurisdiction of the justiciar's court was rarely exercised in Dublin county, the seat of the Irish bench. There is in fact a crudely inverse relation between the amount of time spent at Dublin in the period covered by a given roll and the number of assizes it records. In 34–5 Edward I the justiciar spent much more time than usual at Dublin and one of the two assizes recorded was actually taken there.[2] Apart from this example, indeed, only three Dublin assizes are found in the rolls covered by the printed calendars, and in at least two of these cases there were special features: in one, the tenements were in the liberty of the archbishop of Dublin, in the king's hand at the time, while in the other the assize was taken outside term in the bench.[3] The existence of an example of an assize adjourned from the justiciar's court in its appropriate county to the same court at Dublin suggests the possibility of a practice annoying both to litigants and recognitors.[4] Amongst the ordinances made for Ireland in 1323 was one:

Item qe nostre justice de la dite terre par ses brefs ou lettres ne targe ne ajorne assise de novele disseisine devant lui, fors qe en le conte ou il serra present, e tanc come il demorra en meisme la conte.[5]

However, the more usual procedure was to adjourn an incomplete assize to the next coming of the justiciar to the county[6] or to justices assigned.[7]

[1] Sayles, *Select cases in K.B.*, IV, pp. xxxiii–xxxiv.
[2] *C.J.R. 1305–7*, pp. 311–12.
[3] *C.J.R. 1295–1303*, pp. 251–2; *1308–14*, pp. 45–6 (6 March 1308, which was Wednesday in the first week of Lent; no text survives of a bench roll for Hilary term, but it is inconceivable that the court should be sitting so late). The second reference is unique in the printed calendars in being under the assize heading, but there is another Dublin example of the heading (with two entries) in J.R., 6–7 Edw. II, m. 96. I can make no elucidatory suggestion concerning the assizes in *C.J.R. 1295–1303*, pp. 222–3, and *1305–7*, pp. 311–12.
[4] *C.J.R. 1295–1303*, p. 445 (from Kildare). Only one other example has been found of such an adjournment: *ibid. 1305–7*, pp. 426–7 (Kerry, to come to Kilmallock in Limerick).
[5] *Foedera* (Rec. comm. ed.), II, I, 538.
[6] E.g. *C.J.R. 1305–7*, pp. 92, 93, 131, etc.
[7] E.g. *ibid.* pp. 168, 401; *1308–14*, pp. 8, 10, 121.

(iii) *Procedure without writ*

Assizes apart, most of the litigation in the justiciar's court took the form of procedure without writ. It is referred to in the second element of the writ of summons *venire facias omnes assisas*. Here will be discussed in turn the identification of cases of procedure without writ, the subject-matter of such plaints, the way in which the itinerant character of the court affected the procedure, and finally its popularity and the criticisms levelled at it.

Procedure without writ normally meant procedure by bill, though oral complaints were not unknown.[1] The diplomatic of the Irish justiciary rolls makes actions brought by plaint easier to identify than on the rolls of the English king's bench, for a special heading, *placita querelarum*, was given to the membranes. The resemblance here, as in some other points, was to the English eyre rather than to the court *coram rege*. Not all the business entered under this heading was composed of plaints, and many plaints can be traced elsewhere in the rolls, so that to rely solely on the heading would lead to considerable inaccuracy. But by combining with this guide explicit individual references and the indications which Professor Sayles and Mr Richardson have elucidated—certain initial formulae and the evidence of the membranes of attorneys—a high degree of precision in identification has, it is hoped, been attained.[2]

The justiciary rolls are helpful in another way. In Ireland licence could be secured to plead by bill where a writ was normally required and, in addition to providing a supplemental means of identification of actions without writ, the entry of a note on the rolls that licence has been obtained is of help in classifying the subject-matter in which it was possible to proceed without a writ. We may consider three categories of action: those in which a bill was always admissible, those for which licences to plead by bill could be obtained, and those in which writs were absolutely necessary.

---

[1] E.g. *C.J.R. 1305–7*, p. 215 (Nich. de Nettervill *v.* William de la Ryvere).

[2] Sayles, *Select cases in K.B.* IV, pp. lxxiii–lxxviii, developing Richardson and Sayles, *Select cases of procedure without writ*, pp. xlv–l. The lists of attorneys on the justiciary rolls are less helpful than those on the king's bench rolls, however. The editors of the *Calendar* seem often to have translated *querela* simply as 'plea'; cf. Sayles, in *E.H.R.* LXXIII, 103.

No licence appears to have been required for plaints against the king's ministers brought in accordance with the writ to the sheriff, *venire facias omnes assisas*, for plaints of debt and trespass involving a claim of less than forty shillings, and for a wide range of other bills of trespass. Thus far Irish practice broadly corresponded to English.

It is clear that the most common licence to plead by bill concerned a debt or trespass *de bonis asportatis* above the forty shilling limit. Though that sum had an importance in English law at an earlier time—for example, it was a dividing line between writs *sine* and *pro dono*[1]—and indeed seems to have possessed a peculiar fascination for the law for centuries, the particular rule about bills is evidently connected with the Statute of Gloucester (1278), c. 8. This read:

> E qe nul eit desoremes bref de trespas devaunt justices se il n'afie par fei qe les biens enportez vaillent qarante souz al meins.[2]

Strictly interpreted, this did not do more than prevent writs being pleaded before justices when less than forty shillings was at stake. Six years later, the Statute of Wales declared that trespasses of less than forty shillings should be pleaded in the lesser Welsh courts, while those of more than that sum were to go before the justice, in both cases apparently without writ; where debts were concerned the forty-shilling limit similarly applied, though procedure without writ seems to have been admitted only for the lesser sums and then was optional. A century later, in reply to a petition, the provisions of the Statute of Wales were reiterated in the form of a clear-cut statement that sums over forty shillings must be sought by writ.[3] This interpretation was certainly in harmony with the contemporary opinion of *Britton*;

> ... nous ne voloms qe nul eyt la conisaunce ne poer de teles quereles [*assault, imprisonment, battery*] pleder, ne autres trespas de biens enportez outre la value de xl.s. ne des dettes passantz mesme la summe, sauntz nos brefs.[4]

---

[1] Pollock and Maitland (2nd ed.), I, 553–4.
[2] The interpretation of the statute has been discussed by Richardson and Sayles, *Select cases of procedure without writ*, p. xli, notes 2, 6.
[3] *Record of Caernarvon* (Record comm.), p. 216.
[4] *Ed.* F. M. Nichols, I, 155.

Fleta says:

Aliquando eciam conceduntur huiusmodi placita [*of debt by plaint*] deduci in comitatibus, ciuitatibus, burgis et libertatibus pro parvitate debitorum, set hec causa [*unlike the justification for holding pleas in the exchequer*] non est tantum necessaria regi set populo vt sic laboribus parcatur et expensis. Conceditur eciam quod in hundredis, wapentakiis, tritingis et aliis minutis curiis regis et baronum possunt placita debiti summam xl. solidorum non excedentis sine brevi discuti et terminari.[1]

In other words, the rule in practice was that a writ was needed for trespass *de bonis asportatis* or debt exceeding forty shillings (though it may be noted that English legislation of Edward III seems to recognize the possibility of larger sums being sought without writ).[2]

A plaint *de bonis asportatis* from the earliest (1295) justiciary roll of which we have a text will illustrate the principle. The defendant sought judgment whether he was bound to answer, because:

(*a*) the bill mentioned merely the taking of the goods, without the phrase *contra pacem*;

(*b*) the goods were worth more than forty shillings and there should have been a writ.[3]

The second exception was successful.

The sums recorded in the justiciary rolls as having been paid for licence to proceed by bill in matters beyond the forty-shilling limit vary somewhat, but half a mark occurs with sufficient regularity to suggest a standard rate.

Licences to plead by bill were obtained in other circumstances than those in which the forty-shilling limit presented difficulty. In 1300 a complainant paid a mark for licence to have a plea of false imprisonment by bill.[4] According to *Britton* writs should be required for

trespas de maheign et des playes et de enprisounement et de bateries fetes encountre nostre pes.[5]

---

[1] *Ed.* H. G. Richardson and G. O. Sayles (S.S.), II, 205.
[2] 1 Edw. III, stat. I, c. 6; 5 Edw. III, c. 7; 28 Edw. III, c. 8.
[3] *C.J.R. 1295–1303*, p. 28.
[4] *Ibid.* p. 349.
[5] *Ed.* Nichols, I, 155.

Yet such plaints are found without any mention of payment for licence.[1] There is evidently need of great caution in interpreting the evidence of presence or absence of these notes of payment; probably they were often omitted from the plea roll. In 1323 an ordinance made for Ireland regulated certain fees:

Item pur le seal nostre justice Dirlaund de chescune bille de grace, quatre deners; & pur lescripture de chescune bille deux deners desore seient pris & paiez & nient plus.[2]

It seems most likely that this regulation refers to bills to be pleaded in the justiciar's court, though it must be conceded that the possibility that it refers to the justiciar's 'bills' sent as warrant to the Irish chancellor for the issue of letters under the great seal of Ireland cannot be ruled out. If the bills mentioned were in fact those pleaded in the justiciar's court, the 'bills of grace' were presumably those for which licence had to be sought, though in what way the payment of fourpence covered the licence is obscure. Perhaps the affixing of the seal indicated that the complainant had authorization to proceed by bill. If *chescune bille* in the second clause of the ordinance is to be distinguished from *chescune bille de grace* in the first, it suggests that all bills were written by the clerks of the court (it may be presumed that, sometimes at least, written as well as oral plaints were tendered to them for this purpose). The seal used is the justiciar's—a light on a very obscure part of Irish sphragistics.[3] But plainly the evidence, both of this ordinance and of the rolls which can now be consulted, is very inadequate, and the only litigation which we can definitely say fell normally into the intermediate category for which licence was secured by payment was the plaint of debt or trespass *de bonis asportatis* of more than forty shillings.

Without a writ no man could be compelled to answer concerning his freehold.[4] When the plaint was that the defendant unjustly

---

[1] E.g. *C.J.R. 1305–7*, pp. 251–2, 255–6. There is English evidence that *Britton* cannot be relied upon as a statement of the law in this connection: Richardson and Sayles, *Select cases of procedure without writ*, p. ccvi and references.

[2] P.R.O., C. 66, no. 159, m. 3 (*Foedera* [Rec. comm. ed.], II, I, 538); also printed (from statute roll) in *Stat. realm*, I, 193.

[3] The justiciar's seal may also have been used for judicial writs of his court, but I do not know of any evidence bearing directly on this; cf. Richardson and Sayles, *Administration*, p. 16, n. 7.

[4] Sayles, *Select cases in K.B.* IV, p. lxxix; Richardson and Sayles, *Select cases of procedure without writ*, pp. lxx–lxxii.

prevented the complainant from driving cattle to his pasture, it was enough for the defendant to say that the place where he claimed to have right of way was defendant's freehold.[1] Against this the bill was useless; the complainant was amerced and told to get a writ if he wished. A bill might be met with other arguments to the effect that the defendant did not need to answer. In 1295 a defendant in a plaint of assault said he was not bound to answer 'because a writ in Chancery lies for this'—a restrictive doctrine that did not find favour with the court.[2] In 1308, in reply to a plaint of detinue of a sum of eighteen shillings, the defendant said that the debt had been recovered by judgment against him and the plaint was being improperly used as an alternative process to execution by *fieri facias*. The complainant denied that this was so and the case was adjourned for consultation of the relevant previous roll of the court; unfortunately the outcome is unknown.[3]

It need scarcely be said that no bill, any more than a writ, could oust the lawful jurisdiction of a local or franchisal court or meddle with matters that belonged to the court christian. In a plaint at Tralee in 1295 a local lord claimed his court, since the sum involved did not exceed forty shillings (another view, it would seem, of the Statute of Gloucester, c. 8). The reply was that there was an allegation of fraud: 'it belonged to the King to take cognizance of pleas touching fraud, especially as to tenements committed to farm'; and so he was refused his court. But he persisted and argued that the bill mentioned merely the debt and not the farm or the fraud; he was again refused his court: '[*the bill*] ought reasonably to be explained, and those things not expressly contained in the bill are declared by its reasonable *demonstratio*'.[4] The court also held that the fact that a farm of a

---

[1] *C.J.R. 1295–1303*, p. 394.
[2] *Ibid.* pp. 31–2. Another case, *ibid.* p. 53 (Adam Franceys v. Gilbert son of John Brun) is, at first glance, one going the other way. But in it the goods, the asportation of which was the subject of the plaint, far exceeded forty shillings in value, so the case is really parallel to that cited above, p. 69.
[3] *C.J.R. 1308–14*, pp. 123–4.
[4] *Demonstratio* in the sense of 'statement of claim' is noted in the *Revised Medieval Latin Word-List* (ed. R. E. Latham) as occurring *ante* 1564. In Roman law the first clause of the *formula* was the *demonstratio*. According to Gaius (*Institutes*, IV, 40) its purpose was *ut demonstretur res de qua agitur*. Gaius was, of course, unknown to the thirteenth century and I have not been able to find a convincing reference, either in civil or in canon law, to explain the usage found in 1295. Though a canonist influence is a tempting explanation, the occurrence may, in fact, be the merest chance.

free tenement was involved was a ground for ousting the lord's jurisdiction. The defendant promptly seized on this as an argument equally against procedure without writ; the court, however, with doubtful consistency, accepted the following distinction made on behalf of the complainant:

> To which Ricard answers that it is true that in case where a farm is especially [*specifically*?] demanded, without the King's writ no one is bound to answer, but because Henry [*defendant*] fraudulently withdrew from making his chirograph of the farm, and fraudulently received his money, action for recovery of the farm is not open to him [*Ricard*] but only for restoration of the money received and damages.[1]

In other words, because there could not be, as it were, specific performance and only a remedy in repayment and damages was sought, the fact that the dispute had arisen over a farm of freehold did not preclude the use of a bill.

In 1306 the mayor and bailiffs of Dublin successfully claimed their court of a bill of assault.[2] In 1308, acting under a commission from England, the justiciar, Wogan, reviewed and quashed a judgment of his court upon a bill in 1306, on the grounds that a dispute over tithes belonged to the ecclesiastical forum if the tithes did not exceed the fourth part of the value of the church.[3] Wogan presumably was relying on *Circumspecte agatis* or the customary rule which it clarified.

Like assizes, 'plaints must concern themselves with wrong and wrong-doing within the borders of the county wherein the court was at the moment sitting'.[4] In 1333, a defendant argued that this excluded procedure by bill on contracts and covenants entered into in another county; the complainant replied that the custom was that the physical presence of the defendant in the county was enough to confer jurisdiction.[5] Apart from this point of interpretation, the principle was not rigidly observed by the justiciar's court. The roll for 34–5 Edward I records Meath[6] and Kildare[7] plaints at Dublin, and individual instances of a plaint from

---

[1] *C.J.R. 1295–1303*, pp. 42–3.
[2] *C.J.R. 1305–7*, 238.
[3] *C.J.R. 1308–14*, pp. 93–5; cf. pp. 51, 85. The original plaint (Abbot of Duleek *v.* Prior of Colp) is in *1305–7*, pp. 319–20.
[4] Sayles, *Select cases in K.B.* IV, p. lxxii, and cf. p. lxxx.
[5] J.R., 6–7 Edw. III, in P.R.O.I., RC. 8/17, *Cal. mem. rolls*, XVII, 366–9.
[6] *C.J.R. 1305–7*, pp. 238 (*bis*), 239, 255, etc.; cf. p. 65, above.
[7] *Ibid.* pp. 217, 251, 255.

THE JUSTICIAR'S COURT

Roscommon at Dublin,[1] Louth at Kells,[2] as well as the cross of Carlow at Kildare.[3] Generally, plaints were terminated before the court left the county, but it was possible for one, like any other plea, to drag on with proceedings and adjournments at different places. In January 1306, four members of the Nettervill family apparently brought a bill of trespass at Drogheda, for assault and battery in Meath. The jury came and told an involved story, turning chiefly on the relations of the parties with certain of the Irish. There followed an adjournment to the quinzaine of Hilary at Dublin, then further adjournments, and it was not until Easter 1308, at Dublin, that judgment was given for the complainants.[4] In this case formation of the judgment was the principal cause of delay, but there might be other reasons. The difficulty of getting a jury held up a plaint of events in Cork, which began at Dublin in January 1305, was continued there at Easter, adjourned, for a jury to be taken, to justices assigned, brought back to the justiciar's court in the same state at Castledermot in July, again held up by want of jurors at Castledermot in the quinzaine of Michaelmas and, after further delays amounting to eighteen months, finally resolved by a jury at Cork in the quinzaine of Trinity 1307.[5]

The case last mentioned, it may be observed, contains an example of the court's practice of committing the taking of a jury, like an assize, to justices, though in the case of a plaint the findings of the jury had to be reported back to the justiciar's court for judgment.[6] The court did not itself conclude all plaints brought to it. There are examples of plaints being referred to special commissioners,[7] to arbitrators by consent of the parties,[8] and to the county court.[9]

The great popularity of the procedure is no doubt to be attributed, in the first place, to its relative cheapness and convenience, compared with the expense and trouble of suing a writ from the chancery. Although it has been suggested that the chancellor went before the justiciar, issuing writs, there seems to

---

[1] *Ibid.* p. 255. [2] *Ibid.* pp. 182–3.
[3] *Ibid.* pp. 328–9. [4] *Ibid.* pp. 175–7; *1308–14*, p. 117.
[5] *C.J.R. 1305–7*, pp. 32–3, 109, 132, 284.
[6] Another example: *ibid.* pp. 182–3.
[7] *Ibid.* p. 215 (this group of related written and oral plaints between William de la Ryvere and Neil le Brun is discussed in detail below, chapter VII).
[8] *Ibid.* pp. 238–9. [9] *Ibid.* p. 181.

be no reliable evidence of this, although the chancellor frequently *accompanied* the justiciar.[1] In England, procedure by bill was also speedier, but this advantage may not have been so evident in the Irish court, where a jury does not seem to have been taken if the defendant failed to appear.[2] There may well have been a significantly greater freedom in the conduct of the case: on a writ the count had most carefully to avoid variance, but a bill could seemingly be generously expanded by its 'reasonable *demonstratio*'.[3] While no one today would suggest a special element of equity about bills in eyre, king's bench or justiciar's court, it does seem possible that procedure without writ made escape from some difficulties and limitations easier.[4] In 1299 the children of a testator, by their guardian, brought a plaint against an executor concerning certain goods of the testator's, alleged to have been deposited with the defendant executor by a co-executor. There had previously been proceedings in the ecclesiastical court, in which the defendant executor was successful, as the complainants alleged, by means of forged letters purporting to issue from the ordinary. The case is evidently on the borderline of royal and ecclesiastical jurisdiction. It may even be relevant that the complainants paid ten marks to be allowed to proceed by bill—the largest payment for licence that has been noted; however, it is proper to add that it is the very first payment for licence known on the surviving rolls and it may have been in some way related to the amount at issue (nearly one hundred and forty pounds).[5] In another case the facts were that one Robert had arranged a contest of unspecified nature against the men of a neighbouring town. It was, as it were, an away fixture and one John accompanied Robert there. John wounded one of the townsmen. This man later recovered damages against Robert. (We might well wish to have the record of those proceedings also and an indication of the basis of liability accepted in them.) Robert then used a plaint against John to recoup himself.[6] Again, the complainant in another case said that he had owed

[1] The suggestion was made by Mills, in *C.J.R. 1295–1303*, p. vii, and seems to have been based on a misunderstanding of a passage, *ibid.* p. 47.
[2] Cf. Sayles, *Select cases in K.B.* IV, pp. lxxxii–lxxxiv; *C.J.R. 1305–7*, pp. 3 (*bis*), 51, 57–8, etc.
[3] P. 71, above.
[4] Cf. Sayles, *Select cases in K.B.* IV, p. lxxxv.
[5] *C.J.R. 1295–1303*, p. 275. The parties came to an agreement.
[6] *C.J.R. 1305–7*, p. 232.

small tithes to his vicar, but had paid them. After payment he was excommunicated and put to expense in going to the bishop for absolution; for this he claimed one hundred pounds in damages. The vicar said that he had to declare him excommunicated, because of a general excommunication against those who had not paid their tithes by a given date, which left him no discretion: complainant should have gone to the bishop as soon as he paid. The complainant replied that, when he paid his tithes, the vicar promised to seal letters testifying this to the bishop, but did not do so. The vicar refused to put this to a jury: judgment was rendered against him and he was committed to gaol. A jury to tax damages put them at twenty pounds.[1]

But there was also criticism of the prevalence of procedure without writ in the justiciar's court, and this criticism has a very special interest, because it suggests that there may have been important developments in the use of the procedure under John Wogan. For this critical view we have two documents. The first is a letter of 23 March 1297 on the close rolls:

Rex dilecto et fideli suo Johanni Wogan justiciario suo Hibernie salutem.
Cum intellexerimus quod vos communia placita que totis temporibus retroactis per brevia originalia de cancellaria nostra Hibernie placitari deberent et consueverunt per billas et peticiones vacuas jam de novo coram vobis deduci facitis et etiam terminari per quod feodum sigilli nostri quo utimur in Hibernia et fines pro brevibus dandis ad [*recte* et?] alia commoda que nobis inde solent accrescere diversimodo subtrahuntur in nostri et incolarum parcium illarum dampnum non modicum et gravamen: nolentes igitur huiusmodi novitates fieri per quas nobis dampna gravia poterint evenire, vobis mandamus quod si ita est tunc aliqua placita communia que per brevia originalia de cancellaria nostra predicta de jure et consuetudine hucusque usitata habent terminari per peticiones et billas coram vobis deduci placitari aut terminari de cetero nullatenus presumatis per quod vobis imputari debeat aut possit nostrum incommodum in hac parte. Teste rege apud Shestoniam xxiii die Marcii.[2]

The second is an undated *peticio populi Hibernie*.[3] It evidently is not directly connected with the letters just quoted and complains

[1] J.R., 6–7 Edw. II, m. 101*d*.
[2] P.R.O., C. 54, no. 114, m. 118 (*Cal. close rolls, 1296–1302*, p. 22).
[3] P.R.O., S.C. 8/53, no. 2643.

of the hearing of common pleas by bill in the justiciar's court and by writ in the exchequer. On the first point the complaint is:

la justice Dirlaund lur plede e travayle par biles e petitiouns de trespaces dettes covenauns & tous autres contrats saunz bref nostre seygnur al graunt damage nostre seygnur le roys e lur gref damage & perte e encountre lur usage issint qe le roys pert ses graces e autres profiz . . .

As a remedy they pray the king that he

lur voyle graunter la graunt chartre Dengleterre e les articles desut sun seal dount il pussent estre meyntenuz e bref a defendre la justice e le tresorer qyl sursesent de tous manere de plez e noveleries.

The petition is endorsed

Mandetur justiciario Hibernie quod debita que excedunt xl s. placitent per brevia regis et non per billas; et pro magna carta habenda contribuant secundum quod illi de Anglia.

No consequent letters to the justiciar are in fact known. Plainly, however, the petition belongs to the period of the constitutional crisis of 1297 to 1305. The references to the charter and articles suggest a date shortly after the confirmation and *articuli super cartas* of 1300, for the fourth of those articles concerned common pleas in the exchequer; the possibility of reference to the *Confirmatio cartarum* of 1297 cannot, however, be altogether excluded.[1] It may be added, in passing, that this expression of Irish awareness of what was passing in England may put a puzzling later fourteenth-century variant text of *De tallagio non concedendo*, which inserts a reference to Ireland, in a new light.[2]

Whoever lay behind the phrase *cum intellexerimus* as the source of the information received in England and whoever spoke in the name of 'the people of Ireland', it seems reasonable to suppose that the Irish chancery was in some way involved, as the principal sufferer both from bills and from exchequer writs. Were these complaints directed against innovations made by John Wogan? The

[1] *Statutes of the realm*, I, 138. I am indebted to Professor Harry Rothwell for having discussed these matters with me.
[2] Printed by H. Rothwell, 'The confirmation of the charters, 1297', *E.H.R.* LX (1945), 314–15 (italics indicate departures from the usual text): 'Volumus et concedimus pro nobis et heredibus nostris, quod omnes clerici et laici de regno nostro, *tam illi de marchia Wallie et Hibernie quam illi de Anglia* habeant *iura sua et* libertates *et* leges *suas* et liberas consuetudines suas *secundum ius patrie* . . .'

date of the letters close give him a year in which to have made changes in the jurisdiction of his court, and it would not be wholly surprising if a vigorous administrator, whose higher judicial experience had been largely confined to the eyre, tended to favour the bill against the writ. On the other hand, *novitates*, *noveleries*, are not words to be taken too literally in an age in which the appeal to custom was a very effective one. There are, unfortunately, two obstacles in the way of seeing to what extent plaint jurisdiction in the justiciar's court underwent a change with the arrival of John Wogan. First, the letters of March 1297 do not in fact tell us what were the *communia placita* which, allegedly, had been accustomed to be determined by writ, and, secondly, we have only one justiciary roll from before Wogan's coming and no pleas held by him of earlier date than January 1297, a year after his arrival. Even the forty shilling rule, mentioned in the endorsement to the petition, offers an unsatisfactory line of approach. There was at least one case in 1295 in which the court, under Wogan's predecessor, Thomas fitz Maurice fitz Gerald, expressly accepted the rule.[1] Yet the same roll for 1295 does include what seem to be plaints of more than forty shillings,[2] so that the fact that these occur in 1297 under Wogan[3] really proves nothing. But the first recorded entries of payment for licence to plead by bill come from the month of July 1299.[4] It is to be remembered that this system was peculiar to Ireland.[5] The justiciary rolls underwent various changes of form in the early years of Wogan's administration and we cannot assume with absolute confidence that the system of payments was new in 1299, any more than that the absence of a note of payment at a later date with reference to a particular case means that none was made. None the less, it is possible that Wogan encouraged a more widespread use of

[1] *C.J.R. 1295–1303*, p. 28 and cf. p. 53; p. 69 and p. 71, n. 2, above.
[2] Because the heading *placita querelarum*, like the other specific headings, is little used on the early roll, identification of plaints on it is not easy. But the following entries appear to have been cast in the form *A.B. queritur de C.D. quod*, which is a plaint formula (Richardson and Sayles, *Select cases of procedure without writ*, pp. xlv, cxliii), and to be otherwise relevant; *C.J.R. 1295–1303*, pp. 18 (Adam de Leynz v. Roger de Lesse), 30 (Robert de Notton v. Peter le Petit *et al.*), 30–1 (Will. de Kegworth v. Peter le Petit), 48 (Nich. de Sampford v. Adam de Goules), 52 (Will. de Burne v. Ric. Landre), 59 (Hugh the clerk v. Will Benet).
[3] *C.J.R. 1295–1303*, pp. 78, 91, 93–4, 108, etc.
[4] *Ibid.* pp. 275, 284 (*bis*); the second reference concerns debts of over forty shillings.   [5] Sayles, *Select cases in K.B.* IV, p. lxxix, note 6.

procedure without writ in his court, that this led to protests from the chancery, hidden behind the *cum intellexerimus* of the letters close of March 1297, and that Wogan, or one of his subordinates, then drew the teeth of the dangerous criticism that the king's interests were suffering, by devising the system of payments for licence. After 1300, on this view, the attack was renewed, but without effect, since the matter was tied to the Charter and the articles, and these the king would not grant without a subsidy (*contribuant secundum quod illi de Anglia*). The reason why the endorsement that debts exceeding forty shillings should be pleaded by writ and not by bill was not followed by letters giving it effect was, perhaps, that the justiciar represented that the licensing system minimized the damage suffered by the king.

Since most common pleas in the justiciar's court were by bill, it is probable that the reference to the Great Charter in the *peticio populi Hibernie* is to c. 11 (1225), which stipulated that common pleas should not follow the king but be held *in aliquo certo loco*. If applied to the Irish situation this clause would have struck severely at the jurisdiction of the justiciar's court. In 1305, a hard-pressed litigant, one Adam of Paris, seems to have thought of this:

Adam proffers a writ of the King, by which the King sends to [*rectius* informs] the Justiciar, that, as in the Great Charter of the liberties of England it is contained that common pleas should not follow the King's Court, but be held in some certain place, the Justiciar should not hold this plea by bill.[1]

It is to be regretted that 'by bill' is given a certain emphasis in the English calendared text which we cannot be sure it held in the original,[2] so that the clause is in fact ambiguous; but it is more probable that the objection was to the court's holding the plea at all, rather than to its being held by bill, though this may have added insult to injury. At any rate, the court replied with a bold argument:

And because it appears to the court that the said writ emanated by deceiving (*per surreptionem*) of the King's Chancery, whereas the King has not yet granted to the men of this land the liberties contained in the said Great Charter ...

[1] *C.J.R. 1305–7*, p. 158.
[2] The Latin calendar in P.R.O.I., RC. 8/2, *Cal. mem. rolls*, II, 556–7, 575, totally omits the passages relating to the Great Charter.

An interpretation of this statement has been advanced which would make it the only evidence we have of an intention on the part of Edward I to use the papal bull of 29 December 1305, which annulled his recent concessions, against the Great Charter itself.[1] On the face of it, however, it seems unlikely that so grave a step would first be signified in so obscure a context. It is plain, from the endorsement to the petition, already cited, from the *populus Hibernie*, that the king, *c.*1300, regarded not only his English concessions, but the Great Charter, as not yet extended to his Irish subjects, and there is no evidence of any such extension having occurred in the succeeding years. Admittedly, the loss of the original makes the degree of emphasis to be placed on 'the men of *this land*' uncertain. Yet it seems equally in accord with the text we have and with general considerations to argue that the writ brought by Adam of Paris challenged an extensive part of the justiciar's jurisdiction in a distinctly awkward way and that Wogan got out of a tight corner by relying on the fact that Edward I had never expressly confirmed the Great Charter in his lordship of Ireland. At all events, the incident underlines Wogan's determination not to abandon the wide plaint jurisdiction of the justiciar's court, whether or not he had himself expanded it.

It has been suggested that the modern Irish civil bill procedure stems from the medieval bill.[2] On the whole, however, it seems more likely that the line of descent should not be traced beyond the early seventeenth century.[3]

(iv) *Communia placita*

The third element of the writ *venire facias omnes assisas*, ordering all parties to come who had a day assigned before the justiciar at his next coming, can be used as a somewhat flimsy peg on which to hang the great bulk of business entered on the rolls under the heading *communia placita* (with which may be joined the simple *placita*). Matters covered by that clause in the writ did indeed go under that heading (except in the rare instance of an

---

[1] H. G. Richardson, 'The English coronation oath', *Speculum*, XXIV (1949), 75; cf. H. Rothwell, 'Edward I and the struggle for the charters, 1297–1305', in *Studies in medieval history presented to F. M. Powicke* (Oxford, 1948), p. 331.
[2] F. H. Newark, *Notes on Irish legal history* (Belfast, 1960) (originally published in 7 *Northern Ireland Legal Quarterly*, pp. 121–39), pp. 20–3.
[3] 'His Maiesties Directions for the Irish courts, 1622', ed. G. J. Hand and V. W. Treadwell, *Anal. Hib.* (forthcoming).

adjourned plaint), but they were only a tiny fraction of the total business described by it. Most of this business was dispatched at Dublin and very little at full county sessions. The following figures,[1] obtained by totalling the numbers of membranes with the three principal headings on the rolls for 34–5 Edward I, Easter–Trinity 1 Edward II, and 6–7 Edward II, show the situation at a glance:

	Placita de juratis et assisis	*Placita querelarum*	*Communia placita*, etc.	Total
At Dublin	1	13½	83½	98
Away from Dublin	43	24	15	82
	44	37½	98½	180

What were these *communia placita*? They were not 'common pleas' in the sense of which use is made in speaking of the Westminster and Dublin benches as courts of common pleas; it is not possible to describe them as standing 'apart, on the one hand, from the *placita corone*, the indictable crimes tried locally, and, on the other hand, from the *proprie cause regis*'.[2] The Irish *proprie cause regis* were indeed entered under the heading *communia placita*. As used in headings by the clerks of the justiciar's court, the term *communia placita* really meant 'any business other than pleas of the crown, assizes, and plaints'. 'Common pleas' in the sense of those which 'lie between private individuals',[3] if they were begun by writ and not by bill, *proprie cause regis*, process of execution of judgment (including very often judgments on plaints), proceedings in review (which will receive separate treatment), and the general administrative business which was a peculiar feature of the justiciary rolls, were all entered under the heading *communia placita*. It is only with the first two classes that we need concern ourselves here.

The jurisdiction in common pleas by writ enjoyed by the justiciar's court was broadly similar in kind to that of the English king's bench, although its volume and relative importance were much less. The real actions were left to the bench, and so were

[1] Summarized from Appendix v, below.
[2] Sayles, *Select cases in K.B.* IV, p. xxxii.   [3] *Ibid.*

writs of debt, detinue, covenant, and account.[1] Trespass was the principal 'common plea' dealt with by the court, just as in the English court *coram rege*, but even here procedure by bill was very much more usual. In fact, squeezed between the jurisdiction of the common bench and the justiciar's court's own jurisdiction by bill, the jurisdiction in common pleas by writ was not very important.

Some matters which closely touched the crown went from Ireland to the king's bench in England, but the justiciar's court was the proper place for such proceedings as *quo warranto* (the reservation of this writ to the eyre not applying in Ireland),[2] why a chapter elected without licence,[3] why a king's widow was married without licence,[4] and so forth.

(v) *Jurisdiction in review*

As the highest court of the land of Ireland, the court of the justiciar was that in which the ultimate remedy within the lordship for erroneous judgments in the lower courts lay. Although the Irish jurisdiction of the king's bench in England sometimes modified the operation of this principle, the jurisdiction of the justiciar's court in review was highly important. It was usually exercised at Dublin. For this two special reasons may be adduced. In the first place, the rolls of the royal courts of record were kept in the treasury at Dublin.[5] When a record was required from the treasury for examination of error or for consultation in some other connection a transcript, not the original roll, was produced. But original writs seem to have been produced, although in 1296 a party claimed that transcripts of them also were adequate:

... nec rotuli aliquorum justiciariorum defunctorum liberati in thesaurariam regis cum aliis contingentibus dictos rotulos extra

---

[1] Not all cases of debt and detinue noted in Appendix v, below, are explicitly stated to have been without writ, but the exceptions are merely doubtful—none are known to have been brought by writ.
[2] Cf. *C.J.R. 1295–1303*, pp. 103, 144, 149, etc.; chapters v and vi, below; D. W. Sutherland, Quo warranto *proceedings in the reign of Edward I, 1278–1294* (Oxford, 1963), pp. 99, 181.
[3] E.g. *C.J.R. 1305–7*, pp. 195–6, 275–6.
[4] *Ibid.* pp. 314, 321.
[5] Among many references *Cal. close rolls, 1302–7*, p. 23 (rolls, writs and memoranda of the bench of recent years to be delivered from the treasury to a recently appointed chief justice); P.R.O., E. 163/3, no. 12 (writs to the treasurer and barons).

thesaurariam dictam aliquibus mitti debent nec possunt de jure set transcriptum tam eorundem rotulorum quam brevium originalium sub sigillo regis . . .[1]

Where judgment had been rendered only recently and the roll had not been transferred, the justices apparently checked the transcript prepared by their clerks: in 1301 the sending of a record from the bench was delayed because, in the words of a writ to the chief justice,

. . . primum mandatum nostrum vobis inde directum vobis venit postquam bancus Dublin' clausus fuit et . . . recordum illud et processum mittere non potuistis priusquam fuissent examinata per vos et socios vestros qui tunc absentes fuerunt.[2]

As in England, the time of transfer of rolls appears to have depended largely on the convenience of the justiciar or justice, as the case might be, and quite ordinarily they remained with him until his death.[3] Rolls of an eyre probably came to the treasury more expeditiously, however, upon its conclusion.[4] In 1313 John Wogan had in his custody the rolls of William of Ross, who had been his *locum tenens* in 1301–2, while the roll of pleas of the crown before Wogan himself for Hilary 1311 was in the possession of Edmund Butler, the actual chief governor.[5] A second and weightier probable reason for concentrating this side of the court's business at Dublin was ease of consultation with the justices of the bench and other ministers and persons learned in the law. Difficulty in the way of such consultations was one of the results of the destruction of the king's hall of pleas outside Dublin in the course of the Bruce war.[6] Occasionally, however,

[1] C.P., H. 24 Edw. I, in P.R.O.I., RC. 7/4, *Cal. plea rolls*, IV, 22; cf. *C.J.R. 1295–1303*, p. 418; *1305–7*, p. 144.
[2] C.P., M. 29–30 Edw. I (no. 52), in P.R.O.I., RC. 7/7, *Cal. plea rolls*, VII, 513.
[3] Cf. Sayles, *Select cases in K.B.* I, pp. cxxi–cxxiii. There is an interesting description of the arrangements made for the rolls, etc., of the justiciar Stephen of Fulbourn upon his death in 1288; Cole, *Documents*, p. 60; *Cal. doc. Ire. 1285–92*, pp. 290–2.
[4] *C.J.R. 1295–1303*, p. 418: the keeper of the rolls and writs of the eyre returned (Michaelmas 1302) that 'long before' he had delivered the rolls of the eyre of Louth (early in 1301) into the treasury.
[5] J.R., 6–7 Edw. II, m. 96 d, and 7 Edw. II (no. 105), m. 20. There is a difference of four months between these references (July, November) and Wogan's definite retirement may have had an effect in this respect in the meantime.
[6] P. 52, above.

THE JUSTICIAR'S COURT

writs of 'error' were tried outside Dublin, especially if another place was more convenient to the parties.[1]

In a manner similar to that of the English king's bench, the justiciar's court exercised a jurisdiction in review over both courts of record and courts not of record, but the former class, into which fell the court itself, the bench, the eyre, sessions of justices of assize, and the steward's courts of the great liberties, was much the most important. The court could be commissioned from England to review its own judgments. This might be the case whether or not the same chief governor was in office.[2] Exceptionally, in 1321 the justiciar, John de Bermingham, earl of Louth, was given a general commission to amend errors in all pleas before Roger Mortimer, king's lieutenant, in order to relieve litigants of the dangers and expense of travel to England.[3]

About half the cases which were reviewed by the justiciar's court came to it from the bench. A number of these, of course, had already been transferred into the Dublin court from an eyre[4] or a liberty[5] or had come before it by writ of false judgment from some lesser jurisdiction.[6] The road to the justiciar's court also lay direct from an eyre[7] and, more frequently, was used from justices of assize.[8] A variety of English writ *procedendo ad judicium* in *si difficultas* form was used on one occasion at least, by which the justiciar was ordered to correct the record or send it to the king.[9]

The principal courts of the greater liberties were of record and their judgments could be reviewed by writ of error: for example, a decision of Geoffrey de Joinville, lord of Trim, himself reviewing one of his steward of Trim.[10] This whole matter will be discussed later in another context, since an element of confusion appears to have entered in where a liberty formed a single county for administrative purposes and thus had a single county court with a jurisdiction territorially identical with that of the court of the

[1] *C.J.R. 1295–1303*, pp. 211–14, 379–80.
[2] *Ibid.* pp. 231–2; *1305–7*, pp. 294–5; *1308–14*, pp. 93–5.
[3] *Cal. pat. rolls, 1321–4*, pp. 43, 176. It is strange that only Mortimer's term of office as king's lieutenant (April 1317 to May 1318) and not his later term as justiciar (June 1319 to December 1320) is mentioned, but it may have been intended that both should be covered.
[4] E.g. *C.J.R. 1295–1303*, pp. 211–14, 416–18.
[5] E.g. *C.J.R. 1305–7*, pp. 98–100. [6] E.g. *C.J.R. 1295–1303*, pp. 379–80.
[7] E.g. *C.J.R. 1305–7*, pp. 335, 394, 443–6.
[8] E.g. *ibid.* pp. 60–2, 65–6, 137–8.
[9] *Ibid.* pp. 145–7. [10] *C.J.R. 1295–1303*, p. 223.

steward.[1] At all events, correction of judgments in the courts of liberties was not an important part of the justiciar's jurisdiction.

By writs of false judgment the court reviewed the decisions of courts not of record. These might be, for example, county courts,[2] minor franchisal courts[3] or borough courts.[4] But this type of business was largely left to the bench and proceedings in review of these courts without record were rare in the justiciar's court.[5]

The jurisdiction of the justiciar's court impinged on the lesser courts in other ways than by writs of error or false judgment. For example, an English writ with a *si difficultas* clause was used to bring a case at hearing in a lower court to the justiciar and, at his discretion, *coram rege*.[6] When a royal charter was produced before them, the justices of the bench thought it proper to adjourn the matter into the justiciar's court.[7] The recognitors of an assize were brought into the justiciar's court to answer further questions, since they were alleged not to have been fully examined by the justices assigned.[8] A remedy for wrongs (not the responsibility of the court concerned) in connection with proceedings in a lower court might also be sought before the justiciar. Thus, the chief serjeant of a county was impleaded in the justiciar's court because, in connection with proceedings still before the bench, he had liberated, without authority, a debtor imprisoned under the statute of Merchants. As it happened, he was promptly attacked from the opposite direction, as it were, for the debtor brought a plaint of false imprisonment.[9] A vouchee to warranty in the Dublin bench brought a plaint against his essoiner for warranting against his will.[10]

[1] Pp. 116–19, below.
[2] E.g. *C.J.R. 1295–1303*, pp. 328, 356.
[3] E.g. J.R. 7 Edw. II (no. 105), m. 23.
[4] E.g. J.R. 7 Edw. II (no. 106), m. 4.
[5] Courts in the greater liberties apart, there appear to be only three instances in the printed calendars: *C.J.R. 1295–1303*, pp. 328, 356; *1305–7*, pp. 234, 390–1.
[6] *C.J.R. 1295–1303*, pp. 151–2; chapter VII, below.
[7] C.P., H. 27 Edw. I (no. 42), in P.R.O.I., RC. 7/6, *Cal. plea rolls*, VI, 155–7; the case had already been transferred, for other reasons, from the liberty of Ulster to the Dublin bench.
[8] *C.J.R. 1305–7*, pp. 374–5; on this procedure, cf. Sayles, *Select cases in K.B.* II, pp. l–li.
[9] *C.J.R. 1295–1303*, pp. 317–19.
[10] Ibid. p. 262.

A sample roll of common pleas of the justiciar's court

A sample roll, that for 34-5 Edward I, may be viewed in the light of what has been said of the jurisdiction of the justiciar's court.[1] It has already been mentioned that this roll contains only two assizes and to that degree presents an unbalanced picture, but this is not so great a disadvantage as might be thought, for assize jurisdiction was among the less characteristic of the court's activities.

'Bills are mainly concerned with the kind of action for which a writ of trespass would be appropriate.'[2] Such bills are the most striking feature of the contents of the roll. It is possible to put over sixty plaints into the category. The commonest subject-matters were assault and battery (fourteen cases) and plaints *de bonis asportatis* (eleven cases), but they do not include individual instances of much interest. Among wrongs to interests in land, there are three plaints of ejectment. If we can accept the jury's account of the facts of one of them, the complainant had been given a term by deed by the defendant, who, after a year had elapsed, approached him for a loan. The complainant refused this, but instead offered to surrender his farm, on return of his payment and compensation for improvement. This was agreed between them by word of mouth. Defendant then went to a third party, who agreed to provide the money to buy out the complainant, on condition that he himself was then given the farm. When he raised the money, he and the defendant tendered it to the complainant, who refused to accept it. Knowing, however, that the others intended to eject him, the complainant then transferred the farm to another (apparently more powerful) man. On the same principle, the defendant took himself to a local magnate (one of the Butler family, to whom he was related by marriage), who, for a payment of forty shillings, agreed to threaten the complainant into surrendering the farm (which he seems to have received back in the meantime from his own protector).[3] This was duly done. The defendant re-demised the farm according to his earlier agreement with his financial backer. The complainant brought his bill of ejectment. The parties

---

[1] The contents of the roll are analysed in Appendix v, below.
[2] Sayles, *Select cases in K.B.* IV, p. lxxix.
[3] The tenses in the calendar are not easy to follow.

agreed: the new termor was to pay the old (the complainant) ten marks.[1]

There is what seems to have been a plaint of rape.[2] Amongst the other plaints of trespass, those involving agreements between the parties are worth attention. A colt sold was ill-treated before delivery, to the purchaser's loss; he appears to have recovered damages.[3] A party failed to acquit his pledge, who brought a plaint for damages; as assessed by the jury, the damages are reduced *de equitate* [*curie*].[4] A thousand pounds in damages were (unsuccessfully) sought for the destruction and non-observance of a deed whereby the defendant contracted to secure a dispensation for the marriage of his son and the complainant's niece.[5] An abbot, with the consent of his community, had given letters of freedom to a relative of his who was a *hibernicus* of the abbey; his successor as abbot allegedly seized and destroyed these letters and did other injuries, so the former *hibernicus* brought a bill.[6]

The use of bills did not altogether exclude writs of trespass. They are found for assault and battery of plaintiff's *hibernicus*,[7] for abduction of wife and chattels,[8] *de bonis asportatis* while plaintiff had the king's protection,[9] for wrongs to his person, goods, and men, while proceeding to serve with the king in Scotland,[10] to assert the right of being quit of toll,[11] to vindicate liberty rights against a royal serjeant of adjoining cross-lands who had released prisoners from a liberty prison without authority.[12] On the other hand, the bill alone appears to have been used in the justiciar's court for debt and detinue (twenty-four out of twenty-nine examples on the roll are certainly by bill and the rest are merely doubtful).

Over complaints against the king's ministers, which number ten, there is no need to linger, for the wrongdoing of sheriffs and serjeants is a familiar medieval theme, in Ireland as elsewhere.[13] There are four cases of maintenance and conspiracy. Twice the king prosecuted against liberty officials for remissness in their

---

[1] *C.J.R. 1305–7*, pp. 287–8. [2] *Ibid.* p. 181.
[3] *Ibid.* p. 184. [4] *Ibid.* p. 183. [5] *Ibid.* p. 284; p. 73, n. 5, above.
[6] *Ibid.* pp. 319, 321–3; cf. C. Conway, *The story of Mellifont* (Dublin, 1958), pp. 94–6.
[7] *C.J.R. 1305–7*, pp. 263–4.
[8] *Ibid.* p. 221. It is not quite certain that this was by writ.
[9] *Ibid.* pp. 236–7, 240–1, 246, 281, 318.
[10] *Ibid.* p. 198. [11] *Ibid.* pp. 188, 241. [12] *Ibid.* pp. 283, 310.
[13] Cf. Otway-Ruthven, *I.H.S.* v, 12–13 (sheriffs), 24–5 (serjeants).

duty.[1] Once there was a semi-criminal procedure by information of the chancellor, who came to record how an unknown man from England, claiming to be one John Tel (can this be 'John So-and-so'?) of Nottingham, had sued an original writ from the Irish chancery, requesting also that one Hugh of Nottingham, 'who was accustomed to be sometimes a clerk to the bench, Dublin, and sometimes an attorney in court', who was with him, should be admitted as his attorney. Because Hugh swore to the man's identity, the chancellor did as he was asked; but he later found that he had been deceived by impersonation. Sentenced to a year in prison, the two offenders made fine by ten marks.[2] A complainant by bill sued in the king's name concerning the taking back of wheat seized by a serjeant on a writ to levy a sum previously recovered by the complainant.[3]

The remaining entries on the roll are a mixed bag. Vindication of royal rights in wardships, fisheries, and ecclesiastical matters; enrolments of recognizances, etc.; process of execution; cases that came into the court for review (seventeen in all);[4] summons of records to England (three), and the residue of non-legal administrative business, go to make up the tale. We may conclude with the solitary plaint of defamation on the roll, for it is a reminder, yet again, of the peculiar conditions of life and justice in the lordship. The complainant, Nicholas de Verdun, alleged that, after he had taken with him a force to suppress Irish 'felons' and taken a prey from the Irish in question in the lands of the defendant, John del Auney, where they had been received by other Irish, John had

told the earl of Ulster that Nicholas had robbed faithful Irishmen of the earl, in contempt of the earl, by which the earl was moved beyond measure against Nicholas, and had ill will against him; to his damage of two hundred pounds.

In reply, John alleged the truth of his statement: the Irish were the earl's men and he was the earl's bailiff. The king then joined

[1] *C.J.R. 1305–7*, p. 197.
[2] Ibid. p. 224.
[3] Ibid. p. 267.
[4] These have not been touched on in detail above, because several relevant cases discussed in later chapters will adequately illustrate this side of the court's activity.

with Nicholas to allege that John knowingly received Irish 'felons'. The jurors said that

Doneghuth and his men on whom Nicholas took the prey, were felons of the king, of the company of Malys Orailly, and were with him to slay Peter le Petyt and other faithful Englishmen, and . . . that John, whose tenants they were, and not the earl's, received them, knowing that they were of the company of Molys . . .

Nicholas's damages were taxed at twenty pounds and John eventually secured a pardon for the good service which he did 'in fighting the Irish felons of the king of the mountains of Leinster'.[1]

[1] *C.J.R. 1305–7*, pp. 186–7 (*hibernici* in the calendar has been altered above to 'Irishmen').

CHAPTER IV

THE DUBLIN BENCH AND THE EXCHEQUER

THE early history of the Dublin bench has already been traced.[1] No very important changes occurred in the court during the second half of Edward I's reign or that of his successor. Its personnel and jurisdiction will here be surveyed, with special treatment of its relations with other courts and of the rival jurisdiction exercised in common pleas by the exchequer. But first something must be said of the rolls of the bench.

The small group of five early rolls of the bench (6, 8, 8-9, 9 and 10 Edward I) which survived to 1922 stand apart from the fairly substantial series that began with Michaelmas term, 17-18 Edward I (1289).[2] The terms of the five early rolls are rather uncertain and three of them appear to have reckoned a term of St John Baptist, rather than Trinity.[3] However, at least from 1289, it is evident that the rolls were made up into the four common law terms usual in England, not three, as in the case of the justiciary rolls. The Irish record commissioners, who had the rolls before them, thought that they were formed into annual rolls and later separated.[4] But this is not easy to believe and, if one may go by the earliest surviving roll, the numeration of the membranes on an annual basis was a comparatively modern addition.[5] It is of course possible that the chief justice's rolls for a given year were loosely tied together, perhaps on receipt at the treasury, and later came apart in the course of the centuries. Presumably the rolls of other justices, of which a small number survived to modern times, were always separate.[6]

Until 2.16 in the afternoon of 28 June 1922 the series of bench rolls in the Public Record Office of Ireland was one of the most extensive sources for the history of the lordship. When the dust had settled all that was left from the reigns of Edward I and

[1] Chapter I, above.   [2] Appendix VI, below; cf. p. 9, above.
[3] 8, 9, and 10 Edward I: Appendix VI, below.
[4] *Ir. rec. comm. rep. 1816-20*, p. 80.   [5] C.P., P. 18 Edw. I.
[6] The Irish record commissioners do not seem to have adverted to the problem of identifying these counter-rolls, which they rather loosely called 'duplicates'.

Edward II were the chief justice's roll for the Trinity term of 1308 and a lump of burnt and warped parchment believed to be a roll of one of the terms of the tenth year of Edward II.[1] But through a fortunate piece of negligence at the record office in the course of the nineteenth century a roll for Easter term, 1290, had somehow escaped from its proper custody, and it is now safe and sound at the British Museum.[2] Since no publication of the rolls had been attempted before their destruction, we are dependent upon these chance survivals and on a group of manuscript volumes in the Public Record Office of Ireland. These are what remain of the extensive calendars of memoranda and plea rolls prepared for the Irish record commission. From the Hilary term of 1291 to the end of the reign of Edward I thirty-seven terms are covered in these calendars. The reign of Edward II is less well served, with only sixteen terms. The nature of these curious sources explains much that may seem vague or imprecise in a study such as this. To describe them, one can scarcely do better than quote an official account written when the original rolls were available for comparison.

In these calendars the work has been treated in very different modes. Some of the rolls are transcribed almost in full; others contain short abstracts of the entries; and others have a selection of the entries chosen arbitrarily, without any indication of the omissions. Where the entries have been transcribed, especially in the earlier rolls, the work has generally been carried out with care and accuracy. Where, however, condensation has been attempted, it has usually been carelessly done. In many instances the condensed work is almost worthless, the really important fact of the entry being frequently entirely omitted, and the fact of the omission being obscured by the apparently verbatim nature of what is given, the omitted part being only indicated by an "&c". Several of the volumes have been "prepared for press" by another hand. This preparation consists of striking out about three-fourths of the articles, and shortening, often into unintelligibility, some of the few that are left. This work of revision has been done generally with an utter want of appreciation of the historical value of the materials.[3]

[1] C.P., T. 1–2 Edw. II. [2] Add. Roll 13598, cited as C.P., P. 18 Edw. I.
[3] *P.R.I. rep. D.K. 26*, p. 56; cf. M. C. Griffith, 'The Irish record commission, 1810–30', in *I.H.S.* VII, 17–38, at pp. 31–4. In an attempt to make clear both the nature of the original record and where the version used is to be found, I have adopted the following very full system of reference: (*a*) nature of record (J.R., C.P., etc.); (*b*) term; (*c*) regnal year; (*d*) where necessary to avoid ambiguity, the plea roll number assigned by the record commissioners;

The evidence of the number of membranes in the rolls, which are similar in form to other plea rolls of the time, points to a gradual increase of business to a peak early in the reign of Edward II. Not until 1298 did a terminal roll exceed twenty-five membranes, but in the last years of Edward I a considerably greater number was common and there were fifty-two membranes in the roll for Michaelmas 1304. The rolls continued to increase in bulk until the Bruce wars greatly reduced the volume of the court's business.[1] Though there was some recovery in the last years of Edward II, the court nevertheless was doing substantially less than in the period before the war.[2]

The personnel of the bench

Sometimes the justiciar himself came to the bench to afforce it on a particularly difficult matter. For example, a writ was sent from England ordering the justices to proceed in his presence in a case where difficulty had arisen whether the burgesses of Clonmel were entitled to use the writ *precipe in capite*.[3] Otto of Granson, claiming to be their lord, had first secured a *supersedeas* reciting the Great Charter (c. 24 of the 1225 text), but the justices had wished to postpone his steward's claim to court until after proof. Otto then obtained the writ directing the justiciar's presence; but in fact, when Wogan came to the bench, the steward produced a protection and the matter went *sine die*. Again, Wogan came into court to assist in deciding whether in a particular case the statute of Westminster II, c. 32 (concerning collusive evasion of the statute of Mortmain), made it necessary to take a jury.[4]

(*e*) P.R.O.I., followed by class reference RC. 7 or RC. 8 and item number; (*f*) *Cal. plea rolls* or *Cal. mem. rolls*, as the case may be; (*g*) volume number and page reference. Only recently has a system of class references been introduced at the P.R.O.I.; the second numerical element in the class references gives an item number which is in fact, in the case of these calendars, the volume number. RC. 7/13 is a bundle of papers, really belonging to the plea roll series, with which it is now classed, but mislaid during the nineteenth century and recovered after 1922. It is important to note that the modern volume numbers are not those in use before 1922 and that the plea roll volumes have received a through-pagination only in recent years.

[1] Appendix VI, below; p. 35, n. 5, above.
[2] Compare the following totals for the numbers of membranes in the rolls for given calendar years: 1299, 122; 1305, 149; 1310, 152; 1318, 80; 1321, 72; 1324, 115.
[3] C.P., P. 28 Edw. I (no. 47), in P.R.O.I., RC. 7/7, *Cal. plea rolls*, VII, 24–9.
[4] C.P., M. 28–9 Edw. I (nos. 45, 46), in P.R.O.I., RC. 7/6, *Cal. plea rolls*, VI, 367, 511–12.

Perhaps even on such occasions, certainly on ordinary ones, the chief justice of the bench presided in that court. After more than twenty years' service Robert Bagod retired as chief justice in 1298 and died the same year. His successor, Simon of Ludgate, was an English administrator with some previous experience of Irish affairs.[1] He died in September 1302. Richard of Exeter, knight, son of the former justice of that name and inheritor of his considerable estates in Connaught, followed: he had had experience as a justice of assize. During the Bruce period, when suspicions of disloyalty were prevalent, Richard was suspect because of his relations with the Meath rebel, Walter de Lacy, who had married Richard's daughter, and *autres plusours malveises alliances* of his. The petition which made these charges asked for his replacement by some suitable English or Irish lawyer.[2] Although Roger Mortimer, as justiciar in 1319, had power to remove all ministers of the king in Ireland, the chief justice of the bench, as well as the chancellor, treasurer, and justice of the justiciar's pleas, was excepted from his authority in this regard.[3] It was not until 1323 that Richard of Willoughby was appointed from England to replace Richard of Exeter. The change-over occurred in the course of Hilary term, 1324.

In the last decade of the thirteenth century, the number of puisne judges was two, though it is possible that assistance was lent by justices in eyre when not employed in their ordinary business. In 1300, Robert of Littlebury was sent to Ireland with instructions to the justiciar to assign him to the bench or the eyre, as Wogan might think best.[4] In fact he sent him to the bench because 'the eyre is not yet'.[5] Robert actually presided in the Dublin court in the Michaelmas term of 1302, in the interim following the death of Simon of Ludgate. With the appointment of John de Ponz in 1303 the number of puisne judges came to three, and not long afterwards—probably in 1305—it reached

[1] Although he received payment from Michaelmas 1298 he perhaps had not arrived in Ireland at the beginning of the term, for Thomas of Chedworth appears to have presided: C.P., M. 26–7 Edw. I, in P.R.O.I., RC. 7/5, *Cal. plea rolls*, v, 363.
[2] P.R.O., Ancient petitions, S.C. 8/118, no. 5886; printed in part by Richardson and Sayles, *Administration*, p. 154, n. 4. Neither the petitioner nor the precise date have been ascertained.
[3] *Cal. pat. rolls, 1317–21*, p. 317.
[4] *Cal. pat. rolls, 1292–1301*, p. 494.
[5] *C.J.R. 1295–1303*, p. 306.

four.[1] This considerable number may have been partly caused by—it certainly must have facilitated—the imposition of other duties upon some of the justices. When Hugh Canon, a justice chosen by Piers Gaveston,[2] was impleaded in England in 1310 he obtained letters from the most important men in Ireland—including Wogan, the chancellor, the treasurer, and the earl of Ulster—requesting a protection for him.[3] One of these letter writers who, although anonymous, may well have been Richard of Exeter, then chief justice of the bench, declared that of all the justices of the bench Hugh was *plus sovent . . . chargie de autres diverses busoignes qi touchent le roi*; he had been entrusted with the custody of the vacant office of escheator, as well as being a justice of the eyre of Dublin.[4] But in June 1311 the justiciar was ordered to select the three most competent of the justices of the bench and discharge the others, since their number was excessive.[5] There was no reduction until the lapse of a year, however, when the most junior justice, William of Bardfield, ceased to act. There were thenceforth three puisne judges, occasionally dropping to two.

In the aftermath of the Bruce wars some of the puisne judges came under criticism. In the Michaelmas parliament of 1320 at Westminster a petition from *les liges gentz de Irlaund* complained that the law was badly maintained *par defaut de sages justices* and asked the king to order that there should be in the bench *gentz sachauntz de la ley*.[6] In reply, the treasurer of Ireland was commanded to certify the king as to the justices, which were adequate for their duties and which not, and who would be suitable as replacements. As an administrator, Walter of Islip, the treasurer, was perhaps thought better qualified to advise on this matter than the magnate *locum tenens*, Thomas fitz John, or the chancellor, the archbishop of Cashel. Nothing seems in fact to have been done until a year later when the justiciar, Bermingham, was empowered to remove those appointed by Roger Mortimer when

[1] Doubt is caused by the absence of recorded payments to Thomas of Snitterby during the period 33 Edw. I to 1 Edw. II; but he was certainly in court from time to time: Richardson and Sayles, *Administration*, p. 152, n. 1; J.R. 6–7 Edw. II, m. 77; *Reg. St Thomas, Dublin*, p. 422.
[2] J.R. 6–7 Edw. II, m. 50.
[3] P.R.O., Ancient correspondence, S.C. 1/35, nos. 91, 92, 116 and 210.
[4] P.R.O., Ancient correspondence, S.C. 1/31, no. 171 (printed by Richardson and Sayles, *Administration*, pp. 242–3).
[5] *Cal. close rolls, 1307–13*, p. 354.
[6] *Rot. parl.* I, 386.

justiciar.[1] Seemingly in consequence, the two junior justices were replaced. From 1324 the number of puisne justices definitely dropped to two. Perhaps the appointment of a second justice of the justiciar's pleas had something to do with this reduction in the numbers on the common bench. In 1325, Roger of Birthorpe, the first holder of the office of second justice of the justiciar's pleas, who by the date of the reference was second justice of the bench, was referred to as *nuper secundarius justiciarius loco quarti justiciarii de banco*[2] and this enigmatic phrase may conceal something of relevance. More probably the decline in business was the cause. In 1324-5, in any event, there was a clean sweep made of the personnel of the court: even Robert Bagod, the second justice, who had been on the bench since the beginning of the reign, left office. These changes may reflect the activity of the new justiciar, John Darcy. It may be added that throughout the period the annual fee of the chief justice was forty pounds and of a puisne justice forty marks.

In all, fifteen puisne justices served in the Dublin bench between the Easter term of 1290 and the same term in 1324. The period saw a marked decline in clerical strength on the bench. At its beginning, clerks dominated. Thomas of Chedworth, a justice for more than a quarter of a century before he retired in 1303, was dean of St Patrick's cathedral, Dublin, from 1284, twice vainly elected archbishop, and 'seems to have exercised great influence [in the Irish council] much in excess of his status as a judge'.[3] John of Hatch was promoted in 1283 from the office of keeper of the rolls and writs of the bench. There is no other instance of this rise. He was a justice until 1292. Thomas of Snitterby, who came to the bench in 1295, was, like Thomas of Chedworth, an English clerk who had come to Ireland on the king's service and became a canon of St Patrick's. With possible interruptions after 1304, he remained a justice until 1308. John de Ponz has already been mentioned in connection with the justiciar's court, where he so often sued for the king;[4] he served in the bench in 1295-6 and again in 1303-6. Robert of Littlebury was a former keeper of the rolls of the English bench; he assisted in the Irish court from 1300.[5]

When William le Deveneis was appointed to succeed Thomas

[1] *Foedera* (Rec. comm. ed.), II, 1, 462. [2] *Cal. rot. pat. Hib.* p. 31.
[3] Richardson and Sayles, *The Irish parliament*, p. 28.
[4] P. 49, above. [5] P. 92, above.

of Chedworth in 1303, it was the beginning of a marked change in the personnel of the court. William had first appeared as an exchequer clerk a quarter of a century before and was still styled clerk as late as 1299. In 1301 he was a justice in eyre. He remained on the bench from 1303 to 1313 and was again a justice from 1316 to 1319. He had left his clergy by 1313, when he was described as a knight.[1] In 1305, Walter of Kenley, a knight who had been chancellor of the exchequer in 1289-93 and was very possibly another *nuper clericus*, became a justice, which he remained until 1308. In 1307, the lay element was emphasized by the appointment of Sir Robert Bagod, son of the former chief justice and himself the father of a future justice under Edward III; he was to serve until 1325. The next two appointees were also married men. Hugh Canon, appointed in 1308, was a person of very considerable importance, who, as has been noted, could rely on the support of leading figures in the lordship.[2] He left the bench in 1315, when he was made justice of the justiciar's pleas and permanent chief justice in eyre.[3] William of Bardfield (1308-12, 1316-19) had been a king's pleader.

Most of the five new justices appointed for the first time between 1308 and 1324 seem to have been of lesser calibre. John Benger (1313-15) is a person of whom nothing is known except that he was attorney in Ireland for Aylmer of Valence in 1308.[4] The two justices for whose appointment Roger Mortimer was responsible and who were later removed by Bermingham were evidently undistinguished. William de la Hill (1319-22) had had some experience as a commissioner of oyer and terminer in England before he accompanied Mortimer to Ireland.[5] The other, Rory fitz John (1319-21), a married man, was sheriff of Dublin and Meath in 1319. Of Bermingham's own appointments Robert of Bristol (1322-4) is totally obscure, but Richard le Blond (1322-5) was surely *sachaunt de la ley*, for he had been king's pleader since 1297. Though in Ireland, as in England, 'the close link between bar and bench had not yet been forged',[6] John de Ponz, William of Bardfield and Richard le Blond deserve to be remembered as

[1] On such secularized clerks, cf. F. Pegues, 'The *clericus* in the legal administration of thirteenth-century England', *E.H.R.* LXXI, 529-59, at pp. 556-7.
[2] P. 93, above. [3] *Cal. pat. rolls, 1313-17*, pp. 289, 345.
[4] *Cal. pat. rolls, 1307-13*, p. 48.
[5] *Cal. pat. rolls, 1313-17*, pp. 253, 600; *1317-21*, p. 456.
[6] Sayles, *Select cases in K.B.* VI, p. xxx.

having begun it, together with John of Fressingfield and David le Blond in the justiciar's court.

As for the lesser offices attached to the court, that of keeper of the rolls and writs, at a fee of five pounds a year, was held between 1290 and 1324 by twelve persons. Among names otherwise obscure are those of John of Fressingfield[1] and Henry of Thrapston, who ultimately became chancellor of the exchequer. There was a separate office of chirographer, but it was sometimes combined with that of keeper of the rolls and eventually merged with it.[2] Both the clerks and the marshal of the bench received damages-cleer.[3] A clerk might be 'accustomed sometimes to be... an attorney in court',[4] but references to attorneys in the bench by name are rare.[5]

The jurisdiction of the bench

The correspondence in jurisdiction and procedure which existed between the benches at Dublin and Westminster was closer than that between the Irish justiciar's court and the English court *coram rege*. Nevertheless the justices of the Dublin bench did not regard themselves as slavishly bound to follow the court at Westminster in everything. In 1308 the plaintiff on a writ of error from the bench to Wogan alleged that the continuances in the lower court had not been made according to the pseudo-statute *Dies communes in banco*.[6] Wogan declared:

> such an assignment of common days *in Banco* is not derived from ancient law, nor is it a King's statute, but is an ordinance of the Justices of the Bench at Westminster, which, although useful, it cannot be thought that the present King or any of his ancestors have ever commanded the said ordinance to be observed in this land, and, on inspection of the rolls of the Bench aforesaid from the time of Robert Bagod and others, Justices of the Bench, to the time of the said Robert [*of Littlebury*], it is ascertained that the said Justices at their discretion are wont to adjourn the parties pleading before them as they may deem expedient.[7]

[1] Pp. 46–7, above.
[2] Richardson and Sayles, *Administration*, pp. 39–40, 188.
[3] E.g. C.P., M. 24–5 Edw. I (no. 22), in P.R.O.I., RC. 7/3, *Cal. plea rolls*, III, 316 (out of £80, £10 to clerks, £1 to marshal).
[4] *C.J.R. 1305–7*, p. 224.
[5] E.g. Peter of Hilletoun, 'attorney of the bench at Dublin': J.R., 11 Edw. II (no. 116), m. 25d.   [6] *Stat. realm*, I, 208.
[7] *C.J.R. 1308–14*, p. 72; cf. Richardson and Sayles, 50 *L.Q.R.* p. 564, and Sayles, *Select cases in K.B.* II, p. lxxix, n. 9.

A writ from the justiciar would seen to have been required for a general departure from days already given to litigants in the bench.[1] The bulk of the business of the court was provided by the real actions, which, assizes apart, were not touched by the jurisdiction of the justiciar's court. Even trespass and debt, where there was a measure of overlap, were of much less comparative importance in the bench. There is no evidence of procedure by bill in that court, although the history of research into the subject warns that confidence in making negative statements about it may be misguided. In the contractual and semi-contractual actions of debt, detinue, account, and covenant, the bench had another rival in the exchequer, and of this rivalry more will shortly be said. But analysis of the surviving rolls shows the court preoccupied with the routine actions of the land law.[2]

The court had a considerable jurisdiction in review. Attaint of jury might, for example, be brought in the bench to upset the verdict of an assize before justices assigned.[3] The writ of error, as it emerged as the characteristic means for examining proceedings in courts of record, was left to the justiciar's court, but it is clear that the bench also reviewed proceedings that were technically of record. The roll for Easter 1290 includes references to the summons of parties to be before the court *ad audiendum recordum et processum assise*[4] and essoins *de placito terre unde recordum*,[5] as well as a reference to a litigant who *tulit breve ad faciendum venire recordum et processum cuiusdam assise*.[6] An assize of darrein presentment leading to a fine before justices assigned was brought into the bench by *certiorari* in 1296, but it rapidly went to the justiciar's court.[7] A writ with clause *si difficultas* might be sent from England ordering the justices of the bench to examine a record from an eyre[8] or a liberty court.[9] However, the normal jurisdiction in review exercised by the bench was over courts not of record. By *recordari facias loquelam* the sheriff was ordered to record and

---

[1] C.P., P. 24 Edw. I, in P.R.O.I., RC. 7/4, *Cal. plea rolls*, IV, 59; cf. the general postponement in Hilary term, 1316 (p. 35, above).
[2] Appendix VII, below.
[3] E.g. C.P., P. 18 Edw. I, mm. 3d, 10d. [4] *Ibid.* mm. 4, 6d.
[5] *Ibid.* m. 4d. [6] *Ibid.* m. 4.
[7] *C.J.R. 1295-1303*, pp. 112-14; C.P., H. 24 Edw. I, in P.R.O.I., RC. 7/4, *Cal. plea rolls*, IV, 17-22.
[8] Appendix II (c), below.
[9] P.R.O., K.B. 27/138, m. 57 (*Cal. doc. Ire. 1293-1301*, 100) (also in C.P., T. 19 Edw. I, in P.R.O.I., RC. 7/3, *Cal. plea rolls*, III, 174).

send a plea that had taken place in the county court.[1] To a court, not of record, in a major liberty the writ *accedas ad curiam* was used; the sheriff was to proceed to it and record the plea.[2] Similar writs were directed to him to record proceedings in other minor courts.[3]

With each of the principal courts of the lordship the bench had close connections. An assize might be transferred from the justiciar's court, if it could not be concluded within the county, as an alternative to adjourning it to the justiciar's next coming or to justices assigned.[4] If the tenant in an assize vouched to warranty, the justiciar seems to have adjourned the assize until the bench could determine the plea of warranty;[5] *aliter*, if the vouchee was a party already present in the justiciar's court and warranted there.[6] The overlapping of the jurisdictions of the justiciar's court and of the bench led sometimes to difficulty. In 1299, an assize before the bench had to be respited on receipt of a writ from the justiciar giving the record of a closely related assize in his court and ordering the justices not to proceed without him if difficulty arose, *ne ex surreptione curie contrarietas judiciorum in curia sic redditorum temporibus futuris inveniatur*.[7] The eyre and bench had of course especially close ties, cases being removed to the eyre during its sessions in the relevant county and returned on its conclusion.[8] Even during the sessions of an eyre a case might be brought into the bench for some reason, such as lack of knights for the grand assize[9] or the occurrence of a point of exceptional difficulty in the interpretation of a statute.[10] During

[1] E.g. C.P., H. 19 Edw. I, T. 26 Edw. I (nos 36 and 37), H. 27 Edw. I (nos. 39 and 42), in P.R.O.I., RC. 7/3, 5, 6, *Cal. plea rolls*, III, 45; V, 301, 323; and VI, 189–91.
[2] Pp. 118–19, below.
[3] E.g. C.P., P. 18 Edw. I, mm. 2, 10*d*; C.P., M. 24–5 Edw. I (no. 22), H. 27 Edw. I (no. 42), M. 11 Edw. II, in P.R.O.I., RC. 7/3, 6, 12, *Cal. plea rolls*, III, 293; VI, 123–5; XII, 347.
[4] *C.J.R. 1295–1303*, pp. 321, 337, 344, etc. The references to the bench in the indexes to *C.J.R.* have to be treated with caution, since sometimes *in banco*, meaning 'in court', seems to have been misconstrued.
[5] *C.J.R. 1305–7*, pp. 37, 94–5.
[6] *Ibid.* pp. 368, 439.
[7] C.P., P. 25 Edw. I, in P.R.O.I., RC. 7/5, *Cal. plea rolls*, V, 69.
[8] E.g. *C.J.R. 1308–14*, pp. 68–72, 108–10; C.P., M. 31–2 Edw. I, in P.R.O.I., RC. 8/1, *Cal. mem. rolls*, I, 239, 244.
[9] E.g. C.P., M. 31–2 Edw. I, in P.R.O.I., RC. 8/1, *Cal. mem. rolls*, I, 202, 203; *C.J.R. 1295–1303*, pp. 416–17.
[10] *Select cases in K.B.* II, 77.

the eyre of Dublin in 1311 Irish letters patent were sent to the justices reciting a complaint of the people of that county that pleas were being held on eyre according to the law and custom of England but contrary to that of Ireland: the justices were to cease from dealing with pleas of land which according to Irish custom ought to have been determined in the bench.[1] It is far from clear what was behind this. Perhaps it had not been customary to transfer pleas of land from the bench to an eyre of Dublin, since the courts sat in the same county, but as we have no texts of rolls of the relevant eyres of Dublin nothing can be said with confidence. Proceedings were transferred from the courts of the great liberties to the bench when a person outside the liberty was vouched to warranty,[2] or because of the lack of knights.[3] Little has been found to show to what extent the *nisi prius* system, which grew so rapidly in these years in England, was established in Ireland.[4] In 1318 a sheriff was ordered to have a jury in the bench

nisi Willelmus de Berdefeld justiciarius de banco hic prius in partes illas venerit coram quo fecerit etc.[5]

This may refer to the taking of vacation business by the justices of the bench: two of them are found taking assizes at Drogheda in mid-August, 1304, so the system of vacation assizes was evidently known in Ireland.[6]

Common pleas in the exchequer

The beginnings of the jurisdictional dispute between the bench and the exchequer have already been noticed.[7] Not a great deal is known of the plea side of the Dublin exchequer, though in 1299 it was argued before Wogan and the barons there that

scaccarium est placea equitatis et quod hic placitatur sicut in scaccario Anglie. Et dicit quod licet inventum fuit per inquisicionem quod ipse

[1] *Cal. rot. pat. Hib.* p. 17, usefully supplemented by an English paraphrase in W. Lynch, *A view of the legal institutions, honorary hereditary offices, and feudal baronies established in Ireland during the reign of Henry II* (London, 1830), pp. 22-3.
[2] E.g. C.P., H. 27 Edw. I (no. 42), M. 29-30 Edw. I, in P.R.O.I., RC. 7/6, 7, *Cal. plea rolls*, VI, 155-7; VII, 465-6.
[3] E.g. C.P., M. 29-30 Edw. I, in P.R.O.I., RC. 7/7, *Cal. plea rolls*, VII, 462-5.
[4] An example of the older meaning (Bracton, f. 110) of *nisi prius*, but with *nisi ... interim* as the phrase used, is found, J.I., 44 Hen. III, in P.R.O.I., RC. 7/1, *Cal. plea rolls*, I, 249.
[5] C.P., P. 11 Edw. II, in P.R.O.I., RC. 7/12, *Cal. plea rolls*, XII, 468.
[6] *C.J.R. 1305-7*, p. 18.   [7] P. 11, above.

fuisset plene etatis tempore confectionis predicti scripti adhuc per equitatem et secundum consuetudinem in utriusque scaccario hactenus usitatam admitteretur ipse ad respondendum ulterius in principali. Et unde se ponit discretioni curie et petit judicium.[1]

Whatever the force of the appeal to 'equity', it seems to have been true that English practice was in general followed in the Irish exchequer. However, the plea side was not considerable enough to justify special plea rolls, as in England: a section of the memoranda rolls was given over to pleas. No memoranda roll has been printed, although two survive from the reign of Edward II.[2] There are Latin calendars in manuscript prepared for the Irish record commissioners[3] and some English calendars were also prepared before 1922 with an eye to publication and happily survive.[4] The proceedings were usually before the treasurer and barons of the exchequer. The justiciar sometimes went to the exchequer to deal with matters which presented unusual difficulty: though entered on the justiciary rolls, such business can hardly be regarded as that of the justiciar's court in the ordinary sense.[5]

In 1288 a writ allowed the exchequer to determine common pleas *tam pro mercatoribus quam aliis mota*, since it proceeded more rapidly than the bench.[6] It was alleged later that a saving clause in this writ, *dum tamen negocia nostra in banco minime retardentur*, had been altered by erasing *banco* and substituting *scaccario*. The officials of the exchequer, no doubt, were anxious to secure for themselves discretion in deciding whether a plea might be held there or not. On the other hand, the principle that common pleas should not be pleaded in the exchequer was recited in a writ in a particular case in 1291:

Edwardus dei gratia rex Anglie dominus Hibernie et dux Aquitanie thesaurario et baronibus suis de scaccario Dublin salutem;
Cum communia placita regni nostri coram justiciariis apud Dublin seu

[1] P.R.O., K.B. 27/161, m. 41*d* (*Cal. doc. Ire. 1293–1301*, 737); cf. Sayles, *Select cases in K.B.* II, p. lix.
[2] 3 and 13–14 Edw. II, in P.R.O.I.
[3] In P.R.O.I., RC. 8, *Cal. mem. rolls*.
[4] In P.R.O.I.; they cover 22–3, 31–5 Edw. I, and 1 and 3 (two rolls) Edw. II.
[5] *C.J.R. 1295–1303*, p. 240; *1305–7*, pp. 8–9.
[6] Cole, *Documents*, p. 84.

coram justiciariis nostris itinerantibus et non alibi debeant et consueverunt terminari, ac Mauricius de Carreu Johannem de Barry implacitet coram vobis per breve nostrum de quibusdam consuetudinibus et servitiis sibi faciendis, ut accepimus, contra legem et consuetudinem regni nostri in prefati Johannis dampnum non modicum et gravamen;
Vobis mandamus quod de placito illo in dicto scaccario ulterius tenendo vos in nullo intromittatis intimantes predicto Mauricio quod super hoc secundum legem et consuetudinem regni nostri remedium impetret si sibi viderit expedire.
Teste meipso apud Norham secundo die Junii anno regni nostri nonodecimo.[1]

The Irish exchequer ordinances of 1292–4 do not appear to have directly affected the plea side of the exchequer.[2]

A comparison may be made between the bench roll for Easter 1290 and the two membranes of the memoranda roll for 22–3 Edward I which contain the pleas of Michaelmas term, 1294.[3] The bench roll records only seven cases of the contractual type over which the dispute was chiefly waged. There are fourteen cases in all recorded on the memoranda roll. Nine of these can hardly have been possible subjects of complaint by other jurisdictions. A dispute over the levy of a debt due to the king, a prohibition against interfering with corn forfeited to the king, a complaint that a sheriff did not make proper allowance for a tally, a suit involving a fine made with the escheator, a dispute arising out of a payment to a constable of a castle, acquittance of arrears of scutage, were all matters appropriate to the exchequer.[4] Similarly, it is not surprising that Luccan merchants and the executors of Robert Burnell should have been privileged to plead there. The remaining five cases are less clear-cut. Thomas of Chedworth, as a minister of the exchequer—he was in fact *locum tenens* of the treasurer at the time—was stretching his privilege somewhat in using it to recover a debt due to the common fund of the cathedral of which he was dean. The other four cases are of debt without an evident connection with the exchequer.

[1] Bodleian MS. Laud Misc. 613, p. 140.
[2] On these ordinances, Lydon, *Ir. Comm. Hist. Sc. Bull.* no. 81, p. 2.
[3] The bench roll is analysed in Appendix VII, below; for the memoranda roll the English calendar in P.R.O.I. has been used.
[4] Cf., in general, H. Jenkinson and B. E. R. Fermoy, *Select cases in the exchequer of pleas* (S.S. 49), pp. lxxviii–cxv.

The *Peticio populi Hibernie* of *c.*1300 which attacked the justiciar's jurisdiction by bill also complained

E derichef le tresorer Dirlaund lur plede par bref de Eschekere de jour en jour encountre la commune ley.[1]

But this is not known to have brought a remedy. Other complaints were made from time to time. During a long dispute between Geoffrey de Joinville, lord of Trim, and the Dublin exchequer in 1302, Geoffrey alleged that the exchequer had tried to proceed as if by *quo warranto* against him, though liberties such as his *sapit naturam liberi tenementi* and so ought not to have been called in question there.[2] Though this point was urged by him before the justiciar, it was not mentioned in the judgment in error which he eventually secured in the English council.[3]

For the first year of Edward II a comparison between exchequer and bench records is possible that is more precise chronologically than the comparison already given between records of 1290 and 1294, and it suggests that the bench had made considerable headway against exchequer jurisdiction in contractual matters between party and party. The bench rolls for Easter and Trinity terms, 1 Edward II, may be compared with the L.T.R. memoranda roll for the same regnal year.[4] (No text is available for the K.R. roll of the same year, but the surviving original K.R. roll for 3 Edw. II confirms that such cases as are here in question would not be found upon it, the K.R. heading being *Placita dominum regem tangentia* and the L.T.R. heading *Communia placita*.) The memoranda roll yields only thirteen cases of various kinds in detail; they include no action of debt between private parties in which privilege or a credible allegation of exoneration of the plaintiff's debts to the king were not in question. The ministers of the exchequer were careful of their privilege: one case of detinue of charters began by bill in the justiciar's court, but was sent to the exchequer because the defendant was a remembrancer.[5] But there are quite a lot of entries of attorneys in actions of debt between private parties in which the circumstances are obscure. Awareness of the restrictions on exchequer jurisdiction was

---

[1] P.R.O., S.C. 8/53, no. 2643; pp. 75-6, above.
[2] P.R.O., K.B. 27/171, m. 67 d (*Cal. doc. Ire. 1302-7*, 170).
[3] P. 128-9, below.
[4] Appendix vii, below; English calendar in P.R.O.I.
[5] Mem., 1 Edw. II, m. 17, in P.R.O.I., English calendar, pp. 290-92.

shown by a defendant who challenged it during an action of account in 1310.[1] In the middle of the fourteenth century the struggle over exchequer jurisdiction was still in progress and the holding of common pleas there was forbidden in 1342, 1351 and 1357—repetitions that suggest the ineffectiveness of the ban.[2] There can be little doubt that the plea side had maintained something of its challenge to the bench. Whether this may have helped in a general way towards its development as a court of equity at a later date is an inviting speculation outside the scope of the present study.

[1] Mem. (L.T.R.), 3 Edw. II, m. 10, in P.R.O.I., English calendar, p. 428. The parties—merchants—litigated also before the justiciar, in the borough court of Drogheda, and in that of Dieppe: P.R.O., C. 47/87/2, no. 3 (printed by G. Mac Niacaill, 'The case of Nicholas John', *Louth archaeological society journal*, xv (1963), 273–6); p. 142, below.

[2] *Stat. Ire. John–Hen. V*, pp. 354, 413; *Foedera* (Rec. comm. ed.), III, 1, 216.

CHAPTER V

THE GENERAL EYRE AND OTHER COMMISSIONS

IN Ireland, as in England, the reign of Edward II saw the rapid decline of the general eyre. Eyres were fairly frequent in Ireland in the later years of Edward I: Limerick in 1290, Waterford the same year, Dublin in 1291–2, Kildare in 1297, Louth in 1301, Cork in 1301, Meath in 1301–3 and Tipperary in 1305–7.[1] But after an eyre of Dublin in 1310–11 there is silence for a decade. At the end of 1321 the justiciar was ordered to appoint a commission for Meath.[2] The eyre began in the following March and the burgesses of Drogheda-in-Meath petitioned during the summer for its abandonment.[3] In November 1322 it was therefore suspended.[4] Although commissions were to have been issued for a resumption in 1324, there is no evidence that they took effect.[5] This incomplete eyre appears to have been the last of its kind.

The present chapter will describe, first, the records and personnel of the eyre, then its jurisdiction, and, lastly, the other commissions which were issued from time to time.

Records and personnel of the eyre

Very few eyre rolls survived to modern times and only one is now accessible in a serviceable text, a roll of crown pleas of the exceptional eyre of Kildare held by John Wogan in 1297.[6] Some of the rolls were of common or crown pleas only and some included both, but no conclusions are possible as to the reasons for the difference of practice in this regard. Each justice of an eyre kept his own roll and so there was considerable difficulty

---

[1] This list may not be exhaustive.
[2] *Cal. close rolls, 1318–23*, p. 408.
[3] P.R.O., S.C. 1/61, no. 49.
[4] *Cal. close rolls, 1318–23*, pp. 610, 613.
[5] *Cal. close rolls, 1323–7*, pp. 107, 108.
[6] Appendix VIII, below; *C.J.R. 1295–1303*, pp. 167–208.

when conflicting records were produced of an assize in the eyre of Dublin of 1291:

Et super hoc venit Eustachius le Poer unus socius predictorum justiciariorum itinerantium et protulit aliud recordum eiusdem assise non concordans alio recordo predictorum justiciariorum itinerantium sociorum suorum et expresse dixit idem Eustachius quod illud recordum suum advocat et advocabit non consentiens predicto recordo predictorum justiciariorum itinerantium suorum sociorum.[1]

Unfortunately, in the record commissioners' calendared texts that are, with the exception mentioned, all that now remain to us of the rolls, it is possible to discern the identity of the individual justice to whom the roll belonged in only one instance.[2]

Although a fresh commission was no doubt issued for each eyre there was a marked continuity of personnel. William Barry seems to have been chief justice in eyre in 1289-90. The Dublin eyre of 1291-2 was presided over by Prior William fitz Roger, later *custos*, and John Wogan himself conducted the Kildare eyre of 1297. Walter Lenfant then appears to have become chief justice in eyre, presiding in four eyres from 1301 to 1307. In the last of these, that of Tipperary, Thomas St Leger, bishop of Meath, acted much of the time in place of Walter, who was busy in the justiciar's court. Walter Cusack, a Meath magnate, presided in the eyre of Dublin of 1310-11 and Alexander of Bicknor, archbishop of Dublin, who had a mass of legal and administrative experience behind him, in the suspended eyre of Meath in 1322. The customary number of lesser justices was four. The same justices naturally tended to be called upon for successive eyres. In the four in which Walter Lenfant presided two of his fellows were the same throughout and two more were with him on three occasions each. However, the kind of puisne justice chosen shows a marked difference between the eyres of 1290-2 and those of later date. Of the eight puisne justices in the earlier group of eyres, six were men whose judicial experience was to remain confined to eyre work or the stewardship of liberties; the two exceptions served in the justiciar's court. Of the fourteen in the remaining eyres, one (Alexander of Bicknor) was to become justiciar and all but two at some stage sat in either the justiciar's

[1] P.R.O., K.B. 27/138, m. 18 (*Cal. doc. Ire. 1293-1301*, 92); p. 149, n. 5 below.
[2] The roll (no. 59) of Robert of Littlebury in the eyre of Cork of 29 Edward I.

court or the Dublin bench. (One of the exceptions, Arnold Power, was steward of a liberty, and the other, Master Philip of Yardley, was a clerk of whom very little is known.) It is possible to see in this the emergence of a more professional atmosphere about the eyre bench; but in the absence of adequate information on the activity and jurisdiction of all three courts, Dublin bench, justiciar's court and eyre, before 1290, it would be rash to assume that the change implied a raising of standards in the administration of justice.

The basis of payment on eyre was similar to that in the bench: forty pounds a year to the chief justice, forty marks to his colleagues. The principal lesser officers of the eyre were the keeper of the rolls and writs, at five pounds a year, and the marshal. None of the keepers were persons of any note. The marshalcy was valued at twenty marks a year in 1305, when it was the object of a dispute.[1]

The jurisdiction of the eyre

The only writs of proclamation for an eyre of which texts survive are those for the eyre of Meath of 1322.[2] They bear the date 28 January 1322 and are under the great seal of Ireland. First there is the proclamation addressed to the various freeholders of the county. Alexander, archbishop of Dublin, and four others have been commissioned as justices

ad itinerandum et ad omnia placita hac vice in comitatu predicto attaminata et attaminanda[3] capienda

and

ad omnia placita corone in eodem comitatu deliberanda audienda et terminanda juxta provisiones et ordinaciones per nos factas. Et ad querelas et transgressiones omnium querencium seu conqueri volencium tam de ballivis et ministris nostris quibuscumque quam de ballivis et ministris aliorum et aliis quibuscumque et ad querimonias quascumque audiendas et ad competentes emendas inde faciendas secundum legem et consuetudinem terre nostre Hibernie juxta ordinacionem per nos inde factam et juxta tenorem statutorum eisdem . . . inde traditorum et iniunctorum.

[1] *Rot. parl.* I, 204; P.R.O., C. 47/10/17, no. 17.
[2] 'Muniments of Edmund de Mortimer', ed. Wood, in R.I.A. Proc. XL, 338–41.
[3] So Wood, correctly, prints his source (B.M., Harl. MS. 1240, f. 277d). Emend perhaps to *arrainiata, arrainianda*, or *arramiata, arramianda*.

THE GENERAL EYRE

The wording of this writ is broadly similar to that of the English model of 1278.[1] In the first line of the first of the two extracts just given the text which we have for the Irish writ replaces *communia placita* with *omnia placita*, but this may be no more than a scribal error.[2] More interesting is the absence of any explicit reference to *placita de libertatibus*, and something further will shortly be said in connection with this.

The second writ is addressed to the justices. It commissions them and recites the instructions to the sheriff, which are again recited in the text before the sheriff's formal return. These instructions are almost identical with the English form.[3] As in England, writs of quittance from eyre summons were obtainable.[4]

The common pleas side of the eyre may be dismissed in a few words. Unfortunately, no satisfactory text of an eyre roll of common pleas is now available for analysis, but a general fidelity to English practice is indicated. Thus, the provisions of the statute of Westminster II, c. 10, concerning the delivery of writs in the eyre, were observed.[5] The use of procedure by plaint has already been discussed, in connection with the justiciar's court, and so has the close connection between the common pleas side of the eyre and the Dublin bench.

The paramount interest of the eyre lies in its function as an instrument of searching inquiry, control, and profit, and as dispensing ordinary criminal justice. Here a question of essential importance arises. Were there Irish *capitula itineris*? The writ to the justices in 1322 does mention that complainants are to be done justice *iuxta articulos vobis inde traditos* and a similar phrase in English writs has been interpreted as referring to the articles of the eyre.[6] But examination of the surviving texts of presentments by the juries of cantreds (taking the place of the English hundred juries) does not indicate so exhaustive an inquiry as that outlined by the English articles, though on the other hand it is to be remembered that 'throughout the history of the eyre the majority

[1] H. M. Cam, *Studies in the hundred rolls* (Oxford, 1921), p. 57.
[2] Cf. Meekings, *Crown pleas of the Wiltshire eyre, 1249*, p. 15.
[3] Cf. Bracton, f. 109; a *quo warranto* clause had of course been added by the time of the Irish document of 1322, which includes it.
[4] E.g. *Cal. close rolls, 1288–96*, pp. 254, 255.
[5] E.g. *C.J.R. 1305–7*, p. 317 (writ delivered late); J.I., 18 Edw. I (no. 13), and 29 Edw. I (no. 59), in P.R.O.I., RC. 7/1, 9, *Cal. plea rolls*, I, 171; IX, 20 (assizes on disseisin *infra summonicionem itineris*).
[6] Cam, *Studies in the hundred rolls*, p. 57.

of the articles evoked no presentments'.[1] Many of the articles used in England to inquire into the proprietary rights of the crown and into franchises were not suited to conditions within the lordship of Ireland. It seems probable, though not certain, that there were chapters put to the Irish juries, but that these were not identical with the English articles. A curious fact is that Irish eyre rolls record presentments of offenders against the statute of Mortmain at a period when none are known in England and before the observance of the statute is known to have become an article of the English eyre.[2]

A roll of the eyre of Kildare held by John Wogan in 1297-8 is accessible in an English calendar and may be used for purposes of illustration and analysis.[3] The circumstances of the eyre, and possibly the procedure followed in it, were exceptional, however. William de Vescy had surrendered his liberty of Kildare to the king and Wogan's eyre was partly intended to integrate it in the main structure of the administration of the lordship: thus, the arrangements for coroners had to be re-organized.[4] The eyre lasted from 21 July 1297 to at least the following April. Before its destruction in 1922, the roll consisted of nineteen membranes. Seven were chiefly devoted to pleas of the crown and gaol delivery, the purely judicial side of the eyre. The remaining dozen were taken up with its inquisitorial business. Only about four-and-a-half of them, however, consisted of presentments of the ordinary kind (with which some extracts from coroners' rolls are found closely associated). The rest consisted of material taken from 'ancient inquisitions taken by Will. de Vescy, in the time when the liberty of Kildare was in his hand'. Evidently these 'inquisitions' are founded on some kind of presentments. Almost exclusively, they concern robbery, housebreaking and similar offences. This striking imbalance in subject-matter suggests that they are selective in some way and here attention will be concentrated on the presentments actually made on the eyre.

In turn the jurors of the cantreds of Leys, Offaly, and Omurethy, and of the cross-lands of the county came before the justiciar

---

[1] Cam, *Studies in the hundred rolls*, p. 26.
[2] *C.J.R. 1295-1303*, p. 174; J.I., 33-4 Edw. I (no. 76), m. 33, in P.R.O.I., English calendar; cf. Cam, *Studies*, pp. 65-6.
[3] *C.J.R. 1295-1303*, pp. 167-208.
[4] *Ibid.* p. 167; in general, J. Otway-Ruthven, 'The medieval county of Kildare', *I.H.S.* XI, 181-99.

presiding in the eyre and told their tale. No presentments survive for the fourth Kildare cantred, Offelan, although references are made incidentally to the jurors of that cantred.[1] An odd feature is that, despite the consultation of the coroners' rolls which evidently took place, the jurors of the cantreds do not seem to have been exposed to amercement in the traditional eyre way. 'Death dominates the presentments',[2] as the following summary suggests:

Nature of Presentments	Number of entries
Royal feudal and proprietary rights	5
Royal prerogative, regulations, etc.	15
Homicide	22
Miscellaneous criminal matters	26
Felons' chattels	1
Misadventure	4

As has been mentioned earlier, the surviving writ to the justices in eyre in 1322 omits the reference to *placita de libertatibus* found in the corresponding English form. There is no record on the Kildare roll of formal claims to franchise by proprietors at the beginning of the eyre and it is known that *placita de quo warranto* were associated with the justiciar's court at least as much as with the eyre; however, a membrane was specially devoted to *quo warranto* proceedings in a roll of the eyre of Cork of 1301.[3] The jurors of the cantred of Offaly presented the exercise of some franchises, nevertheless.[4] Returns of a type familiar in England, though looming less large, concern some of the proprietary rights of the crown and the misdoings of local officials.[5] The articles put to the Kildare jurors may well have included one concerning breach of the common-law rule, reiterated by the statute of Marlborough, c. 2, against distraint outside the fee.[6] Obstruction of highways was presentable.[7] More than once the jurors drew attention to the important matter of keeping passes cleared through

[1] *C.J.R. 1295–1303*, pp. 194, 195, 197.
[2] Meekings, *Crown pleas of the Wiltshire eyre, 1249*, p. 95; my indebtedness to the table printed, *ibid*. p. 37, and in other respects, will be evident.
[3] J.I. 29 Edw. I (no. 59), in P.R.O.I., RC. 7/9, *Cal. plea rolls*, IX, 205; p. 81, above.
[4] *C.J.R. 1295–1303*, p. 174.
[5] *Ibid*. pp. 174, 181–2.
[6] *Ibid*. pp. 168, 171.
[7] *Ibid*. p. 168.

the woods.[1] Presentments for failure to have 'horses at arms' at various places as assessed evidently also reflected peculiarly Irish conditions, although the precise nature of the service involved is not quite clear,[2] and the same can be said of a presentment that two Irishmen 'took pledges from the faithful people of the country for victual and extorted money'.[3] From time to time valuations of deodands occur. In 1290 the priory of St Catharine at Waterford had secured letters granting it the deodands of Irish courts during pleasure, but the only assignment expressly recorded on the eyre roll of Kildare was to the friars minor of Kildare town.[4] In the reign of Edward II the Hospital of St John without the New Gate at Dublin secured this right to deodands.[5]

The general judicial business of the eyre is represented by membranes headed 'pleas of the crown before John Wogan',[6] 'delivery of gaol . . . before John de Ponte and Gilbert de Sutton, justices assigned',[7] 'delivery of gaol in the eyre of John Wogan',[8] and 'delivery of gaol . . . before John Wogan'.[9] These differences of wording suggest that the gaol delivery was, as usual, largely entrusted to subordinate justices. John de Ponz has already received mention for the part he played in the justiciar's court and the Dublin bench. He may indeed have been on the ordinary judicial commission for this eyre, for the names of Wogan's associates are not precisely known. Gilbert of Sutton was then sheriff of Kildare and later became steward of Wexford and a justice in the liberty of Kilkenny.[10] Robbery, burglary, larceny, and receiving stolen chattels formed almost two-thirds of the cases on these membranes and in most instances the accused made fine immediately.[11] If he did go to a jury, acquittal generally resulted. Indeed, if comparison of sample rolls is a guide, the proportion of acquittals to the total number of cases was much

---

[1] *C.J.R. 1295–1303*, pp. 168, 173, 175.   [2] *Ibid.* pp. 168, 175.
[3] *Ibid.* p. 168.
[4] *Cal. pat. rolls, 1281–92*, p. 356; cf. P.R.O., S.C. 8/88, nos 4351 and 4352; *C.J.R. 1295–1303*, p. 208.
[5] *Cal. rot. pat. Hib.* p. 25; P.R.O., S.C. 8/181, no. 9006; *Chartae, privilegia et immunitates* (Ir. rec. comm.), p. 51; cf. J.R. 9–11 Edw. II (no. 114), m. 9 d.
[6] mm. 4, 5 d, 6, 10, 18 (*C.J.R. 1295–1303*, pp. 200, 191, 196, 202, 205).
[7] m. 9 d (*ibid.* p. 175).
[8] mm. 12, 15 (*ibid.* pp. 191, 193).   [9] m. 13 (*ibid.* p. 207).
[10] There are various references to him in *C.J.R.*: also, P.R.O., K.B. 27/185, m. 14 d, and C. 47/10/17, no. 14 (*Cal. doc. Ire. 1302–7*, 367); *Cal. close rolls, 1302–7*, p. 256.   [11] Appendix IX, below.

higher than in the justiciar's court: forty-nine out of one hundred and seventy-two, as against thirteen out of seventy-six. This would confirm that the eyre was a more searching inquiry.

Other commissions

References to the commissions of assize, gaol delivery, and oyer and terminer at work in the lordship of Ireland have chiefly to be gleaned from the records of the central courts. Until 1922 there survived a roll formed from various assize membranes of 25 Edward I and it is now represented by a record commissioners' calendar.[1] There is an almost full text available of the writs for the taking of an assize by special commissioners in 1286, which suffices to show, as might be expected, that the English forms were followed.[2] In Ireland there seems to have been a nucleus of one or more quasi-permanent justices of assize, with whom others were joined in each county as occasion and convenience demanded. So, in 1295, David of Uffington is mentioned as the king's justice appointed to take assizes in Ireland.[3] A little later, after David seems to have become chiefly occupied as a baron of the exchequer, the roll of assize membranes that survived until 1922 shows that John de Ponz was invariably one of different groups of justices taking assizes in counties Tipperary, Louth, Cork, and Limerick. The first Irish statute to deal with justices of assize was apparently enacted in 1310 (3 Edw. II, c. 5);[4] it decreed that there should be certain justices for the task in all the counties and that they should also deliver the gaols. Early in the reign of Edward II, one Henry Cogan, in association usually with David le Blond, was accustomed to act as a justice of assize in the Munster counties.[5] Henry's good services in holding pleas of juries and assizes in the counties of Cork, Limerick, Tipperary and Waterford were mentioned when a fine incurred by him was remitted in 1312.[6] It is possible that he was the predecessor of Adam le Breton, who in May 1319 was appointed chief justice of assizes in the counties of Munster and

---

[1] J.I., 25 Edw. I (no. 27), in P.R.O.I., RC. 7/4, *Cal. plea rolls*, IV, 233-48.
[2] C.P., H. 24 Edw. I, in P.R.O.I., RC. 7/4, *Cal. plea rolls*, iv, 19-20.
[3] *Cal. close rolls, 1288-96*, p. 428.
[4] Not numbered in *Stat. Ire. John–Hen. V*, p. 269, since no medieval source was found for the text; c. 5 in the conventional enumeration of Irish statutes.
[5] J.R. 6-7 Edw. II, mm. 83, 84, 84d, and 7 Edw. II (no. 105), m. 16.
[6] J.R. 6-7 Edw. II, m. 10.

the cross-lands of Leinster.[1] This appointment followed hard upon the statute 13 Edw. II, c. 5 (Ir.).[2] By this, provision was made for three justices in each county before whom assizes should be held and the gaol delivered. One justice was to be *un homme de court sage et loial et puissant* and the other two knights of the county. Two might act, but *celuy de court* had to be of this quorum. The same justices were empowered to inquire, at least twice a year, into the conduct of sheriffs and serjeants and their underlings and hear complaints against them. There is no information on the workings of this system, but it may have been to a great extent a re-statement of existing arrangements. It was plainly convenient to have a single 'man of court' working with different local associates in a group of counties. This had probably been the role of John de Ponz, almost certainly that of Henry Cogan, and henceforth was to be that of Adam le Breton.

Two examples may be given of the seeking of special commissions of oyer and terminer. In 1307, in the last months of Edward I's reign, the influence of the prince of Wales and the earl of Ulster secured the appointment of Wogan and Quantock, bishop of Emly and chancellor, to deal with trespasses committed against Geoffrey of Morton, one of the most litigious persons in the colony.[3] In 1323 a petitioner sought the appointment of four named persons as commissioners to deal with wrongs alleged to have been suffered by him when he was absent on the king's service in Scotland.[4]

[1] *Cal. pat. rolls, 1317–21*, pp. 332–3. He had been a justice of assize in Carlow in 1311: *Cal. rot. pat. Hib.* p. 17.
[2] *Stat. Ire. John–Hen. V*, p. 287; the statute is not included in the *Irish Statutes at Large*.
[3] *Cal. chancery warrants, 1244–1326*, p. 261.
[4] *Ibid.* p. 542.

CHAPTER VI

LIBERTIES AND FRANCHISES

THE great Anglo-Irish liberties resembled those of England, rather than the marcher lordships of Wales.[1] Proceedings in their courts were amenable to writs of error and false judgment. Their jurisdiction by 1290 was, except in the case of east Meath (Trim), limited by the reservation to the crown of the four pleas of rape, arson, forestalling, and treasure-trove.[2] Thus, a liberty official chose to erase an indictment for *forstallum* in order to arrange the payment of a fine for the accompanying offence of simple robbery;[3] a plaint alleging *forstallum* and assault was remitted from the justiciar's court to that of the liberty when it was found that there was in fact only simple assault.[4] In 1293 it was alleged that liberty jurisdiction ceased upon indictment or appeal of one of the four pleas, even when the accused was in process of outlawry already in the liberty court:

consuetudo universalis Hibernie talis est quod si quis positus fuit in exigendis in libertate alicuius et pendente illa exacione si ille qui exactus est indictus fuerit sive appellatus de incendio forstallo thesauro invento sive raptu vel male suspectus habeatur communiter quod ex tunc cessare debet potestas huiusmodi libertatum de huiusmodi exactionibus.[5]

As in the case of the Welsh lordships and the greater English liberties, prerogative wardship did not apply within the Irish liberties, though of course the king retained the marriage of heirs.[6]

A highly important limitation on liberty jurisdiction in Ireland was the exemption from it of certain church-lands—cross-lands—and their relation instead to a convenient royal county. Grants of liberty reserved these 'crosses' to the crown, but this did not

[1] J. Otway-Ruthven, 'The constitutional position of the great lordships of South Wales', *R. Hist. Soc. Trans.* 5th ser. VIII (1958), 1–20, *passim*.
[2] P. 11, above.   [3] *C.J.R. 1295–1303*, p. 171 (Kildare).
[4] *C.J.R. 1305–7*, pp. 156–7 (Carlow, Wexford).
[5] P.R.O., K.B. 27/138, m. 57*d* (*Cal. doc. Ire. 1293–1301*, 100).
[6] Otway-Ruthven, *R. Hist. Soc. Trans.* 5th ser. VIII, 14, and 'Knight-Service in Ireland', *R.S.A.I. Jn.* LXXXIX (1959), 1–15, at p. 9; *C.J.R. 1295–1303*, pp. 402–3 (Kilkenny, Wexford, and Carlow), 431 (Wexford).

necessarily mean that lands subsequently conveyed to the church acquired a similar privilege. For that, the consent of the lord of the liberty was required. The existence, within the apparent territorial bounds of the liberties, of enclaves not subject to their jurisdiction was inevitably a source of dispute.[1] An exceptionally illuminating case arose in 1292 as to whether certain lands of the abbey of St Thomas, Dublin, and of the abbey of Clonard, were cross-lands or subject to the liberty of Kildare. The case appears to be evidence for the following propositions: (*a*) that merely general words, such as those giving freedom from all exactions and free and peaceable possession, in a charter from a lord of a liberty could not operate to exempt the lands from his jurisdiction, to 'incroceate' them; (*b*) that gifts from tenants of the lord *non potuerunt esse incrociate rite vel juste* without the lord's consent.[2] The first proposition, as a canon of interpretation, is of course in broad accordance with the arguments advanced on behalf of the king in the *quo warranto* inquiries in England; but ironically this particular application strengthened the franchises against the king.[3] It is clear from the *Articuli cleri* presented to the justiciar in 1291 that Irish churchmen valued the position of the cross-lands.[4] On the other hand, practical difficulties in enforcing the law in these scattered areas may have lain behind the Irish statute 13 Edw. II, c. 11, which enjoined the stewards of liberties to assist the lords of crosses, or the king's serjeants therein, in the arrest of felons.[5]

Although the organized scrutiny of English franchises between the inquiry of 1274–5 and the statute of 1290 does not seem to have had an Irish parallel, procedure by *quo warranto* was available as a check to the claims of the proprietors of Irish liberties.[6] The best-documented cases concern ecclesiastical liberties in Ulster and Connaught, on which an attack appears to have been launched early in the justiciarship of John Wogan. In 1297, the bishop of

[1] For a useful map of church-lands (not necessarily cross-lands) in the liberty of Kildare, *c.*1300, Otway-Ruthven, *I.H.S.* XI, 196.
[2] P.R.O., K.B. 27/136, mm. 27, 27*d*, 40; 137, m. 47*d*; 138, mm. 59, 62*d*; 140, m. 7; 141, mm. 33, 40, 40*d* (*Cal. doc. Ire. 1293–1301*, 22, 43, 82, 101, 133, 146). The ultimate decision is unknown; the statement (Otway-Ruthven, *I.H.S.* v, 7–8) that it was decided against the lords of the liberty is perhaps due to the misleading version given in *Cal. doc. Ire. 1293–1301*, 146.
[3] Sutherland, Quo warranto *proceedings*, chapter v, *passim*.
[4] Articles VI, VII, in *Stat. Ire. John–Hen. V*, pp. 183–4.
[5] *Ibid.* p. 289. [6] Cf. pp. 81, 109, above.

Down, who claimed to have all but the four great pleas of the crown, surrendered the liberties claimed for ever when he was impleaded before Wogan.[1] He was an Irishman and his successor later argued that the surrender had been made *per suam simplicitatem* and without the assent of the chapter, so that in 1312 an inquisition was ordered.[2] It found that the pleas had been held since the limit of legal memory and the bishop appears in consequence to have recovered them. A by-product of this case was a similar one concerning the cathedral priory of Down, but its course is obscure.[3] At the same time, the primate, Nicholas Mac Maoil Íosa, was called to account for the liberties claimed by him. The proceedings no doubt formed part of the general friction between him and the Dublin administration, and the precise outcome is unknown.[4] The proceedings in which John de Ponz sued for the king against the archbishop of Tuam in 1300 raised a matter of peculiarly Irish interest.[5] The archbishop submitted a detailed list of his franchises, which he claimed to have been held by his predecessors from the limit of memory. It was replied that, since Connaught had been conquered only in the time of King John and therefore within the limit of legal memory, the defence could not suffice. Once more we are in the dark as to the judgment. That all four cases just mentioned concerned the claims of churchmen is significant, for any residue of jurisdictional rights that survived from pre-invasion society was more likely to be found in connection with the continuing church, and in the three Ulster instances vindication of the king's claims would have strengthened royal administration in the cross-lands adjoining the earl of Ulster's great lordship.

The cross-lands formed a territorial limit to the greater liberties and *quo warranto* was a possible check to a widening of franchises: how were the lordships thus defined administered? The great liberties were organized on the model of the royal administration, and so there was little detailed adaptation required, for example, when Kildare became a royal county in 1297.[6] Ulster was so large

[1] *C.J.R. 1295–1303*, p. 103.
[2] J.R., 6–7 Edw. II, m. 95 (cf. *C.J.R. 1308–14*, pp. 40–1).
[3] *C.J.R. 1295–1303*, p. 149; *1308–14*, p. 40; P.R.O., C. 47/87/2, no. 2.
[4] *C.J.R. 1295–1303*, p. 103; A. Gwynn, 'Nicholas Mac Maol Íosa, archbishop of Armagh', *Féil-Sgríbhinn Eóin Mhic Néill* (ed. S. Ó Riain; Dublin, 1940), pp. 394–405.   [5] *C.J.R. 1295–1033*, pp. 316–17; cf. p. 176, below.
[6] Otway-Ruthven, *I.H.S.* v, 6.

that it was subdivided into five shires.[1] At the head of each liberty, the lord was represented by a steward, distinct from the sheriff of the county even though the liberty and the county might be (and at this time in all cases but that of Ulster were) conterminous.[2] The steward had to take an oath to the king as well as to the lord of the liberty.[3] The county court, where the sheriff of the liberty presided, was distinct from the court where the steward sat as judge in those pleas which exceeded the jurisdiction of the shire but were not reserved to the crown. For judicial business the steward was accompanied by other members of the lord's council, justices, or assessors.[4] In Ulster, with its five counties, there seems to have been an itinerant bench.[5] The liberties had their exchequers and chanceries, treasurers (or receivers) and chancellors. There were writs in the name of the steward as well as in that of the lord.[6] As in England, the higher personnel of liberty and seignorial administrations belonged to a managerial class for whom the transition to the king's service was easy.[7] Ordinances sent to Ireland in 1293 forbade that a steward of liberty should also serve as justice in eyre or of the bench *ou aylours ou fraunchises deyvent estre tryez*.[8] An ordinance of 1331 made this more sweeping by prohibiting that a steward be given any task in the royal administration.[9]

Three aspects of the position of the liberties in the legal system of the lordship are of special interest: the execution of writs of the Dublin chancery and the royal courts, the procedure for rectifying

[1] Otway-Ruthven, *R. Hist. Soc. Trans.* 5th ser. VIII, 5.
[2] For a deed of appointment of a steward of Carlow in 1299, see *Cal. doc. Ire. 1293–1301*, 594.
[3] Nugent, *R.S.A.I. Jn.* LXXXV, 68; cf. *C.J.R. 1295–1303*, pp. 103, 242; J.R., 9–11 Edw. II (no. 114), m. 13 (steward of Kilkenny heavily amerced for wrong return 'against his oath'); but contrast the special claims of Geoffrey de Joinville in his petition of 1302, p. 129, below.
[4] *C.J.R. 1295–1303*, p. 89 (Kilkenny); *Chartul. St Mary's, Dublin*, I, 393, 395 (Trim); but references to such justices do not seem to be found at Carlow: W. F. Nugent, 'Carlow in the middle ages', *R.S.A.I. Jn.* LXXXV (1955), 62–76.
[5] *Cal. close rolls, 1296–1302*, p. 124; P.R.O., C. 47/10/22, no. 10; C.P., M. 31–2 Edw. I, in P.R.O.I., RC. 8/1, *Cal. mem. rolls*, I, 197–8.
[6] C.P., T. 28 Edw. I, in P.R.O.I., RC. 7/7, *Cal. plea rolls*, VII, 245–6, seems to bear on this difference: judgment quashed because a record which had been vouched had been summoned by writ of the steward of the liberty of Kilkenny and not by writ of the lord.
[7] Cf. N. Denholm-Young, *Seignorial administration in England* (Oxford, 1937), pp. 162–4; for Irish examples, pp. 46, 95, 105–6 above, and 153, below.
[8] *Stat. Ire. John–Hen. V*, p. 192.   [9] *Ibid.* p. 326.

errors of the liberty courts, and the question of protections and pardons of suit of peace.

If it became necessary for a writ to be executed within one of the Leinster liberties, the sheriff of Dublin was charged with seeing that this was done by the liberty administration, the possibility of default by the liberty being met by a *non omittas* clause.[1] The stewards of the Leinster liberties made return through the sheriff of Dublin.[2] The lord of east Meath (Trim) claimed the special privilege that all writs should be directed immediately to him or his steward.[3] In Ulster and the attenuated liberty of west Meath (Loxeudy) a position similar to that in the Leinster liberties prevailed until 1297, when the Irish parliament under Wogan provided for separate royal sheriffs of Ulster and Meath, both in order to cover cases of default by the liberty administrations and for the cross-lands.[4] But the Ulster arrangements did not change in practice and since the sheriff of Dublin was in fact usually also the king's sheriff of Meath the change there was slight also.[5]

In the liberty of Trim there was a court higher than the steward's—the lord might himself correct the proceedings of his minister.[6] If this was the case elsewhere, as seems reasonable, the fact that only Ulster had a normally resident lord throughout this period may have helped to reduce the practical importance of the principle. In 1297, a former steward of Kilkenny declared that his successor in office could not correct his acts.[7] Recourse was easily had to the king's courts, but in this connection some discussion of the difference between courts of record and courts not of record is first desirable.

The essential difference between a court of record and a court not of record was that the rolls of the latter 'could not be used to prove themselves in a court of law'.[8] Consequently the remedies available to dissatisfied litigants differed. If a court was of record, a writ might be sued to order the justices to send the record and process. Most commonly this writ was some sort of *certiorari*, from which, at the time with which we are here concerned, the

---

[1] E.g. *C.J.R. 1295–1303*, pp. 106, 124, 140, 149, 242, 250, etc.
[2] E.g. *ibid*. pp. 105, 106, 111 (all Kildare), 358, 359, 380 (all Kilkenny), 258, 259 (both Wexford), 442 (Carlow).
[3] Pp. 124–30 *passim* below.   [4] *Stat. Ire. John–Hen. V*, pp. 196–8.
[5] Otway-Ruthven, *I.H.S.* v, 4–6.   [6] *C.J.R. 1295–1303*, p. 223.
[7] *Ibid*. p. 89.   [8] Turner, *Brevia placitata*, p. xlv.

specific writ of error was becoming differentiated.[1] If a court was not of record, various writs of false judgment were used, which had as their common feature the recording of the plea by the sheriff on the verbal testimony of four persons. 'Speaking generally we can hardly doubt that [this record] usually followed the entries on the rolls of the court', but these entries were none the less in law mere memoranda.[2] The writ *recordari facias* was the writ of false judgment used when a county court was in question: the sheriff was to record the plea with four knights who had been present. Similarly, *accedas ad curiam* was used to a seignorial court: the sheriff was to go with four knights of the shire and record the plea by four suitors who had been present. In England, the king's bench alone dealt with proceedings on writs of record; it had also a jurisdiction in false judgment, but in the early fourteenth century this was declining to the point of disappearance. The English bench had a jurisdiction in false judgment, but none in record.[3] We have already seen that a broadly similar division of labour prevailed between the justiciar's court and the Dublin bench, though there is some indication that ways may have been found for the bench to examine the proceedings of courts of record.[4] It is against this background that the status of liberty courts must be considered.

The theoretical position was clear enough. The proceedings of the county courts in liberties were not of record, those of the stewards' courts were.[5] But in practice there was some confusion, perhaps induced by the fact that all the liberties except Ulster were by 1290 organized as single shires, so that the jurisdictions of the shire court and the steward's court were territorially conterminous. In 1297 a record of assizes before the steward of the liberty of Kilkenny was brought into the justiciar's court by a writ of 'mere record':

[*defendant*] demands judgment if he ought to answer to such a writ, which is of mere record, in this case from a court of liberty which has

[1] Professor S. F. C. Milsom has made a study of judicial review and I am indebted to him for his advice, while of course I am alone responsible for any error in what is said above.   [2] Turner, *ibid*.
[3] Cf., in general, Sayles, *Select cases in K.B.* II, pp. xliv–l; N. Neilson, 'The court of common pleas', *English government at work, 1327–36* (Medieval academy of America, 1940–50), II, 259–85, at pp. 270–1; Holdsworth (7th ed.), I, 37*, 200–2.
[4] Pp. 83–4, 97–8 above.   [5] Pp. 83, 98 above.

not full record. And because it appears to the court that the king is seised of the pleading of such pleas by writ of False Judgment and it appears to the court to be more useful to the king to plead by such writs, than by writ of record, [*plaintiff*] is directed to proceed by writ of False Judgment if he thinks fit.[1]

Three years later the identical record was sent by the steward, apparently in the same fashion, but unfortunately we do not know what happened in the interim.[2] It looks suspiciously as if it was realized that the proceedings were after all of record. Also, in 1297, the claim that the court of Kildare was of record seems to have been accepted,[3] and so was, in 1309, a similar statement concerning Wexford.[4]

The evidence from the Dublin bench is more puzzling. For example, there is an unmistakable case of *accedas ad curiam* being directed to the sheriff of Dublin to record a real action before the steward of Kilkenny in 1300.[5] The same procedure is found in use for proceedings headed

Placita de communibus assisis ... coram Ricardo de Pevenshey tunc senescallo Weysford ... et aliis de consilio domine Johanne de Valencia.[6]

It may be, however, that this apparent inconsistency reflected an ambition on the part of the Dublin bench to extend its jurisdiction to include review of proceedings in courts of record, as well as confusion about the status of the various liberty courts.

It may be added that it was of course possible for a case at hearing in a liberty to be referred elsewhere for some such reason as the voucher to warranty of a person holding no land there,[7] and in addition a certain number of cases from Irish liberties found their way to the court *coram rege* in England by various means.[8]

The admission of a felon to the king's peace does not seem necessarily to have compelled the lord of a liberty to abstain from prosecuting him for offences committed in the liberty and falling

---

[1] *C.J.R. 1295–1303*, pp. 88–90.   [2] *Ibid.* p. 316.   [3] *Ibid.* p. 118.
[4] *C.J.R. 1308–14*, p. 138. *C.J.R. 1295–1303*, pp. 85, 112, affords an example of *accedas ad curiam*, but unfortunately it is not clear whether the proceedings had been in the shire court or the liberty court of the steward.
[5] C.P., T. 28 Edw. I, in P.R.O.I., RC. 7/7, *Cal. plea rolls*, VII, 245–6.
[6] C.P., M. 28–9 Edw. I, in P.R.O.I., RC. 7/6, *Cal. plea rolls*, VI, 337.
[7] E.g. *C.J.R. 1295–1303*, p. 214; p. 99 above.
[8] Chapter I, above, and VII, below.

within its jurisdiction. Amongst the many complaints against William de Vescy, lord of Kildare, were two that he had refused to admit to his peace persons admitted to that of the king. The ruling of the king and council in the English parliament was

concorditer ordinatum est quod pax domini regis concessa valere debet tam infra libertatem quam extra ...[1]

But William replied that he had proceeded against those concerned

pro feloniis factis infra libertatem de Kildare et quarum cognicio ad ipsum et participes suos pertinet racione libertatis sue predicte

and the matter was left for further inquiry.

* * * * * * * *

In the remainder of this chapter the individual major liberties will be discussed in turn, with special attention to that of Trim (east Meath). In conclusion something will be said of lesser liberties and franchises.

The Leinster liberties

By 1290 what had been the liberty of Leinster was divided into those of Wexford, held by the Lady Joan, wife of William of Valence, Kilkenny, held by the earl of Gloucester, Carlow, held by Roger Bigod, earl of Norfolk, and Kildare, held by co-parceners, of whom the most important was Agnes de Vescy, who was succeeded in the course of 1290 by her son William. Wexford alone emerged from the next thirty-five years substantially as it had been before. The liberty was taken into the king's hand in 1301, but seems to have been almost immediately replevied through the prompt action of the steward.[2] On the death of Aylmer de Valence in 1324 Wexford went to his nephew and remained in the descendants of the Lady Joan until the end of the middle ages.[3]

[1] *Rotuli parliamentorum Angliae hactenus inediti*, ed. H. G. Richardson and G. O. Sayles (R. Hist. Soc. Camden, 3rd ser. II), pp. 44–5.
[2] *Cal. close rolls, 1296–1303*, pp. 516–17; Richardson and Sayles, *Administration*, p. 235 (steward's claim for expenses). The episode does not seem to have left any trace on the Irish pipe rolls: 31 Edw. I, *P.R.I. rep. D.K. 38*, p. 70, and 33 Edw. I, *ibid.* pp. 100–1.
[3] Curtis, *Medieval Ireland*, p. 203; D. B. Quinn, 'Anglo-Irish local government, 1485–1534', *I.H.S.* I (1938–9), 354–81, at pp. 375–7.

Apart from a brief seizure by the crown about 1301,[1] the de Clare liberty of Kilkenny retained its position until Earl Gilbert died at Bannockburn. It was then inevitably involved in the vicissitudes of the husbands of the three co-heiresses, Hugh Audley the younger, Roger Amory, and the younger Despenser, though in fact very little is known.[2] A few glimpses of the administration at work in 1324 are afforded by the well-known narrative of the proceedings against Dame Alice Kyteler for sorcery: the arrest of Bishop Richard Ledred by a serjeant under a writ of the steward, the court held by the steward *in aula judiciali sua . . . coram ipso militibus omnibus nobilibus et aliis libere tenentibus insimul congregatis*.[3]

The survival of account rolls of the Bigod liberty of Carlow has enabled a fairly detailed account to be given by a modern scholar of its administration before it went to the king upon the death of Earl Roger without heirs of his body in 1306.[4] In 1312 the liberty was revived for Thomas of Brotherton.[5] Carlow suffered severely in the Bruce wars: the earl of Norfolk complained that his stewards, treasurers, and many free tenants were among the dead.[6]

In 1290 the succession of William de Vescy to his mother's interest in the lordship of Kildare, quickly followed by his appointment as justiciar,[7] began a stormy time for this part of the old liberty of Leinster. William was superseded as chief governor in 1294 and proceedings followed concerning the charges brought against him by his many enemies. Whether justified or not, some

---

[1] *Cal. chancery warrants, 1244–1326*, p. 158; *Cal. close rolls, 1302–7*, pp. 54, 136; but cf. pipe rolls, 30 Edw. I, *P.R.I. rep. D.K. 38*, pp. 62–3 and 33 Edw. I, *ibid*. pp. 96–7.

[2] Cf. Orpen, III, 95–6; IV, 149, 223. From Earl Gilbert's death until January 1315 the liberty was wholly in the king's hand, and then as to two-thirds until, presumably, the partition in 1317: pipe roll, 16 Edw. II, in *P.R.I. rep. D.K.*, 42, p. 50.

[3] *Proceedings against Dame Alice Kyteler for sorcery*, ed. T. Wright (Camden Soc. 1843), pp. 4, 13, 26. Some records of the liberty found their way into the Ormond collection: *Red book of Ormond* (Irish MSS. Comm.), pp. 67–9; *Cal. Ormond deeds* (Irish MSS. Comm.), I, nos. 435, 577.

[4] Nugent, *R.S.A.I. Jn.* LXXXV, 62–76.

[5] Curtis, *Medieval Ireland*, p. 203; from Hilary 1313 the pipe rolls treat Carlow once more as a liberty: 3 Edw. II, *P.R.I. rep. D.K. 39*, p. 31, 6 Edw. II, *ibid*. p. 44, and 10 Edw. II, *ibid*. p. 73.

[6] P.R.O., S.C. 8/130, no. 6480, apparently leading to the letters in *Cal. close rolls, 1318–23*, p. 80.

[7] *Cal. fine rolls, 1272–1307*, p. 279; *Cal. pat. rolls, 1281–92*, pp. 387–8.

of these accusations indicate ways in which the lords of a liberty might offend. John of Malton, William's steward, was alleged to have declared that the king's letters of protection could not stay a suit in the liberty.[1] When the servants of an ecclesiastical tenant of cross-land were bringing a felon to Dublin, the sheriff of Kildare allegedly seized him from them and did justice on him in the liberty.[2] This complaint was from the abbot of St Thomas, Dublin, who was plainly at bitter feud with William and made other charges concerning the treatment of cross-lands: distraint in them,[3] failure to obey a prohibition against holding a plea of advowson of a cross-land church in the liberty court.[4]

In the months before his death in 1297, William de Vescy, who was without living legitimate issue, negotiated the surrender of his Irish property to the king, as part of a transaction that was to permit provision to be made elsewhere for his bastard, Sir William of Kildare.[5] Consequently, upon his death Kildare became a royal county. In the making of these arrangements the claims of his mother's co-parceners were treated very cavalierly. Under Agnes de Vescy, the steward, treasurer, and sheriff had been appointed by her, but had taken an oath to the other co-parceners, who were entitled to substantial shares in the profits of the county.[6] (These shares were not equal, because the profits of the county had been used to balance inequalities in the partition of other property.) William had largely ignored these claims and the change of status of the county of course imperilled them further. For the next twenty years, various representatives of the original co-parceners sought unsuccessfully to establish their rights.[7] A further complication arose with the need to provide dower for William's widow.[8] In a far stronger position than any of these people was

[1] *Rot. parliamentorum hactenus inediti*, pp. 33–4.
[2] *Ibid.* pp. 31–3; cf. *Cal. doc. Ire. 1293–1301*, pp. 52–3.
[3] *Rot. parliamentorum hactenus inediti*, p. 41.
[4] P.R.O., K.B. 27/136, mm. 30, 30*d*; 137, mm. 1, 1*d*, 47*d*; 138, m. 55 (*Cal. doc. Ire. 1293–1301*, 26, 43, 46, 102).
[5] *Cal. pat. rolls, 1292–1301*, pp. 238, 256; *Cal. close rolls, 1296–1302*, pp. 15–16, 21, 38; *Cal. doc. Ire. 1293–1301*, 365, 375, 426; *Red book of Kildare*, pp. 129–30.
[6] P.R.O., C. 47/10/15, no. 10; S.C. 1/12, no. 159.
[7] *C.J.R. 1295–1303*, pp. 282–3; *Cal. close rolls, 1296–1302*, pp. 322, 603, *1302–7*, p. 353, and *1313–18*, p. 189; *Rot. parl.* 1, 182–3; P.R.O. K.B. 27/189, m. 68 (*Cal. doc. Ire. 1302–7*, 660); C. 47/10/15, no. 10; S.C. 1/12, no. 159.
[8] *C.J.R. 1295–1303*, pp. 357, 401; *Cal. close rolls, 1296–1302*, pp. 212–13, and *1302–7*, p. 35; *Cal. rot. pat. Hib.*, p. 9; P.R.O., C. 47/87/2, no. 24.

LIBERTIES AND FRANCHISES

the man on the spot, John fitz Thomas, who had been the principal sub-tenant, and perhaps bitterest enemy, of William de Vescy. In 1316 he became the first earl of Kildare and in the following year the liberty was revived for his son, Thomas, the second earl.[1] One of the representatives of the co-parceners of Agnes de Vescy made a last futile attempt to recover a share in 1318.[2] There was therefore established in Kildare during the reign of Edward I the lordship of the greatest of late medieval Anglo-Irish houses.[3]

Ulster

Territorially the greatest of the liberties, Ulster was ruled from 1280 to 1326 by Richard, the 'Red Earl'. Tantalizingly little is known of its administration. The distant sheriff of Dublin was charged with execution in default of the steward, and it is likely that this arrangement was not very efficient, for the chief serjeant of the cross-lands was unwilling to act upon the sheriff's orders:

in libertate comitis Ultonie non vult nec audet se intromittere nec aliquis serviens regis dictam libertatem unquam ingredi consuevit.[4]

Early in the reign of Edward II the earl unsuccessfully sought to have the reservation of the four pleas of the crown abolished. This he hoped to secure, not only for his Ulster lands (including Derry, which he had reduced to 'peace'), but also for those in Connaught, of which otherwise little is heard; in any event he wished to have his existing liberties extended to those areas.[5] Ulster bore the chief brunt of the Bruce wars and the earl's rights were renewed afterwards in parliament.[6] But the strength of his position was as much political and geographical as legal.

Meath

Already before 1290 the de Verdun lords of the western purparty of Meath (Loxeudy) had ceased to enjoy their franchise.[7] In 1310 Theobald II de Verdun made an unsuccessful attempt to recover

---

[1] Otway-Ruthven, *I.H.S.* XII, 197-9. [2] Cole, *Documents*, p. 15.
[3] Technically, the liberty of Kildare ceased in the mid-fourteenth century. Otway-Ruthven, *I.H.S.* XI, 199, should be read in conjunction with, and partial correction of, Quinn, *I.H.S.* I, 377-8.
[4] C.P., M. 34-5 Edw. I, in P.R.O.I., RC. 7/11, *Cal. plea rolls*, XI, 345; for the attempt to remedy matters in 1297, see pp. 26, 117, above.
[5] B.M., MS. Cotton Titus B, XI, f. 1. [6] *Cal. rot. pat. Hib.* p. 27.
[7] P. 13, above; 'western' and 'eastern' are of course only approximate descriptions of the divisions.

it and another equally failed, c.1328, following his death.[1] In 1330 the de Verdun lordship was merged with the eastern purparty (Trim).[2] The situation and history of Trim were very different. It possessed in 1290 a jurisdiction wider than that of any other Irish liberty, for the four pleas were not reserved. The richness and importance of the area and its (to royal officials) irritating privileges combined to keep its lord and lady, Geoffrey de Joinville and Matilda de Lacy, his wife, in repeated quarrels with the Dublin administration. But Geoffrey maintained an unwearying defence into old age, hardly less remarkable in its way than the achievement of his brother, Jean, in setting down as an octogenarian his memoirs of St Louis.

In 1281 an inquisition, which was often to be quoted in later years, was held into the claims of Geoffrey and Matilda de Joinville. It found that the liberty was *extra fines cuiuslibet comitatus* and that all writs should be directed to Geoffrey and Matilda or their steward for execution, and not to the king's sheriff, which was to the king's advantage:

eo quod graviores misericordias habere poterit de ipsis quam de vicecomitibus suis et precepta domini regis citius per ipsos et melius expedientur quam per vicecomitem.[3]

In 1289 the king and council declared a judgment of the Dublin bench on an assize of novel disseisin in error because: (i) Geoffrey had his liberty in which *exercere debet regiam potestatem per suum sigillum et suum senescallum loco justic' sui*; (ii) in any liberty in England, to the laws of which those of Ireland ought to conform, the lord of the liberty might be judge of his own act; (iii) the Great Charter had declared that an assize should be taken in its proper county—Trim was a county and more than a county; (iv) the jurors of the assize were not from the liberty.[4] In 1290

[1] *Cal. chancery warrants, 1244–1326*, p. 317; P.R.O., S.C. 8/81, no. 4007.
[2] Wood, *R.I.A. Proc.* XL, 317.
[3] P.R.O., C. 47/10/14, no. 1 (*Cal. doc. Ire. 1252–84*, 1666).
[4] P.R.O., K.B. 27/121, m. 37 (*Cal. doc. Ire. 1285–92*, 525); also K.B. 27/114, m. 44 d, and 120, mm. 4, 9 d, 36 (*ibid.* 453, 494). The facts in this case were that Thomas de Leonn on the point of death enfeoffed his uncle Geoffrey de L. of his land. Thomas held of Geoffrey and Matilda de Joinville *in capite* and upon his death G. de J. held an inquisition into the circumstances, and then gave seisin to Joan, the sister of T. de L. G. de L. then arraigned an assize of novel disseisin against G. and M. de J., J. de L., and others, in the Dublin bench. G. de J. submitted to the assize being taken as an inquisition into what he himself had done, and after it had been taken the bench gave judgment for G. de L.

there was a further vindication of the rights claimed by Geoffrey. A writ declared that men of the liberty must not be called upon to answer outside, except for pleas touching the king.[1] It was invoked in a dispute with the justiciar a little later in the year.[2] In these years Geoffrey had also a couple of running battles with that jealous defender of cross-land claims, the abbot of St Thomas, Dublin.[3] However, these could only produce a finding of fact whether particular lands were of the cross or not—the earlier statements had set out the general rights of the lord of the liberty unmistakably.

In 1293 a serious storm arose in the relations of the liberty with the Dublin administration. One Nicholas Bacon had been imprisoned at Trim in circumstances unfortunately now obscure. In June 1293, the justiciar ordered Geoffrey to inquire into the actions of his steward in the matter; he did so, but upheld the steward. A further writ ordered the parties before the justiciar and council at Dublin, and as a result the liberty was taken into the king's hand. Geoffrey and Matilda then addressed a long petition to the king, consisting of a recital of a writ of 1284 ordering the justiciar to respect the findings of the inquisition of 1281, a claim to franchises similar to those of the Welsh liberties, and a request that the record of the Bacon case should be brought *coram rege* at the next parliament.[4] This was granted in time for the Trinity parliament of 1294.[5] Geoffrey appears to have crossed to England at the beginning of May.[6] His mission was successful. The liberty was replevied in June[7] and fully restored in May 1295, in consideration of his services in the Welsh wars.[8]

New difficulties arose in 1297. In January, the justiciar instructed the steward of Meath to have a jury before him to answer articles touching the rights of the crown, but the steward

[1] P.R.O., C. 47/35/14, no. 3.
[2] P.R.O., C. 47/35/14, no. 2; S.C. 1/20, no. 123 (*Cal. doc. Ire. 1285–92*, 635); cf. *Chartae, privilegia, et immunitates*, p. 36.
[3] P.R.O., K.B. 27/114, m. 44, 121, m. 13, and 122, m. 21 (*Cal. doc. Ire. 1285–92*, 452, 526, 599); C. 47/10/15, no. 4 (*ibid.* 1075); if the petition of the abbot in 1302 found in S.C. 9/25, m. 2 d, concerns this matter, the outcome was inconclusive and satisfactory to neither party.
[4] P.R.O., C. 47/10/15, no. 7.
[5] P.R.O., C. 81/6/540 (*Cal. doc. Ire. 1293–1301*, 125).
[6] P.R.O., S.C. 8/325, no. E. 691 (endorsement).
[7] *Cal. close rolls, 1288–96*, p. 352.
[8] *Cal. pat. rolls, 1292–1301*, p. 135.

did not obey.[1] Among the duties imposed on the royal sheriff of Meath created by the Irish parliament held that spring was that of making execution in the liberty of Trim in default of the officials of the liberty.[2] The surrender and shiring of Kildare may well have been disturbing news for the lord of Trim. But the constitutional crisis in England, in which the king made use of the loyalty of his old associate, came indirectly to Geoffrey's rescue, for in July, when Edward had made him his marshal, he secured writs to the justiciar and chancellor of Ireland reminding them to respect the procedure set out in the inquisition of 1281.[3] Early in October, this was followed by the reference of his complaints against Wogan to John Langton, the chancellor of England, and Roger Brabazon, the chief justice of the English king's bench.[4] While matters were thus apparently *sub judice* friction continued. The steward of Trim refused in 1299 to obey a writ to have a jury before the justiciar, on the grounds that no certain place was named in it and the liberty ought to return writs only to Dublin.[5] A little later in the year another Trim bailiff put up a similar claim on behalf of his lord.[6] Again, in 1300 the steward replied to a writ only 'from respect to the king' and 'saving the profit of Geoffrey de Joinville', then in England.[7] In fact, Edward had been obliged to call upon the services of 'his friend' Geoffrey de Joinville in difficult diplomacy at Rome in 1300.[8] In April 1301, writs were issued reiterating the principle of the inquisition of 1281 and ordering the justiciar to allow Geoffrey the full enjoyment of his liberty.[9] (There had been proceedings in the English parliament on the matter, but the schedule which contained them has disappeared and the details are unknown.)[10] These writs appear to have relieved the liberty

[1] *C.J.R. 1295-1303*, p. 79.   [2] Pp. 26, 117, above.
[3] Rishanger, *Chronica* (Rolls ser.), p. 173; *Chronicle of Pierre de Langtoft* (Rolls ser.), II, 291; *Cal. close rolls, 1296-1302*, pp. 49-50 (possibly in response to a complaint by Geoffrey to John Langton: P.R.O., S.C. 1/26, no. 196 (*Cal. doc. Ire. 1285-92*, 1186)).
[4] P.R.O., S.C. 1/45, no. 82 (*Cal. doc. Ire. 1293-1301*, 447).
[5] *C.J.R. 1295-1303*, p. 242.
[6] *Ibid.* p. 293.
[7] *Ibid.* p. 308; for another dispute about the same time, p. 289.
[8] *Cal. close rolls, 1296-1302*, p. 444; *Cal. doc. Ire. 1293-1301*, 744; *Cal. pat. rolls, 1292-1301*, p. 508; the phrase 'his friend' is Powicke's (*The thirteenth century*, p. 681).
[9] *Cal. close rolls, 1296-1303*, pp. 443-4; *Cal. pat. rolls, 1292-1301*, p. 589.
[10] P.R.O., K.B. 27/161, m. 54 (*Cal. doc. Ire. 1293-1301*, 738).

from pressure by the justiciar and the chancellor, but it was soon attacked on two new fronts, the Dublin bench and the exchequer.

In 1301 the justices of the bench were forbidden to meddle with the liberty of Trim by hearing an assize of novel disseisin that had been brought against Geoffrey and Matilda.[1] In addition they had instructed the (royal) sheriff of Meath to record a plea in the court of Geoffrey's steward of Trim. The steward refused to co-operate and his lord came to the bench at Dublin, claimed to have *correctionem judiciorum redditorum*, and produced an Irish writ of June 1301 affirming his rights in terms similar to those of the English writs of April.[2] Although the justices did not yield and merely adjourned the case, no more is known of it.

In Michaelmas term, 1301, the exchequer at Dublin, in the course of proceeding against those who dealt in 'pollards' without the king's licence required under recent legislation concerning the coinage, ordered the steward of Trim to have certain persons before the barons of the exchequer.[3] The steward returned *nichil actum est quia contra libertatem*. A writ with clause *non omittas propter libertatem* was then sent to the sheriff of Dublin to have the steward, to answer for his contempt, as well as the original offenders, before the court. The steward obstructed the sheriff and a writ was issued for his arrest. In Hilary term he came to the exchequer and defended what he had done: his lord had cognizance of all pleas and the liberty was outside all counties. Geoffrey de Joinville, who was present in person, referred to the inquisition of 1281. He and the steward left to consult outside the court. An adjournment was given in their absence to another day and on that day to the morrow of Ash Wednesday. When this day came, only the steward and a general attorney of Geoffrey and Matilda appeared. The attorney refused to answer further without an original writ. Judgment was given that the liberty should be forfeited: Geoffrey and Matilda were amerced and their steward committed to gaol.

The exchequer had gone too far. After Easter, Wogan came to

---

[1] C.P., M. 29–30 Edw. I, in P.R.O.I., RC. 7/7, *Cal. plea rolls*, VII, 486–8.

[2] C.P., T. 29 Edw. I, in P.R.O.I., RC. 7/8, *Cal. plea rolls*, VIII, 112–17. The Irish writ was warranted *per breve de Anglia* (cf. p. 39, above) and perhaps the English writs were its warrant.

[3] P.R.O., K.B. 27/171, mm. 67, 67d (*Cal. doc. Ire. 1302–7*, 170, is hopelessly inadequate); cf. p. 161, below.

the exchequer and in the presence of the treasurer and barons the affair was recited before him. Geoffrey alleged that the morrow of Ash Wednesday was *extra terminum placitandi* and that his attorney had claimed this. There should have been a writ *quo warranto* and the exchequer was no place for such a question, which *sapit naturam liberi tenementi*. The king's serjeant, Richard le Blond, argued that the steward was sworn after the manner of a sheriff and therefore [*ad eum*] *non spectat judicare que spectant ad cognicionem curie domini regis*. The justiciar then instructed the treasurer, barons, chancellor, justices of the bench, and Walter Lenfant, justice of the justiciar's pleas, who were all present, to make record orally and they confirmed the written record of the exchequer on most points. But they said that Geoffrey's attorney had objected to the morrow of Ash Wednesday as out of term and also to the lack of an original writ, *qualitercunque minus plena contineatur in primo recordo*. Later in the summer, the record of these proceedings of Wogan was called to the Michaelmas parliament to be held at Westminster. This summons was the fruit of a lengthy petition of great interest submitted by Geoffrey de Joinville.

This petition forcefully and meticulously set out the wrongs and grievances he had endured.[1] The first complaint was about the procedure followed by the exchequer in trying to exercise jurisdiction in the matter of false money. Seven reasons were advanced against what the exchequer had done. First, the king, in his grant of Meath, had reserved nothing but his lordship and knight service. Secondly, since the first grant of the franchise, the lords had held such pleas as that of false money. Thirdly, this position had not been altered by the recent ordinances and statutes. Fourthly, respect for the liberties held by Geoffrey and Matilda had been enjoined by the king in various writs (notably those of April, 1301), but the treasurer had not allowed these orders the worth even of blank parchment (*la value dun blaunk parchemin*). Fifthly, it seemed to Geoffrey that the treasurer and barons administered justice like the judge who hanged the accused before dinner and tried him after (*qui pendit avaunt manger et prist lenqueste apres manger*), because they attached the steward for his return without first making inquiry whether he was entitled to make such a return; had he then successfully defended his act before

[1] P.R.O., S.C. 8/48, no. 2389.

them he would have been in the position of the man who was first hanged and then acquitted. Sixthly, the stewards had always been entitled to make the return, *nichil actum est quia contra libertatem.* Seventhly, the sheriff of Dublin had no more right to act upon default of the steward of Meath than he had upon default of, say, the sheriff of Limerick.

After this vigorous attack on the conduct of the exchequer, two more complaints were made in the petition. The argument as to the steward's oath which had been advanced by Richard le Blond before Wogan was undermined by Geoffrey's complaint that the treasurer and barons had wrongly distrained the steward to take it *come sil fust un des viscountes le Roy.* Thirdly, the treasurer and barons had declared the liberty forfeit and sent the steward to prison, as well as detaining the sheriff of the liberty.

In November 1302, the liberty, already replevied by the treasurer and barons, was to be further replevied to Pentecost 1303.[1] The king and council in England, however, decided about the same time, without giving a decision on the substance of the claims advanced on either side, that the Irish exchequer had followed an erroneous procedure. The exchequer had enlarged proceedings against the steward into proceedings against his lord; the seizure of the liberty *originem sumpsit de quadam transgressione personali imponita senescallo.*[2] All the continuances recorded until the morrow of Ash Wednesday were against the steward and then the attorney of Geoffrey and Matilda had appeared only to take exception to what was being done. The restoration of the liberty was therefore ordered.

At the Lent parliament of 1305 Geoffrey submitted a group of seven petitions on various matters.[3] Four concerned the exchequer. Three of these were questions of allowances, and of them two were granted after inquiry by Wogan.[4] The fourth was a double complaint against the treasurer: stewards had been amerced for contempt without any formal accusation, and the return *nichil actum est quia contra libertatem* had been made a ground for

---
[1] *Cal. close rolls, 1296–1302,* p. 564.
[2] P.R.O., K.B. 27/171, m. 67 d.
[3] P.R.O., S.C. 8/114, no. 5664; S.C. 9/12, m. 16; calendared from justiciary roll, *C.J.R. 1305–7,* pp. 72–3; part of justiciary roll text in Mayart, 'Answer ...', in Harris, *Hibernica,* pt 2, pp. 149–50.
[4] *C.J.R. 1305–7,* p. 73; *Cal. close rolls, 1302–7,* pp. 416, 477. The fate of the third is obscure.

amercement despite the letters patent secured from the king.[1] He professed himself willing that the system of returning writs should be reviewed, but all amercements of the time of the then treasurer, Richard of Barford, should first be pardoned. Richard had been treasurer since 1300 and perhaps there was an element of personal feud in his relations with Geoffrey de Joinville; in any event, no result of this particular petition is known. The fifth petition concerned encroachments by the justices in eyre in Meath in 1301-2 and the sixth some allegedly committed by the justices of the Dublin bench. This last complaint received a satisfactory explanation from the justices and a compromise was arranged without prejudice.[2] Geoffrey's last petition was a personal one, that, as he was *de graunt age*, he should not be asked to travel without special reason. Later in 1305, Wogan upheld the contention of Geoffrey's steward that he need find pledges only to the sheriff of Dublin with the king's writ and not to any serjeant with a mere sheriff's warrant.[3] In 1306, Geoffrey once more had to insist that all writs should be directed to himself or to his steward.[4] His wife was by then dead and in 1307 he surrendered his interest by the curtesy to her heiress, their granddaughter Joan, and her husband, Roger Mortimer of Wigmore.[5]

The change of personalities did not mean a change in the problems of the liberty, though the new connection with a mighty marcher lord of Wales perhaps strengthened it. The findings of the inquisition of 1281 were again aired in 1310;[6] the abbey of St Thomas, Dublin, raised anew the question of the cross-lands.[7] In 1322 the most determined onslaught yet was made in the eyre of Meath. The eyre opened when Mortimer's fortunes were at a low ebb—just two months had passed since his surrender to Edward II.[8] In the *quo warranto* proceedings the attorneys of Roger and Joan traced their claim to Walter de Lacy (earl of Meath, 1194-1241) and argued that they could not answer without the de Verdun representatives of the other purparty,

---

[1] Evidently those of April 1301 were meant: *Cal. pat. rolls, 1292-1301*, p. 589, of which P.R.O., S.C. 8/114, no. 5665, is a transcript sent with the petition to the Lent parliament.

[2] *C.J.R. 1305-7*, p. 74. [3] *Ibid.* pp. 132-3.
[4] *Ibid.* p. 241. [5] *Cal. pat. rolls, 1307-13*, p. 33.
[6] *Cal. rot. pat. Hib.* pp. 11, 16. [7] J.R., 6-7 Edw. II, m. 97.
[8] Cf. Stubbs, *Constitutional history* (3rd ed.), II, 366-7.

some of whom were under age.[1] It was easy to answer on the king's behalf that no such claim had been made in the last eyre in 1302, when Geoffrey and Matilda claimed to hold, not by descent from Earl Walter, but by grant from Henry III. This was of course the true history of the matter.[2] The court examined the rolls of that eyre and told the claimants to answer further. The restitution of the liberty after seizure in 1295 and 1302 was appealed to on behalf of Roger and Joan and the aid of the de Verdun co-parceners was again sought. But the court was unsympathetic; the attack on the liberty may have been one of the principal motives for holding the eyre in the first place. Alexander of Bicknor, who was presiding, was at this time loyal to the king whom he later deserted; Arnold Power, another justice, was steward of the younger Despenser's liberty of Kilkenny;[3] yet another, Richard le Blond, had conducted the exchequer proceedings of 1301–2.

Et quia predicti Rogerus et Johanna prius petierunt auxilium a predictis participibus suis etc. de quo quidem auxilio per consideracionem curie hic etc. ammoti et abiudicati fuerunt ut patet superius in recordo et super illa abiudicacione exierunt ad interloquendum et in eorum reditu nichil aliud dicunt nisi quod petunt auxilium de participibus suis ut prius petierunt: consideratum est quod predicta libertas capiatur in manum domini regis et annexa sit et gueldabilis decetero huic comitatui.[4]

On the fall of Edward II, the liberty was restored after a judgment in error in the king's bench—no doubt even more influenced by the power which Mortimer then enjoyed than the eyre had been by his previous weakness—and Joan also recovered it after her husband's death.[5]

Other greater liberties

A liberty that never properly established itself was the de Clare lordship of Bunratty, originally granted to Robert de Muscegros in 1252 and confirmed to Thomas de Clare in 1276.[6] In 1292, when this lordship was in the king's hand during a minority, there was reference to a writ of the liberty and to the record of

---

[1] *R.I.A. Proc.* XL, 341–5.   [2] Pp. 12–13, above.
[3] Cf. Orpen, IV, 223–5.   [4] *R.I.A. Proc.* XL, 344–5.
[5] *R.I.A. Proc.* XL, 323–4, 345–7; P.R.O., S.C. 8/173, no. 8638.
[6] *Cal. chart. rolls, 1226–57*, pp. 377–80, *1257–1300*, p. 198; Orpen, IV, 60–1, 66–7.

its justice, but no purported text of either survives.[1] The catastrophe of Dysert O'Dea in 1318 put an end to the de Clare power in Thomond: for two centuries it was to be true of Bunratty *nach táinic nech dá sliocht dá héiliugad ó sin illé*.[2] By contrast, there was a liberty which, though territorially small indeed, not only had a jurisdiction limited solely by the usual reservation of the four pleas, but survived in an attenuated form to the nineteenth century: the archbishop of Dublin's liberty of St Sepulchre.[3] Some important claims to liberties on the part of other prelates have already been mentioned in connection with *quo warranto*.

In addition to the establishment of the Geraldine liberty of Kildare, two other new earldoms with attached liberties appeared in the Bruce period. In September 1315 the earldom of Carrick was created, with return of writs in three cantreds of Tipperary.[4] In fact, the letters seemed to have failed in creating the intended beneficiary, Edmund Butler, earl, but in 1328 his son became earl of Ormonde.[5] After the death of Bruce, the victor in the battle of Faughart, John de Bermingham, was created earl of Louth, securing liberties as full as those granted in the case of Kildare.[6] After his murder in 1329, the liberty was united to that of the Mortimers.[7] With the creation of the liberty and earldom of Desmond in 1329,[8] the way was paved for the growth of 'feudal honours and liberties ... in the Anglo-Norman colony to an extent rarely paralleled in England'.[9]

[1] P.R.O., K.B. 27/142, m. 46 (*Cal. doc. Ire. 1293-1301*, 161).

[2] 'Never a one of their breed has come back to look after it': *Caithréim Thoirdhealbhaigh*, I, 145. Actually this branch of the de Clares became extinct in 1321: Curtis, *Medieval Ireland*, p. 195.

[3] C. McNeill, 'The secular jurisdiction of the early archbishops of Dublin', *R.S.A.I. Jn.* XLV (1915), 81-108; introduction by H. Wood to *Court book of the liberty of St Sepulchre* (R.S.A.I. 1930); P.R.O., S.C. 8/174, no. 8685; *C.J.R. 1295-1303*, pp. 102, 148, 291, etc.

[4] *Cal. chart. rolls, 1300-26*, pp. 284-5.

[5] *Complete peerage*, II, 449-50; III, 60; Orpen, IV, 225.

[6] *Foedera* (Rec. comm. ed.), II, 1, 393, 397; P.R.O., S.C. 8/81, no. 4049; Orpen, IV, 208.

[7] *Cal. chart. rolls, 1327-41*, pp. 175-6.

[8] Curtis, *Medieval Ireland*, p. 202.   [9] Quinn, *I.H.S.* I, 363.

Minor liberties

The lordship of Ireland was studded with the courts of individual lords and communities who claimed franchises of one kind or another. Thus at the eyre of Kildare in 1297

> John son of Thomas, Peter de Bermingham, and all others who hold courts in this county, claim to hold pleas of *Vetitum namium*, and bloodshed of Englishmen, and to take fines from Irishmen, except felonies, etc.[1]

A very full statement of the liberties accorded by the lords of Meath to their 'magnates' is found in a general charter of Geoffrey de Joinville, *c*.1266, which is preserved in no less than three cartularies.[2] Since so full a statement is unique in Ireland, some analysis of it is of interest.

The charter concerns those magnates of Meath who either came with Hugh de Lacy to the first conquest or were enfeoffed by Walter de Lacy (d. 1241) and who had had the plea of replevin and the chattels of their criminous Irishmen. The following eight clauses can be assembled by conflation of the versions:

(i) The magnates may have all pleas of replevin between their tenants; but if such a plea arises between two magnates, tenants *in capite* of the lord of Trim, it must be held in his court.[3]

(ii) If hue and cry is raised in their lands, the sheriff of Trim is to take inquisition whether the offences pertain to the crown. If they do, they are to be dealt with in the court of the lord of Trim. If they do not, they are to be left to the appropriate seignorial court.[4]

(iii) The magnates may have the chattels of convicted Irishmen, even if they were tried in the court of the lord of Trim.[5]

(iv) If an Englishman wounds another Englishman, the magnate in whose lands the deed was done may attach him and detain him and his chattels found in that jurisdiction, until the fate of the

---

[1] *C.J.R. 1295–1303*, p. 174.
[2] *Reg. Tristernagh* [T], pp. 52–4; *Chartul. St Mary's, Dublin* [M], I, 275–7; *Cal. Gormanston reg.* [G], pp. 176–7. T has no list of witnesses and M apparently an incomplete version of the list in G. Bodleian MS. Rawl. B. 504 contains a copy of T, printed by C. McNeill in *Anal. Hib.* I, 170; this version is collated in *Reg. Tristernagh*. B.M., MS. Cott. Titus B, XI, ff. 187–8, is another copy of T. As between each other T and M have only verbal differences, but those between them and G are substantial enough to suggest that two issues of the charter are in question.
[3] Fullest text in M, T practically identical, but G omits the clause concerning tenants *in capite* of the lord of Trim.   [4] T, M, G.   [5] T, M, G.

injured is certain. If death or mayhem transpire, justice belongs to the lord of Trim; if only light injury has been sustained, the matter is to be left to the magnate's court.[1]

(v) If an Englishman kills an Irishman and is found with the mainour, the magnate may detain him until he finds security for the payment of compensation.[2]

(vi) The magnates may have waifs (stolen chattels abandoned by felons) and the profits of assize of measures, except in cases of false measures.[3]

(vii) The sheriff is to have his tourn twice a year in their lands and possibly more often, though the versions vary as to the circumstances.[4]

(viii) Those *limites* which are not royal may remain to the magnates. The obvious emendation to *libertates* lacks a manuscript authority.[5]

In addition to the franchises enjoyed by lords, great and small, the customs and privileges of the towns deserve a passing mention.[6] One of the borough privileges most frequently invoked was freedom from being impleaded outside the borough, except where 'foreign' tenements were concerned.[7] Compurgation, instead of battle, in appeals seems to have been somewhat earlier a valued right.[8] Lastly, a case in the justiciar's court in 1313 gives us a momentary glance at the administration of justice in another type of court—that of the fair of Any, co. Limerick: the steward of the fair, hearing a plea of debt by custom of the fair, appears, together with the serjeant of the fair, who executes the judgment.[9]

[1] T, M only.   [2] T, M only; cf. pp. 202-3, below.   [3] G only.
[4] *Cum a dictis magnatibus fuerit requisitus*, T, M; *cum necesse fuerit*, G.
[5] T, M only. Wood, in giving an English summary (*R.I.A. Proc.* XL, 316) and McNeill (*Anal. Hib.* I, 170) emend to *libertates*. Clarke and Macaulay (*Reg. Tristernagh*, p. 54) print *limites* without comment. Though *limes* seems unknown in any suitable sense to du Cange and the *Revised medieval word-list*, there is surely some risk in emending so odd a word, found in two texts which there is no particular reason to believe have a common exemplar, to one so common and unmistakable as *libertates*.
[6] Curtis, *Medieval Ireland*, Appendix III, pp. 408-16; much valuable Irish material is to be found in: *Borough customs*, ed. M. Bateson (S.S. 18, 21); *Hist. & mun. doc. Ire.*; G. Mac Niocaill, *Na buirgéisí XII-XIV aois* (2 vols; Dublin, 1964).
[7] E.g. *C.J.R. 1295-1303*, pp. 225, 244-5 (Cork), *1305-7*, pp. 25-6 (Drogheda-on-the-side-of-Uriel), 277 (Dublin), 458 (Limerick); J.R., 6-7 Edw. II, m. 88 d (Cork).
[8] *Close rolls, 1251-3*, p. 232 (Drogheda-on-the-side-of-Uriel); C.P., 6 Edw. I, in P.R.O.I., RC. 8/1, *Cal. mem. rolls*, I, 4-5 (Dublin).
[9] J.R., M. 7 Edw. II (no. 105), m. 20.

CHAPTER VII

THE IRISH JURISDICTION OF ENGLISH COURTS

WHAT a later age would regard as the constitutional relationship of England and Ireland was not a problem which agitated minds in the thirteenth and fourteenth centuries. Ireland was not a kingdom nor was her ruler, as such, a king; he was *rex Anglie, dominus Hibernie*. Ireland was a 'land', like Scotland during the Edwardian conquest. In 1304 a punctilious clerk seems to have altered the last two words of the phrase *solenc la ley e lusage de nostre roiaume* in a draft writ to *celes partes*.[1] Only once about this time was any question of a difference between the ruler's position in England and in Ireland raised in official circles. In 1329 a conciliar memorandum posed—and left unanswered—the problem whether, because the king *est nomme seignur Dirlaunde e nient roy*, his prerogative changed in crossing the Irish sea.[2] But, though he might not be styled king of Ireland, the king was nevertheless normally referred to as *dominus rex*. Though the administration of his land of Ireland was structurally independent of its English model, the fact that the ruler, at this time, was usually in England and never in Ireland meant that the English organs of his will were constantly used to direct and supervise Irish affairs. Some aspects of this dualism, as found in the relations of the Irish and English chanceries, have already been discussed.[3] One of great practical importance in the administration of justice concerned the appointment of sheriffs. In the earlier years of Edward I Irish sheriffs might be appointed in Ireland on the initiative of the chief governor, or appointed in the Irish exchequer following a mandate from England, or directly commissioned in the English chancery.[4] The Irish exchequer ordinances of 1293 recited that such appointments by the English chancery had brought into office sheriffs not sufficiently obedient to the Irish exchequer, and therefore

[1] P.R.O., S.C. 1/12, no. 158.
[2] Sayles, *Select cases in K.B.* III, p. xliii, n. 4.
[3] Pp. 26–9, above.
[4] E.g. *Cal. fine rolls, 1272–1307*, p. 271; *Cal. pat. rolls, 1281–92*, pp. 355, 382.

entrusted future appointments to the Irish treasurer and barons.[1] Apart from some appointments in 1302–3, this seems to have been enforced in the rest of the reign.[2] But the troubles of the reign of Edward II put the principle of devolution under too great a strain and sheriffs were frequently appointed or nominated in the English chancery.[3]

Yet, though it was often obscured in particular instances, the independence of the Irish legal and administrative system under the king's *alter ego*, the justiciar, was the fundamental principle of the government of the lordship. The justiciar was by right both the channel of instructions to the Irish administration and the first recipient of the complaints and petitions of the king's Irish subjects. Only on his default, ran the theory, should there be recourse to the king himself; when in 1290 the burgesses of Shandon petitioned the king in parliament the reply they received reminded them *ce chose ne fut unkes mostre a la justice*—to him it must first go.[4]

Before considering how the courts nearer the king exercised a jurisdiction in Irish matters, a few words may be devoted to the co-operation necessary between the two legal systems. For example, a person indicted of robbery in England was attached by the justiciar and found mainprise before him.[5] In the Middlesex eyre of 1294 the tenant in an assize of mort d'ancestor vouched to warranty a vouchee who was in Ireland.[6] Berwick J. refused to accept this voucher:

... je mandace bref issant hors de roules a Yrelaunt pur fere le venir e je dese *teste J. de Berewike*, yl ne savereyt ques coe fut: par ques il semble ki le vocher ne vaut nent.

Bracton, on the other hand, had been clear that a person in Ireland might be vouched.[7] A partial solution was found in the use of the

[1] *Stat. Ire. John–Hen. V*, pp. 190–2.
[2] *Cal. doc. Ire. 1302–7*, 10, 24, 274.
[3] *Cal. fine rolls, 1307–19*, pp. 11, 24–5, 42, 48, 51, 55, 135, 151, 163, 248, 380, 398; *Cal. close rolls, 1318–23*, pp. 19, 81; J.R., 6–7 Edw. II, m. 88 d. Dublin is not found among the counties involved.
[4] Cole, *Documents*, p. 70.
[5] *Cal. close rolls, 1296–1302*, p. 449.
[6] *Y.B., 21 & 22 Edw. I* (Rolls ser.), p. 309. A cursory search of the rolls of the eyre (P.R.O., Just. Itin. 1/543, 544) has failed to find the case (*Quintyn* v. *de la Berue et al.*).
[7] F. 380 b.

king's bench as a clearing-house when a person vouched to warranty in one jurisdiction had lands only in the other. Bracton had held that Ireland and England were distinct for the purpose of abjuring the realm.[1] *Britton* took a similar view in connection with attorneys:

Et si acun attourne moerge pendaunt le play adounc fet a distincter, si cist, a qi le attourne fust, soit passe la meer ou noun. Car si il ne soit point en Engleterre ou en Hirelaund, si le plee i soit, adounc est la parole suspendable sauntz jour jekes al retourn celi . . .[2]

The admission of attorneys for proceedings in the other jurisdiction was a commonplace activity, though in 1304 the treasurer of Ireland inquired if he had acted rightly in admitting attorneys for parties in a case *coram rege* without a writ of *dedimus potestatem* in that behalf.[3] At least until 1305[4] English letters of protection had to be reckoned with in Irish proceedings: a writ might be sought to overrule one[5] or to reinforce one that had been ignored by an Irish court.[6]

Petitions to the king

In the relations of the two legal systems an important part was played by petitions to the king, especially those considered in his highest court, in his council in his parliaments. 'The development of petitory procedure in parliament, which characterizes the reign of Edward I, made it easy for the king's Irish subjects to approach him with grievances which the ordinary processes of law would not remedy'[7] and the subject-matter of petitions was perhaps wider than this phrasing, narrowly considered, would suggest. The roll for the Hilary parliament of 1290 has eighteen Irish petitions and that for Easter of the same year thirty-eight.[8] There were sixteen

---

[1] f. 136.
[2] *Ed.* Nichols, II, 361.
[3] P.R.O., S.C. 1/28, no. 3; cf. *Memoranda de parliamento, 1305*, nos. 442, 444 (petitions for general letters of attorney in England).
[4] P. 28, above.
[5] *Rot. parl.* I, 466 (uncertain date, but if P.R.O., S.C. 1/27, no. 19 is, as seems likely, related, *c.* 1295).
[6] P.R.O., S.C. 8/138, no. 6867; the original letters are in *Cal. pat. rolls, 1302–7*, p. 139.
[7] Richardson and Sayles, *The Irish parliament*, p. 247.
[8] Cole, *Documents*, pp. 55–67, 68–82. Since some petitions concern more than one matter, these figures may be variously calculated: thus, Richardson and Sayles, *The Irish parliament*, p. 247, n. 23, give thirty-nine as the number at the Easter parliament, 1290.

petitions complaining of William de Vescy taken at the Michaelmas parliament of 1293.[1] A membrane of Irish petitions at the Michaelmas parliament of 1302 has twenty-eight items.[2] Forty-four *peticiones de Hibernia* are given by the roll for the Lenten parliament of 1305[3] and fifteen more by a detached membrane which apparently relates to the same parliament.[4] The only other group of Irish petitions surviving from this period is one of five from the Michaelmas parliament of 1320,[5] but there are many individual petitions from Ireland presented in and out of parliament.

The subject-matter of these petitions was very varied. A rough-and-ready analysis of those in the groups just enumerated (excepting the complaints against William de Vescy) suggests that they may be divided in the proportion of two requests for offices, lands, or privileges, and two financial petitions, to one of each of the following classes: complaints against ministers, strictly legal matters and miscellaneous.[6] Some petitions which cannot strictly be classified as legal none the less arose out of circumstances in some way connected with the administration of justice. A widow petitioned for remission of amercements incurred by her husband in an assize: the justiciar was ordered to see to this in whole or in part at his discretion.[7] Behind petitions over the advowson of Dungarvan in the later years of Edward II lay half-a-century's endeavour to construct a prison at Cashel in the face of the archbishop's opposition, which had eventually been overcome by the compensatory grant of the Dungarvan advowson.[8] Those petitions which did have a more definitely legal content frequently

[1] *Rot. parliamentorum hactenus inediti*, pp. 30–45.
[2] P.R.O., S.C. 9/25, m. 2.
[3] *Memoranda de parliamento, 1305*, pp. 232–54.
[4] P.R.O., S.C. 9/12, m. 16. One answer reads: '. . . *nunc* [*in isto parliamento* interlineated] *post festum sancti math'i apostoli* . . .' a.r. 33. The saint's name is certainly not written as *mathiae*, but it seems that the reference can only be to the Lenten parliament of 1305. Also, letters of 28 March 1305 found in *C.J.R. 1305–7*, p. 72, are plainly in pursuance of the reply, given on the membrane, to petitions of Geoffrey de Joinville.
[5] *Rot. parl.* I, 385–6.
[6] The actual figures of this analysis of 148 petitions are, for the subject-matters in the order given above, 40, 44, 21, 23, 20. But these figures are merely crude indications.
[7] *Rot. parliamentorum hactenus inediti*, pp. 23–4 (Michaelmas parliament of 1283).
[8] P.R.O., S.C. 8/104, nos. 5178 to 5181, 165, no. 8203, and 309, no. 15449; S.C. 1/14, no. 66; *Rot. parl.* II, 74; *Cal. chart. rolls, 1257–1300*, p. 204; *Cal. pat. rolls, 1321–4*, p. 114, *1327–30*, p. 436, and *1330–4*, p. 214.

THE ENGLISH COURTS 139

claimed considerations such as judicial prejudice as reasons for reliance upon the king's grace. In 1272 William Picot complained that *non potuit habere narratorem nec consultorem nec ... pre timore [Ricardi] de Exonia* and so he had lost a plea in the borough court of Dublin.[1] Similarly, John Cogan complained at the Easter parliament of 1290 that he could not have execution of judgment given in his favour in the Dublin exchequer *pur favur fet a la partie* (Theobald de Verdun).[2] In 1308 a petitioner complained that he could not have justice in county Cork because David le Blond, who had disseised him, was a judge and allied to the great lords of the land, so that petitioner and his wife, and their ten children, were *destruz e mendyncantz*. His appeal to the king, *qi ad les poeuvres a governer auxi bien come les riches*, for two named persons to be assigned as justices was referred to the chancellor of England for swift action.[3]

A small but highly important class of petitions was composed of those which led to a record and process from an Irish court being called to England. This might be merely for certification as to the facts on which an extra-legal remedy should be given, or it might lead to pleadings in the English court *coram rege*. Thus, of the fifty-nine Irish petitions at the Lenten parliament of 1305, the reply to three was that the record should be sent and in a fourth instance it had already been sent after an earlier petition. Judgment had been given against the prior and convent of an English house in an Irish eyre, allegedly without sufficient summons: the record was sent and examined in the king's bench.[4] Petitioners who complained of judgments in, respectively, the Dublin bench and the eyre of Louth were told they could have writs to bring the records; but they are not known to have proceeded further.[5] In proceedings before an Irish eyre and in the Dublin bench an English abbey had lost lands to the king; an earlier petition and record were in the chancery and the king now

[1] P.R.O., C. 47/10/13, no. 8; for Richard of Exeter, see pp. 41–3, above. This document is damaged and very faded.
[2] Cole, *Documents*, p. 70.
[3] P.R.O., S.C. 8/164, no. 8180; *Cal. chancery warrants, 1244–1326*, p. 276; cf. p. 47, above.
[4] *Memoranda de parliamento, 1305*, 408; P.R.O., K.B. 27/185, m. 18*d* (*Cal. doc. Ire. 1302–7*, 532); *C.J.R. 1305–7*, pp. 228, 317; cf. p. 148, n.2 below.
[5] *Memoranda de parliamento, 1305*, 413; P.R.O., S.C. 9/12, m. 16 (Emma of Kent).

granted re-seisin of special grace.[1] The reply to a petition presented at the Michaelmas parliament of 1320, concerning an allegedly collusive action by writ of entry used to defeat a title which the petitioner derived from the king's grant, puts the procedure neatly:

Veigne le record devant le roi issint que veue le record le roy puisse faire outre ceo que fait a faire pur lui e pur la partie.[2]

The Irish jurisdiction of the king's bench

The varied Irish business of the king's bench down to the end of the seventeenth regnal year of Edward I was discussed in an earlier chapter and some tentative efforts made to elucidate the ways in which it arose. Here, the account will be carried down to the end of the reign of Edward II. A greater wealth of material is available on the individual cases of this period, permitting a more systematic presentation. General trends and principles will first be considered. Then the cases will be analysed according as they were initiated in the king's bench, were transferred thither from Irish courts, or were examined in review. Some questions that arise will be discussed and a group of three cases, really forming a single protracted course of litigation, will be described as an illustrative example.

(i) *General trends and principles*

The first seventeen years of Edward I saw forty-three Irish cases appear in the king's bench, the remainder of the reign forty, and the reign of Edward II fifteen. A pattern of rise and fall emerges from the following figures of new cases appearing, in sexennial periods:

1–6 Edw. I: 13	31 Edw. I to 1 Edw. II: 18
7–12 Edw. I: 13	2–7 Edw. II: 9
13–18 Edw. I: 19	8–13 Edw. II: 2
19–24 Edw. I: 17	14–20 Edw. II: 2
25–30 Edw. I: 5	

Evidently there was a peak in the middle years of Edward I and a decline at the turn of the century, with a new peak at the end of

[1] *Memoranda de parliamento, 1305*, 419; P.R.O., S.C. 8/271, nos. 13505 to 13510; *C.J.R. 1305–7*, p. 83; *Cal. close rolls, 1302–7*, p. 257.
[2] *Rot. parl.* I, 376.

Edward's reign, while after the first years of Edward II the Irish cases almost disappear. Indeed, the figures given above do not adequately convey this last point: after 8 Edward II the only two Irish cases in the reign appear in the fifteenth year.[1] The causes of the declines can only be surmised, though this is not a difficult task. The fall in the later years of the century is almost certainly related to Wogan's arrival and the improvement in administration which followed. The decline under Edward II is attributable to the political troubles of the reign in both countries and especially to the dislocation of Irish government in the Bruce period. In neither case is there convincing evidence of a change in principle, merely one of circumstances.

There were, however, three statements of principle during this period which are relevant to any account of this jurisdiction. The first arose in 1305. Agnes de Valence was a doweress, the widow of Maurice fitz Gerald, third baron of Offaly, who had died in 1268; John fitz Thomas was his first cousin and second successor.[2] John, alleging that she was dead (she in fact lived on until 1310, but she can hardly have been young in 1305), seized the property she enjoyed in Ireland. Agnes attempted to proceed against him in the justiciar's court by English writs of trespass. A united protest was made by the Irish magnates, who secured the ruling from the king and council that writs for pleas of trespass to be pleaded in Ireland should be purchased in the Irish chancery and those for use in England in that of England. It may be noted that this statement did not preclude an original jurisdiction in Irish matters being enjoyed by an English court with English writs before it.[3]

The second and most important statement arose, like the first, in connection with a case involving powerful magnates. Edmund Butler brought a writ of escheat in the Dublin bench to recover the manor of Hollywood from the archbishop of Dublin, on the grounds that Geoffrey Marsh, who had held it and died a felon, held of Edmund's ancestor, Theobald.[4] The archbishop had taken

---

[1] Year-by-year figures to 17 Edw. I are given above, p. 15, n. 2. From 18 Edw. I: 2, 5, 2, 5, 4, 1, 0, 0, 1, 0, 2, 1, 1, 2, 1, 4, 5, 4; from 1 Edw. II: 2, 6, 0, 1, 2, 0, 0, 2, 0, 0, 0, 0, 0, 0, 2 (no more in this reign).

[2] Orpen, IV, 65, 129.

[3] *C.J.R. 1305-7*, pp. 75-8; *Cal. chancery warrants, 1244-1326*, pp. 253-4; pp. 27, 51, above; for her proceedings against him in the king's bench, p. 146, below.

[4] Cf. Powicke, *The thirteenth century*, p. 58, and references; Orpen, III, 264, for the fate of Geoffrey Marsh.

it as escheat to himself. Licence to agree was given, but execution of the concord, by which the archbishop was to put Edmund in seisin, was delayed while an inquisition found as to Theobald's tenure—whether he had held of the archbishop or of the king *in capite*. It was found that he had held of the archbishop. This was in 1305. In 1308 a new and influential archbishop-elect, the king's clerk Richard of Havering, had the record called into the king's bench. There it remained until 1312, when Butler secured a writ to have it returned to Ireland, on the grounds that the custom of Ireland was that records in which error was alleged should first go

coram capitali justiciario nostro terre illius qui pro tempore fuerit ad errorem illum si quis fuerit corrigendum et partibus plenam justitiam faciendam antequam recorda et processus huiusmodi placitorum coram nobis venire fecimus . . .

In producing this writ, Edmund's attorney alleged that the archbishop had given Edmund seisin of only half the manor and had sued the record into England merely in order to delay execution of the concord. Although Brabazon C. J. does not seem to have been at all too pleased with the procedure adopted, he duly obeyed the writ.[1]

The principle of *Butler's Case* was stated in Ireland in 1314. A writ had been sent from England summoning the record of a plea of account in the Irish exchequer. After discussion with the earl of Ulster and other members of the Irish council it was decided not to send the record

pro eo quod esset contra consuetudinem Hibernie per diversa mandata regis etc. . . . Quia huiusmodi recorda et processus prius et principaliter venire debent coram justiciario Hibernie aut eius locum tenentibus si in eadem terra corrigendi etc. Et deinde si necesse fuerit venire debent coram rege in Anglia . . .

and the writ, endorsed to this effect, was returned to England.[2]

The rule expressed in these quotations has value as a general principle, not as a statement of unvarying practice. A small

---

[1] *Y.B., 5 Edw. II (1312)* (S.S. 33), pp. 152–4, where the record is also given. The final concord is *Cal. Ormond deeds* (Irish MSS. Comm.), I, no. 394; cf. also *Cal. close rolls, 1296–1302*, p. 555.

[2] Mem., 7 Edw. II, in P.R.O.I., RC. 8/9, *Cal. mem. rolls*, IX, 182–5; printed in part by Sayles, *Select cases in K.B.* II, p. lx, where, however, the date 1315 is given: cf. p. 103, n. 1, above.

number of cases had until 1312 by-passed the justiciar, though from the middle of the reign of Edward I it was more usual for his court to play its part than it had been before. It is unfortunately impossible to draw conclusions as to the effect of *Butler's Case*, though its place in the Year Books and the affirmation of the same principle in 1314 suggest that it may have made an impression. The Irish business of the king's bench in the reign of Edward II after 1312 was negligible, but this can so easily be explained by the political and administrative crises of the time that no other significance can safely be placed upon it. Yet whatever the precise extent of its application the rule did express the general principle that the justiciar was supreme in internal Irish administration.

(ii) *Original jurisdiction*

During this period nine matters may be said to have originated *coram rege*, rather than in Irish courts.[1] But one of these is doubtful and another really a matter of process (the enforcement of a debt by statute merchant against lands in Ireland),[2] so that the effective number of such cases may be put at seven.

Of these seven one case of a criminal character arose in a narrow sense in the court itself. Walter of Bodenham had allegedly persuaded the abbot of Mellifont to promise him a sum of money wherewith to bribe a justice of the king's bench in a case which was to be brought by error from the justiciar's court. When the abbot failed to pay the balance, Walter sued him in the Irish exchequer and found himself arraigned *coram rege*.[3] What was done to him is not clear, but two years later he brought a plaint

---

[1] Although what is said above is based on examination of the original rolls, references to them have been omitted in footnotes in the following circumstances: where the text has been printed; where there is an adequate calendar in *Cal. doc. Ire.* (all *Cal. doc. Ire.* references are in any event given); generally, where entries of attorneys and process are in question. Full references to all the material with the marginal note *Hibernia* on the king's bench rolls during the reigns of Edward I and Edward II will be found in my D.Phil. thesis (University of Oxford), 'English law in Ireland, *c.*1290–*c.*1324', pp. 18–25, 187–206. *Cal. doc. Ire. 1285–92*, 843, is an editorial error, *ii brevia* having been misread as *Hibernia*; but some of the parties had Irish connections.

[2] *Cal. doc. Ire. 1285–92*, 546, 613; *1302–7*, 446; cf. *C.J.R. 1305–7*, pp. 119, 296–7; Mayart, 'Answer... to a book entitled, *A declaration...*', in Harris, *Hibernica*, pt 2, pp. 100–7.

[3] P.R.O., K.B. 27/152, mm. 54, 58*d* (*Cal. doc. Ire. 1296–1301*, 445, 446, is inadequate).

of defamation in the justiciar's court against the abbot, alleging the damage done him by the proceedings in the king's bench.¹ Three cases record proceedings closely connected with parliament. One was a criminal matter, heard *coram ipso domino rege et consilio suo* in parliament in 1305—the causing of an affray in Tipperary in which six people had been killed. The accused claimed that he was *autrefois acquit* in the justiciar's court, and certification as to this was requested from Ireland, but does not seem to have been in his favour.² The dispute between the co-parceners of Kildare and the abbots of St Thomas, Dublin, and Clonard over crosslands began with a complaint by the co-parceners, which secured a writ commissioning the justices of the Dublin bench to inquire into the affair. It then became involved with the petitions complaining against William de Vescy at the Michaelmas parliament of 1293.³ The last 'parliamentary' case had its origin in a petition to the king and council in parliament in 1305, alleging expulsion from a prebend by the chancellor of Ireland, who had had himself presented, *sede vacante*.⁴

The remaining three cases which made their appearance on the rolls of the king's bench without having been litigated upon in Ireland were inquiries into special matters. Geoffrey of Morton had been accused by unnamed *emuli* of withholding and misusing the common seal of the city of Dublin; he wished to clear himself.⁵ One of the co-parceners of Kildare tried proceedings *coram rege* in the hope of recovering her share of the profits of the county.⁶ Return was made of an inquisition into the dispute between the king and the archbishop of Tuam concerning the status and temporalities of the see of Annaghdown.⁷

(iii) *Cases transferred from Irish courts*

Seventeen cases were transferred from hearing in Irish courts. Five were from the Dublin bench, one from an eyre, one from special commissioners of oyer and terminer, five from the justiciar's

---

[1] *C.J.R. 1295–1303*, pp. 255–7; eventually he did not prosecute.
[2] P.R.O., K.B. 27/182, 75*d* (*Cal. doc. Ire. 1302–7*, 448); *C.J.R. 1305–7*, p. 230.   [3] Pp. 121–2, 137–8, above.
[4] *Cal. doc. Ire. 1302–7*, 447.
[5] *Ibid.* 606; printed in full in *Hist. & mun. doc. Ire.* pp. 228–30; cf. *C.J.R. 1305–7*, pp. 315–16.
[6] *Cal. doc. Ire. 1302–7*, 660; cf. *Cal. close rolls, 1296–1302*, p. 603.
[7] P.R.O., K.B. 27/190, m. 10*d*; C. 47/19/3, no. 9; *C.J.R. 1305–7*, pp. 244–6.

THE ENGLISH COURTS 145

court as court of origin, and five from the justiciar after reference from lower courts. Three of the matters originating in the bench are examples of the clearing-house function of the king's bench when a vouchee to warranty had no land in Ireland.[1] The other two from the Dublin bench were called by writs *procedendo ad judicium* in the *si difficultas* form. One of these cases had started in the eyre of Limerick of 1290 but raised so important a question of interpretation of a statute that the justices dared not proceed *sine saniori consilio* and it went to the king's bench.[2] Curiously, a case on identical lines brought by the same demandant against a different tenant in the Dublin bench was sent for error to the justiciar by a writ with *si difficultas* clause and apparently began its journey to the court *coram rege*, but has left no trace on the rolls of that court.[3] One case was transferred direct from an eyre by *certiorari*, since the disputed lands were held of the king in chief.[4] Another had been brought against the treasurer of Ireland for trespass, heard before commissioners of oyer and terminer there, and transferred to England because the treasurer was required there to state his account.[5] Apart from one of the warranty cases, this is the only one transferred after Wogan took up office which did not go through the justiciar's court.

The five cases which were transferred to the king's bench while at hearing before the justiciar as a court of first instance have in

[1] (*a*) *Cal. doc. Ire. 1285–92*, 614, 615, 1077, 1092; (*b*) *1293–1301*, 134, 224, 291 (a doubtful example) and (*c*) 765, 766, 767, 814.
[2] *Emelina fitz Maurice* v. *Thomas fitz Maurice*, who vouches Gilbert de Clare: *Select cases in K.B.* II, 72–9 (discussed, *ibid.* III, pp. xxvi–xxviii); *Cal. doc. Ire. 1285–92*, 1022, 1023, 1093, 1150, *1293–1301*, 3, 144, 205, 262, 292, 331, 444. Unfortunately *Cal. doc. Ire.* omits K.B. 27/154, m. 34*d*, which records the discontinuance of the case in 1298 upon the death of Thomas. For the original proceedings in eyre, J.I., 18 Edw. I (no. 14), in P.R.O.I., RC. 7/2, *Cal. plea rolls*, II, 331–7; for those in the Dublin bench, C.P., H. 19 Edw. I, *ibid.* RC. 7/3, *Cal. plea rolls*, III, 79–80; C.P., P. 18 Edw. I, m. 9. The phrase *sine saniori consilio* comes from a letter which almost certainly relates to this, and the case mentioned in the next note, printed *Select cases in K.B.* II, Appendix XII (l), p. cxxxvi. The other case mentioned above as coming from the Dublin bench in this way is *Cal. doc. Ire. 1285–92*, 883; the writ is given in Appendix II (*b*), below.
[3] P.R.O., C. 47/87/2, no. 20. These cases in which Emelina fitz Maurice was demandant are discussed below, pp. 170–1.
[4] P.R.O., K.B. 27/125, m. 41 (*Cal. doc. Ire. 1285–92*, 800, is inadequate and omits the reasons for transfer given in the writ: *rege inconsulto* none of his ministers *se debet intromittere*, etc.).
[5] P.R.O., K.B. 27/189, m. 69*d*, m. 102; 198, m. 141; cf. *C.J.R. 1308–14*, p. 60.

common the importance of the parties concerned. The first occurred in 1294. It was a political *cause célèbre* of the highest order. William de Vescy, still justiciar, at least in name, complained before Walter de la Haye, who was acting as chief governor because, it seems, of the very crisis the proceedings were about, that John fitz Thomas had defamed him. It was at least as much the substance of what John fitz Thomas was supposed to have alleged as that he had said it of the justiciar which made it unthinkable that the case should be left to Walter de la Haye. William de Vescy had been accused by John of having said that the king was a coward and had shown this by his conduct before Kenilworth during the Barons' War.[1] The king's bench found sufficient error in Walter's conduct of the proceedings to annul them without prejudice to either party, but it may be suspected that this decision was politically convenient; the affair seems to have been the occasion of William finally losing the justiciarship.

The history of plaints brought by Geoffrey of Morton against the treasurer and barons of the Irish exchequer in 1304 is not altogether clear, but it seems likely that they began with a petition to the king and council in England which was referred to the justiciar and council in Ireland.[2] This case was the subject of two writs in *si difficultas* form before the justiciar sent it. Once in England Morton found the tables rapidly turned: when he sought an adjournment because he had not *consilium ad querelas suas debito modo formandas*, he was committed to the Tower for contempt and was later arraigned for larceny.[3] The remaining three cases were proceedings taken by Agnes of Valence against John fitz Thomas: judgment had actually been given in Ireland, but execution had proved very difficult and so writs of *elegit* were sent from England.[4]

Of the five cases transferred from the justiciar's court which had not originated there, one came from an eyre by reason of

[1] *Rot. parl.* I, 132–4 (in part also *ibid.* I, 127–8) duplicates P.R.O., K.B. 27/141, mm. 36, 36 d. No historian seems to have examined why the charge made by John fitz Thomas should have taken this form: cf. Curtis, *Medieval Ireland*, pp. 170–1.

[2] P.R.O., S.C. 8/176, no. 8773, is probably the petition.

[3] *Hist. & mun. doc. Ire.* pp. 223–7; cf. *C.J.R. 1305–7*, pp. 17, 316–17; *Cal. chancery warrants, 1244–1326*, p. 244.

[4] P.R.O., K.B. 27/197, m. 82; cf. *Cal. chancery warrants, 1244–1326*, p. 212; *Memoranda de parliamento, 1305*, 420; P.R.O., S.C. 8/145, no. 7242; *C.J.R. 1305–7*, pp. 221, 231, 236–7, 240–1, 282, 393, 399–400; cf. p. 141, above.

THE ENGLISH COURTS

alleged failure to execute the judgment and was then called to the king's bench by the use of a writ *procedendo ad judicium* with clause *si difficultas*.[1] In two cases, closely related to each other, royal charters had been vouched in the court of a liberty and then in the justiciar's court; the means by which one at least was freed from the consequent delay in the justiciar's court was a parliamentary petition.[2] The remaining two cases falling into this group were instances of the justiciar and council sitting with the treasurer and barons in the exchequer.[3] One was an action of debt of which it was said *quodammodo tangit ipsum regem*.[4] The other was highly unusual. One of the chamberlains of the Dublin exchequer committed an offence which was given the description *quasi-felonia*. *Cepit et asportavit de denariis domini regis in thesauraria* was the charge, but this was a simplification of the facts of a species of embezzlement in order to fit them into a familiar category of crime. Wogan and the council were in the circumstances unwilling to proceed to sentence of death, *rege inconsulto*, and a writ of *certiorari* brought the record to the king's bench.[5]

(iv) *Jurisdiction in review*

The twenty cases in which the king's bench reviewed the judgments of courts in Ireland included six from inferior courts there, two from the justiciar's court as of first instance, and twelve in which he had exercised his corrective jurisdiction, though in some instances hearings had not ended before him.

The cases which by-passed the justiciar first appeared in the king's bench in 1291 (two), 1293, 1305, 1306 and 1312. The last to arise was *Butler's Case* itself. Another is very obscure[6] and a third was summoned from before justices of assize because it touched the subject-matter of a previous decision in the king's

[1] P. 132, n. 1, above.
[2] P.R.O., S.C. 9/25, m. 2*d*; *Cal. doc. Ire. 1302–7*, 565; *C.J.R. 1305–7*, pp. 63–4; *1308–14*, pp. 50, 56–7.
[3] Cf. p. 100, above.
[4] P.R.O., K.B. 27/161, mm. 41, 41*d* (*Cal. doc. Ire. 1293–1301*, 737); *C.J.R. 1295–1303*, pp. 240–1, 363, 383; cf. also P.R.O., C. 47/10/17, no. 3; p. 177, n. 4, below.
[5] Richardson and Sayles, *Administration*, pp. 238–42; P.R.O.I., Mem. 31–5 Edw. I, m. 21, and 1 Edw. II, m. 26; *C.J.R. 1305–7*, pp. 225–6, *1308–14*, pp. 44, 59; pipe roll, 3 Edw. II, *P.R.I. rep. D.K. 39*, p. 33.
[6] *Cal. doc. Ire. 1285–92*, 886, 959, 960.

bench.[1] Yet another, though brought by petition in parliament from an Irish eyre, appears to have been later returned to the justiciar's court.[2] There remain in this category two cases of more substantial interest.

A writ of right was brought in the liberty of Trim in 1286. Because the four knights to choose the twelve for the grand assize could not find sufficient knights, free from affinity to the parties, in the liberty, the case was removed to the Dublin bench. Two of the twelve chosen then defaulted. In the absence of the chief justice (Bagod), the second justice of the bench substituted two (one of the electors and another by consent of the parties) and took the assize, which found for the demandant. The tenants then sued a writ to England and error was found in that the puisne justices of the bench exceeded their authority in Bagod's absence, had wrongly substituted the two knights, thereby disregarding the statute of Westminster II, c. 30, and had not followed a recognized form for the tenant's putting himself to the assize. The fact that these irregularities were by consent of the parties could not save the proceedings

maxime ubi de mero jure agitur, cum sit modus et mensura et fines certi ultra que citraque nequid consistere rectum.[3]

The other case in this group was one of those which arose from the hostility between the abbot of St Thomas, Dublin, and William de Vescy. The abbot was defendant in an action of *quare impedit* in the court of the liberty of Kildare and produced a writ of prohibition. But the Irish council gave the liberty court permission to continue. The abbot, when judgment was given against him, secured a writ of *certiorari* form into the king's bench, where the plaintiff was committed for contempt. The dual capacity of William de Vescy as justiciar and as lord of Kildare is neatly illustrated by the writ of prohibition in this case, which was attested by himself at Kildare.[4]

---

[1] This is one of the group of cases involving Master William de la Ryvere and is discussed in detail in the second next section, below, pp. 152–6.

[2] P. 139, n. 4, above.

[3] P.R.O., K.B. 27/127, mm. 50, 50*d*, 51 (in part, *Select cases in K.B.* II, 45–50); *Cal. doc. Ire. 1285–92*, 891, 962, 1091; *1293–1301*, 85.

[4] *Cal. doc. Ire. 1293–1301*, 26, 42, 43, 102, 131, 132, 141, 145, 146; cf. the case mentioned above, p. 144, with which this is closely connected.

THE ENGLISH COURTS

Assizes of novel disseisin came by writ of error from the justiciar's court as of first instance in 1302[1] and 1315.[2]

In one case the justiciar's corrective jurisdiction was recognized only in that a writ ordered him to correct errors of a lower court (the bench), but included a *si difficultas* clause on which he acted.[3] The eleven cases that unquestionably were first reviewed by the justiciar before going to the king's bench fall into two groups: six in which the work of review had not been completed before him and five in which it had been. Of the first group one took the form of a plaint against justices in eyre for wrongful imprisonment: complainant had never been properly presented for his alleged offence. The justiciar and council were ordered to hear the case, but referred it to the king's bench, which in turn adjudged some of the eyre proceedings to have been erroneous, but sent the matter back for further consideration in Ireland.[4] In another instance the justices of the bench in Ireland, together with the chancellor and treasurer, had been ordered to examine the record by a writ of *procedendo* with a *si difficultas* clause; although the justiciar also lent his aid, the records of the justices in eyre were found to conflict and the case was sent to England.[5] An examination of a process of outlawry in a liberty court, first entrusted to the Dublin bench by a writ with *si difficultas* clause and then sent to the justiciar and certain members of the Irish council, was by them sent, in pursuance of another writ with clause *si difficultas*, to England.[6] The proceedings in the Dublin exchequer over the seizure of the liberty of Trim in 1302 have been included here because Wogan went to examine what the treasurer and barons had done.[7] The last two cases of the six were closely related and will shortly be discussed in more detail; here

---

[1] Some doubt exists whether the record came from the bench or the justiciar's court, but the latter seems to have been the case: *Cal. doc. Ire. 1302–7*, 127, 301; *C.J.R. 1295–1303*, pp. 380–2, 447.

[2] P.R.O., K.B. 27/219, m. 106; 221, m. 81.

[3] *Cal. doc. Ire. 1285–92*, 1094.

[4] *Select cases in K.B.* II, 125–35; some discussion, *ibid.* IV, p. lxxxi, especially n. 2.

[5] P.R.O., K.B. 27/138, mm. 17, 18, 18*d* (*Cal. doc. Ire. 1293–1301*, 92, is much abbreviated); the writ of *procedendo ad judicium* is given in Appendix II (*c*), below, and an extract from the record at p. 105, above.

[6] *Cal. doc. Ire. 1293–1301*, 100, 81, 142; *Rot. parliamentorum hactenus inediti*, pp. 40–1; C.P., T. 19 Edw. I, in P.R.O.I., RC. 7/3, *Cal. plea rolls*, III, 174. An extract from the record is given above, p. 113.

[7] Pp. 127–8, above.

it may be said that one was called to England by writ *procedendo ad judicium* with *si difficultas* clause and the other by *certiorari*.[1]

Finally, there is the group of five cases in which full use was made of the justiciar's court as a court of review. They are widespread in time: one each year in 1290, 1303 and 1305, and two in 1309. Some doubt attaches to the first, a plaint brought in the justiciar's court concerning proceedings in the borough court of Dublin.[2] The next three cases had come from the Dublin bench to the justiciar's court. One was an action of waste which turned on the assessment of damages contrary to the statute of Gloucester.[3] Another, upon a writ of entry *dum non fuit compos mentis*, had originated in the liberty of Kilkenny, but was sent to the Dublin bench when a vouchee to warranty had nothing in the liberty.[4] The third, also on a writ of entry, was of quite exceptional complexity and appears to have been moved from court to court by *certiorari*.[5] Lastly, a plea of advowson that began before an eyre and was adjudged in error by the justiciar's court came before the king's bench in 1309.[6]

(v) *Special questions*

How extensive was the use of the writ of *procedendo ad judicium* in *si difficultas* form? Excluding the use of such writs in the course of the proceedings within the Irish jurisdictions, there are eight examples. Although in one case two writs had to be sent to the justiciar before he obeyed,[7] the writ really operated to transfer cases, and courts did not proceed further after its receipt.

When a case was brought *coram rege* what part did the king and council play, according to the evidence of the rolls? Excluding

[1] These were the first and third cases involving Master William de la Ryvere, discussed further below, pp. 152–6.
[2] *Cal. doc. Ire. 1285–92*, 820.
[3] *Cal. doc. Ire. 1302–7*, 255; *C.J.R. 1295–1303*, pp. 386–9; C.P., M. 29–30 Edw. I, in P.R.O.I., RC. 7/7, *Cal. plea rolls*, VII, 507–8.
[4] P.R.O., K.B. 27/182, m. 96*d*; *Cal. doc. Ire. 1302–7*, 533; *C.J.R. 1305–7*, pp. 10, 140, 223.
[5] P.R.O., K.B. 27/197, m. 83*d*; 202, mm. 101–2*d*; *C.J.R. 1295–1303*, pp. 408, 431–9; J.R., 7 Edw. II (no. 106), m. 6*d*; C.P., T. 25 Edw. I (no. 34), H. 28 Edw. I, M. 28–9 Edw. I (no. 45) and (no. 46), T. 29 Edw. I, in P.R.O.I., RC. 7/5, 6, 7, 8, *Cal. plea rolls*, V, 202–11; VI, 304, 394–5, 437–8, 551–3; VII, 377–81; VIII, 98–100.
[6] P.R.O., K.B. 27/202, m. 88*d*; 210, m. 99*d*; 212, m. 35; 214, m. 26; 216, m. 35; 220, m. 65.
[7] P. 146, n. 3, above.

THE ENGLISH COURTS 151

the cases in which petitions in parliament are known to have been addressed, conciliar interventions were few. The restoration of the de Joinville liberty after its seizure in the Irish exchequer was of course directed by the council,[1] there is one case of a person being *arrenatus et inculpatus* before the king and council,[2] and *loquendum cum rege* was noted with regard to a difficult problem of interpretation of a statute.[3] In other words, in Irish as in other matters, the court retained close relations with its progenitor, the *curia regis*, but usually displayed its independent standing.[4]

Last, but not least, what was the fate of Irish judgments reviewed in the king's bench? The delays and hazards of medieval justice, with its preoccupation with procedural detail, meant that in only nine cases judgments are recorded on the substance of records examined for error. In all the Irish proceedings were annulled. These included two cases from justices of assize,[5] two from eyres,[6] two from the Dublin bench,[7] one from the Irish exchequer,[8] and two judgments in error delivered in the justiciar's court.[9]

Probably the safest generalization that can be made concerns, not the legal subject-matter of the cases nor the course of their passage through the Irish judicial system, but the standing of the interested parties. Obviously persons of wealth and influence were most likely to be able to secure this highest form of justice. Leaving aside ten shadowy cases known only from entries on membranes of attorneys,[10] it is possible to list twenty cases in each of which one or other of seven persons had an interest. The seven were: the king's cousin, Agnes de Valence, the magnate justiciars, William de Vescy and Edmund Butler, the mayor of Dublin and great merchant, Geoffrey of Morton, the abbot of the royal abbey of St Thomas, Dublin, the king's clerk, William de la Ryvere, and the English magnate, Otto of Granson.

Among the other names that occur are those of the magnates Geoffrey de Joinville, John fitz Thomas, Theobald de Verdun, Thomas fitz Maurice 'an ápa', and Walter de Lacy of Rathwire; of prelates such as the archbishops of Armagh, Dublin and Tuam,

[1] P. 129, above.   [2] P. 144, n. 2, above.   [3] P. 145, n. 2, above.
[4] Sayles, *Select cases in K.B.* II, pp. lxiii–lxx, especially at p. lxvi.
[5] Pp. 155–6, below.   [6] P. 149, notes 4–5, above.
[7] P. 148, n. 3, above and pp. 154–5, below.
[8] P. 129, above.   [9] P. 150, notes 3 and 5, above.
[10] These cases have been omitted from the detailed discussions above, though included in the totals on p. 141, n.1.

the abbot of Mellifont and the prior of Lanthony; and of the administrators Quantock, chancellor, Barford, treasurer, and Neil le Brun, escheator. In fact, only nine cases, six of which appeared in the court between 1289 and 1293, were concerned solely with people who are otherwise unknown to the general historian of the period.[1]

(vi) *An illustrative example*

In the eyre of Dublin of 1291 William de la Corner recovered certain lands on a writ of entry brought against Richard, son of Robert, son of John. William (son of Richard de la Corner, bishop of Meath 1230–51) was bishop of Salisbury and died in 1291. On 2 August 1299, Richard son of Robert brought an assize of novel disseisin before justices assigned at Drogheda against William de la Ryvere and his bailiff, William of Ballygorman. William de la Ryvere was apparently a nephew of Bishop William de la Corner: he first appears as a student in 1283 and was later canon of Salisbury and a royal clerk (collector of the biennial tenth of 1306–7 in Ireland).[2] Before the justices it was argued for William de la Ryvere that the statute of Westminster II, c. 30, forbade assizes to be taken other than at three specified times in the year, but the justices did not allow this exception. It was then argued that Richard had sued a writ of error from England on the proceedings in the eyre of 1291. Richard claimed that his writ had been useless owing to the absence of some justices and the illness of the justiciar (William Dodingeseles?). The case was adjourned for a fortnight to 16 August and in the meantime the justiciar sent a writ associating Simon of Ludgate, chief justice of the Dublin bench, with the justices already assigned. William now produced a new exception—that he had been attached only the day before the proceedings began. Consequently the justices ordered the sheriff to attach him for a fortnight later (31 August). On that day the assize came and said that, before the serjeant came to execute the eyre judgment in favour of William de la Corner, two servants of William de la Ryvere, of

[1] Except in the case of administrators, the test of fame has been mention in Orpen, III and IV.

[2] For biographical details: *Cal. pat. rolls, 1281–92*, pp. 58, 467, 468; *1292–1301*, pp. 571, 609; *1301–7*, p. 429; *1307–13*, p. 142; *1313–17*, p. 99; *1317–21*, p. 163 (William de la Ryvere dead by 12 June 1318); P.R.O., C. 47/87/2, no. 1 (*Cal. doc. Ire. 1285–92*, 503); S.C. 8/70, no. 3479.

whom William of Ballygorman was the second, had successively entered on the lands. After some discussion between them, the serjeant had said to William of Ballygorman that he was putting him in seisin *ad opus* William de la Corner. William of Ballygorman had never been the attorney of William de la Corner, but had been substituted by the latter's attorney, who had become a leper. The jury assessed damages at three hundred and forty marks, if the court were to hold that the facts constituted disseisin. (This kind of special verdict was permitted by the Statute of Westminster II, c. 30.) The case was adjourned to a month from Michaelmas in the Dublin bench and on that day further adjourned to the quinzaine of Martinmas.

On 28 September an Irish writ ordered the justices to certify on certain matters and, after two continuances in county Meath, this was attended to at Dublin on the octave of Martinmas. Richard claimed that William of Ballygorman had ploughed the land and taken fealty without waiting to be put in seisin by the serjeant; he also argued that damages should have been taxed on the basis of the yearly value of the tenements and the number of years the disseisin had lasted. The jurors said that there had been no ploughing, but that fealty was taken; allowing for improvements, they taxed damages at four hundred marks. The matter was then adjourned to the bench at the quinzaine of Martinmas. Judgment was given for Richard on that day. If William de la Corner had entered without a writ of execution and the king's bailiff, Richard could have recovered against him by novel disseisin; all the more was this remedy available against William de la Ryvere, *qui est extraneus*.

William de la Ryvere now sought a review before Wogan of the proceedings and Richard was summoned to answer him, together with one Neil le Brun, whom Richard had apparently enfeoffed. Neil was probably the person of that name who had been steward of the liberty of Kildare and who from 1308 to his death in 1310 was to be escheator of Ireland.[1] The errors alleged in the justiciar's court on behalf of William de la Ryvere were: (i) he had not been properly attached; (ii) the writ of error sued by Richard after the proceedings of 1291 had named, as well as William de la Corner, William de la Ryvere as tenant of the land, and so conceded that

[1] Cf. *C.J.R. 1295–1303*, pp. 168, 171, etc.; Richardson and Sayles, *Administration*, p. 126.

the judgment had been executed; (iii) though the earlier proceedings were annulled on the arrival of Simon of Ludgate the sheriff was then ordered merely to bring the assize and *tot et tales*, instead of a new assize having been empanelled; (iv) the justices had neither allowed nor rejected William's exception as to the writ of error; (v) if anyone had been disseised it was William de la Corner and not Richard. Four other errors of a more verbal kind were alleged in the record. This was in the quinzaine of Hilary 1301. Richard had not brought his warrant for a previous essoin for the king's service, so that he was amerced and excluded from replying to these arguments.[1] But for Neil it was argued, point by point, that: (i) Simon had rectified the attachment when he came; (ii) the writ of error had never had any effect and could not preclude a recovery *per competenciorem et leviorem viam*; (iii) in the circumstances the justices were entitled to order the sheriff merely to empanel more jurors; (iv) William had pleaded further, so that the justices were free to ignore that exception; (v) livery of seisin depends upon acceptance—William of Ballygorman was unwilling to accept seisin *ad opus* William de la Corner.

William de la Ryvere now obtained a writ of *procedendo ad judicium* with clause *si difficultas*, which was acted upon by the justiciar, who was about to set out for Scotland. In the Easter term of 1302 in the king's bench William's allegations of error were re-stated: (i) once the proceedings before the other justices were quashed on Simon of Ludgate's arrival there was no jurisdiction—the justices were *sine fundamento et querela*; (ii) the assize was thus taken simply *ex officio curie* and against custom; (iii) the justices answered the questions on which certification was required after they had terminated their own authority by adjournment into the Dublin bench: the certificate concerned damages and a court should first establish the fact of injury and then inquire into damages; (iv) by the judgment in eyre Richard had lost all claim—how could he recover a *pristinam seisinam* he had not had?

The king's bench gave on this matter the most scathing judgment found on any Irish case in the period:

inveniuntur in eisdem errores diversi multiplices et graves tam per predictum magistrum Willelmum de la Ryvere assignati et proponiti ut predictum est quam alii de quibus non est necesse mencionem facere,

---

[1] Cf. Bracton, ff. 338*b*, 340.

THE ENGLISH COURTS 155

for if they were mentioned there could be as many judgments as errors. However, since

unus error manifestus satis sufficiat et sufficere debeat ad unicum judicium in curia regis minus rite redditum adnullandum,

the justices selected one simple error, that had not even been mentioned in the pleadings—the record did not specify the tenements or the vill wherein they lay. Judgment was accordingly given for William with restitution of damages.[1]

In August, 1304, Neil le Brun brought a new assize of novel disseisin against William de la Ryvere before two justices of the Dublin bench, apparently engaged in taking vacation assizes at Drogheda. For William, it was argued that no assize should lie to a person enfeoffed while a plea to reverse the judgment secured by his feoffor was pending. Neil replied that he had gone *sine die* in the justiciar's court and had not been summoned to the king's bench, and so was without notice of the proceedings there. For William, it was asked that the record of the king's bench should be called, but this the justices refused and they took the assize. It found that Neil had been enfeoffed immediately upon the success of Richard in the first assize. Judgment was given for Neil, with forty marks damages.

In November, an English writ of error was sent to the senior justice of assize, John de Ponz, ordering a return in Hilary 1305, and including a *supersedeas* of the levying of damages. John replied that he could not fix a day in the king's bench, since the case had concluded before him, and consequently in April Wogan was ordered to have the parties in the king's bench in Trinity term. The court, on the principle *fraus et dolus nemini debeant patrocinari*, declared the feoffment and assize both null and ordered restitution of damages.[2] Once again the king's bench had given judgment for William.

At the same time as Neil le Brun had brought his assize, Richard son of Robert had tried again also. The jurors told the same story as in 1299, but this time there were no procedural complications

[1] P.R.O., K.B. 27/168, mm. 50–51*d* (*Cal. doc. Ire. 1302–7*, 57, is useless); 197, m. 102; 205, m. 74*d*; 208, m. 44*d*; *C.J.R. 1295–1303*, p. 356; *1305–7*, p. 19; C.P., M. 27–8 Edw. I (no. 50), and 28 Edw. I (no. 47), in P.R.O.I., RC. 7/7, *Cal. plea rolls*, VII, 22–3, 262–4.

[2] P.R.O., K.B. 27/181, mm. 56, 56*d* (*Cal. doc. Ire. 1302–7*, 485); *C.J.R. 1305–7*, p. 71.

and judgment was given for Richard, with one hundred and eighty marks damages. The record was called into the justiciar's court and, in pursuance of a writ from England, declaring that, in view of the previous judgment, the alleged errors might be amended only *coram rege*, the *custos* of Ireland, Butler, on the quinzaine of Hilary 1305, ordered the parties to be *coram rege* in the octave of the Purification. This was such exceptionally short notice that the fact was noted on the record:

> Et licet de consuetudine terre Hibernie nullus adjornari solet extra terram Hibernie ad minus spacium quam quadraginta dierum dictum tamen est partibus predictis quod sint coram domino rege ad diem predictum si sibi viderit expedire et commode possint interesse.

In the king's bench, it was held that no free tenement could have remained to Richard after the writ giving William de la Corner seisin had been executed. The assize judgment was therefore held to be erroneous and restitution of damages was ordered.[1] It may here be added that Master William de la Ryvere encountered great difficulty in recovering the damages he had paid in all three cases and had not fully succeeded by 1313.[2]

It is clear that Richard, son of Robert, and Neil le Brun could rely on a very sympathetic hearing in Irish courts and in 1306 they tried new devices. They brought bills of trespass and conspiracy in the justiciar's court which were committed to the treasurer, Richard of Barford, and John of Fressingfield. After some adjournments, Richard, son of Robert, in November failed to prosecute, while Neil reached a settlement; the inevitable writs to summon the plaints on William's behalf to the king's bench were already on their way. An attempt to have the justiciar's court review the original proceedings of 1291 also failed.[3]

---

[1] P.R.O., K.B. 27/181, mm. 57, 60 (not *Cal. doc. Ire.*); *C.J.R. 1305–7*, pp. 17, 18–19, 71.

[2] *C.J.R. 1305–7*, pp. 165, 339–40; *1308–14*, pp. 32–3; P.R.O., K.B. 27/186, m. 30 (*Cal. doc. Ire. 1302–7*, 564); 197, m. 102 (doubtful); 205, m. 74 d; 208, m. 44 d; J.R., 6–7 Edw. II, mm. 44, 63 d. The Irish pipe roll for 7 Edw. II notes payments to him and to William of Ballygorman in recompense for amercements: *P.R.I. rep. D.K. 39*, p. 48.

[3] *C.J.R. 1305–7*, pp. 215, 231, 260, 276, 313, 342.

THE ENGLISH COURTS

Irish cases in the English exchequer of pleas

There is no known evidence that the English bench of common pleas exercised any direct jurisdiction in Irish affairs, though of course matters in it might be of incidental Irish interest.[1] But the plea rolls of the exchequer do contain Irish cases, though they are extremely few and far between.[2] In the whole course of the reigns of Edward I and Edward II seven cases may be distinguished.[3] Four of these were actions of account by persons in England against Irish bailiffs and stewards. The first arose in 1276 and was brought by the Queen-mother and Christina Marsh against a Florentine merchant who had had custody of Christina's Irish lands.

Quia vero visum fuit baronibus quod de huiusmodi contractibus factis in Hibernia non est procedendum coram eis sine domino rege et suo consilio

the barons adjourned the matter

interim loquendum est cum rege et suo consilio super premissis[4].

Eventually the parties put themselves on the record of the justiciar and chancellor of Ireland as to what had happened there. There was a further action of account brought by Christina against a bailiff in 1278.[5]

The third action of account concerning Ireland was much the most important. It was brought by Agnes de Valence against her husband's and her bailiff, John de Valle, for his management of receipts and issues amounting to over £5,000. The English audit of the account made it clear that John still owed over £400, while another £1,000 was in dispute. The case was adjourned to permit the parties to agree on the choice of special auditors in Ireland and John was released on mainprise of nine mainpernors, among them Geoffrey de Joinville, William Dodingeseles, John fitz Thomas, and Walter Lenfant, junior—four very impressive names in the Ireland of the day. Some delay was caused by a vacancy in

---

[1] A small number of feet of fines were calendared by Sweetman from the reign of Henry III and the early years of Edward I.
[2] It is possible that further enlightenment might be had from the memoranda rolls.
[3] This does not include the case printed in *Select cases concerning the law merchant*, II, 93–6, which had only a very tenuous Irish connection.
[4] P.R.O., E. 13/4, m. 10 (*Cal. doc. Ire. 1252–84*, 1207, is not very good).
[5] P.R.O., E. 13/7, m. 7; 8, m. 6d (*Cal. doc. Ire. 1252–84*, 1588).

the treasurership of Ireland, but at Easter 1292 the treasurer and Robert Bagod were chosen as auditors. John defaulted in 1293 and Agnes, and later her executors, devoted considerable pains to attempts in the next twenty years to extract money from the nine mainpernors.[1] Another Irish action of account appeared in 1297.[2]

Two cases concerned the Irish exchequer. In 1291 the wife of an Irish sheriff who had been committed to the marshalsea of the exchequer at Dublin complained that the treasurer of Ireland had refused to admit mainpernors produced in accordance with a writ secured in England and had also refused to take into account certain writs of *allocate*.[3] In 1309, when Richard of Barford was rendering his account as treasurer of Ireland, there was a dispute over a payment made, involving a chamberlain of the Dublin exchequer.[4] The remaining Irish case was an action of debt brought in 1293 by Luccan merchants against an Irish rector.[5]

[1] P.R.O., E. 13/17, mm. 6, 6 d (*Cal. doc. Ire. 1285–92*, 993, is very incomplete); 53, m. 7d; 33, mm. 34d, 44d; 35, m. 3; *C.J.R. 1295–1303*, pp. 102, 104–5, 263–4, 322, 327–8; *1305–7*, pp. 6–8, 45, 198, 205–13. There is a reference to this case in Denholm-Young, *Seignorial administration in England*, p. 158, but the author does not seem to have pursued the entries beyond the very first reference in this footnote. The writ of 14 November 1304 calendared in *C.J.R. 1305–7*, p. 6, was used by Mayart ('Answer ... to a book entitled, *A declaration* ...', in Harris, *Hibernica*, pt 2, pp. 145–7) to establish that the English exchequer had power to send writs into Ireland.
[2] P.R.O., E. 13/21, m. 72 (*Cal. doc. Ire. 1293–1301*, 433).
[3] P.R.O., E. 13/17, m. 8 (*Cal. doc. Ire. 1285–92*, 963).
[4] P.R.O., E. 13/33, m. 24 d.
[5] P.R.O., E. 13/18, m. 42 (*Cal. doc. Ire. 1293–1301*, 45).

CHAPTER VIII

STATUTES

IN theory Irish courts had to administer two bodies of statutes, Irish and English, but there is no question as to the far greater importance of English statutes in the reigns of the first two Edwards. The earliest Irish legislation in parliament now surviving dates from 1278.[1] There are other groups of enactments from 1297, 1299, 1310 and 1320.[2] For the most part this Irish legislation was concerned with the maintenance of order in the lordship and the relations of its subjects with the native Irish.[3] Technical legal matters were left to English legislation. Consequently, while pleadings in Irish courts made frequent reference to the great Edwardian English statutes, mention of Irish legislation is very rare. In this chapter what little can be said will first be said of Irish statutes. The general principles governing the application of English statutes in Ireland in this period will then be discussed. Examples will be given of the use and interpretation of English statutes in Irish courts.

Irish statutes

Although many statutes and ordinances made during this period in Ireland have probably been lost to view, those that survive sufficiently indicate that, in the words of Mr Richardson and Professor Sayles, 'little of [the legislation] can have been memorable or can have possessed more than transitory importance'.[4] This is also shown by the few references to Irish statutes on the plea rolls; they concern statutes dealing with the various disorders of the lordship. For example, the Irish statute 25 Edw. I, c. 4,[5] permitted those who had been robbed by felons to recover the value of their property from persons who failed to obstruct the escape of the robbers. A plaint was brought under this statute in

[1] Richardson and Sayles, *The Irish parliament*, pp. 291–3.
[2] *Stat. Ire. John–Hen. V*, pp. 194–212, 212–18, 258–76, 280–90. The old collections of Irish statutes began with those of 3 Edw. II.
[3] Cf. Richardson and Sayles, *The Irish parliament*, pp. 68–9, 92–6.
[4] *Ibid.* p. 92.
[5] *Stat. Ire. John–Hen. V*, pp. 200–2.

1313.¹ Again, three years later, two men charged with the death of a robber were acquitted on the strength of an otherwise unknown statute against 'idlemen' unwilling to render themselves to the king's peace 'who should immediately be killed without those so killing such malefactors incurring any penalty'.² In 1317, an 'ordinance made by the magnates of Ireland' about purveyance of horses and carts was invoked.³

A few Irish statutes did deal, however, with legal matters of wider concern. Among the statutes of 1278 was one about the writ of replevin. It provided that instead of the sheriff making deliverance of the beasts to the plaintiff the distrainor might be left in possession of them upon finding pledges.⁴ At the next county court the sheriff should hold inquisition and there could be no essoin. This was an interesting modification of English law in a matter which had lately been the subject of legislation in the statutes of Marlborough and Westminster I.⁵ Though the application of another chapter of the statute of Marlborough in Ireland is indicated in this same year, 1278, there is no record of its formal extension until 1320 and the statute of Westminster I was not extended to Ireland until 1285.⁶ The English legislation had been directed at the protection of the tenant, but the Irish enactment could hardly have gone further in favour of the lord, since in fact it removed the essential feature of replevin—return of the distress pending the plea in the county court. It may be, however, that the Irish statute was influenced by official anxiety to ease the burdens of sheriffs and serjeants, as well as by the strength of the magnates in the councils of the lordship. Certainly the ultimate sanction of the statute of Westminister I, c. 17 (*qe le Roy . . . face a batre le Chastiel ou le forcelet saunz relever*) must have been peculiarly impracticable and inexpedient in Ireland. There is no evidence to show that the Irish enactment was followed in later years and it seems on general grounds unlikely.⁷

¹ J.R. 6-7 Edw. II, m. 56.
² J.R. 9-11 Edw. II (no. 114), m. 3; cf. *Stat. Ire. John–Hen. V*, p. 269.
³ J.R. 11 Edw. II (no. 119), m. 2.
⁴ Richardson and Sayles, *The Irish parliament*, p. 292.
⁵ T. F. T. Plucknett, *Legislation of Edward I* (Oxford, 1949), pp. 57-63; *Brevia placitata*, pp. cxlv–cxlvii.
⁶ Pp. 4-5, above.
⁷ *C.J.R. 1305-7*, pp. 182-3, has a plaint arising out of an action of replevin in which the English procedure was evidently followed; but of course the Irish statute in any event merely afforded the distrainor an alternative course.

STATUTES

In 1299 and 1300 there was a curious overlap when Irish and English statutes successively dealt with the problem of bad coinage and the English legislation was ordered to be observed in Ireland.[1] According to Dr A. G. Donaldson, who has examined the matter in detail, 'it seems that the English enactment was enforced [in Ireland] rather than the prior Irish one'.[2] The Irish parliament of 1299 also produced a statute concerning servants and wages that may be said to have anticipated the statutes of Labourers in a small way by half a century.[3] It may be that this, and the statute of 1278 about replevin, reflected the degree to which the magnates dominated the Irish parliament.

The application of English statutes in Ireland: general principles

Dr Donaldson has shown that before Poynings's Law English enactments might apply in Ireland in various ways. It was rarely clear from its terms that a statute was to apply to Ireland. This was however the case with the statute of Merchants in 1285, that of Carlisle in 1307, and the ordinances of the Staple in 1326.[4] It is to be remembered, also, that important sets of ordinances for Ireland were sent by the king and council in 1293, 1323, and 1325.[5] In the second place, an English statute might be transmitted to Ireland with a writ ordering its observance there. This procedure had been used in 1285 for the statutes of Westminster I and II and the statute of Gloucester.[6] It was again used in 1299 for the statute of False Money of that year, as well as for the statute *De illis qui ponendi sunt in assisa* of 1293.[7] In 1308, the statute of Winchester of 1285 was transmitted and in 1324 the statutes of Lincoln (1316) and York (1318).[8] Thirdly, English statutes were confirmed in 1310 in the Irish parliament and on a wider scale by the Irish statute 13 Edw. II, c. 2, ten years later.[9] By this, both statutes of Westminster and those of Merton, Marlborough, and Gloucester were confirmed, and it was declared that other English

---

[1] *Stat. Ire. John–Hen. V*, pp. 212–14, 220–6, 236–8; *C.J.R. 1295–1303*, pp. 265–6.
[2] 'Application of English legislation', p. 74.
[3] *Stat. Ire. John–Hen. V*, pp. 214–16.
[4] *Ibid.* pp. 103, 240–2, 314–20.   [5] *Ibid.* pp. 190–4, 293–5, 310–12.
[6] P. 5, above.   [7] Note 1, above; *Stat. realm*, I, 113.
[8] *Stat. Ire. John–Hen. V*, pp. 244–52, 296–304; Donaldson, 'Application of English legislation', pp. 95a–6, 97.
[9] *Stat. Ire. John–Hen. V*, pp. 266, 280–2; for a reference in the legislation of 1278, p. 4, above.

statutes should be examined by the council before the next parliament and that

les points qe couenables sount pur le poeple e la pees de la terre Dirlande soient illuesqes confermetz et tenutz, salues toutz iours les bones custumes et usages de la terre.

It does not appear, however, that the projected examination ever took place, although the proceedings of 1320 were further confirmed in 1325.[1]

In addition, some English statutes were unquestionably used in Ireland though no record survives of their extension or confirmation there. This is sufficiently explained by the pressure of the general principle of uniformity of law and by the fact that many judges and administrators served in both jurisdictions. In 1290 the *Districciones scaccarii* of 1275 was in use.[2] There is little evidence to show the statute of Consultation of 1290 at work in Ireland; but in 1299 a bishop successfully petitioned the Irish council for permission to proceed despite a prohibition.[3] *Quia emptores* was pleaded, apparently with success, in the justiciar's court in 1302.[4] However, the Irish ordinances of 1293 had permitted tenants in chief to subinfeudate in marchlands for their better defence.[5] The statute of Fines of 1299 was pleaded in the same court in 1307 and 1312.[6] A puzzling reference to a statute about champerty in 1305 appears to have been to the *Articuli super cartas* of 1300, c. 11.[7] In the case in question, the treasurer and barons of the exchequer, for various reasons, including the introduction of the allegation of champerty, dared not proceed further 'until they had better counsel' and the record was summoned into England; no more is known. Yet there is some reason to believe that the king wished to make any extension of the *Articuli super cartas* to Ireland dependent on a grant of subsidy and no evidence that the extension was made.[8]

---

[1] *Ibid.* pp. 310–12.
[2] J.I. 18 Edw. I (no. 13), in P.R.O.I., RC. 7/2, *Cal. plea rolls*, II, 177; C.P., P. 18 Edw. I, m. 5 *d*.
[3] *C.J.R. 1295–1303*, p. 269.
[4] *Ibid.* pp. 383–5.   [5] *Stat. Ire. John–Hen. V*, p. 192.
[6] *C.J.R. 1305–7*, pp. 418–19 (no conclusion recorded); J.R. 6–7 Edw. II, m. 77 (apparently successfully).
[7] *C.J.R. 1305–7*, pp. 8–10. This view of the case was arrived at independently by Dr Donaldson ('Application of English legislation', p. 81) and myself, but there is some doubt.   [8] P. 78, above.

STATUTES

Irish lawyers were not uncritically deferential to documents alleged to be English statutes. The justices of the Dublin bench did not consider themselves bound by the pseudo-statute *Dies communes in banco* and their attitude met with Wogan's support.[1] Similarly, the distinction between making a statute in England and publishing it in Ireland was understood.[2] As we shall see, this distinction was of particular importance where the statute of Mortmain was concerned.

Though 1290 saw the end of the great legislative period of the reign of Edward I, the provisions of the Edwardian statutes were being constantly applied in the years that followed, in Ireland as in England. To illustrate their impact in Ireland and the approach of the Irish courts, an Irish case on the interpretation of the statute of Gloucester, c. 5, will be considered, the question of the application to Ireland of the statute of Mortmain examined, and the use made in Ireland of the statute of Westminster II surveyed.

*The application of English statutes in Ireland:
examples of user and interpretation*

The statute of Gloucester, which was amongst those sent to Ireland in 1285, provided (c. 5) that a writ of waste should be available against tenants by the curtesy, tenants for life, tenants for term of years, and doweresses; triple damages should lie. It also reinforced the Great Charter (c. 4 of the issue of 1225), which had prohibited waste by guardians under pain of losing the wardship; henceforth damages should also be given, if the value of the wardship lost did not amount to the damage (i.e. if the residue of the wardship was less in value than the waste done?). In an action of waste in 1300–1 the Dublin bench awarded triple damages against a guardian, *secundum formam statuti domini regis*.[3] The defendant brought the record to the justiciar's court for error, amongst his grounds being that damages against a guardian

[1] P. 96, above.
[2] P.R.O., S.C. 8/44, no. 2183 (*Hist. & mun. doc. Ire.* pp. 212–13); discussed by Richardson and Sayles, *R.I.A. Proc.* xxxviii, 138, n. 4. C.P., M. 26–7 Edw. I, in P.R.O.I., RC. 7/5, *Cal. plea rolls*, v, 421–3, makes a distinction between *confectio* and *publicatio*, but the text, in its surviving calendared form, does not make it clear whether the emphasis was on publication in *Ireland*; cf. also *Cal. doc. Ire. 1285–92*, 666.
[3] For references, see p. 150, n. 3, above; for some further remarks, see p. 169, below, in connection with the statute of Westminster II, c. 14.

should be simple, not threefold. The party successful in the Dublin bench could only answer to this *ponit se totaliter in discreccionem curie*. In fact the justiciar's court substantially upheld the judgment (damages were slightly modified on one head, for a reason not here relevant), and the disgruntled party went *coram rege* in England. There it was repeated on his behalf that only simple damages lay against a guardian, threefold against a tenant for life or a doweress. The king's bench upheld this, declaring the assessment to be wholly against the tenor of the Great Charter (though this was not the only error found). Evidently the Dublin justices had erroneously read the provision as to triple damages into the second part of the chapter. They can scarcely have consulted the text with much care, if at all, for it sufficiently indicated a difference in the basis of assessment and also referred back to the Great Charter.

The statute of Mortmain (1279) is one of those which are not known with certainty to have undergone any formal extension to Ireland. The earliest reference to it in connection with the lordship is in a writ of 29 December 1284 addressed to the justiciar. The prior of Lanthony had complained that certain lands had been taken into the king's hand by reason of the statute, although they had been given long before it. In his return the justiciar declared that the lands had not been taken

pretextu alicuius statuti vestri in Anglia nuper editi de terris vel tenementis in manum mortuam non ponendis

but for another specified reason.[1] This is unenlightening. The fact that a prior on the other side of the Irish sea thought that lands in Ireland had been seized on account of the statute, whereas the justiciar alleged another reason, tells us nothing of the application of the statute in Ireland. An involved story on a pipe roll of forty years later seems to mean that at an uncertain date between 1285 and 1289 the escheator of Ireland seized some lands allegedly given in mortmain.[2] This should bring us beyond the statute of Westminster II, c. 32, which met attempts to defeat the statute of Mortmain through collusive proceedings. This statute was sent to Ireland in the year of its enactment, although no Irish reference to the chapter

[1] P.R.O., S.C. 1/17, no. 189 (*Cal. doc. Ire. 1285–92*, 39).
[2] Pipe roll, 19 Edw. II, *P.R.I. rep. D.K. 42*, p. 69. The archbishop of Cashel referred to died in 1289 and the escheator took office in 1285.

STATUTES

has been found earlier than 1300.[1] In 1290, however, the first known licence in mortmain for an Irish applicant is found and a writ was issued in 1296 with a *non obstante* clause relating to the statute.[2]

A letter of 25 November 1296 recited that the chancellor of Ireland (Quantock) had testified that the statute of Mortmain had not yet been published in that land.[3] Although there is no direct evidence, it seems either that the omission was then rectified or else that the chancellor's views were not finally accepted, for there were proceedings under the statute in the justiciar's court in 1297, as well as a presentation of lands alienated after the statute in the eyre of Kildare of that year.[4] After that, references to the statute in Ireland become fairly frequent.[5] During the eyre of Louth of 1301 a vigorous attempt appears to have been made to enforce the statute, leading to a number of petitions addressed to the king in the Easter parliament of 1302. After one reply, telling a religious house to make fine in the English exchequer after inquisition *ad quod damnum*, there is the note

Consimili modo fiat de omnibus terris et tenementis captis in manum regis coram justiciariis itinerantibus pro eo quod ponebantur in manum mortuam.[6]

Nevertheless, no record survives of the formal extension of the statute to Ireland and it is not clear that the Irish chancery ordinarily had authority to issue licences in mortmain.[7] In modern times it has been convenient to regard the statute as applying by virtue of Poynings's Law.[8]

[1] C.P., M. 28–9 Edw. I (no. 45) and (no. 46), in P.R.O.I., RC. 7/6, *Cal. plea rolls*, VI, 511–12; cf. C.P., T. 1 Edw. II, m. 20 (1308).

[2] *Cal. pat. rolls, 1281–92*, p. 365; *Cal. close rolls, 1288–96*, pp. 492–3.

[3] *Cal. close rolls, 1296–1302*, pp. 3–4.

[4] *C.J.R. 1295–1303*, pp. 84, 87–8, 100, 165, 174.

[5] E.g. *Cal. pat. rolls, 1292–1301*, pp. 422–3, and *1301–7*, p. 51; *Cal. doc. Ire. 1293–1301*, 801, 827; P.R.O., S.C. 9/25, m. 2. These references concern licences; for proceedings in the justiciar's court see later notes.

[6] P.R.O., S.C. 9/25, m. 2.

[7] There is a possible example from 11 Edw. II: *Cal. rot. pat. Hib.*, p. 22 (grant to the Augustinians of Adare).

[8] 10 Hen. VII, c. 22 (Ir.). This was the course followed in the Mortmain (Repeal of Enactments) Act, 1954 (Schedule, pt I). There is a good account in Donaldson, 'Application of English legislation', pp. 76–9, but not all the material cited here is used; the conclusions are summarised by V. T. H. Delany, *The law relating to charities in Ireland* (Dublin, n.d. [1956?]), pp. 5–7. In 1636 Wentworth reported that the statute of Mortmain was not in force in Ireland, but the meaning may be that it was not enforced: *Cal. State Papers, Ireland, 1633–47*, p. 131.

Uncertainty about the circumstances of the extension of the statute may have made for practical difficulties in its application. What was to be taken as the relevant date? An inquiry, with uncertain result, in 1297 seems to have taken the date of enactment as operative.[1] Yet in 1302 the escheator returned that, though certain lands were given after the date of the statute,

die adepcionis eiusdem terre statutum predictum pupplicatum non fuit in Hibernia aut intellectum.[2]

Some years later an inquisition found that tenements were occupied *diu ante statutum predictum promulgatum in hac terra*.[3] A pardon in 1306 referred to entry made 'after the publication of the statute'.[4] This phrase occurs again in 1309 and in an inquisition a couple of years later.[5] The publication of the statute seems therefore to have been the operative date, though none of the references are sufficiently precise to permit a calculation of when this was considered to have occurred, and the passage of years no doubt made the matter rather unimportant. The discussion may conclude with a curious case from 1312. A prior brought an assize of novel disseisin against a person whose defence was that he had entered as immediate lord when the lands were alienated contrary to the statute. The jurors upheld the prior's claim that his predecessors had been seised for more than twenty years before the statute.[6] No other reference to the immediate lord's right of entry has been noted from the Irish plea rolls.

The statute of Westminster II, made at the Easter parliament of 1285, was sent to Ireland in the following September.[7] There are many references to its provisions on the Irish plea rolls, in forms such as *per formam statuti*, and the account which follows is largely confined to the cases which contain such express references. As a result, only eighteen of the fifty chapters will be

[1] *C.J.R. 1295–1303*, p. 100 ('before the said statute, made *a.r.* vi' [*sic*]); cf. ibid. p. 174 ('after the statute').
[2] *Ibid.* p. 386, and 'Introduction', p. viii.
[3] *C.J.R. 1305–7*, pp. 173–4 (in part, Mayart, 'Answer... to a book entitled, *A declaration...*', in Harris, *Hibernica*, pt 2, pp. 139–40).
[4] *C.J.R. 1305–7*, p. 310.
[5] Writ printed by M. H. MacInerny, *History of the Irish Dominicans* (Dublin, 1916), pp. 546–7, from Irish memoranda roll, 3 Edw. II, m. 50*d*; J.R. 6–7 Edw. II, m. 20*d* (in part, Mayart, *op. cit.* pp. 140–1).
[6] J.R. 6–7 Edw. II, m. 3*d*.
[7] P. 5, above.

STATUTES   167

mentioned here, although it is probable that the operation of others could be illustrated from a very close search of the evidence.

Various new remedies and improvements in procedure given by the statute can be shown to have been adopted in Ireland. Thus the extension of the scope of the writ *cessavit per biennium* (c. 21) can be seen in a case in the Dublin bench in 1290,[1] and on the roll of the same court for Michaelmas 1295 the writ is referred to as *per formam statuti nuper inde provisi*.[2] The procedure of receit, conferred on wives and reversioners by c. 3, was evidently popular,[3] and if any testimony to the favour in which creditors held the writ of *elegit* (c. 18) is required it may be had in plenty from Irish records.[4] The provisions of c. 11 regarding the action of account were mentioned in the justiciar's court in 1305.[5] The manner of calculating damages in assizes of darrein presentment and in *quare impedit* laid down in c. 5 of the statute was followed in Ireland,[6] and the rule of priority of wardship established by c. 16 was used in an action in the Dublin bench in 1300.[7]

The justiciar's court applied itself to the enforcement of those chapters relating to abuse of legal procedure. Appellors in malicious appeals were imprisoned by it in 1297 and 1300, in accordance with c. 12 of the statute.[8] In 1295 a woman successfully brought a plaint against the sheriff of Kerry because he had imprisoned her without a properly sealed indictment.[9] Though c. 13 gave a writ of false imprisonment in such a case, it is typical of the justiciar's court that a plaint should have been the mode of action. Treble damages, in accordance with c. 36, were awarded in 1310 against a steward who harassed one of his lord's tenants by

[1] C.P., P. 18 Edw. I, m. 4. On m. 3*d* there is a case within the scope of the earlier provision, statute of Gloucester, c. 4; cf. Plucknett, *Legislation of Edward I*, pp. 90–1.
[2] C.P., M. 23–4 Edw. I, in P.R.O.I., RC. 7/3, *Cal. plea rolls*, III, 351; for two cases in Hilary 1298 (roll missing in modern times), Mayart, *op. cit.* pp. 83–4.
[3] E.g. *C.J.R. 1308–14*, pp. 109–10 (reversioners); C.P., M. 23–4 Edw. I and H. 28 Edw. I, in P.R.O.I., RC. 7/3, 7, *Cal. plea rolls*, III, 350–1 (wife); VII, 404–5 (wife, reversioners).
[4] E.g. *C.J.R. 1295–1303*, pp. 78, 79, 125, 157, 211, etc.
[5] *C.J.R. 1305–7*, p. 19.
[6] C.P., M. 27–8 Edw. I, and M. 28–9 Edw. I (no. 45), in P.R.O.I., RC. 7/6, 7, *Cal. plea rolls*, VI, 322–4; VII, 279.
[7] C.P., M. 28–9 Edw. I (no. 45), in P.R.O.I., RC. 7/6, *Cal. plea rolls*, VI, 320–1.
[8] *C.J.R. 1295–1303*, pp. 120–1, 347–8 (in part Mayart, *op. cit.* pp. 92–3).
[9] *C.J.R. 1295–1303*, pp. 26–7.

procuring pleas against him.[1] The operation in Ireland of c. 32 has already been mentioned in connection with the statute of Mortmain,[2] and c. 41, directed at religious houses who alienated lands given to them in frankalmoin, is also known to have been applied to Irish cases.[3] In a sphere touching criminal law, a man was presented in the eyre of Kildare of 1297 for abducting a woman with her husband's goods (c. 34).[4]

Those chapters which concerned the judicial system in general may perhaps have been applied with a little latitude, because the structure of the Irish system did not precisely correspond to that of England. Nevertheless, in 1306 the justiciar's court annulled a judgment in an eyre because c. 10, providing for a fixed term for the delivery of writs, had not been duly observed.[5] Similarly, the qualifications for jurors laid down in c. 38 were observed in Ireland.[6] But c. 30, which concerned the assignment of two justices in each county to take assizes, can scarcely have been regarded as fully applicable, since the system envisaged does not seem to have been established in Ireland until a later date. Certainly, in 1299 the exception, based on this chapter, that an assize ought not to be taken outside three specified periods of the year, was ignored by justices assigned; but it is far from clear that the chapter would have applied to a precisely similar case in England, since one of the justices assigned was a justice of the bench on vacation work.[7] Another part of the same chapter, concerning the manner of taking inquisitions in pleas before the justices of the bench, was mentioned in an Irish writ of 1301.[8]

In fact, there are recorded only three major cases on the interpretation of the statute in this period in Ireland. In all three instances, the matter eventually was called into the king's bench in England, though in only one case was a decision reached there —and even in it the point of statutory interpretation did not appear

[1] Mayart, *op. cit.*, pp. 97–9 (from justiciary roll missing in recent times).
[2] P. 164, above.
[3] J.R., 11 Edw. II (no. 118), in P.R.O.I., RC. 7/12, *Cal. plea rolls*, XII, 223; cf. *C.J.R. 1295–1303*, pp. 134–6.   [4] *Ibid.* p. 175.
[5] P. 107, above; cf. *Cal. close rolls, 1307–13*, p. 310 (writs to be received notwithstanding the statute).
[6] E.g. *C.J.R. 1295–1303*, pp. 296, 298 (insufficient property); C.P., P. 11 Edw. II, in P.R.O.I., RC. 7/12, *Cal. plea rolls*, XII, 477 (septuagenarian).
[7] In the first assize brought by Richard, son of Robert, against Master William de la Ryvere: p. 152, above.
[8] C.P., M. 29–30 Edw. I, in P.R.O.I., RC. 7/7, *Cal. plea rolls*, VII, 473.

in the eventual judgment. The regulation by c. 14 of the manner of taking an inquisition of waste by a guardian was a ground of error in the case involving the statute of Gloucester, c. 5, which has already been discussed.[1] In the Dublin bench the defendant urged, after the sheriff had taken inquisition, that

> de tam arduo negotio inquisicio debet fieri coram justiciariis de banco et non coram vicecomite.

The plaintiff replied

> predictus vicecomes est familiaris predicti Theobaldi [*the defendant*] ad robas et ad eius feodum et minus favorabiliter inquisivit de predicto vasto,

but none the less argued that it was the sheriff's task to take the inquisition: he ought, however, to be joined by some suitable official. Consequently, the justices ordered the sheriff to proceed with the coroners of Fingal.[2] When, after doing so, the sheriff again made return, the defendant objected to certain of the jurors, and by consent of the parties the chief justice of the bench and a puisne justice themselves went with the sheriff for the taking of the inquisition upon which judgment was in fact given. In the justiciar's court, it was argued that the sheriff should take the inquisition in waste only if the defendant made no appearance. This argument was no doubt founded on c. 14, which detailed the procedure, including inquisition by the sheriff, in cases where the defendant did not come after summons, attachment, and distress, but did not enter into similar detail with regard to the case where the defendant did appear. In the justiciar's court the argument was unsuccessful and it was not expressly included in the grounds of the later annulling judgment of the king's bench.

Chapter 25 was a lengthy collection of provisions on novel disseisin and more than one aspect of it occurred in Irish cases: the extension of the assize to cases of alienation by tenants for term of years[3] and by guardians,[4] the penalty of imprisonment

---

[1] Pp. 163–4, above.
[2] In Ireland there seems to have been a coroner for each cantred: Otway-Ruthven, *I.H.S.* v, 26.
[3] *C.J.R. 1305–7*, pp. 404–5; Mayart, 'Answer... to a book entitled, *A declaration*...', Harris, *Hibernica*, pt 2, pp. 93–4 (from justiciary roll missing in recent times).
[4] *C.J.R. 1305–7*, pp. 424–5.

imposed on those advancing false exceptions by voucher of rolls.¹ A thorny point in the latter connection came before the justiciar's court in 1305. After ordaining the penalty of imprisonment for falsely alleging the exception that an assize of the same tenements had passed between the parties or that a writ of a higher nature was pending between them for them, the chapter went on to consider the position when bailiffs put forward such exceptions on behalf of their absent lords. It decreed that the justices should not delay in taking the assize because a mere bailiff advanced that exception: but if the lord should come, even after judgment, and offer to vouch a record in proof of the exception put forward by his bailiff, he should be permitted to do so.

Now, in an assize of novel disseisin before justices assigned in 1301 a bailiff of the tenant put forward the exception that an assize of the tenements had already been taken before the justiciar. The justices, in accordance with the statute, refused to receive this. But later the tenant came by his general attorney and the justices still refused to receive the exception, because they 'could not direct the justiciar, their superior, to make the assize come before them'. The tenant then secured an English writ, with *si difficultas* clause, to bring the matter to the justiciar's court, where another difficulty was revealed. The tenant had never come before the justices in person—did appearance by attorney satisfy the statute? The justiciar's court, finding the point not expressly mentioned in the statute, adjourned the matter into the king's bench, but unfortunately no further proceedings are known.²

The most impressive Irish case on the interpretation of this statute concerned c. 40.³ The pleadings on a writ of *cui in vita* brought in the eyre of Limerick of 1290 presented the justices with three important questions. The chapter ordained that if a man alienated his wife's right she could recover after his death and her suit should not be delayed *per minorem etatem heredis qui warantizare debet*. Did this refer only to the pure and separate right of the wife or did it also concern common right, where husband and wife had been conjointly enfeoffed? Did the statute apply where a defendant vouched a person under age who

¹ *C.J.R. 1305–7*, pp. 168–9 (three years, however, instead of the statutory one).
² *Ibid.* pp. 145–7, 265.
³ P. 145, n. 2 above; see especially the concise account by Sayles, *Select cases in K.B.* III, pp. xxvi–xxviii.

was not the heir of the plaintiff's husband, but of a purchaser from the husband? Should the statute, in the light of c. 50, declaring that it should operate from Michaelmas 1285, apply to alienations made before then?[1] The case was evoked from the eyre to the Dublin bench and from the bench, by a writ in *si difficultas* form, to the king's bench in England. There it lingered unresolved until the death of the tenant brought it to an end in 1298. A later English decision held for the narrower interpretation of the statute with regard to the second question; that is to say, that it favoured the wife only against a first purchaser who vouched the heir of her husband.[2] English cases also went to establish that the statute was not retrospective and did not apply to alienations made before Michaelmas 1285.[3]

It is plain that the Irish courts adhered with fidelity to those English statutes which applied in that land. Only on the rare occasions when the somewhat different structure of the Irish judicial system made modification desirable do exceptions appear to have occurred. Further, the disinclination of the Irish courts to meddle with disputes over the interpretation of statutes made its small contribution to the role of the king's bench in such matters.

[1] Broadly similar pleadings had occurred in another case brought by the same demandant that cannot be traced beyond the Dublin bench: p. 145, n. 3, above.

[2] *Y.B. 33–5 Edw. I* (Rolls ser.), pp. 242–4 (notwithstanding a previous case, there referred to, where the other view had prevailed); T. F. T. Plucknett, *Statutes and their interpretation in the fourteenth century* (Cambridge, 1922), pp. 59, 123–4.

[3] Plucknett, *op. cit.* pp. 118–19, 187.

CHAPTER IX

THE CUSTOM OF THE LAND OF IRELAND

ALTHOUGH an elaborate corpus of written law had existed in Ireland from at least the eighth century, 'the early records of the English administration have little to say' about it.[1] Even the condemnatory approach of the sixteenth and seventeenth centuries is scarcely found;[2] the Brehon law was simply ignored. To such a generalization there are a very few exceptions. One of the statutes of the Irish parliament of 1278 used a technical term of Irish law, *cin comfocuis*, in the disguise of *kynkonges*; but this is a matter best explored in connection with the status of the native Irish at English law.[3] There are occasional reflections of the great part played in Gaelic society by obligations of hospitality and entertainment.[4] It was noted with regard to Meath in 1311 that

> the notables of the county for their money [*rent?*] in past times were often accustomed to take from the tenants victuals for their hospitality and this taking has not hitherto been forbidden to the notables.[5]

A few years later an Irish harper was found to have got felons (bearing the Norman surname of Caunteton) to revenge him upon those who refused him hospitality.[6] In 1316 a recent Irish statute against idlemen who committed robberies under the pretence of seeking hospitality (*civilitas*) was mentioned in the justiciar's court.[7] A case in 1308 tells how, after one man wounded another,

> he took him into his own house to heal him of his wound, but after a few days [*the wounded man*] left for want of sustenance and a surgeon.[8]

---

[1] D. A. Binchy, 'The linguistic and historical value of the Irish law tracts', *Brit. Acad. Proc.* XXIX (1943), 195–227, at 227.
[2] But cf. *Foedera* (Rec. comm. ed.), I, II, 540, where Edward I denounces Irish laws as 'detestable to God'.
[3] Pp. 193, 203, below.
[4] Cf. the regulations in *Crith Gablach*, ed. D. A. Binchy (Dublin, 1941) and the editor's notes on the words *biathad*, *cóe* and *esáin* (pp. 76–7, 81, 87–8).
[5] *C.J.R. 1308–14*, p. 211.
[6] J.R. 8–9 Edw. II, m. 8 d.
[7] J.R. 9–11 Edw. II (no. 114), m. 3; cf. p. 160, above.
[8] *C.J.R. 1308–14*, p. 41.

THE CUSTOM OF THE LAND OF IRELAND 173

There is a faint possibility that this is a late reflection of the archaic law of *folog* or *othrus* ('sick-maintenance'), already obsolete some centuries before.[1]

In 1299 there was an elaborate agreement between two members of the Rochfort family which sought to oust the rules of primogeniture in favour of the Irish law of succession to chieftaincies. Henry son of Henry Rochfort, being ill, enfeoffed Henry son of Simon Rochfort, by a sort of *donatio mortis causa*, with a condition subsequent that the feoffee should reconvey if the feoffor recovered his health. In fact Henry son of Henry did recover and Henry son of Simon gave the lands back, to be held of himself in tail male. It was provided that, if Henry son of Henry died without male issue, all should revert to Henry son of Simon and the heirs male of his body, who, however, undertook to provide marriage portions for any daughters left by Henry son of Henry. If, after this, Henry son of Simon were in turn to die without heirs male of his body, then

... the most noble, worthy, strong, and praiseworthy of the pure blood and name of Rochfordeyns, issued from the blood of Sir Walter de Rupeforti and lady Eva de Herford his wife, shall have the barony of Okethy with all other lands; unless the four nearest of our blood and name choose to elect one better and more worthy of the Rochfortdeyns, to whom so elected the whole barony ... shall remain: so that the inheritance shall never pass to daughters.[2]

As it happened, the validity of this ingenious attempt to fit English forms to Gaelic realities was not directly at issue in the litigation which caused it to be enrolled. Consequently the justiciar's court was not called upon to anticipate the famous judgment of the Irish king's bench in the *Case of Tanistry* three centuries later.[3]

More than once in the first half of the thirteenth century, when conformity of law on both sides of the Irish Sea was receiving attention, procedure on the writ *de divisis faciendis* or *de rationabilibus divisis* was the subject of letters from England.[4] This

[1] Cf. Professor Binchy's note in *Críth Gablach*, pp. 91–3.
[2] *C.J.R. 1295–1303*, p. 326; the connected proceedings, not here strictly relevant, are at pp. 322–5.
[3] Sir John Davies, *Reports* (edition of London, 1674), pp. 28–42; cf. *Críth Gablach*, ed. Binchy, pp. 107–8 (note on *tánaise* [*ríg*]); F. H. Newark, 'The case of Tanistry', 9 *N.I.L.Q.* (1952), 215–21; W. F. T. Butler, *Gleanings from Irish history* (London, 1925), pp. 80–91.
[4] Pp. 1–3, above.

writ was a variety of the writ of right, but a letter in 1222 stated that, instead of the correct procedure being followed, actions were sometimes decided in Ireland simply on the verdict of perambulators.[1] Pleas of bounds were ordered henceforth to be held as in England, battle and the grand assize being thus made available to the defence. That the influence of native custom lay behind this is suggested by further letters close early in the succeeding year. These distinguished between lands *inhabita Hyberniensibus*, where the Irish custom was to be followed, and those inhabited by *Anglicis exclusis Hyberniensibus*, where bounds should be made according to English custom.[2] In 1227 the writ *de divisis* was included in the *Register* sent to Ireland.[3] Seven years later, however, the justiciar was sent a copy of it with an order that it should be followed, *in forma qua currit in terra nostra Anglie*.[4] The matter is not known to have arisen again.

Because it bridged both the divide between pre-invasion and post-invasion Ireland and that between territories in the obedience of the lordship and those of the Gaelic chiefs, the Church occupied an exceptional position. Some dioceses were cut through by the territorial division, with peculiar results. When in 1299 a writ of *quare impedit* was brought against the bishop of Derry the exception was advanced on his behalf that he was not named in the writ, as he ought to have been, *Gofridus* (i.e., apparently, *Goffraid*), but *Galfridus*. The jury said

episcopus vocatur Galfridus et eo nomine cognoscatur inter Anglicos et eodem nomine baptizabatur set Hibernici nesciunt vocare ipsum in partibus suis nisi Gofridus secundum modum Hibernicorum.[5]

But the questions raised by the continuity of the Church through the invasion were more serious. The claim was not infrequently brought forward that the Irish church had retained from preconquest days canonical rights more generous in scope than those which the English church enjoyed, especially with regard to the *privilegium fori* and the jurisdiction of courts christian in matters other than testamentary and matrimonial. There is no need to explore here topics which have been the subject of recently

---

[1] *Rot. litt. claus. 1204–24*, p. 497; cf. *Brevia placitata*, ed. Turner, p. civ.
[2] *Rot. litt. claus. 1204–24*, p. 352.
[3] Maitland, *Collected papers*, II, 132.
[4] *Close rolls, 1234–7*, p. 157.
[5] C.P., H. 27 Edw. I (no. 39), in P.R.O.I., RC. 7/5, *Cal. plea rolls*, V, 473.

THE CUSTOM OF THE LAND OF IRELAND 175

published studies.[1] The royal administration was determined not to concede anything to attempts to resist the application of the English relationship of royal and ecclesiastical jurisdictions to Ireland. 'On one occasion [Edward I] replied to an Irish episcopal complaint: *Fiat eis secundum quod fit prelatis in Anglia*. It was a concise summary of his whole attitude to the legal position of the Irish Church'.[2] But a somewhat more flexible position appears to have been taken on a question of tenure. How should lands devoted to ecclesiastical purposes before the conquest be integrated in the new legal system? The invasion necessarily brought uncertainty and loss to some ecclesiastical landowners. In a case in which Innocent III appointed judges-delegate in 1205 it was alleged that the English had a law whereby a grant made by an Irishman to a religious house might be invalidated by a subsequent grant of the property concerned by the king of England to another grantee. Whatever the details of the case, the pope understandably declared that such a law *nec naturalis nec scripti juris contineat equitatem*.[3] But our concern here is with lands that the church was successful in retaining, though the tenure might remain to be adapted and clarified. A petition of uncertain date, very possibly from the reign of Edward I, put forward the ecclesiastical claim that such lands were in general held in frankalmoin. The Irish rulers had given all the lordship they themselves possessed:

ut nichil juris humani sibi retinerent in eisdem sed sicut ipsi in terrarum suarum regimine nullum preter Deum superiorem agnoverant, sic nec ecclesie quibus predia ecclesiastica in liberam, puram et perpetuam contulerant elemosinam.[4]

[1] The most important is by J. A. Watt: 'English law and the Irish Church: the reign of Edward I', *Medieval studies presented to Aubrey Gwynn, S.J.*, ed. J. A. Watt, J. B. Morrall and F. X. Martin (Dublin, 1961), pp. 133–67; see also his 'Negotiations between Edward II and John XXII concerning Ireland,' *I.H.S.* x (1956), 1–20. M. P. Sheehy, 'English law in Medieval Ireland', *Arch. Hib.* XXIII (1960), 166–75, prints two interesting documents. G. J. Hand, 'The Church and English law in medieval Ireland', *Proceedings of the Irish Catholic Historical Committee, 1959*, is a brief introduction, expanded in '*Ecclesia inter Anglos:* the English lordship at its height, 1216–1307' (a fascicle of *A history of Irish Catholicism*) (forthcoming).
[2] Watt, *Studies presented to Aubrey Gwynn*, p. 160; the reference is apparently to B.M., MS. Cott. Aug. II, no. 104, printed by Sheehy, art. cit. p. 173 (*sit* in Dr Watt's quotation has been emended to *fit*, which is Dr Sheehy's reading and seems superior).
[3] M. P. Sheehy, *Pontificia hibernica* (Dublin, 1962), I, 134.
[4] Lambeth Library, MS. 619, f. 206 (printed in *Arch. hib.* XXIII, 174, but I read *contulerant* for Dr Sheehy's *contulerunt*).

In practice, a distinction came to be made between the temporalities of the sees and of the pre-invasion religious houses. After the invasion, the archbishops of Armagh and Dublin in fact acquired land to be held of the king by knight service, but this was not the case with the other bishops.[1] None the less, the king maintained that the temporalities of every Irish see were held of him and regalian rights were consequently exercised, where possible, in the same way as in England. But the pre-invasion religious houses appear to have been ultimately successful in the claim to hold in frankalmoin.[2]

In Ireland it was natural to approach the question of prescription by reference to the conquest. Clearly, lands and liberties enjoyed *a principio conquesti Hibernie* were beyond the limit of legal memory.[3] But enjoyment since the conquest had to be shown. A complaint from the archbishop of Tuam in 1255 led to the following statement of the law, which might well be classed among the early statutes of Ireland:

Super hoc provisum est et statutum quod si aliqui petentes narraverint de seisina suorum predecessorum ante tempus predicti Henrici regis avi et ante conquestum Anglicorum et de nulla seisina narraverint de tempore predicti avi nec post tempus dicti conquestus, eo ipso cadit a causa sua et a jure suo, et, si tenens in magnam assisam se posuerit cum mencione de tempore predicto et per recognicionem ejusdem assise constiterit quod petens vel ejus antecessores nunquam seisinam habuerint tempore dicti regis avi, seu post conquestum nec aliquando postmodum, tunc petens cadat a causa et tenens ab ejus impeticione absolvatur.[4]

In 1300 it was inconclusively argued in the justiciar's court that seisin since the conquest was not enough to put forward in the case of liberties in Connaught, because Connaught had not in fact been conquered until after the accession of King John.[5]

[1] Richardson and Sayles, *The Irish parliament*, pp. 18, 120–1.
[2] Most of the evidence is later in date than the limits of the present study and has been summarized in *Proc. Ir. Cath. Hist. Comm. 1959*, pp. 12–13; cf. also G. J. Hand, 'Christ Church, Dublin, and the common law, 1277–1382', *R.S.A.I. Jn.* (forthcoming). In 1313 the earl of Ulster tried to secure the custody of sees in his liberty during vacancy: B.M., MS. Cotton Titus B XI, f. 1.
[3] E.g. J.I. 29 Edw. I (no. 59), in P.R.O.I., RC. 7/9, *Cal. plea rolls*, IX, 211–12.
[4] *Close rolls, 1254–6*, p. 413.
[5] *C.J.R. 1295–1303*, p. 317; p. 115, above.

THE CUSTOM OF THE LAND OF IRELAND 177

What were usually meant by 'customs of the land of Ireland' had, however, little to do with the Gaelic world or with the special problems of conquest; they were merely older or local variations of English custom brought thither by the early colonists.

Some slight doubt may have existed about the application of the curtesy of England to Ireland, although in 1226 its observance there had been decreed.[1] In 1295 the justiciar and chancellor were instructed to deliver the wife's lands in a particular case, if they ascertained that the custom existed in Ireland as in England.[2] In fact, what evidence there is goes to show that curtesy was faithfully followed in Ireland, even in the precedence given to a second husband over the right of the issue of the first in lands held by the wife *in liberum maritagium*.[3]

The customary rule of succession by which the goods of testators and intestates were divided into three parts *inter virum, uxorem, et prolem*, if wife and issue survived, and two parts *inter virum et uxorem*, if there was no surviving issue, was in 1300 unanimously declared by the king's council in Ireland, including the bishops, to be *consuetudo in Hibernia usitata*.[4] The custom survived in Ireland down to the seventeenth century, its English origin having been obscured by time, so that it came to be regarded as peculiarly Irish.[5]

It was argued in the justiciar's court in 1295 that great whales were, by ancient custom of Ireland, reputed wreck of the sea and consequently covered by a general grant of wreck.[6] This attempt to oust the ordinary doctrine that such fish must have special mention in the charter of franchise was evidently unsuccessful.[7]

On a roll of pleas of the crown in the justiciar's court in 1311 there are two very curious entries. Both concern the undertakings of mainpernors. In the first, the mainpernor undertook that [the principal] would henceforth bear himself well and faithfully to the king's peace. [He also] undertook without delay to put out the eyes of [the principal] and to ... [bring?] him to the sheriff.[8]

[1] *Patent rolls, 1225–32*, p. 96.   [2] *Cal. close rolls, 1288–96*, p. 413.
[3] J.R. 11 Edw. II (no. 116), m. 21; cf. Plucknett, *Legislation of Edward I*, p. 118, n. 1.
[4] *Stat. Ire. John–Hen. V*, p. 226; p. 147, n. 4, above; for other cases, *C.J.R. 1305–7*, pp. 157, 254; for the English law, Bracton, ff. 60b, 61.
[5] H. J. M. Mason, *An essay on the antiquity and constitution of parliaments in Ireland*, ed. J. O'Hanlon (Dublin, 1891), Appendix 1, pp. viii–x.
[6] *C.J.R. 1295–1303*, p. 29.   [7] *Ibid.* pp. 54–5, 264; cf. Bracton, f. 14.
[8] *C.J.R. 1308–14*, p. 197; cf. p. 31, n. 3, above.

In the second instance the undertaking is that those mainprised will

bear themselves well and faithfully towards the king's peace, and if not they [the mainpernors] will restore [their] bodies to the king's prison, for judgment, or utterly blind them. And it is granted by the justiciar here that it be at the election of the said mainpernors either to blind [them] after a renewal of their misdoing or to restore their bodies to the king's prison, as aforesaid.[1]

No other evidence has been found for the survival in the criminal law of the lordship of mutilation in this way.[2] It seems to have been a reflection of the difficulty of securing the administration of justice in the outlying areas.

Much the most important custom of the land of Ireland concerned the custody of the heir of a socage tenant and it was at the heart of a remarkable Irish case which claimed the attention of the court *coram rege*. The matter is one on which Bracton was emphatic. According to him, the incidents of feudal wardship and marriage depended on knight service, not on the doing of homage.

Et sciendum quod [*homage is due*] de terris et tenementis, redditibus et omnibus aliis que tenentur per servitium militare, sive servitium militare magnum sit vel minimum, etiam si non daretur ad scutagium nisi obolus unus, et semper sequetur tale servitium custodia heredis et maritagium, et non tantum propter homagium factum, sed propter regale servitium, et quia non ad omne homagium sequitur custodia et maritagium, quia homagium fit aliquando de tenemento quod tenetur in socagio.[3]

He recognized that homage, instead of simply fealty, was sometimes done for lands held in socage, but insisted that this left the rule unaffected:

Et si de facto fiat homagium, non tamen sequitur propter hoc quod ad dominum capitalem pertineat custodia et maritagium, quia custodia et maritagium non semper sequitur homagium, quia ad quem huiusmodi pertineant per homagium non determinatur, sed per servitium, secundum quod tenementum tenetur per servitium militare vel per socagium.[4]

---

[1] *C.J.R. 1308–14*, p. 215.
[2] Cf. Pollock and Maitland (2nd ed.), II, 461–2.
[3] F. 79b.
[4] F. 34b; cf. also f. 77b.

THE CUSTOM OF THE LAND OF IRELAND

In another passage, however, he was obliged to admit the existence of customary exceptions:

... licet in quibusdam partibus de consuetudine et per abusum observetur contrarium, sicut in episcopatu Wintoniensi et alibi. Et cum ita factum sit quamvis per abusum, oportet quod de custodia et relevio fiat secundum quod fit de feodo militari.[1]

Plainly, Bracton disliked a custom which gave a lord the wardship and marriage of his tenant in socage. It is known, however, that the custom in England was not confined to the bishopric (i.e. barony of the bishop?) of Winchester,[2] and it was tenaciously defended by the magnates of the lordship of Ireland.

In 1277, John Comyn, who held the manor of Kinsaley, in north county Dublin, from the Dublin cathedral priory of Holy Trinity (Christ Church) was slain by a lay-brother and some men attached to a near-by grange of the abbey of St Mary, Dublin.[3] According to the ordinary common law, his widow should have had the wardship of his lands, and, as against the priory, the marriage of his son and heir, an infant. But homage had been done for Comyn's lands and his lord, the prior of Holy Trinity, could therefore found a claim on the alleged custom of Ireland that homage gave wardship and marriage. To complicate matters, however, not only was the office of Prior of Holy Trinity vacant at the time of John Comyn's death, but so was the see of Dublin. The temporalities of the see were consequently in the king's hand, and the escheator alleged that the vacancy in the priory, occurring at the same time, meant that the prior's claim to the Comyn wardship fell to the king. The escheator's intervention was contested and custody sought, both by the sub-prior and convent, and by Mabel, the widow. A further complication was the claim of the abbot of Malmesbury, of whom John Comyn was alleged to have held land in England by knight-service, to have the wardship of those lands and the marriage of the heir.

After an inquisition had shown that the vacancy in the priory gave no rights to the archbishop or, *sede vacante*, the king, the

---

[1] f. 85 b.
[2] Pollock and Maitland (2nd ed.), I, 321.
[3] E. St John Brooks, 'The early Irish Comyns', *R.S.A.I. Jn.* LXXXVI (1956), 171–86, at pp. 176–82; *Chartul. St Mary's, Dublin*, I, 1–3; C. Ó Conbhuí, 'The lands of St Mary's abbey, Dublin', *R.I.A. Proc.* LXII (1962), 21–84, at pp. 43–4.

escheator withdrew and the canons were put in seisin.[1] But Mabel, the widow, did not relax her claims. The exact course of events is not altogether clear from the records. Proceedings seem to have taken place before Ralph Hengham in the English king's bench, but the immediately contemporary rolls are silent about them.[2] In October 1279, a writ ordered the justiciar to take the lands once more into the king's hand and inquire into the facts.[3] The resulting inquisition, held in the following May, was favourable to the prior. The custom was said to be that if homage was 'contained in a charter or chirograph' the lord had wardship. Although John Comyn had never done homage, homage was contained in a fine of the lands made between a former prior of Holy Trinity and John's father (who had done actual homage in court). Apparently on this basis, the king's bench gave judgment for the prior, awarding him the wardship of the lands, probably in late Trinity or early Michaelmas term, 1280.

Meanwhile, the abbot of Malmesbury had not been idle. In the Hilary term of 1279 he sought the wardship of the heir in the English bench, in virtue of lands held of the abbey by knight service in Wiltshire.[4] The case was pleaded in Michaelmas term, 1279. Mabel's defence was that John had held lands by knight service (!) in Ireland of the priory of Holy Trinity by feoffment prior to that by the predecessors of the abbot of Malmesbury. (Though the statute of Westminster II, c. 16, was of course still in the future, the rule implied seems to have been one of the current theories).[5] It was therefore in Mabel's interest to point out that judgment had been given before Hengham in the prior's favour:

Et petit judicium utrum ipsum heredem reddere debeat ipsi abbati donec discussum fuerit inter ipsum et predictum priorem, ad quem illorum predicta custodia pertinere debeat.[6]

[1] The weakness of the archbishop's claim is not primarily relevant here; it has been discussed in: G. J. Hand, 'The two cathedrals of Dublin' (unpublished M.A. thesis, National University of Ireland, 1954), pp. 13–14, 123.
[2] P.R.O., K.B. 27/98, mm. 28 d, 29 (*Cal. doc. Ire. 1285–92*, 210); C. 47/10/14, no. 7 (*Cal. doc. Ire. 1252–84*, 2150); *Registrum Malmesburiense* (Rolls ser.), I, 255.
[3] *Cal. doc. Ire. 1252–84*, 1596 (also, *Cal. inq. p.m. 1–19 Edw. I*, no. 331).
[4] P.R.O., C.P. 40/31, m. 36; *Reg. Malmesburiense*, I, 251. On the other hand, the heir successfully brought an assize of mort d'ancestor of lands in Warwickshire, held in socage: *ibid.* II, 397–9 and cf. I, 250–1.
[5] Plucknett, *Legislation of Edward I*, pp. 112–13.
[6] *Reg. Malmesburiense*, I, 253.

THE CUSTOM OF THE LAND OF IRELAND 181

After further pleading, Hengham certified the proceedings before him into the bench. The justiciar of Ireland was ordered to summon the prior for Michaelmas term, 1281, and in the meantime to take an inquisition as to the facts and the custom of Ireland.[1]

During this time, Mabel seems to have been seeking an extra-judicial remedy. There is an undated letter from the justiciar to the king that seems to fit this period of the litigation best. In it he expressed unwillingness to override the custom claimed by the prior, because it was generally claimed by the Irish baronage:

> Quia barones terre vestre Hybernie communiter tam prelati quam alii ex antiqua consuetudine continuata donec in hec tempora semper habere consueverunt custodias terrarum et heredum illorum qui de eis tenent in socagium dum cum illo socagio fuerit homagium quamquam nullum servicium militare inde debeatur mandatum vestrum nuper mihi factum per litteras vestras quas excellencie vestre presentibus remitto inclusas pro Amabilia que fuit uxor Johannis Comyn exequi distuli donec mihi plenius constiterit de voluntate vestra utrum contra consuetudines Hybernie dictum mandatum exequi debeam maxime cum in eisdem litteris vestris inseratur quod secundum consuetudinem terre Hybernie fiat in hac parte quod de jure fuerit faciendum.[2]

Perhaps it was to overcome this reluctance on the part of the justiciar that Mabel obtained a writ, dated 16 May 1281, ordering restoration of the lands to be made to her, with a *salvo jure nostro et alterius cujuscunque*.[3] Together with this writ was a memorandum of great interest:

> Memorandum quod non est lex nec justa consuetudo quod domini feodorum habeant custodias heredum et terrarum que tenentur de eis in socagio, quamvis aliqui hucusque habeant tales custodias per pigriciam et defaltam tenencium suorum qui noluerunt sibi perquisisse in curia domini regis per breve.[4]

The memorandum continues that this is manifest from a case before justices itinerant in Tipperary in 1267, in which the justices

---

[1] *Ibid.* I, 252–6; P.R.O., K.B. 27/98, m. 29 (*Cal. doc. Ire. 1285–92*, 210); P.R.O., C. 47/10/14, no. 7 (*Cal. doc. Ire. 1252–84*, 2150). It is not clear that a judicial writ of the bench issued to the justiciar.

[2] P.R.O., S.C. 1/21, no. 21. This may date from an earlier stage of the case, c.1277–9. It would also be tempting to fit it in after the writ of May 1281, but there does not seem to have been time for it in the course of events about mid-1281, and consequently it appears that we lack the text of the letters which provoked it.   [3] P.R.O., S.C. 1/14, no. 67.

[4] *Ibid.* printed by Sayles, *Select cases in K.B.* III, p. xxx, n. 5.

had followed the common law rule though the custom was pleaded.

Probably even before receipt of this writ, with its strong declaration of policy, the justiciar seems to have had the prior ejected (if the judgment in his favour had indeed ever been executed), for the prior, alleging ejectment, obtained a summons of parties, records, and writs before the king and council for the quinzaine of St John Baptist, 1281.[1] In his return to this writ ordering the summons, the justiciar included a fresh inquisition which, broadly speaking, reiterated in its findings that of May 1280.[2] He also noted that:

nullus processus seu placitum in partibus Hibernie super hoc habebatur set tantummodo quedam inquisicio capta [i.e. *that of May 1280*].

The next development was the taking, in July, 1281, of the inquisition ordered some time before in connection with the action of the abbot of Malmesbury in the bench at Westminster.[3] This produced findings similar to those of the earlier inquisitions and the Malmesbury case marked time for the next three years, possibly on account of the council's deliberations on the Irish aspect.

In November 1281, a writ ordered a search of Irish rolls for relevant cases on the custom.[4] The return certified that the only one which could be found was the judgment in 1267 against the Irish custom which had already been brought forward on Mabel's behalf. This caused the Irish council some concern, for they favoured the custom, and Stephen, bishop of Waterford and justiciar, and Richard of Exeter, sent a covering letter to Robert Burnell. In this they alleged that

omnes archiepiscopi episcopi abbates et ceteri magnates dictam consuetudinem a tempore conquestionis terre predicte usi sunt et dominus noster rex eandem consuetudinem tempore vacacionis custodiarum hucusque usus est.[5]

[1] P.R.O., K.B. 27/92, m. 7 (*Cal. doc. Ire. 1285–92*, 58). There could hardly be time for the receipt in Ireland of the writ dated 16 May, execution of it by the justiciar, and petition by the prior in England in time for a summons to be sent for early July. Perhaps, however, the prior's representatives in England moved as soon as the writ of 16 May issued.
[2] P.R.O., K.B. 27/92, m. 7 (*Cal. doc. Ire. 1285–92*, 58).
[3] P.R.O., C. 47/10/14, no. 7 (*Cal. doc. Ire. 1252–84*, 2150); *Reg. Malmesburiense*, I, 256–7.
[4] P.R.O., K.B. 27/92, m. 7 (*Cal. doc. Ire. 1285–92*, 58).
[5] P.R.O., S.C. 1/23, no. 85.

They went on to ask Burnell to see that the king's council was not swayed, by the single judgment in a contrary sense found on the rolls, in *prejudicium et dampnum ac exheredacionem* of the magnates of Ireland. After this, the matter hung fire until 1285, apart from adjournments and attorneys in the king's bench.[1]

In February 1285 a jury was summoned to the bench at Westminster for Easter term concerning the tenure of the Wiltshire lands held of the abbot of Malmesbury.[2] There was, however, an eyre of Warwick in this year and the case went to the justices there, apparently through some error; however, judgment was finally given for the abbot in the bench in Easter term.[3] In the following term, judgment was also at last given in the Irish case before the king and council. The fear of the Irish council proved to have been well founded. *Cum una et eadem lex debet esse* in both jurisdictions, and, since an Irish court had in 1267 refused to admit the custom, Mabel was given the wardship of the lands her husband had held of Holy Trinity.[4] A financial settlement for the time the prior of Holy Trinity had been in possession of the manor of Kinsaley was reached late in 1286.[5] No doubt encouraged by her success in the Irish case, Mabel brought a writ of error in the king's bench to overthrow the judgment of the common bench in favour of the abbot of Malmesbury. But this attempt failed and early in 1288 she bought the marriage of her son back from the abbot.[6] The whole long course of litigation must have consequently appeared to be at an end.

Then, at the Easter parliament of 1293, a new prior of Holy Trinity presented a petition alleging error.[7] A writ in pursuance of this petition ordered the parties to be summoned *coram rege* in

---

[1] *Cal. doc. Ire. 1252–84*, 1904, 1906, 1975, 2076, 2128, 2190, 2191; *1285–92*, 55.
[2] *Reg. Malmesburiense*, I, 257.   [3] *Ibid.* I, 259–60.
[4] P.R.O., K.B. 27/92, m. 7d (*Cal. doc. Ire. 1285–92*, 58).
[5] 'Calendar of Christ Church deeds', no. 143, *P.R.I. rep. D.K. 20*, p. 60.
[6] P.R.O., K.B. 27/98, mm. 28d, 29 (*Cal. doc. Ire. 1285–92*, 210); *Reg. Malmesburiense*, I, 260, 261–4.
[7] From this point the material used above (as well as recitals of much already used from other sources) is in P.R.O., K.B. 27/139, mm. 43, 43d. Although this membrane is now in a very bad condition, there survives an excellent transcript made by Thomas Madox: B.M., Add. MS. 4525 (vol. xlvii of Madox's Collections), ff. 115–38. Even Madox, however, had to confess 'This entry is, at the latter end of it, obliterated and some words hardly legible'. Objections to be urged on behalf of the prior are also noted in 'Calendar of Christ Church deeds', no. 91 (*P.R.I. rep. D.K. 20*, p. 51); unfortunately the original was destroyed in 1922 and the document had not been transcribed before then.

Hilary 1294. When they came, it was argued on Mabel's behalf that the prior's petition alleged error only *in principali* and not *in processu* and that therefore the justices should consider only the content of the previous judgment, which was good because

magis tenenda est consuetudo Anglie diu approbata... quam consuetudo Hibernica que juri non concordat.

For the prior it was said that the justices were exercising their ordinary jurisdiction, and could examine both the process and the content of the judgment for errors. (The stress on the distinction between 'principal' and 'process' is a reminder that too mechanical and procedural a view can be formed of the medieval search for error on the record.) In any event,

erratum est in processu et in principali eo quod invenitur quod processum fuit ex officio et non per oppositionem et responsionem partium prout decet.

It was further argued that the custom was also known in Cumberland, Westmorland and the diocese of Winchester. Successive adjournments followed.

In the octave of St John Baptist 1294, it was conceded by Mabel's representative that the prior of Holy Trinity had been seised immediately upon the death of John Comyn and that, after the escheator's intervention, he had been re-seised upon an inquisition *ex officio curie*.

Et pretera predicta Amabilia requisita si ministri regis iterato ad sectam suam ejecerunt predictum priorem, ad quod nichil respondit.

The court held that, when the prior was once re-seised after an inquisition upholding his right, *curia amplius inde ex officio se intromisse non debuit*. Instead, procedure ought to have been by a recognized form of action: Mabel should have sued a writ of wardship or the heir should have brought an assize of mort d'ancestor. The decision of 1285 was therefore *extra formam judicii*. Certain lesser errors were also found in the record, but the heart of the matter seems to have been that *ex officio* procedure could not be used to deprive anyone of right:

hujusmodi processus habitus est magis ex officio curie quam per figuram judicii, quod quidem officium jus alicujus terminare non debet.

THE CUSTOM OF THE LAND OF IRELAND 185

The judgment of 1285 was therefore declared null, but Mabel and her son were left to seek another remedy if they willed. In fact, the younger John did bring a writ of mort d'ancestor in the Dublin bench against the prior, which was compromised by a financial settlement reached in February 1296.[1]

Even though the unfavourable judgment given in 1285 was ultimately ineffective for other reasons, the Comyn case must have weakened the Irish custom. It certainly did not kill it, however. The custom was unsuccessfully pleaded before Wogan in 1307.[2] But in 1300 a plaintiff who based his claim to a wardship in the Dublin bench on tenure by homage and suit of court *secundum consuetudinem Hibernie* was successful.[3] The surviving justiciary roll for 6–7 Edward II includes four assizes of novel disseisin in which the tenant pleaded the custom. In three no result valuable for the present purpose is recorded.[4] But in one the Irish custom appears to have been upheld by Walter of Thornbury and William Alexander, assigned to the place of Edmund Butler.[5]

In 1331 the king was petitioned about the matter by *ses liges gent de sa terre de Irlaund*.[6] This petition referred back to the Irish judgment of 1267 against the custom and complained

voz justices de la dite terre par lour lasches soeffrent les seignurs de la dite terre occuper les gardes des tieles tenures ... atort e encontre la lei e en oppression du poeple.

The petition was answered by letters sent both to the justiciar and to the justices of the Dublin bench.[7] After references to the contrary judgments of 1267 and 1285, the king expressed his will that the law and custom of his realm and not the Irish custom was to be observed. However, a conciliar memorandum of probably slightly later date, giving what seem to be draft ordinances for

---

[1] 'Calendar of Christ Church deeds', no. 153, *P.R.I. rep. D.K. 20*, p. 64; cf. C.P., M. 23–4 Edw. I, in P.R.O.I., RC. 7/3, *Cal. plea rolls*, III, 412.

[2] *C.J.R. 1305–7*, pp. 364–5; doubtful or inconclusive cases are to be found in *1295–1303*, p. 341, and *1305–7*, pp. 388, 457.

[3] C.P., T. 28 Edw. I, in P.R.O.I., RC. 7/7, *Cal. plea rolls*, VII, 236.

[4] J.R. 6–7 Edw. II, mm. 33, 72, 73 d.

[5] m. 81d. There is an inconclusive reference on J.R. 11 Edw. II (no. 116), m. 7d.

[6] P.R.O., S.C. 8/262, no. 13051.

[7] *Cal. close rolls, 1330–3*, pp. 203–4.

Ireland, suggests that the king and other lords should have wardship and marriage of tenants in socage

en manere come de viel fu acustume nient contresteant briefs qe y soit avant mande du contraire.[1]

It is hard to believe that the Irish administration under Edward III could in fact have suppressed a custom, lucrative to the magnates, which had survived Edward I and John Wogan.

[1] P.R.O., C. 49/6, no. 30.

CHAPTER X

THE STATUS OF THE NATIVE IRISH AT ENGLISH LAW

EVEN in recent times, the question of the status of the native Irish at English law when the medieval lordship of Ireland was at its height has appeared in political polemic.[1] This controversial atmosphere may indeed have helped to secure for it rather more attention from serious historians than other aspects of medieval Irish legal history have received. The interest of the matter is more than narrowly Irish, however. It shows English law, itself a young system, grappling with one of the problems presented by a subject people possessing a different legal tradition.

In different ages and circumstances the pride of a conquering race will show itself in different forms. Now-a-days the victor may regard the conflict as one between civilization and barbarism, or between a high and a low morality, and force his laws upon the vanquished as the best, or the only reasonable laws. Or again, he may deliberately set himself to destroy the nationality of his new subjects, to make them forget their old language and their old laws, because these endanger his supremacy... In older and less politic days all will be otherwise. The conquerors will show their contempt for the conquered by allowing such of them as are not enslaved to live under their old law, which has has become a badge of inferiority... A scheme of 'personal laws' would have seemed to them [the Norman invaders of England] a natural outcome of the conquest... But it was too late for a system of 'personal', that is of racial laws.[2]

Maitland's alternative situations, of territorial and personal law, very broadly—though only very broadly—correspond to the contrasting policies pursued by Edward I as conqueror of Wales and as Lord of Ireland.[3] The Statute of Wales, because it integrated much native law and custom in the compromise code

[1] E.g. J. Connolly, *Labour, nationality and religion* (Dublin, 1910), p. viii. The topic even finds mention in L. Kohn, *The constitution of the Irish Free State* (London, 1932), p. 129.
[2] Pollock and Maitland (2nd ed.), I, 90–1.
[3] J. Otway-Ruthven, 'The native Irish and English law in medieval Ireland', *I.H.S.* VII (1950), 1–16, at p. 5, probably makes the Wales/territorial, Ireland/personal, contrast too clear-cut, but it remains substantially convincing.

which it set out, made for a situation, at least in North Wales, very different from that in Ireland, where native law retained no significant accepted foothold in those areas in which the invaders had been able to prevail. 'The Welsh', it has recently been written, 'were clearly regarded as a race apart, if not entirely a lesser breed without the law';[1] the latter description is more appropriate to the native Irish. If they lived where a native chief still held sway, they were perforce left to their own law; if they lived within the effective influence of the governors of the lordship, they were treated as members of an unfree class not entitled to use the king's courts. For the classes already unfree at native law the change of master cannot have mattered greatly. But the formerly free Irish caught up in the spread of Anglo-Norman power, by being treated as unfree, endured many disabilities. Probably the most important was their inability to bring actions in the king's courts, but it is another, often misunderstood, aspect of the problem that has done most to drag it into the domain of partisan history: the killing of an Irishman was no felony. It is not surprising to find that to say a man was Irish was a defamatory statement, actionable by plaint.[2] One is here reminded of the part in the origins of slander believed to have been played by accusations of villeinage.[3] When in 1289 a man discovered that a jury had in his absence found him to be Irish

accessit ad locum tenentem capitalis justiciarii Hibernie et huiusmodi iniuriam sibi in absentia sua factam graviter conquerendo ostendit.[4]

Likewise, jury findings that a person was English were worth preserving in the form of letters patent from the Irish chancery certifying the fact.[5] Here again there is a reflection of the ordinary English law of villeinage: in certain circumstances a finding on an exception of villeinage was decisive as to the plaintiff's status.[6]

Because of the exceptional attention paid to it by historians, it seems advisable to preface a discussion of the substance of this question by a historiographical review.

[1] R. R. Davies, 'The Twilight of Welsh Law, 1284–1536', *History*, LI (1966), 143–64, at p. 151.
[2] *C.J.R. 1295–1303*, pp. 18, 390; *1308–14*, pp. 41, 102–3.
[3] T. F. T. Plucknett, *Concise history of the common law* (5th ed., London, 1956), p. 491.
[4] P.R.O., S.C. 1/14, no. 31 A.
[5] *Cal. rot. pat. Hib.* pp. 16, 26.   [6] *Britton*, ed. Nichols, I, 327.

The historiography of the question

In his *Discoverie of the true causes why Ireland was never entirely subdued* (1612), Sir John Davies, King James's attorney-general in Ireland (to some, perhaps, better known as the author of *Nosce teipsum*), attempted to show the defects of government and policy that had impeded the conquest until his own days. Since amongst those errors he ranked the failure to extend English law to the native Irish, he was at no pains to minimize the difficulties under which the native race was placed. Even today the extracts from the public records which he printed in order to illustrate the position of the Irish at English law are of considerable interest and value.[1]

Two-and-a-half centuries after Davies, A. G. Richey, Deputy Regius Professor of Feudal and English Law in the University of Dublin, 'by far the fairest, and, had his life been prolonged, by far the greatest of Irish historians',[2] relied largely upon the *Discoverie* in discussing the status of the Irish in *Lectures on the history of Ireland down to 1534*, published in 1869.[3] But Richey realized that what the native Irish thought should not be left out of the picture. He consequently also drew attention to certain relevant clauses in the *Remonstrance* addressed by Domnall Ua Néill and other Irish chiefs to Pope John XXII at the time of the war brought about by the Bruce invasion.[4]

The publication of the five volumes of the *Calendar of documents relating to Ireland*, in 1875–86, and, still more, of the first two volumes of the *Calendar of justiciary rolls*, in 1905 and 1914, made available important material not accessible to Richey. The editor of the justiciary rolls, James Mills, had already offered some

---

[1] *Works of Sir John Davies*, ed. A. B. Grosart (privately printed, 1869–76), II, 65–70; the edition most commonly used is that edited by H. Morley in *Ireland under Elizabeth and James the First* (London, 1890). There seems to be a distinct likelihood that Cambridge University Add. MS. 3104, a volume of abstracts of Irish public records, was used by Davies in this connection. On Davies and his approach to the problem of the two laws in general, J. G. A. Pocock, *The ancient constitution and the feudal law* (Cambridge, 1957), pp. 59–63.

[2] A. V. Dicey, *A fool's paradise* (London, 1913), 'Preface', p. ix.

[3] Pp. 143–6; this passage remained unchanged in the *Short history of the Irish people*, brought together by R. R. Kane from Richey's writings (Dublin, 1887), pp. 172–7.

[4] Pp. 162–4 (*Short history*, pp. 190–2); for texts of the *Remonstrance*, see p. 198, n. 3, below.

useful comments in a study of the agricultural classes.[1] In editing the rolls he devised the convention that, where *hibernicus* seemed to be used as equivalent to 'villein', it should be allowed to stand in the English text, and, where it simply meant 'Irishman', it was to be translated.[2] Whatever the wisdom of this particular editorial convention it certainly at once laid bare the importance of distinguishing between the unfree Irish tenants, 'betaghs' and others, and the formerly free Irishmen who had not been admitted to English law.

The first scholar to make use of the new sources in the present connection was G. H. Orpen, in the first two volumes of *Ireland under the Normans* (1911). It was Orpen's belief that his closely documented study made it manifest that

> the most prominent effect of the Anglo-Norman occupation was ... the introduction over large parts of Ireland of a measure of peace and prosperity quite unknown before.[3]

The pages he devoted to the Irish at English law were not altogether free from over-anxiety to prove this point. While justly pointing out that the 'betaghs' and their like merely changed masters and that the rule that it was no felony to kill an Irishman must be related to the native law, which knew only a 'wergild' payment, he erred in implying that the formerly free Irish automatically enjoyed the ordinary privileges of English law.[4]

In his reply to Orpen in *Phases from Irish history*, published in 1919,[5] the leading historian of the nationalist school, Eoin MacNeill, rather surprisingly avoided this topic, though he touched briefly on it some years later.[6] In the next year, 1920, Orpen's second two volumes appeared. He traced the attempts at extension of English law from 1277 to 1331 and argued, against Davies, that the native Irish would have fiercely opposed their own subjection to English law.[7] It does not seem unjust to say that in this Orpen unduly confused the position of Irishmen living in the colony proper with that of those who were in unconquered

---

[1] 'Tenants and agriculture near Dublin in the fourteenth century', *R.S.A.I. Jn.* XX (1890), 54–63.
[2] *C.J.R. 1295–1303*, 'Introduction', pp. viii–ix.
[3] Orpen, I, 10–11.   [4] Orpen, II, 332, especially note 1.
[5] 'The Norman Conquest' (pp. 300–22) is the chapter chiefly relevant.
[6] *Early Irish laws and institutions* (Dublin, n.d. [1935]), p. 144.
[7] Orpen, IV, 21–7, 300.

THE STATUS OF THE NATIVE IRISH

or in effect autonomous areas. None the less, the account he gave of the matter remained the best for almost twenty years.

In 1923, Miss Olive Armstrong, in the course of a somewhat inadequate study of the Bruce wars, discussed the position of the native Irish.[1] Although she made a creditable attempt to establish the position by examination of the primary sources in print, her presentation was artificially schematic and to some extent vitiated by a lack of discrimination in relating evidence drawn from widely different periods of the history of the lordship. It is not surprising that her book has, in this respect, been passed over in silence by later writers. But in the same year the first edition of *Medieval Ireland* by Edmund Curtis appeared. 'The unique place that he holds as a historian of Ireland was due in part ... to his appreciation alike of Gaelic and Anglo-Norman civilization.'[2] He found himself, though from moral and nationalist considerations, in agreement with Sir John Davies in condemning the lack of 'emancipation', 'a general and generous enfranchisement'.[3] He explicitly took Orpen to task on the matter.[4] But Curtis's book did not include any real attempt at a detailed assessment of the position at English law of the Irish of the formerly free classes, and in any event his ignorance of the technicalities of English law was at times startling.[5] However, both in this book and, still more, in an article published in 1936, Curtis enlarged knowledge of the 'betagh' class.[6] In his re-arranged and re-written second edition of *Medieval Ireland* (1938) Curtis relegated the question of the legal position of the Irish to an appendix.[7] His treatment remained much more satisfactory where the unfree 'betagh' class was concerned, however. In this second edition, he also consolidated into an appendix the valuable work he had done since 1908 on the Scandinavian element in the population and its position at English law.[8]

[1] *Edward Bruce's invasion of Ireland* (London, 1923), pp. 35-52.
[2] T. W. Moody, 'The writings of Edmund Curtis', *I.H.S.*, III (1942-3), 393-400, at p. 393.
[3] *Medieval Ireland* (1st ed.), p. 174. [4] P. 206.
[5] E.g. p. 137 (a comment on *C.J.R. 1295-1303*, p. 271, in which he refers to disseisin as a felony).
[6] 'Rental of the manor of Lisronagh, 1333, and notes on "betagh" tenure in medieval Ireland', *R.I.A. Proc.* XLIII (1936), 41-76.
[7] *Medieval Ireland* (2nd ed.), pp. 417-21; cf. pp. 412-13.
[8] *Ibid.* pp. 403-7; cf. 'The English and Ostmen in Ireland', *E.H.R.* XXIII (1908), 209-19.

The second edition of *Medieval Ireland* provoked a more learned study of the technicalities of the problem than had yet appeared. This formed part of a review article by Mr H. G. Richardson.[1] In it the evidence, especially of the justiciary rolls, was meticulously examined and the conclusion reached:

> The evidence seems to suggest that in the early fourteenth century the disabilities of Irishmen in the royal courts were on their way to becoming technical points of procedure.[2]

In 1949 Professor Otway-Ruthven published documents concerning the negotiations of c.1277-80 in which the archbishop of Cashel and other prominent Irishmen endeavoured to get a general grant of English law.[3] This was merely a preliminary to the survey of the whole question which came from her pen in the following year.[4] Her conclusion was:

> Though... the Irishman not admitted to English law was neither rightless nor deprived of legal protection, the position for those resident amongst the English must have had many practical inconveniences.[5]

In 1960 some of the political and personal background to the negotiations of 1277-80 was further elucidated by Professor Aubrey Gwynn.[6]

If a certain difference of emphasis is discernible between the quotations just given from Mr Richardson and Professor Otway-Ruthven, it can probably be explained by the former's preoccupation, at the time of writing, with the opinions of Edmund Curtis. At all events, the present account in many respects can only be a reflection, with glosses and expansions, of the work of these two scholars. Yet of that work one general criticism—admittedly marginal—can be made. It is that, unlike Richey and Orpen, they have not made much effort to see whether understanding of the subject can be increased from native Irish sources. In the first place, this means the Brehon law. The six volumes of

---

[1] 'English institutions in medieval Ireland', *I.H.S.* I (1938-9), 382-93, at pp. 386-91.   [2] *Ibid.* p. 390.
[3] 'The request of the Irish for English law, 1277-80', *I.H.S.* VI (1948-9), 261-70.
[4] 'The native Irish and English law in medieval Ireland', *I.H.S.* VII (1950-1), 1-16.   [5] *Ibid.* p. 14.
[6] 'Edward I and the proposed purchase of English law for the Irish, c.1276-80', *R. Hist. Soc. Trans.* 5th ser., X (1960), 111-27.

THE STATUS OF THE NATIVE IRISH 193

the *Ancient laws and institutions of Ireland* (1865-1901) were an over-ambitious and premature project and historians not specially versed in the old Irish language could well be excused from using them, especially when the inadequacy of the translations provided became known.

In 1929, however, Mr Richardson and Professor Sayles pointed out that a technical term of the Brehon law, *cin comfocuis*, had found its way into the earliest extant parliamentary legislation of the English lordship.[1] Six years before, in 1923, an aspect of Irish law, the law of status, had been clarified by a new translation of relevant texts, with commentary, published by Eoin MacNeill.[2] In 1941 Professor D. A. Binchy re-edited one of these texts, *Críth Gablach*. The notes and legal glossary appended to his edition have frequently been relied upon in this account for guidance in the relevant fields of Irish law.

Here the economic and tenurial basis of the relationship between the conquered Irish and their lords, as clarified by reference to the Brehon law, will first be discussed. The apparent absence at this period of literary evidence of the feelings of the native Irish towards English law, such as is known to exist for the sixteenth century,[3] gives the *Remonstrance* to Pope John XXII particular importance. It will therefore be used in the second part of the discussion as a guide to the aspects of the treatment of the Irish at English law that were most resented by them. Afterwards there will be an account of the grants and projected extensions of English law, with a final word on the fast-disappearing third race, the Ostmen.

The basis of the relationship between the conquered Irish and their lords

At the bottom of the scheme of status set out in the Brehon treatise *Críth Gablach* was the *sen-cléithe*, a hereditary serf or villein who passed as an appurtenance with the land.[4] Next came the *bothach*

---

[1] 'The Irish parliaments of Edward I', *R.I.A. Proc.* XXXVIII (1929), 128-47, at p. 142 (replaced now by *The Irish parliament*, p. 292).
[2] 'Ancient Irish law: the law of status or franchise', *R.I.A. Proc.* XXXVI (1923), 265-316.
[3] E.g. A. S. Green, *The making of Ireland and its undoing* (Dublin, 1908), p. 280.
[4] *Críth Gablach*, ed. Binchy, p. 105. It need hardly be said that the summary given above is much simplified (though not, it is hoped, too much distorted), as well as deliberately anglicized.

and the *fuidir*, tenants-at-will who were bound to render uncertain services to their lord, but who were not bound to the soil and could terminate the relationship.[1] After nine generations had lived on the same land, however, a *bothach* or *fuidir* family sank to the *sen-cléithe* level.[2] *Sen-cléithe*, *bothach* and *fuidir* were all members of the unfree classes. Amongst freemen there was the relationship of *célsine*, clientship. The *céle giallnaí* or *dóer-chéle* received from his lord both a grant of stock or land and a payment equal to his honour-price (*énech*), thereby conceding to the lord a share in legal compensatory payments made to him for injuries inflicted.[3] He rendered an annual food-tribute and other fixed services. This relationship was essentially contractual and terminable. In a higher form of clientship, *sóer-rath*, there was no honour-price payment, but a grant of stock by the lord, repaid by heavy payments of rent or interest by the *sóer-chéle*, who was also bound to some personal attendance on the lord.

The invaders were from the free classes of their own society. The words they used for the native unfree classes were *betagius*, *nativus* and *hibernicus*. *Villanus* was practically unknown in medieval Ireland. *Betagius* (betagh) was more common than *nativus*, which none the less was in occasional use throughout the medieval period. *Hibernicus* was used technically to mean an unfree Irishman, as well as used generally to mean an Irishman. The classical instance is a case in 1300:

Walterus hibernicus est de cognomine des Offyns, et ipse Walterus et pater suus fuerunt molendinarii ipsius Johannis et patris sui apud Fersketh, set non hibernici predicti Johannis.[4]

'Here', as the editor, Mills, wrote, '*hibernicus* is used in two distinct senses in the same sentence.'[5] It is not intended, however, to follow Mills's convention of using *hibernicus* for an unfree

[1] *Críth Gablach*, pp. 78, 93.
[2] *Ibid.* pp. 13, lines 326–7: *co nómad n-aó*. This is Professor Binchy's interpretation on p. 93; on p. 105 he renders it *ten* generations, meaning, presumably, that the tenth is no longer free to move. MacNeill thought the phrase meant 'nine nines' of years, i.e. eighty-one years.
[3] *Críth Gablach*, pp. 80, 96–8.
[4] *C.J.R. 1295–1303*, p. ix.
[5] *Ibid.*; but an alternative interpretation of the passage cannot be wholly excluded (p. 200, n. 7, below).

THE STATUS OF THE NATIVE IRISH

Irishman and translating it only when the racial sense alone is evidently meant.[1] The usual derivation of *betagius* has been from *bíatach*, 'a food-provider'.[2] But Professor Binchy suggested a possible alternative from the Irish technical term *bothach*: the *bothach*, it will be remembered, was a tenant-at-will whose right to leave the land might be lost by long residence of his family upon it.[3] The betagh more precisely corresponded to the *sen-cléithe* of the Irish scheme, but it is conceivable that many of the *bothach* and *fuidir* classes were forced into betaghry by the native lords or their post-invasion successors and in any event there is always a distinct measure of uncertainty about the fidelity of the Irish law tracts to actual conditions, especially in the twelfth and thirteenth centuries.[4] A betagh was bound to the land. A grant of land might specify *omnia servicia betagiorum suorum hibernicorum*.[5] Services of betaghs might be had by a creditor of their lord upon a writ of *elegit*.[6] A constant threat to such a system of unfree tenure was the acquisition by men hitherto personally free of land hitherto held as unfree. In 1309 the Dublin exchequer had to decide between two claimants to twenty-seven acres of land held *in betagio* of the king. One claimant was Irish and traced his claim from his father and a brother; the other was English and claimed in right of his wife (who was apparently the sister of the Irish claimant). The court preferred the Irishman, who was *verus betagius* and bound to the soil, whereas the Englishman

pro voluntate sua ammovere potest et elongare bona sua et catalla extra tenementum domini regis predictum quo minus eidem domino regi

[1] In any event, *hibernicus* has been let stand in the *Calendar* in cases where the Irishman was a tenant or dependant (like Walter the miller mentioned in the above quotation) but was certainly not, in the ordinary sense, unfree: e.g. *C.J.R. 1308–14*, pp. 230–1.
[2] So Orpen, II, 330, n. 5, and references; Curtis, *Medieval Ireland*, p. 417; Otway-Ruthven, *I.H.S.* VII, 7. The derivation from *bíatach* has been urged again by L. Price, 'The origin of the word *betagius*', *Ériu*, XX (1966), 185–90; and it may be that there was confusion between *bíatach* and *bothach*. Dr Price's argument, that *bíatach* underwent a change of meaning in the thirteenth century, is not wholly convincing, however. See Additional Note, p. 213.
[3] *Críth Gablach*, p. 13.
[4] Were there, for example, Irish equivalents to the 'new tenures' in Wales? Cf. T. Jones Pierce, 'Social and historical aspects of the Welsh laws', *Welsh history review* (Special number, 1963: 'The Welsh laws'), pp. 33–49.
[5] J.I. 18 Edw. I (no. 13), in P.R.O.I., RC. 7/2, *Cal. plea rolls*, II, 255.
[6] *C.J.R. 1295–1303*, pp. 356–7.

responderi poterit de firma sua et aliias serviciis de predicta terra debitis et consuetis.[1]

It appears that by the early fourteenth century, around Dublin at any rate, the betaghs 'held their land at fixed rents, apparently not very excessive, and rendered service definitely regulated by custom, and generally little more than nominal in amount'.[2]

Nativus was a technical term of English law for one *adscriptitius glebe* and it was in use in Ireland beside *betagius*, probably through the influence of the writ of naifty.[3] As early as 1204, the justiciar was empowered to issue the writ and the capture of Dublin (1170) was set as the period of limitation.[4] Both the writ *de nativo habendo* and the closely related, and generally interlocutory, writ *de libertate probanda* were sent to Ireland in the register of writs dispatched in 1227.[5] In a case in 1290 eleven Irishmen brought the writ *de libertate probanda*, which suggests that the ordinary procedure of English law in this matter was followed in Ireland.[6] In Ireland the words *hibernicus* and *nativus* might be coupled:

Jurati dicunt quod predictus Willelmus et eius antecessores sunt hibernici et nativi predicti prioris. Ideo consideratum est quod predictus prior habeat prefatum Willelmum tanquam hibernicum et nativum suum cum tota sequela sua et omnibus rebus suis.[7]

In 1312 an action of trespass was brought against a sheriff for having failed to arrest two men named McArny, alleged to have been fugitive Irishmen of the complainant. The jury declared that they were *meri anglici*. In view of the form of the names of the men concerned it is possible that *anglici* was being used for Irishmen who were not unfree *nativi* or *betagii*.[8]

Many Irishmen were tenants or dependants of English lords without being bound to the soil. On the manors of the archbishop of Dublin there was a class of Irish *firmarii* apparently not so

[1] Mem. 3 Edw. II, m. 7.
[2] Mills, *R.S.A.I. Jn.* xx, 54; cf. extents in *Red book of Kildare*, pp. 99–101, 121–2.
[3] For the writ in general, R. C. Van Caeneghem, *Royal writs in England from the conquest to Glanvill* (S.S. 77), pp. 336–43.
[4] *Rot. litt. pat.* p. 47.
[5] Maitland, *Collected papers*, II, 132.
[6] J.I. 18 Edw. I (no. 14), in P.R.O.I., RC. 7/2, *Cal. plea rolls*, II, 349; cf. Van Caeneghem, *op. cit.* pp. 343–4.
[7] C.P., M. 31–2 Edw. I, in P.R.O.I., RC. 8/1, *Cal. mem. rolls*, I, 228.
[8] J.R. 6–7 Edw. II, m. 12.

THE STATUS OF THE NATIVE IRISH

bound.[1] Perhaps it was such an Irish *firmarius* who answered a messenger of his lord in 1305 or 1306:

I and my household have so much labour in the service of G. de B., our lord, in divers his works and labours, that I cannot bear this more, nor will bear it henceforth,

and decamped with his wife, household and cattle to the land and protection of another Englishman, 'who did not love G. de B. and his people'.[2] There were even Irish free tenants, either survivors of the higher classes of Gaelic society or betaghs or *firmarii* who had risen in the world.[3] Further, outside such a settled neighbourhood as Dublin there was also a system of 'avowries', rather like that in Wales and Chester: Irishmen paid English lords small sums to be under their protection.[4] The 'avowries' may well in part reflect the remnants of semi-nomadic pastoral elements in society, moving with their cattle from place to place.[5] In one instance, when their lord was slain, a number of Irish tenants, for fear of those who had slain him, took themselves to another Englishman, whom he had knighted, and 'besought him to admit them to his protection and avowry'. He agreed, 'wherefore they brought all their goods and other chattels with their wives and households' to his manor. He then directed them to go to waste-lands held by him in an adjoining county, and arranged that they should be massacred *en route*.[6] Such Irishmen as these, while feeling the need for an English protector (however unfortunate their choice), were certainly not, in the ordinary sense, unfree. Their action was not unlike that of a freeman in the native system in becoming a *céle*, a client. And that is to say nothing of those Irish chiefs, rulers of semi-autonomous areas, who were loosely dependent on such great lords as the earl of

---

[1] Mills, *R.S.A.I. Jn.* xx, 55.
[2] *C.J.R. 1305–7*, pp. 326–7; cf. p. 379 (lord fails to recover Irishman who had left him for another because he 'did not fully pay his wages'; but the status of this 'hired' Irishman is puzzling—he passed on a conveyance of the lands).
[3] Mills, *R.S.A.I. Jn.* xx, 59–60.
[4] *Red book of Ormond*, pp. 40–1; Nugent, *R.S.A.I. Jn.* LXXXV, 74; R. A. Griffiths, 'Royal government in the southern counties of Wales, 1422–1485' (unpublished Ph.D. thesis, University of Bristol, 1962), pp. 86–7; R. Stewart-Brown, 'The advowries of Chester', *E.H.R.* XXIX (1914), 41–55.
[5] I am indebted to Dr Griffiths for this view of the matter, expressed to me in correspondence.
[6] *C.J.R. 1308–14*, pp. 230–1.

Ulster.[1] Yet, the general rule, where capacity to sue in the king's courts was concerned, was that any Irishman, of whatever consequence, was theoretically in the same position as a betagh.

The legal capacity of Irishmen in civil proceedings

The *Remonstrance* addressed by Domnall Ua Néill and other Irish chiefs to Pope John XXII in 1317 was intended to suit the purposes of the Bruce brothers, and its literary form may, it has recently been suggested, have been the work of Bernard of Linton, abbot of Arbroath and author of the Declaration of Arbroath.[2] Nevertheless, there can be little question that its substance was provided by the Irish chiefs and is authentic.[3] It contains statements of four legal grievances which can serve as headings to the present inquiry.

The first complaint concerning English law in the *Remonstrance* reads as follows:

Quod omni homini non hibernico licet super quacunque indifferenter actione convenire hibernicum quemcumque; sed hibernicus quilibet, sive clericus sit sive laicus, solis prelatis exceptis, ab omni repellitur actione eo ipso.

Theoretically the tenure of an Irishman was a matter for his lord's court and injury to his goods and chattels could be the subject of an action by the lord alone.[4] The absence of manorial records precludes discussion of the former matter. But since an injury to his Irishman was usually, in fact as well as in theory, one to his lord also, the lord was generally anxious to exercise his right of action, and actions by lords for goods taken from their Irishmen

---

[1] Otway-Ruthven, *I.H.S.* VII, 3; Orpen, IV, 148–9; Nugent, *R.S.A.I. Jn.* LXXXV, 74 (payments of 'fees' and 'gifts' to Irish chiefs); *C.J.R. 1305–7*, pp. 186–7.

[2] R. G. Nicholson, 'Magna Carta and the Declaration of Arbroath', *Univ. of Edinburgh Journal* (Autumn 1965), pp. 140–44 at p. 143.

[3] The text is found only in a continuation of the work known as *Fordun's Scotichronicon*. It has been printed in two editions of Fordun: ed. Thomas Hearne (5 vols; Oxford, 1722), III, 908–26, and ed. W. Goodall (2 vols; Edinburgh, 1759), II, 259–67. The text given above is based on these editions, with reference also to two of the manuscripts used by Hearne: B.M., Harleian 712 and Royal 13 E X. English translations have appeared in: R. King, *Primer of the church history of Ireland* (3rd ed., Dublin, 1845–51), II, 1119–35; *Irish historical documents*, ed. E. Curtis and R. B. McDowell (London, 1943), pp. 38–46. In general, see Curtis, *Medieval Ireland*, pp. 191–3, and Watt, 'Negotiations between Edward II and John XXII concerning Ireland', *I.H.S.* X, 4.

[4] Richardson, *I.H.S.* I, 388; Otway-Ruthven, *I.H.S.* VII, 10–12.

THE STATUS OF THE NATIVE IRISH

are therefore found on the rolls fairly frequently.[1] An interesting example is a plaint against a sheriff for having wrongfully distrained chattels of plaintiff's Irishman. The sheriff's unsuccessful defence was that the Irishman also held of another lord (B), that the sheriff had to levy money from B, that he had tried to do so from the holding held by the Irishman from B, that he had met with difficulty in doing this and consequently thought it in order to distrain the Irishman's chattels found on the land he held from the plaintiff.[2] A lord might sue for trespass to the person of his Irishman.[3] But of course an action might fail if the writ did not specify that those who suffered the immediate injury were plaintiff's Irishmen, since no such action lay to him if they were free Englishmen.[4] An Irishman might be joined as plaintiff with his lord, and such cases may well indicate one who was otherwise free, perhaps one who had bought his way into the 'avowry' of an Englishman.[5] There is a certain parallel in these connections to the receit of a lord in matters of warranty, though there of course the defence was in question.[6] Even if an Irishman's lord had himself done him injury the Irishman might sometimes have a remedy, through the king being joined with him.[7]

The manner in which an Irishman's action was defeated in practice was by the defendant alleging that he was Irish. This peremptory exception was akin to the ordinary English exception of villeinage. A typical form in Ireland was

quod non tenetur ei inde respondere, eo quod est hibernicus et non de libero sanguine.[8]

In the case of the exception of villeinage, according to *Britton*, the procedural effect varied according to the form of action employed.[9] Upon writs *qe touchent la proprete et le dreit* judgment would go against a demandant who refused to let the exception be tried. But in the possessory assizes the demandant could refuse to

---
[1] E.g. *C.J.R. 1295–1303*, pp. 221, 426; *1305–7*, p. 479.
[2] *C.J.R. 1295–1303*, p. 40.
[3] *Ibid.* pp. 333–4; *1305–7*, pp. 56, 175–7, 263–4, 415.
[4] *C.J.R. 1305–7*, p. 198. Quaere, how did this apply if procedure was by bill? Cf. p. 74, above.
[5] *C.J.R. 1295–1303*, p. 162; J.R. 7 Edw. II (no. 105), m. 19.
[6] S. J. Bailey, 'Warranties of land in the thirteenth century', 9 *C.L.J.* p. 86, n. 26 and references.   [7] Richardson, *I.H.S.* I, 390 and cases there mentioned.
[8] Davies, *Works*, ed. Grosart, II, 66 (from roll of the eyre of Louth, 1301).
[9] *Britton*, ed. Nichols, I, 326–7.

allow his status to be left to the assize; in that event, if the tenant would not waive the exception, the court could, acting *ex officio*, take the assize upon the disseisin. The few relevant Irish cases do not make practice altogether clear. In one assize of novel disseisin the court seems to have treated the exception according to the rules suggested by *Britton* for a writ of right; in another the rule for the possessory assizes seems to have been followed.[1] In a plaint of assault, it seems to have been thought that only the question of status should go to a jury.[2] In any event, the most clear-cut and effective reply to the exception was the production of a charter of enfranchisement or a grant of English law.[3] In this connection, a curious point was raised upon an assize of mort d'ancestor in the Dublin bench in 1298. The tenant, the archbishop of Tuam, alleged that the demandant was Irish. In replication it was said that a charter having the force of enfranchisement had been given by the archbishop's predecessor, but had since been accidentally destroyed. Could the demandant be admitted to prove this story? The court reserved its opinion and the result has not been traced.[4]

There is evidence that the exception of Irishry was regarded as *odiosa* so that, if the jury found that the plaintiff was English, the defendant was committed to gaol;[5] simple amercement was also a possibility.[6] Such punitive action may also have followed where the exception was that the plaintiff was defendant's own Irishman and the jury, though confirming that he was Irish, found against the defendant's claim over him.[7] The existence of such deterrents to pleading the exception must have encouraged Irishmen to try their luck by bringing actions. Certainly, there are cases of parties with unmistakably Irish names appearing as plaintiffs, though the possibility that they had grants of English law must be remembered.[8] It is easy to understand that one Irishman might

[1] *C.J.R. 1295–1303*, pp. 158, 336–7.
[2] *Ibid.* pp. 453–4.   [3] On these, pp. 206–10, below.
[4] C.P., M. 26–7 Edw. I, in P.R.O.I., RC. 7/5, *Cal. plea rolls*, v, 413–14.
[5] *C.J.R. 1295–1303*, pp. 158, 453–4; *1308–14*, p. 41.   [6] J.R. 6–7 Edw. II, m. 68.
[7] This is a possible alternative explanation of the passage quoted above, p. 194, from *C.J.R. 1295–1303*, pp. ix, 342–3.
[9] Otway-Ruthven, *I.H.S.* vii, 11, especially references in n. 39; but the demandant in *Cal. doc. Ire. 1252–84*, 360, was the archbishop of Tuam, who was probably privileged by reason of his office (p. 206, below), and *C.J.R. 1295–1303*, p. 209, must have involved privilege, for the proper handling of payments of a subsidy was in question.

safely implead another.[1] The Irish close roll for the fourteenth year of Edward II noted payments for writs made by persons named Ohalwy, McGildowy, McCody, Idefucoboll, Onethe, Oharill and Gilbarry.[2]

An Irish *defendant* apparently suffered only one disability: he could not be admitted to wager of law. In the middle of the thirteenth century this had been the subject of complaint by the archbishop of Cashel and his suffragans.[3] Wager of law no doubt declined in importance during the thirteenth century, in Ireland as in England, but the objection that a defendant was Irish could still appear in reply to an attempt at wager under Edward II.[4] The *Remonstrance* is silent on the point. Otherwise, Irish defendants in the king's courts appear to have been under no legal disability.[5]

The status of the Irish in the criminal law

The second legal complaint in the *Remonstrance* concerned the punishment of those who killed Irishmen and may be used to introduce the question of the position of the Irish in criminal law.

Item sicut plerumque accidere solet, quando aliquis Anglicus perfide et dolose interficit hominem hibernicum, quantumcumque nobilem et innocentem, sive clericum sive laicum, sive regularem sive secularem, etiam si prelatus hibernicus interfectus fuerit, nulla correctio vel emenda fit in dicta curia de tali nephario occisore ...

When in 1228 King John's charter of English law was ordered to be read to the magnates of Ireland, the death of Irishmen was already presenting a problem, which the letters close declared had been reserved for further consideration.[6] What was decided is unknown, but by the end of the century an Irish statute could state that *anglicorum et hybernicorum occisio diversos modos postulat*

---

[1] All parties to an assize are called Murthy: J.R. 6–7 Edw. II, mm. 31, 72.
[2] *Cal. rot. pat. Hib.* pp. 29–30; cf. p. 203, n. 3, below.
[3] *Cal. papal letters, 1198–1304*, p. 283.
[4] J.R. 6–7 Edw. II, m. 76d.
[5] E.g. J.R. 7 Edw. II (no. 105), m. 15d (three McBrens answer by Reginald McCotyr, apparently a *narrator*); J.R. 11 Edw. II (no. 117), m. 2 (John Ocarran, defendant in an action of trespass).
[6] *Close rolls, 1227–31*, p. 45; cf. p. 3, above.

puniendi.[1] An indictment for the death of an Irishman was met as follows:

[accused] venit et non dedicit mortem predictam; sed dicit quod [the deceased] fuit hibernicus et non de libero sanguine et de bono et malo ponit se super patriam.[2]

If the jury found that the deceased was Irish the accused was acquitted. It is not surprising that a coroner's jury might be charged with having falsely found that a dead man was Irish,[3] or a coroner himself charged with accepting a bribe to secure such a finding.[4] Despite all this, it is possible that occasionally an Englishman did hang for the death of an Irishman.[5]

This state of the law is more intelligible when it is remembered that at native law the penalty for homicide was *éraic*, a payment akin to *wergild*.[6] This law was acknowledged and accepted by the invaders inasmuch as the lord of an Irishman who had been slain (though not the kin) might sue the slayer for compensation. This was a civil proceeding and acquittal on a charge of felonious killing on the grounds that the deceased was Irish did not automatically lead to the payment, unless, perhaps, the deceased was the king's own Irishman.[7] The writ used to the sheriff has been printed by Mr Richardson:

Precipimus tibi quod si, per inquisicionem quam fieri facies, tibi constiterit quod A. interficit B. Hibernicum [C] et quod idem B. fidelis homo ipsius fuit tempore quo interfectus fuerit et ad pacem nostram, tunc ipsum distringas ad solucionem mortis predicti B. eidem [C] secundum consuetudinem Hibernie sine dilacione faciendam.[8]

The amount recoverable in this way seems to have become fixed at five marks and forty pence.[9] In the charter of liberties given by

---

[1] *Stat. Ire. John–Hen. V*, p. 210.
[2] Davies, *Works*, II, 70 (from roll of the eyre of Louth, 1301); cf. *C.J.R. 1305–7*, p. 520, *1308–14*, pp. 203, 291; J.R. 8–9 Edw. II, m. 5; *Liber primus Kilkenniensis*, ed. C. McNeill (Irish MSS. Comm.), pp. 6–9.
[3] *C.J.R. 1308–14*, p. 168. In this case it was found that the jury did, honestly but mistakenly, believe that the deceased was Irish.
[4] *Ibid.* p. 309. He was found guilty.
[5] J.R. 8–9 Edw. II, m. 2 d (John Bodenham, who had slain Gilbert McCurryn).
[6] *Crith Gablach*, p. 86; *Ancient laws of Ireland*, III, 98–106.
[7] *C.J.R. 1308–14*, pp. 203–4 (in part, Davies, *Works*, II, 69).
[8] *I.H.S.* I, 387 (from B.M., MS. Lansdowne 652, f. 200).
[9] References are given by Richardson, *I.H.S.* I, 387, n. 2; to them may be added J.R. 7 Edw. II (no. 105), m. 18 d.

Geoffrey de Joinville to his magnates of Meath there was a provision that they might detain an Englishman, who had killed an Irishman and was found with the mainour, until compensation had been paid.[1]

There is certainly some measure of exaggeration in this second legal complaint in the *Remonstrance*.[2] It is true, however, that an Englishman who killed an Irishman, *quantumcumque nobilem et innocentem*, might hope to escape with impunity, if there was no lord to sue for compensation. There is, as against this, a solitary plaint in which the king joined a widow suing on the death of her Irish husband while he was going to the king's court at Dublin 'to sue writs on divers trespasses done to him'—the object of the journey is itself highly significant.[3] The element of contempt may here be relevant; in any event it was found that payment had already been made to the Irishman's lord, the bishop of Ardfert.

Wrongs such as robbery and burglary in which the victims were Irish were sometimes matter for indictment. Usually, though not always, the Irishman's lord was specified in the indictments.[4]

In the Irish parliament of 1278 it was enacted:

En dreit des Irreys udyfs, qe mauveys genz sunt e suvent se mespernent encuntre la pes, asentu est par les riches hommes qe il seent justicez par lur lignages qe sunt a la pes, si les lignages reduablement ne puissent mustrer qe il ne les pussent chastier ne justicer, issint qe les kynkonges curgent sicum il soleyent fere.[5]

This obscure statute appears to have meant that the Irish of the semi-autonomous areas were to be the responsibility of the heads of their clans, if these were at peace with the English and could not show inability to punish them, but that the alternative of the native system of liability of the kin in order (*kynkonges, cin comfocuis*) was not excluded. An act of 1310 made a similar provision that every *cheif de graunt lygnage* should punish those of his lineage, but it seems to have been concerned with the great Anglo-Irish, rather than native, families, and the text is very

[1] P. 134, above.
[2] No evidence has been found on the death of Irish prelates.
[3] *C.J.R. 1305–7*, pp. 413–14; Richardson, *I.H.S.* I, 390.
[4] *Hibernicus* of the king: Cambridge U.L., Add. MS. 3104, f. 49*v*; of other named lords: *C.J.R. 1308–14*, pp. 287, 297, 298, and J.R. 11 Edw. II (no. 119), m. 3; of lords not named: *C.J.R. 1295–1303*, p. 68, and *1308–14*, pp. 175–6.
[5] Richardson and Sayles, *The Irish parliament*, p. 292.

defective.[1] The later history of *kynkonges* or *kincogus* was a long one, but lies outside our scope here.[2]

Generally speaking, an Irishman was justiciable in his lord's court and if he was charged before the justiciar he was handed over to his lord.[3] In certain circumstances, however, Irishmen were brought to book in the king's courts, even if they had an English lord. Escape and outlawry[4] seem to have been amongst these. On this account, and since there were many lordless Irish in the marches, the justiciary rolls frequently record indictments of Irishmen.[5] The punishment meted out to Irish felons departed from normal English practice. It was stated in 1316 that, although an Irishman convicted of the death of an Englishman or of arson was customarily hanged,

> Hibernicus de latrocinio vel depredacione cuicunque anglico vel hibernico facto convictus ad voluntatem sui judicis relinqui solet redimendus, vel ultimo supplicio condempnandus.[6]

But this law, it was complained, had not been faithfully observed and fines had been permitted, even for the death of English and for arson. To have a gallows to hang Irishmen seems to have been a special franchise and, as a rule, lords did not hang Irish felons, but admitted them to a pecuniary fine or ransom.[7]

Refusal of dower to Irish widows

The remaining two legal grievances of the *Remonstrance* are of lesser scope and importance. The first is the refusal of dower to Irish widows of Englishmen:

> Item omnis mulier hibernica, sive nobilis vel alia, que nubuit anglico cuicumque, post decessum mariti, tertia parte terrarum ac possessionum viri sui, eo ipso quod hibernica est, omnino privatur.

This was also mentioned in 1290 when the archbishop of Armagh petitioned in parliament for English law to be granted to a named

---

[1] *Stat. Ire. John–Hen. V*, p. 266.

[2] 'His Maiesties Directions for the Irish Courts, 1622', ed. Hand and Treadwell, *Anal. Hib.* 'Introduction' and Direction no. 34 (forthcoming).

[3] Richardson, *I.H.S.* I, 387–8; e.g. *C.J.R. 1295–1303*, p. 34.

[4] *C.J.R. 1295–1303*, pp. 95, 254–5; cf. the Irish statute of 1278 concerning the escape of Irish; Richardson and Sayles, *The Irish parliament*, p. 292.

[5] J.R. 8–9 Edw. II is especially rich in them.

[6] *Foedera* (Rec. comm. ed.), II, 1, 293–4.

[7] Cole, *Documents*, p. 72; *C.J.R. 1295–1303*, p. 95; Richardson, *I.H.S.* I, 388.

THE STATUS OF THE NATIVE IRISH 205

Irishwoman in order to protect her from the custom *quod mulieres Hybernice non recipiunt dotem*.[1] There may, in fact, have been more than one grievance in connection with dower. In Wales, the Welsh were not permitted to grant dower; but there the problem seems to have concerned the English widows of Welshmen.[2] The Irish complaints may have meant no more than that an Irish widow was open to the exception that she was Irish, if she attempted to obtain dower by bringing an appropriate action. Thus in 1295 the exception was pleaded to a writ of dower before the Dublin bench

[demandant] est hibernica et non de quinque progeniebus hibernicis quibus licite est portare brevia in curia domini regis.[3]

The testamentary incapacity of the native Irish

The last grievance concerned the testamentary incapacity of the Irish:

Item anglici, ubi possunt hibernicum violenter opprimere, nullo modo permittunt quod in ultimis voluntatibus hibernici [*sic*] de suis rebus disponat, aut testamentum condat quoquomodo; ymmo omnia bona ipsius appropriant sibiipsis, privantes ecclesiam jure suo, et sanguinem ab antiquo liberum facientes auctoritate propria violenter servilem.

This was an old complaint with the Irish church. In 1255 it was brought to the king's attention by the archbishop of Tuam and others.[4] It seems that the complaint was against the seizure by lords of the chattels of Irishmen on the grounds that they were unfree: *sanguinem ab antiquo liberum facientes... servilem*. The lack of adequate surviving records of the medieval Irish ecclesiastical jurisdictions makes it impossible to say much more.

The partial enfranchisement of the native Irish

We have seen something of the ordinary disabilities of the native Irish at English law. There were, however, certain classes and individuals of Gaelic race who enjoyed English law as a privilege.

---

[1] Cole, *Documents*, p. 58.   [2] Davies, *History*, LI, 152.
[3] C.P., M. 23–4 Edw. I, in P.R.O.I., RC. 7/3, *Cal. plea rolls*, III, 450; for the 'five bloods', see below, p. 206.
[4] *Close rolls, 1254–6*, p. 214; cf. Sheehy, *Pontificia Hibernica*, ii, no. 417 (1256). The complaint may lie behind some of the Irish ecclesiastical *gravamina* at the Council of Vienne: *ed*. R. Ehrle, *Archiv für Literatur und Kirchengeschichte*, IV (1888), 382, 398–9.

From a very early date this was the case with the 'five bloods'—the royal families of Ua Néill of Ulster, Ua Maíl Shechnaill of Meath, Ua Conchobuir of Connaught, Ua Briain of Munster, and Mac Murchada of Leinster.[1] Thus, in a record which has already been quoted, it was said

[demandant] est hibernica et non de quinque progeniebus hibernicis quibus licite est portare brevia in curia domini regis.[2]

That Irish bishops and prelates enjoyed a degree of privilege *ex officio* is undoubted, but its scope is less certain. Although the *Remonstrance*, in reference to the exception of Irishry, uses the vague phrase *solis prelatis exceptis*, a petition from Irish ecclesiastics, probably *temp.* Edward I, suggests (the text is now very defective) that the only exemption was in favour of bishops litigating on behalf of their church.[3] Apart from these two classes, there is evidence that enfranchisement of individual Irishmen occurred at quite an early date in the history of the lordship. In 1299 a charter granted by William I Marshal ninety years before was produced in the justiciar's court by the great-grandson of the original grantee, in order to answer the exception that he was Irish.[4] The king, however, generally reserved the right to grant charters of English law to himself in his English chancery. But any lord might enfranchise one of his Irishmen as regards himself, so that he would be unable to plead the exception against the man thus freed.[5] Within the towns there was little discrimination until a later period.[6] So it was stated in 1307:

Whereas by the custom used hitherto as well in said burgh as in other cities and burghs in this land, Irishmen made burgesses are free in the same as Englishmen, especially as to the disposition of their goods and tenements which they had in such burghs and cities . . .[7]

It seems to have been the case that, though individual betaghs were unfree, their communities had some sort of collective legal

---

[1] Otway-Ruthven, *I.H.S.* VII, 6; Davies, *Works*, II, 65-6 (from various rolls).
[2] P. 205, above.
[3] B.M., MS. Cotton Augustus II, no. 104 (printed by Sheehy, *Arch. hib.* XXIII, 173).
[4] *C.J.R. 1295-1303*, p. 271.   [5] E.g. *C.J.R. 1305-7*, pp. 321-3.
[6] Curtis, *Medieval Ireland*, pp. 412-13; cf. Richardson, *I.H.S.* IV, 363 (a review of M. D. O'Sullivan, *Old Galway*).
[7] *C.J.R. 1305-7*, p. 352; I have substituted 'Irishmen' for *hibernici*, retained in the printed calendar.

capacity and, if the king's own, could sue in his ordinary courts.[1]

In 1253 the king granted a petition that certain faithful Irishmen should be exempt from the effect of the usual exception, if pleaded against them: the justiciar was not to permit them to be prevented

quin possint terras vendicare in quibus jus habent sicut quilibet anglicus; quia ... injustum est ... quod excepcione, qua repellantur Ibernenses a vendicacione terrarum aliis, repellantur.[2]

One of the few extant texts of a letter of Edward I as lord of Ireland before becoming king is a grant of English law, conferred at the request of Walter de Burgh, earl of Ulster.[3] Early in Edward's reign, from about 1277 to about 1280, a determined effort was made by the Irish of Munster, under the leadership of David MacCarwell, archbishop of Cashel, to purchase a grant of English law.[4] Though these negotiations ultimately broke down, there was no expression of unwillingness on the part of the king to make such a grant, or to make grants to individual petitioners. Such individual grants appear to have issued from the English chancery, for the chief governor was not usually authorized to make them. The sum eventually offered in 1280 for a general grant was ten thousand marks and a petitioner in 1290 alleged that in a single day the king had obtained three thousand pounds, apparently for a grant to a class of persons.[5] Yet enrolments of such grants on the patent rolls are very few. They are most numerous for the years 1290 to 1293: seventeen, affecting twenty-six named persons. In eight instances (seventeen persons) the grant was for the life of the grantee only,[6] although one such grantee later secured an extension in favour of his children.[7] In one case the children of a specified wife only were included,[8] and in seven (eight persons) there was a general grant to the named grantee and his children.[9]

[1] *Ibid.* pp. 180–1.   [2] *Close rolls, 1251–3*, pp. 458–9.
[3] Cambridge U.L. Add. MS. 3104, f. 50.
[4] Otway-Ruthven, *I.H.S.* vi, 261–70, is the fullest account, with select documents; Gwynn, *R. Hist. Soc. Trans.* 5th ser. x, 111–27, provides more general background; cf. also Richardson and Sayles, *The Irish parliament*, pp. 290–2.
[5] Cole, *Documents*, p. 69; the petitioner was an Ostman (pp. 210–12, below) and the letter referred to was probably to benefit his race (if there is anything in the story).
[6] *Cal. pat. rolls, 1281–92*, pp. 364, 366, 370, 380, 427; *1292–1301*, pp. 21, 23, 57.
[7] *Cal. pat. rolls, 1281–92*, p. 439.   [8] *Ibid.* p. 368.
[9] *Ibid.* pp. 419, 420, 462 (*bis*), 487; *1292–1301*, pp. 22, 28.

About 1296, a petitioner declared that it had been shown to the king in the parliament held at Westminster in November 1295 that it was to his profit that English law should be granted to all who sought it.[1] Despite this, there was a sharp falling-off in the number of grants enrolled in the years that followed, together with an absence of any recorded demand for a wide extension, and one is forced to suggest, either that John Wogan disapproved of the extension of English law or that the legal treatment he accorded the Irish made them less anxious for formal grants. From 1296 to 1316 there are only fifteen enrolments, naming twenty-one persons. Grants for the life of the grantee only disappear after 1302[2] and, apart from one to benefit only children 'henceforth procreated',[3] the majority were for the benefit of the grantee and his posterity.[4] In two cases the original petition by chance survives.[5] In two instances, also, a petition is known to have been granted (from entries on the parliament roll) but no letters patent in consequence can be found.[6]

About the middle of the reign of Edward II the question of the Irish at English law came once more into prominence. But, whereas the initiative in 1276–80 had come from Irishmen desiring equality before the law, it now came from the English of the lordship, perturbed at the effect of the dual system in softening the rigours of the criminal law. In 1316 a petition was sent to England to complain that fines and ransoms were being taken for all felonies, even the death of Englishmen. In response to this the justiciar was ordered (8 August 1316) to gather the prelates, barons and commons together to advise on what should be done.[7] In November the appointment of Roger Mortimer as king's lieutenant gave him power to grant to Irishmen the use of English law, a power that seems to have been enjoyed by the earlier

---

[1] *Cal. doc. Ire. 1285–92*, 1174; for the date and the parliament, Richardson, *I.H.S.* IV, 363, n. 2.

[2] *Cal. pat. rolls, 1292–1301*, p. 208 (a clerk?); *1301–7*, p. 22.

[3] *1313–17*, p. 346.

[4] *1292–1301*, pp. 245, 352; *1301–7*, pp. 22, 319 (*bis*), 324, 325, 504; *1307–13*, pp. 183, 458 (*bis*); *1313–17*, p. 463.

[5] P.R.O., S.C. 8/133, no. 6621 and S.C. 8/258, no. 12875 (*Memoranda de parliamento, 1305*, no. 447), leading respectively to *Cal. pat. rolls, 1301–7*, pp. 22, 324.

[6] *Memoranda de parliamento, 1305*, no. 432; P.R.O., S.C. 9/25, m. 2 (David and John, sons of Emma the nurse of Coolock).

[7] *Foedera* (Rec. comm. ed.), II, 1, 293–4; cf. p. 204, above.

holder of the title of king's lieutenant, Gaveston, also.[1] Five grants of English law are known to have been entered on the rolls of the Irish chancery during Mortimer's chief governorship before he left Ireland in May 1318; all included the grantee's posterity.[2] Probably early in 1318, Thomas fitz John, earl of Kildare, and John de Bermingham, soon to be earl of Louth, jointly submitted a dual petition to the king.[3] Firstly, the justiciar should always be commissioned to receive to English law those Irish *qi desirent et prient estre a la pace e a la foi nostre seignur le roi*, so that they should be treated according to English law for the future. Secondly, the petitioners themselves should be empowered to receive the Irish of their lands and marches. The second part of the petition was granted in letters patent dated 7 June 1319 and at the same time the justiciar, Roger Mortimer, was also given authority to admit Irishmen to English law.[4] The rolls do not show much use of this power by Mortimer,[5] nor do they afford any evidence at all that the two earls fulfilled a clause in their letters patent that they should notify the king of any such grants made by them, to have them confirmed. Another petition about the same time requested the grant of English law to all Irish faithful to the king, saving, however, the rights of lords in their betaghs.[6]

One of the anomalies of the situation seems to have been that Irishmen admitted to the benefit of English law were no more liable to the usual penalties of the criminal law, if they offended, than they had been before. This class had thus, in a way, the best of both worlds. In 1320 the *liges gentz* of Ireland requested, firstly, that there should be no pardon for death of English except by special grace of the king, and, secondly, that the Irish who wished to come to English law should have it as to life and limb:

Et saunz ceo qe ce deux pointz soient ordeinetz, james ne serra finable pes en la dite terre de Irlaund.[7]

This law should be kept as well within liberties as outside them. In consequence of this petition, letters patent dated in the

[1] *Ibid.* II, 1, 301; cf. *Cal. rot. pat. Hib.* p. 24.
[2] *Ibid.* pp. 21, 24, 25; for an English grant in 1318, *Cal. pat. rolls, 1317–21*, p. 155.   [3] P.R.O., S.C. 8/119, no. 5944.
[4] *Cal. pat. rolls, 1317–21*, pp. 339, 342.   [5] *Cal. rot. pat. Hib.* pp. 26, 28.
[6] P.R.O., S.C. 8/177, no. 8820 (faded). Richardson, *I.H.S.* 1, 390–1, suggests that this is probably a little later in date than the petition of Kildare and Bermingham. It can hardly be later than the petition of the *liges gentz* in 1320.
[7] *Rot. parl.* 1, 386; cf. p. 29, above.

following January ordered that those Irish admitted to English law should use it as to life and limb—in other words, they should be subject to the same penalties as the English.[1] This order was to the advantage and greater security of the English of the lordship, rather than of the native Irish.[2]

Early in the next reign, under the guidance of John Darcy, there was a more general extension of English law to the Irish.[3] The ordinances made for Ireland in 1331 included one:

> Ita quod una et eadem lex fiat tam hibernicis quam anglicis, excepta servitute betagiorum penes dominos suos eodem modo quo usitatum est in Anglia de villanis.[4]

The racial distinction was thus to be ignored within the lordship, except where it coincided with that of the social system. But the measure had come too late. Fifty years before, there had been a sizeable body of native Irish anxious for English law. Twenty years later, in the Ordinances of Kilkenny, it was necessary to forbid the use of Brehon law amongst the English of the colony themselves.[5]

The Ostmen

By the end of the thirteenth century the Ostmen, as the descendants of the Scandinavian invaders of an earlier time were called, were rapidly losing their identity.[6] The Normans, and especially those who acted on the king's behalf, seem to have viewed the Ostmen with favour and accorded them substantial equality of status, despite their vigorous resistance to the actual invasion. In the towns they retained much of their old position, though in the countryside they were often in danger of degradation to the level of the Gaelic Irish. Most of the evidence concerning the legal position of the Ostmen in the period here studied has reference to those of Waterford. In 1283 the king ordered a charter of

[1] *Cal. pat. rolls, 1317–21*, p. 563.
[2] The context leaves little room to doubt the above interpretation, which is that of Mr Richardson and Professor Otway-Ruthven: *I.H.S.* I, 388, and VII, 15–16. Curtis (*Medieval Ireland*, p. 162, n. 1) understood it, however, in quite the opposite sense. See Additional Note, p. 213.
[3] The background has been given by Curtis, *Medieval Ireland*, pp. 205–6; Otway-Ruthven, *I.H.S.* VII, 16; Richardson and Sayles, *The Irish parliament*, p. 98. See Additional Note, p. 213.
[4] *Stat. Ire. John–Hen. V*, p. 324.
[5] C. XVI (Statutes of Kilkenny, 1366, c. IV).
[6] In general, Curtis, *E.H.R.* XXIII, 209–19, and *Medieval Ireland*, pp. 403–7.

THE STATUS OF THE NATIVE IRISH 211

Henry II, according the right to use English law to the Ostmen of the city and county of Waterford, to be observed in favour of named members of the family of MacGillemory and others.[1] At the Easter parliament of 1290 one Philip McGothmund sought to have his Ostman and English status confirmed, *ne de anglico et custmanno* [sic] *fiat hibernicus*.[2] Another petition at the same parliament was from Maurice Macotere (Cotter), *residens in fine mundi in partibus Hibernie*.[3] Making a similar request, and relying on the precedent of other cases, he submitted the text of letters of the Irish chancery declaratory of his right to use English law. Both petitioners were successful.[4] In 1316 another Ostman obtained a grant of English law.[5]

The printed justiciary rolls record only two cases in which the status of an Ostman was at issue. The first was an assize of novel disseisin in Tipperary in 1295. The tenants put forward the exception that the demandant was Irish. He replied that he was an Ostman of Limerick. What the jurors said is at once so interesting and so obscure that it is best quoted at length.

Jury says that Thomas, father of [demandant] all the days of his life was held for Irish, and after his death Olyna [*sic, recte* Olyva?], mother of [demandant], seeing her son reduced to the servitude of his father, went to Limerick and obtained the liberty of the Ostmen for her son, on account of which [demandant] complained in a plea of *Vetitum namium* in the county court, and as an Ostman was answered, and hitherto has enjoyed that liberty, on which it is adjudged that [demandant] be answered to this writ.[6]

Perhaps the demandant's mother was Ostman, though his father was Irish. But what precisely took place at Limerick—especially as it appears his own presence was not necessary? And was the

[1] *Cal. pat. rolls, 1281–92*, p. 78.   [2] Cole, *Documents*, pp. 68–9.
[3] *Ibid.* pp. 69–70. Where did Maurice live? Perhaps at Waterford, like McGothmund. Curtis repeated a suggestion of D. F. Gleeson that by 'the world's end' was meant the Limerick district, but he himself seems to have favoured Tipperary; *Medieval Ireland* (1st ed.), pp. 198–9, and (2nd ed.), p. 406. J. I. Young, 'A note on the Norse occupation of Ireland', in *History*, xxxv (1950), 11–33, at p. 17, suggested Kerry or Limerick. But there is a place near Kinsale, co. Cork, called 'World's End'; this was the identification made by the Munster antiquarian, T. J. Westropp, entered in the margin of the calendar of the petition in his copy of *Cal. doc. Ire. 1285–92*, p. 306, now in my possession.
[4] *Cal. pat. rolls, 1281–92*, p. 368.
[5] *Ibid. 1313–17*, p. 463; cf. P.R.O., S.C. 8/135, no. 6742.
[6] *C.J.R. 1295–1303*, p. 59; cf. p. 14.

plea of *vetitum namium* a collusive one, to establish his claim by exercise? The other Ostman case occurred in 1311 and was a criminal one. A man accused of killing one John MacGillemory answered that this was no felony, for John was Irish. It was replied for the king that the MacGillemory family were free Ostmen and the letters of 1283 were produced. The jury gave a lengthy account of the resistance of the Norse under Reginald MacGillemory at the capture of Waterford during the Norman invasion and stated that John MacGillemory was of the stock benefited by the charter of Henry II. The further outcome of these proceedings is unknown.[1]

Conclusions

Great uncertainty must attach to generalizations about the status of the native Irish at English law in medieval Ireland. The formidable deficiencies in the evidence raise considerable problems. Why are so few letters of English law enrolled in either chancery? Were such letters always enrolled? Is it possible that a distinction was made between letters formally conferring the right to use English law and letters declaratory of an alleged existing right to use it? Had the Irish chancery greater authority to issue the latter class and did it enrol them? Questions like these must first be put, even though they remain unanswered, before an attempt at general statements can be made. Again, how often in plea rolls does an Irishman lurk behind an English-seeming name? A change of name is the most obvious course of self-help towards assimilation and historians have discovered some startling examples in medieval Ireland.[2]

The preceding survey has left its writer with the impression that Orpen and Curtis, in their treatment of the problem, were too much influenced, albeit in part unconsciously, by political events and passions of their own time. 'Those who develop emotion over such a conflict as that over Home Rule read history in the light of their emotions'.[3] In turn, Mr Richardson, in anxiety to modify the unbalanced picture given by Curtis, probably went too far in a

[1] *C.J.R. 1308–14*, pp. 185–8; in full, A. Bugge, 'Nordisk Sprog og Nordisk Nationalitet i Irland', *Aarbogr for Nordisk Oldkyndighed og Historie*, ser. 2, XV, 219–32, at pp. 227–32; extracts in Davies, *Works*, II, 68–9.

[2] Richardson, *I.H.S.* IV, 363; for an O'Driscoll who passed himself off as a Caunteton, *C.J.R. 1308–14*, p. 203 (cited also by Davies, *Works*, II, 69).

[3] W. I. Jennings, *The stuff of politics* (Cambridge, 1962), p. 298.

minimizing direction when he wrote of the disabilities of the Irish as 'on their way to becoming technical points of procedure'.[1] Professor Otway-Ruthven's stress on 'many practical inconveniences' is most satisfactory of all.[2] In short, willingness to accord individual grants of English law, the leaning of the king's courts towards freedom, the self-interest of English lords, the spirit of urban solidarity, and the demands of everyday life, all served in different ways to make matters more tolerable for the native Irish; but their severe legal disabilities could be bitterly felt, as the *Remonstrance* showed, and, like the religious penal laws of a later Ireland, must have remained a constant invitation to malice and greed.

ADDITIONAL NOTE

Since the above was written Dr G. Mac Niocaill has published a new account of the word 'betagh': 'The origins of the betagh', (1966), 1 *Ir. Jur.* (N.S.) 292–8. On grounds different from those of the late Dr Price (p. 195, n. 2, above) he has argued for an origin in *bíatach* rather than *bothach*; and this I accept. Dr Mac Niocaill's note contains other comments relevant to the question of betagh status. In addition, Professor Bryan Murphy has prepared a paper, to be published in (1967), 2 *Ir. Jur.* (N.S.), which, amongst other points, deals with the extensions of 1321 and 1331 (pp. 209–10, above). With regard to the first of these, he argues for Curtis's interpretation, against that followed above, which, however, I still favour.

[1] *I.H.S.* I, 390.   [2] *I.H.S.* VII, 14.

CHAPTER XI

'UNA ET EADEM LEX': THE PLACE OF LAW IN THE HISTORY OF THE LORDSHIP

TERRA *Hibernie gubernari debet per leges et consuetudines in Anglia usitatas*, declared litigants in an Irish case before the king's bench in 1278.[1] The phrase *una et eadem lex*, used in the judgment by which, in 1285, the English council condemned the Irish custom of wardship,[2] still more concisely summarizes the policy pursued by the administrators of the lordship after the coming of King John. One and the self-same law should prevail on both sides of the Irish sea. The operation of that policy has now been examined during the period which may deservedly be called 'the climax of medieval Ireland'.[3] In that period—approximately a generation— English law was administered over a wider area of Ireland than was to be the case again, in all probability, until the seventeenth century. To-day, Dunquin, at the extremity of the northernmost of the Kerry peninsulas, is as remote a place as any in Ireland and forms part of the surviving Irish-speaking 'Gaeltacht'. Yet in 1307 John Wogan, sitting at Ardfert, heard a plaint concerning a letting of land at Dunquin.[4]

The structure of the legal system corresponded to the English model. It is true that the justiciar's court had something of the earlier itinerant *curia regis* and something of the eyre about it, and until after 1324 was not as exact a replica of the English king's bench as the Dublin bench was of that at Westminster, but this difference was not enough to alter the general picture. The variations in the rules of law used in the Irish courts brought about by specially Irish conditions were few and those that betrayed the influence of native law fewer still. Even the existence of established English parallels did not save the Irish custom of wardship from

[1] P.R.O., K.B. 27/39, m. 16 (*Cal. doc. Ire. 1252–84*, 1450).
[2] P. 183, above.
[3] Extending somewhat the phrase of the late Professor Redford (in his thesis mentioned in the 'Preface', above, p. viii), which he applied to the reign of Edward II.
[4] *C.J.R. 1305–7*, p. 409; cf. Orpen, III, 133.

condemnation, though in practice it probably survived. If the curious statute of 1278 dealing with replevin is excepted,[1] local legislation dealt with peculiarly local problems and more general questions were left to English statutes. The jurisdiction of the English king's bench in Irish matters, by transfer or in review, provided a certain supervision over the law administered in Ireland.

The elaborate legal system of the lordship none the less declined. Gradually the sway of English law contracted, Brehon law and convenient amalgams of both came into customary use, and the amount of business with which the king's courts had to deal in the fifteenth century was, by earlier standards, derisory.[2] All this was but one aspect of the general decline of the lordship. It prompts two questions: were there any specifically legal causes contributory to the decline, and how far does the study of legal history aid understanding of the other causes that have been assigned?

The answer given to the first question by Sir John Davies still stands in essentials. The failure to bring all men, English and Irish, in the lordship under a single law prevented the consolidation of the colony. The crucial episode was Archbishop David MacCarwell's attempt to secure a general grant in 1277–80. If, as there is some reason to believe, the magnates of the lordship obstructed the proposals then made for the extension of English law, they did their descendants and successors a grave disservice.[3] Able administrator though he was, John Wogan seemingly did not possess the penetration of mind to see this weakness in the colony he ruled and nothing was done during his tenure of office. The more far-seeing John Darcy helped to bring about the grant of *una et eadem lex* to all free men in the lordship, but it was too late.[4] The long refusal of the full benefits of English law, and the infiltration of native custom into the criminal law which, paradoxically, it assisted, were the only specifically legal factors in the decline of the lordship. Other legal elements in the situation, such as the rise of the new liberties of Kildare, Ormonde, and Desmond, were more directly by-products of the course of political history.

---

[1] P. 160, above.
[2] The shrinking of the rolls can be traced in *Ir. rec. comm. rep. 1816–20*, pp. 90–113.
[3] Cf. Otway-Ruthven, *I.H.S.* vi, 264.   [4] P. 210, above.

Irish historians have advanced other reasons for the 'Norman' failure in generous variety. Richey, the most balanced in outlook amongst them, suggested seven: too rapid and too wide dispersal of the invaders, unsuitability of their military methods to much of the Irish terrain, internal strife in the colony, the demands of English kings for men and supplies to assist their wars elsewhere, the absenteeism of English magnates married to Anglo-Irish heiresses, the infiltration of Gaelic ways, and the ease with which adventurers might cross to Ireland to take what they could.[1] These causes, in his view, though already undermining the structure of the colony, did not come into full play until the fourteenth century, when the system of the lordship, already 'rotten', was 'shivered to pieces' by the Bruce invasion.[2]

At the end of the first part of *Ireland under the Normans*, a book that showed immensely more precise and detailed knowledge than was at Richey's command, Orpen noted two weak points in the organization of the colony: the incompleteness of the conquest and 'the alternate neglect and capricious interference' of King John as lord of Ireland.[3] This promising beginning was not sustained in the corresponding pages of the second half of the work. Orpen's writing reflected his own position as a member of a later colony in decline and he tended to blame Gaelic Ireland for not having known when it was beaten. His reasons for the decline of the lordship were that the Irish were 'regarded as an inferior race', that looking back was 'a defect of the Celtic temperament', and so the Gaelic Irish failed to come to terms with a new age, that there were 'defects of feudalism' in comparison with 'tribalism', and that the invaders lost their initial military advantage.[4]

Although Edmund Curtis made no adequate attempt to tackle the problem of the failure of the English colony as a whole, Eoin MacNeill devoted some thoughtful pages to it.[5] According to him, 'the tide was turned more than half a century before the Bruce invasion'. In this, 'the principal factor was national sentiment'. A more tangible element, the introduction of a new military force on the Irish side, the Hebridean mercenaries known as *gallóglaich*,

[1] *Lectures*, pp. 149–58 (*Short history*, pp. 179–86).
[2] *Ibid.* p. 158 (p. 186).
[3] Orpen, II, 340–1.
[4] Orpen, IV, 299–306 (the quotations are from the marginalia).
[5] *Phases of Irish history*, pp. 323–6.

joined with national feeling to bring about an effective Irish rally.

To most of these alleged reasons for the weakness of the colony legal history plainly has no relevance. Recently, however, Dr J. F. Lydon has brought new life to a suggestion made by Richey[1] which had also been thought deserving of mention by Curtis.[2] Dr Lydon has argued that 'the simple fact is that by withdrawing large sums of money from Ireland ... the king left the Irish administration without the financial means necessary for good government in Ireland'; again, 'there can be no doubt that the continued use of Irish revenues for purposes which were far removed from the best interests of the colony in Ireland was at least partly responsible for the eventual breakdown of law and order'.[3] A full appreciation of this view necessarily must await the appearance in print of the unpublished work upon which it is based.[4] It is proper to point out that Mr Richardson and Professor Sayles have contended that the change in the finances of the colony in the first half of the fourteenth century was that it ceased to be 'very profitable' to the English crown rather than that it became so exhausted as to be a burden.[5] Nevertheless, this general line of interpretation points to a truth as much psychological as financial or legal, to an attitude of mind which formed a weakness in the governing policy of the lordship, not least, perhaps, under John Wogan. Ireland was treated as a conquered country when it was not. The technicalities of English law might be pleaded in the courts, even as far from Dublin as Ardfert or Roscommon, but there were large tracts dominated, not merely by another race, but by something like a rival civilization. In the long run, completion of the conquest was a more vital task than merely securing the meticulous observance of the fine points of the common law in the areas already occupied.

[1] *Lectures*, pp. 152–3 (*Short history*, pp. 181–2).
[2] *Medieval Ireland*, p. 176.
[3] J. F. Lydon, 'Edward II and the revenues of Ireland in 1311–12', *I.H.S.* XIV (1964), 39–57, at p. 43.
[4] 'Ireland's participation in the military activities of English kings in the thirteenth and early fourteenth century' (Ph.D. thesis, University of London, 1955). Dr Lydon's principal conclusions were used by the late M. D. O'Sullivan in her *Italian merchant bankers in Ireland in the thirteenth century* (Dublin, 1962), pp. 131–6.
[5] H. G. Richardson and G. O. Sayles, 'Irish revenue, 1278–1384', *R.I.A. Proc.* LXII (1962), 86–100, at p. 90; cf. Dr Lydon's criticism of certain of their calculations, *I.H.S.* XIV, 43, n. 12, and his table of sums of Irish treasure received by the king, *ibid.* pp. 53–7.

The resources of government were applied to purposes that were premature. When a Gaelic revival, a new invasion, and, very possibly, some measure of internal economic decline, were brought to bear, the medieval lordship began its two centuries of crumbling decay.

Yet the 'first adventure of the common law', to use the happy phrase of a twentieth-century Irish judge,[1] proved more enduring than most of the fabric of the lordship. The judges of the two jurisdictions in Ireland today rightfully claim succession to those of Wogan's time. Much of the public law aspects of the common law has been written into the constitutions which mark the political changes of the last half-century in Ireland.[2] The continuity of law has been shown also in conscious judicial reference to the medieval common law. A substantial part of the modern Irish law of religious charities is drawn from pre-Reformation common law, as interpreted by Palles C. B. in *O'Hanlon* v. *Logue*,[3] and Gavan Duffy J. in *Maguire* v. *Attorney-General*.[4] While this study was in preparation, the Lord Chief Justice of Northern Ireland, Lord MacDermott, referred in *R.* v. *Bailey*[5] to a plaint of trespass brought before John Wogan at Cashel in June 1297.[6] The Bar of the Republic of Ireland is still educated at an Inn which owns the motto, derived from the declaration of the barons at Merton in 1236, *nolumus* (*leges Angliae*) *mutari*.

[1] W. J. Johnston (then a county court judge and later a judge of the High Court of the Irish Free State), 'The first adventure of the common law', 36 *L.Q.R.* 9.
[2] Cf. F. E. Moran, 'The migration of the common law: 7: The Republic of Ireland', 76 *L.Q.R.* 69, at 72.
[3] [1906] 1 I.R. 247, at 262.
[4] [1943] I.R. 238, at 242.   [5] [1956] N.I.L.R. 15, at 28.
[6] *C.J.R. 1295–1303*, p. 133 (*Ric. de Boyton* v. *John de Turbervill*).

APPENDIX I

THE JUSTICES ITINERANT, 1248 TO 1269

THE table which follows is largely based on that given by Mr Richardson and Professor Sayles in their *Administration of medieval Ireland*, to which reference should be made for authorities.[1] A change from *curia domini regis* to *curia domini Edwardi illustris regis Anglie primogeniti* occurred in 1256 with the definitive grant of the lordship to Edward.[2] Terms have been indicated by the initials M, H, P and T. An asterisk (*) beside a term indicates that the justices are known to have held pleas of the crown, while a lower case 'x' is intended to convey that this is probable but not certain. The order in which the justices are mentioned in the sources is that obtained by reading the columns from left to right.

[1] Pp. 134–9. In most cases the evidence comes from final concords.
[2] Cf. Richardson and Sayles, *The Irish parliament*, pp. 57–8.

Year	Term, etc.	Place	Names of Justices			Comments
1248	H	Dublin	Robert of Shardlow	Walrand of Wellesley	Robert of Belvoir	
1251	T	Limerick	,,	,,	Geoffrey of St John	
1252	P	Dublin	,,	,,	,,	
	T*	Limerick, Waterford	,,	,,	,,	Peter de Repentigny
1252–3	—	Limerick, Connaught	,,	and companions		
1252–3	—	Dublin, Tipperary	,,	and companions		*Magistro Roberto de Nicandell* [lege *Schardelawe*] *et sociis suis ultimo itinerantibus apud Dublin' [et] coram justiciario apud Tiperariam* (Pipe roll, in *Anal. hib.* II, 252)
1253	M	Limerick	Geoffrey of St John	Walrand of Wellesley	Alexander of Nottingham	
1254–5	—	Dublin	Geoffrey of St John, bishop of Ferns	and companions		Geoffrey became bishop of Ferns in 1254
1255	M	Dublin	Walrand of Wellesley	Alexander of Nottingham	William of Bacquepuis	
1257	H	Limerick	Geoffrey of St John	,,	William of Weyland	Richardson and Sayles suggest that the third justice's name is an error for Walrand of Wellesley (both 'W. de W.'); but compare entry for 1259 (T?), below; cf. also *R.I.A. Proc.* XXXV, 95–6

1258	P	Dublin	Walrand of Wellesley	"	William of Bacquepuis	Richard of Exeter		Richardson and Sayles attribute to Easter 1259 a reference that in fact concerns this term Extracts from receipt roll, 42 Hen. III, ed. Lydon, *R.I.A. Proc.* LXV, 25
	T?	Tipperary	Alexander of Nottingham	William of Bacquepuis	Robert fitz Warin	William of Weyland	
1259	T	Dublin	Walrand of Wellesley	Alexander of Nottingham	William of Bacquepuis	—	
1260	H*	Cork	"	"	"	Hugh of Kingsbury	Robert fitz Warin	See under 1264 (M)
	M (a)	Dublin	Walrand of Wellesley	"	"	—	
	M (b)	Dublin	Hugh of Taghmon, bishop of Meath	Walrand of Wellesley	Arnold of Berkeley	Alexander of Nottingham	—	The bishop of Meath was then treasurer
1261	Px	Dublin	Walrand of Wellesley	Alexander of Nottingham	William of Bacquepuis	Philip de Hynteberg	Richard of Exeter
	T*	Limerick	"	—	"	"	"	Roll, probably of eyre of Limerick, before preceding and *aliis regis itinerantibus* (P.R.O.I., RC. 7/1, *Cal. plea rolls*, I, 119–221)
1262	Mx	Dublin	"	Alexander of Nottingham	"	"	"
	P	Dublin	"	"	"	"	—
	T	Dublin	"	"	"	Richard of Exeter	
1264	M	Dublin	"	"	"	"	
	H	Dublin	"	"	"	"	
	P	Dublin	"	"	"	"	

Year	Term, etc.	Place	Names of Justices					Comments
			Alexander of Nottingham	William de Bacquepuis	Richard of Exeter	Hugh of St Albans [Kingsbury]		
1264	M	Dublin						Kingsbury was a manor of St Albans
1265	M	Dublin	,,	,,	,,	,,		
1266	H	Dublin	,,	,,	,,	,,		
	P	Dublin	,,	,,	,,	,,		
	T	Dublin	,,	,,	,,	,,		
	M	Dublin	,,	,,	,,	,,		
	H	Limerick	,,		,,	,,	Griffin fitz Alan	
1267	P	Dublin	,,	William de Bacquepuis	,,	,,	,,	
1268	M	Dublin	,,	,,	,,	,,	,,	
	T	Dublin	,,	,,	Richard of Exeter	William of Caister		
1269	P	Dublin						
	Mx	Dublin	Alexander of Nottingham	William de Bacquepuis	,,			Roll calendared in P.R.O.I., RC. 7/1, *Cal. plea rolls*, I, 415–89: *apud Dublin' de itinere justiciariorum ad omnia placita in eodem comitatu tenenda*

APPENDIX II

EXAMPLES OF THE WRIT 'PROCEDENDO AD JUDICIUM' WITH CLAUSE 'SI DIFFICULTAS'

ONLY one example of a writ of this type addressed to an Irish court has hitherto been printed (*Hist. & mun. doc. Ire.* pp. 223-4, from P.R.O., K.B. 27/181, m. 53*d*). Another is recited in indirect speech in *Select cases in K.B.* II, 72-3 (from P.R.O., K.B. 27/130, m. 14). In this Appendix three texts are given: (*a*) the general form of the writ in the sixteenth-century printed *Registrum brevium*; (*b*) a simple text addressed in 1290 to the Dublin bench; (*c*) an adaptation in 1292 to a more complicated situation.

(*a*) *Reg. brevium*, f. 222.

Cum A. arrainaverit coram vobis quandam assisam novae disseisinae per breve nostrum versus I. de tenementis in N. ac licet vos assisam illam secundum legem et consuetudinem regni nostri Angliae ceperitis judicium tamen inde adhuc restat reddendum ad grave damnum ipsius A. et juris sui retardationem et exheredationis suae periculum manifestum sicut ex querela sua accepimus;

Vobis mandamus quod ad judicium inde reddendum cum ea celeritate qua de jure et secundum legem et consuetudinem regni nostri Angliae poteritis procedatis;

Et si aliqua difficultas subfuerit quare ad judicium praedictum nobis inconsultis secure procedere non possitis tunc recordum et processum assisae praedictae coram vobis habitae cum omnibus ea tangentibus nobis sub sigillo vestro vos prefat[a]e A. [*sic*] mittatis et hoc breve ita quod ea habeamus tali die coram nobis ubicumque tunc fuerimus in Anglia partibus eundem diem praefigendo quod tunc sint coram nobis facturi et recepturi in praemissis quod de jure et secundum legem et consuetudinem regni nostri Angliae fuerit faciendum.

Teste etc.

(b) P.R.O., K.B. 27/127, m. 8d. *Cal. doc. Ire. 1285–92*, 883, is inadequate and does not reveal the nature of the writ.

Edwardus dei gratia etc. justiciariis de banco Dublin' salutem. Cum Alicia de Crombe implacitaverit Philippum de Crombe coram vobis per breve nostrum de recto de uno mesuagio et quatuor carucatis terre cum pertinentiis in Conktilin et Dermothyr et per aliud breve nostrum de recto de centum acris terre et quinque marcatis et quadraginta denariatis redditus cum pertinentiis in Selioc et [villa] Palmeri ac placita illa diutinam coram vobis ceperunt dilationem prout ex gravi querela ipsius Alicie accepimus:

Nos eidem Alicie justiciam fieri volentes in hac parte vobis mandamus quod in placitis illis quam citius secundum legem et consuetudinem partium predictarum poteritis procedatis et predicte Alicie super hoc fieri faciatis plene et celeris justicie complementum ne pro defectu justicie in premissis ipsam Aliciam recursum ad nos habere oporteat iteratim per quod sollicitari debeamus amplius ex hac causa.

Et si subsit aliqua difficultas per quod in placitis illis nobis inconsultis procedere non possitis tunc recorda et processus placitorum illorum cum omnibus ea tangentibus nobis sub sigillis vestris distincte et aperte mittatis et hoc breve ita quod ea habeamus in octabis sancte trinitatis ubicumque tunc fuerimus in Anglia partibus eundem diem prefigentes quod tunc sint ibi facture et recepture quod curia nostra considerabit in hac parte.

Teste meipso apud Queninton iiii die martii anno regni nostri xviii.

(c) P.R.O., K.B. 27/138, m. 18. *Cal. doc. Ire. 1293–1301*, 92, does indicate the nature of the writ.

Edwardus dei gratia rex Anglie dominus Hibernie et dux Aquitanie dilectis et fidelibus suis Roberto Bagod et sociis suis justiciariis de banco Dublin' salutem. Cum ad gravem querelam abbatis sancti Thome iuxta Dublin' et Johannis de Cogan sibi iniuriatum fuisse asserentium in assisa mortis antecessoris quam Alexander le Chamberleyn arramiavit coram dilectis et fidelibus nostris priori hospitalis sancti Johannis Jerusalem in Hibernia et sociis suis justiciariis nostris ultimo itinerantibus apud Dublin' per breve nostrum versus predictum abbatem de uno mesuagio duabus carucatis et sexaginta acris terre

APPENDIX II 225

uno molendino et sex acris bosci cum pertinentiis in Balymakelly unde idem abbas predictum Johannem versus predictum Alexandrum vocavit ad warrantizandum ut dicitur eisdem priori et sociis suis mandaverimus quod recordum et processum eiusdem assise cum omnibus ea tangentibus sub sigillis suis vobis mittant:

Vobis mandamus quod cum contingat recordum illud et processum vobis mitti ut predictum est tunc vos ea in presencia dilectorum clericorum nostrorum magistri Thome Cantok cancellarii nostri Hibernie et Willelmi de Estden thesaurarii nostri Dublin' examinetis et auditis rationibus predictorum abbatis et Johannis super injuriis eis in hac parte illatis si quid in premissis quod correctione indigeat inveneritis tunc id de consilio predictorum Thome et Willelmi prout justum fuerit corrigi et eisdem abbati et Johanni inde exhiberi faciatis debitum et festinum justicie complementum secundum legem et consuetudinem partium illarum:

Et si quid difficultatis subsit quare nobis inconsultis id secure facere non possitis tunc recordum et processum negocii supradicti cum omnibus ea tangentibus ad aliquem certum diem nobis sub sigillis vestris distincte et aperte mittatis et hoc breve partibus eundem diem prefigentes quod tunc sint coram nobis facture et receptute quod justicia suadebit.

Teste meipso apud Heywra xx die septembris anno regni nostri xx.

APPENDIX III

LIST OF JUSTICIARY ROLLS, EDWARD I–II

THE following list is based on those in *Ir. rec. comm. rep. 1816–20*, pp. 79–101, 522–7, and *P.R.I. rep. D.K. 26*, Appendix III, pp. 57–60, together with examination of the surviving sources. References to rolls for which no calendar of any kind survives have been omitted. In referring to the manuscript calendars prepared by the Irish record commissioners, only the form 'RC. 7' or 'RC. 8', for *Cal. plea rolls* or *Cal. mem. rolls*, as the case may be, with item number and page reference, has been adopted here; the item number is also a volume number. The list gives the following information: (*a*) regnal year; (*b*) earliest and latest dates found in headings of pleas; (*c*) chief governors named in the headings; (*d*) plea roll number (if any) assigned by the Irish record commission; (*e*) number of membranes known to have been in the roll; (*f*) form in which the roll survives. The list has been divided vertically into sections, composed of rolls including, A, pleas of the crown and common pleas; B, common pleas only; and, C, pleas of the crown only.

[226]

Regnal years	Dates	Chief governors	Record commission number	Number of membranes	Surviving form
Edward I			A. *Pleas of the crown and common pleas*		
23	24 Jan. 1295–26 Nov. 1295	Thomas fitz Maurice	21	26	*C.J.R. 1295–1303*, pp. 1–77
			B. *Common pleas only*		
25	8 Jan. 1297–1 April 1297	John Wogan	28	11	*Ibid.* pp. 78–97; RC. 7/4, pp. 251–69
25	22 April 1297–22 Sept. 1297	,,	29	36	*C.J.R. 1295–1303*, pp. 97–166; RC. 7/4, pp. 273–402
27	13 Jan. 1299–13 Nov. 1299	John Wogan and Earl of Ulster	—	40	*C.J.R. 1295–1303*, pp. 209–98
28	16 April 1300–3 Oct. 1300	John Wogan	—	31	*Ibid.* pp. 299–366
30–31	19 Mar. 1302–6 Jan. 1303	John Wogan and Maurice de Rochfort	65	43	*Ibid.* pp. 367–458; RC. 7/9, pp. 481–546
31	6 and 13 Jan. 1303	John Wogan	Fragment 4	2	*C.J.R. 1295–1303*, pp. 458–64
33–4	14 Jan. 1305–20 Jan. 1306	Edmund Butler and John Wogan	—	73	*C.J.R. 1305–7*, pp. 1–179
34–5	19 Jan. 1306–7 Jan. 1307	John Wogan	—	66	*Ibid.* pp. 180–330
35	3 April 1307–21 July 1307	,,	—	53	*Ibid.* pp. 331–462
Edward II					
1–2	8 Jan. 1308–16 Aug. 1308	,,	—	79	*C.J.R. 1308–14*, pp. 1–118: *see note at end*
2	14 Jan. 1309–16 Feb. 1309	William de Burgh	90	10	*Ibid.* pp. 119–42

Regnal years	Dates	Chief governors	Record commission number	Number of membranes	Surviving form
Edward II		B. *Common pleas only (cont.)*			
6–7	30 Sept. 1312–28 Aug. 1313	Edmund Butler	—	104	Original surviving in P.R.O.I.
7	29 Sept. 1313–31 Dec. 1313	,,	105	24	P.R.O.I., MS. English calendar
7	9 April 1314–21 April 1314	,,	106	7	Similar
11	10 Aug. 1317–13 Feb. 1318	,,	116	25	Similar; RC. 7/12, pp. 1–57
11	14 Nov. 1317–8 April 1318	Roger Mortimer	115	36	RC. 7/12, pp. 107–82 (incomplete)
11	27 Jan. 1318–4 April 1318	Edmund Butler	117	16	P.R.O.I., MS. English calendar; RC. 7/12, pp. 63–104
11–12	7 April 1318–25 Sept. 1318	William, archbishop of Cashel	118	39	P.R.O.I., MS. English calendar (mm. 1–7 only); RC. 7/12, pp. 185–254
		C. *Pleas of the crown only*			
Edward I					
33–5	8 July 1305–27 Feb. 1307	John Wogan	77	23	*C.J.R. 1305–7*, pp. 463–521
Edward II					
3–7	10 May 1310–3 June 1314	John Wogan and Edmund Butler	108	87	*C.J.R. 1308–14*, pp. 143–326
8–9	13 Aug. 1314–10 Mar. 1316	Theobald de Verdun and Edmund Butler	109	13	P.R.O.I., MS. English calendar
9–11	31 Mar. 1316–4 Aug. 1317	Edmund Butler	114	20	Similar (incomplete)
11	3 Nov. 1317–7 May 1318	Roger Mortimer	119	14	Similar; RC. 7/12, pp. 261–76

APPENDIX III

Note: *Justiciary roll, 1–2 Edward II*

In *C.J.R. 1308–14*, an error of identification has been made concerning the roll for 1–2 Edward II, a calendar of certain membranes of which is printed (pp. 1–118). This roll was unknown to the Irish record commission, but was noted in *P.R.I. rep. D.K. 26* (p. 57), which appeared in 1894. It is there given the shelf reference 1Q. 48. 9, which seems to have been reserved for rolls that had come to light in the course of the nineteenth century. The roll is not to be identified, as in *C.J.R. 1308–14*, with the rolls numbered 84–87 by the record commissioners. These rolls were in fact rolls of the Dublin bench and indeed no. 87 still survives (see Appendix VI, below). Consequently the division made of the justiciary roll in order to correspond with this numeration, indicated in *C.J.R. 1308–14* (p. iii) and followed in the arrangement of the calendar, ought to be ignored. The following should be substituted:

Membranes	Dates	Reference in *C.J.R. 1308–14*
29–36	8 Jan. 1308–20 Jan. 1308	Pp. 1–23. This and the next group of membranes represent the Hilary section
40–50	20 Jan. 1308–1 April 1308	Pp. 23–46
52–79	28 April 1308–16 August 1308	Pp. 47–118. This is the Easter–Trinity section and begins with the attorneys, etc., for that term

It should also be noted that there is no justiciary roll for Michaelmas term, 1307, known to the Irish record commission but since then lost, which might yet appear, contrary to a suggestion made, on the basis of the erroneous identification, by Professor Sayles in his review of *C.J.R. 1308–14* (*E.H.R.* LXXIII, 102).

APPENDIX IV

SESSIONS OF THE JUSTICIAR'S COURT DURING THE LIEUTENANCY OF ROGER MORTIMER, 1317-18

THE list which follows gives the dates and places of sessions before Roger Mortimer and Edmund Butler between 7 April 1317, when Mortimer took up office, and 6 May 1318, when William, archbishop of Cashel, was appointed Keeper. Sessions at Dublin with the heading of the quinzaine of Easter (7 May) 1318 were recorded before both Mortimer and Archbishop William, but this duplication occurred at the time of transfer of authority and hence falls into a different category from the others noted below. Except in instances where printed references are available, the authority given below is simply the number of the justiciary roll, further particulars of which can be had from Appendix III. The descriptions of business are based merely on the headings of pleas, not upon detailed analysis of the contents. An 'X' in the Table indicates that business of the kind shown at the head of the appropriate column was taken.

The references to *I.H.S.* x are to G. O. Sayles, 'The siege of Carrickfergus Castle, 1315-16', in *I.H.S.* x, 94-100.

Year	Dates	Chief governor	Place	Essoins	Common pleas	Juries and assizes	Pleas of plaints	Pleas of the crown	Gaol delivery	References
1317	8 April	Butler	Cashel					X		114
	11 April	,,	Brittas					X		114
	2 May	,,	Drogheda					X	X	114
	13 May	,,	Castledermot					X	X	114
	19 May	,,	Ballygaveran					X		114
	24 May	,,	Ross					X	X	114
	13 June	,,	Thomastown					X		114
	8 July	,,	Dublin					X		114
	23 July	Mortimer	Drogheda					X		119; *I.H.S.* x, 99
	25 July	,,	?							J. T. Gilbert, *History of the Viceroys of Ireland*, pp. 531–2
	4 Aug.	Butler	Waterford					X	X	114
	10 Aug.	,,	Thomastown				X			116
	22 Aug.	,,	Dublin		X		X			116
	27 Sept.	,,	Limerick							116
	13 Oct.	,,	Dublin	X	X					116
	20 Oct.	Mortimer, Butler	,,				X	X		119; *I.H.S.* x, 100
	27 Oct.	Butler	,,	X						116
	3 Nov.	Mortimer, Butler	Thomastown					X		115, 119; *P.R.I. rep. D.K.* 26, p. 58
	7 Nov.	Mortimer	New Ross					X		115, 119
	9 Nov.	,,	Waterford			X		X	X	115, 119

Year	Dates	Chief governor	Place	Essoins	Common Pleas	Juries and assizes	Pleas of plaints	Pleas of the crown	Gaol delivery	References
1317	14 Nov.	Mortimer	Cork				X	X	X	115, 119
	14 Nov.	Butler	Limerick	X		X	X			116
	21 Nov.	Mortimer, Butler	Cork							115; *P.R.I. rep. D.K. 26*, p. 58
	24 Nov. to 1 Dec.	Butler	Limerick	X	X	X				116
	5 Dec.	,,	Kilmallock			X	X			116
	14 Dec.	Mortimer	?			X				115
1317–1318	14 Dec. to 7 Jan.	Butler	Cashel	X		X	X			116
1317	19 Dec.	Mortimer, Butler	Cork							115
1318	7 Jan.	Butler	Clonmel	X						118
	13 Jan.	Mortimer	,,					X	X	115, 119
	26 Jan.	,,	Thomastown		X			X	X	115, 119
	27 Jan.	Butler	Cashel		X					117
	3–20 Feb.	,,	,,	X	X					117
	16 Feb.	Mortimer	Dublin				X			115
	23 Feb. to 18 Mar.	Butler	Limerick	X	X	X	X			117
1318	24 Feb.	Mortimer	Dublin					X	X	119
	13 Mar.	,,	Drogheda	X		X	X	X	X	115, 119
	3 April	Butler	Cashel			X	X			117
	4 April	,,	Limerick							117

APPENDIX V

ANALYSES OF JUSTICIARY ROLLS

JUSTICIARY rolls may be analysed in three ways, two of which may be regarded as supplementary to the third and most important, analysis on the basis of the individual entries on the roll. The two supplementary ways are the division of the roll according to the place and type of session and that according to the headings of pleas used. All three are interrelated: a high proportion of sessions at Dublin reduced the frequency with which the heading *placita de juratis et assisis* was used and increased that of the heading *communia placita*, and these varying proportions are reflected in the analysis of entries and pleas.

For the purposes of the present study, analysis of one roll of pleas of the crown and of three of common pleas has been attempted.

The selected roll of pleas of the crown is that of 33–5 Edward I, because it is the only roll of its kind accessible in the printed calendar which is open to comparison with a roll of common pleas likewise available. In order to make it correspond precisely to the common plea roll for 34–5 Edward I, only membranes 11–20 of the roll of crown pleas, which originally had twenty-three membranes, have been analysed below (m. 8 was missing before the calendar was made). This means that, by taking together the analyses of the business on the two rolls, as precise a picture as possible can be had of the work of the court in a single year of Wogan's justiciarship. It also means that a single sessional analysis serves for the two rolls. Analysis of headings is of course unnecessary with rolls of pleas of the crown; the only ones used were *placita de corona* and *deliberacio gaole*.

The choice of the justiciary roll of common pleas for 34–5 Edward I was dictated, as has just been explained, by the desire to provide a composite picture of all the court's business in a single year. All three types of analysis of this roll are given below, the analyses of headings and of individual entries being presented in tabular form with those of other justiciary rolls of common pleas.

The second roll of common pleas chosen is the Easter–Trinity section of that for 1 Edward II. The choice was here commanded by the desire to provide a comparison with what can be made out of the contents of the rolls of the Dublin bench for those terms, analysed in Appendix VII. Both this roll and that for 34 Edward I rather weight the balance in favour of sessions held at Dublin, and so do not give an altogether exact impression of the average proportions of the court's business, as a cursory glance at their nearest neighbours in the series of surviving texts will show. However, their value for comparative purposes has been thought to compensate for this disadvantage. As a further corrective, the surviving roll, 6–7 Edward II, has been called in. A sessional analysis of this roll, supplemented from the corresponding record of pleas of the crown, will be found in chapter III (p. 58), above. An analysis of headings is given below. Since the roll is still in manuscript and the help of an index is lacking, a plea analysis has not been attempted.

A few points of procedure in making the analyses may be explained before presenting them. In the detailed analysis of pleas of the crown, indictments of more than one person for the same offence have each been counted once only, unless different accused took different courses (e.g. one was immediately pardoned suit of peace, another put himself upon the country). In such a case each individual has been counted separately. If more than one charge is found in an indictment, that considered most important has alone been reckoned.

Plaints without writ present problems of identification and classification. It has been presumed that cases under the heading *placita querelarum* were by bill, in the absence of evidence to the contrary. Otherwise, the guides indicated by Professor Sayles and Mr Richardson are followed (*Select cases in K.B.* IV, pp. lxxiii–lxxviii, and *Select cases of procedure without writ*, pp. xlv–xlvi). Two special categories, 'plaints concerning officials' discharge of their duties', and 'exceptional plaints', have been devised, and in all other classes the number of cases believed to have been without writ has been bracketed after the total. These figures are not absolutely reliable, however, because of the difficulties in classification.

Another difficult classification problem is presented by 'trespass' and it has been somewhat arbitrarily treated here. In general, the guide has been the categorization used by Professor S. F. C. Milsom ('Trespass from Henry III to Edward III', 74 *L.Q.R.* (1958), 195–224, 407–36, 561–90). But instances of cases called

APPENDIX V 235

'trespass' on the rolls will also be found under the headings 'ecclesiastical matters' and 'maintenance, conspiracy, etc.'. It unfortunately is not possible to tell whether the omission of *vi et armis* and *contra pacem* in any given instance is traceable merely to the editors of the calendar.

If a judgment or recognizance occurs on the roll itself, it has not been also reckoned under the heading 'process of execution, etc.', which has been reserved for judgments and recognizances of earlier date or of other courts. In a solitary instance in which a case was on the rolls of the year in which it was summoned to England, it has been included under both its own appropriate heading and that of 'records summoned to England', but otherwise each case has been reckoned only once.

Sessional analysis, 34–5 Edward I

The roll of common pleas (*C.J.R. 1305–7*, pp. 180–330) covers sessions from 19 January 1306 to 7 January 1307. The relevant section of the roll of pleas of the crown (*ibid.* pp. 490–514) covers 24 January 1306 to the same date. Two headings of pleas at the same place within a fortnight of each other have been treated as a single session, unless of course the justiciar is known to have been elsewhere between those dates. Where the dorso of a membrane is blank it has been credited to the heading of the recto.

Type of Session	Number held	Membranes of common pleas	Membranes of pleas of the crown
Full county session	1	2	1
Sessions at Dublin, with pleas of the crown	4	40	$3\frac{1}{2}$
Sessions at Dublin, without pleas of the crown	4	11	—
Casual sessions, with both common pleas and pleas of the crown	5	4	4
Casual sessions, with common pleas only	6	$6\frac{1}{2}$	—
Casual sessions, with pleas of the crown only	3	—	$1\frac{1}{2}$
[*Attornati*, etc.]	—	[$2\frac{1}{2}$]	—
TOTAL	23	66	10

Pleas of the crown, 34–5 Edward I

HOMICIDE

Benefit of clergy
  (*a*) delivered as convicted   4
  (*b*) pardoned   1
Pardoned suit of peace before putting himself on country   4
Made fine after putting himself on country   2
To be hanged   1
Acquitted   1
Mainprised to next coming   3
To be mainprised if he surrenders   1
To be outlawed as fugitive   1
         18

RAPE

Pardoned suit of peace before, etc.   1
Made fine after, etc.   1
To be outlawed as fugitive   1
         3

ROBBERY AND 'FORSTALLUM'

Pardoned suit of peace before, etc.   4
To be hanged   1
Acquitted   1
Doubtful result   1
         7

LARCENY

Benefit of clergy (delivered, etc.)   1
Pardoned suit of peace before, etc.   8
Made fine after, etc.   3
To be hanged   2
Acquitted   3
Exceptional cases (pp. 61–2 above)   2
To be outlawed, etc.   1
Mainprised to fight Irish   1
Incomplete   1
         22

HARBOURING FELONS

Pardoned suit of peace before, etc.   3
Made fine after, etc.   6
Acquitted   7
Mainprised (principal not yet convicted)   1
Incomplete   1
         18

MISCELLANEOUS INDICTMENTS

Escape (do not appear)   2
Breach of sanctuary (acquitted)   1
Rescue from stocks (made fine, etc.)   1
Return after abjuration of the land (benefit of clergy, delivered)   1
Appellor slain on way to Dublin bench (incomplete)   1
Woman appellor carried off on way to (justiciar's?) court
  (made fine, etc.)   1
Ravishment of ward (incomplete)   1
         8

MISCELLANEOUS ENTRIES

Fines, mainprises, and amercements in unspecified circumstances	17
Report on negotiations with Irish of the marches	1
Licence to receive back chattels	2
	20

Sessional analysis of roll of common pleas, Easter–Trinity, 1 Edward II

The sessions on this roll (*C.J.R. 1308–14*, pp. 47–118) range from 28 April to 16 August 1308.

Type of Session	Number	Membranes
Full county session	1	$3\frac{1}{2}$
Sessions at Dublin	3	$23\frac{1}{2}$
[*Attornati*, etc.]	—	[1]
TOTAL	4	28

Sessional analysis of roll of common pleas, 6–7 Edward II

For this, see chapter III, p. 58, above.

Analysis of membranes by headings used: rolls of common pleas, 34–5 Edward I, Easter–Trinity, 1 Edward II, and 6–7 Edward II

	34 Edw. I		1 Edw. II		6–7 Edw. II		
Heading	Dublin	Elsewhere	Dublin	Elsewhere	Dublin	Elsewhere	TOTAL
Attornati, etc.		$2\frac{1}{2}$	1		5		$8\frac{1}{2}$
Essonia	2	—	$1\frac{1}{2}$	$\frac{1}{2}$	1	$4\frac{1}{2}$	$9\frac{1}{2}$
Placita	7	1	—	—	—	1	9
Communia placita	$34\frac{1}{2}$	$2\frac{1}{2}$	$19\frac{1}{2}$	1	22	$9\frac{1}{2}$	89
'Pleas of the council'	$\frac{1}{2}$	—	—	—	—	—	$\frac{1}{2}$
Placita querelarum	$6\frac{1}{2}$	8	$2\frac{1}{2}$	$\frac{1}{2}$	$4\frac{1}{2}$	$15\frac{1}{2}$	$37\frac{1}{2}$
Placita de juratis et assisis	$\frac{1}{2}$	1	—	$1\frac{1}{2}$	$\frac{1}{2}$	$40\frac{1}{2}$	44
Totals by location	51	$12\frac{1}{2}$	$23\frac{1}{2}$	$3\frac{1}{2}$	28	71	$189\frac{1}{2}$
TOTAL		66		28		104	198

Common pleas, 34–5 Edward I and Easter–Trinity, 1 Edward II

	34 Edw. I	1 Edw. II
TRESPASS		
A. *Wrongs to the person*		
Assault and battery	14 (14)	4 (2)
False imprisonment	3 (3)	1 (1)
Assault, etc. on *hibernicus* of plaintiff	1 (—)	—
Abduction of wife and chattels	1 (—)	—
Rape	1 (1)	—
B. *Wrongs to land*		
Ejectio firme	3 (3)	—
Reaping crops, taking timber	4 (4)	—
C. *Wrongs to goods and chattels*		
De bonis asportatis	13 (11)	7 (7)
Injury by bailee	1 (1)	—
D. *Wrongs against those under royal protection*, etc.	3 (—)	—
E. *Wrongs against exercise of rights and franchises*		
Rescue of cattle	1 (1)	—
Quit of toll	1 (—)	—
Wrongful release by royal servant from franchisal prison	1 (—)	—
F. *Non-performance of miscellaneous obligations and agreements*	7 (7)	1 (1)
G. *Unspecified* (chiefly known from membranes of attorneys)	25 (19)	7 (2)
Total trespasses	79 (64)	20 (13)
DEBT AND DETINUE	29 (24)	12 (9)
PLAINTS CONCERNING OFFICIALS' DISCHARGE OF THEIR DUTIES	10 (10)	—
MAINTENANCE, CONSPIRACY, etc.	4 (3)	2 (—)
PROSECUTIONS IN THE KING'S NAME FOR OFFENCES IN THE ADMINISTRATION OF JUSTICE, etc.	5 (2)	1 (—)
ASSIZES		
Novel disseisin	2	7
Mort d'ancestor	—	3
ACQUITTANCE OF RENTS AND SERVICES	1 (1)	—
LAW MERCHANT, STATUTE MERCHANT	2 (1)	—
PROCEEDINGS RELATING TO ROYAL WARDSHIPS, etc.	3	—

APPENDIX V

	34 Edw. I	1 Edw. II
ECCLESIASTICAL MATTERS		
Election without licence	2	—
Why archbishop removed royal presentee and made church prebendal	1	—
Why plea drawn into court christian	1	—
Why proceeded against prohibition	—	1
Plaint of trespass concerning manner of episcopal visitation	—	1
BY WHAT TITLE FISHERIES HELD	1	—
EXCEPTIONAL PLAINTS		
Defamation	1	1
Disclosure of counsel	1	—
Recovery of damages paid to third party by plaintiff for injury inflicted by defendant	1	—
Deceit by arbitrator in not keeping promise to favour particular party	1	—
INCOMPLETE AND UNCERTAIN ACTIONS	7 (4)	—
PROCESS OF EXECUTION		
(*a*) of judgments previously rendered in justiciar's court	21	24
(*b*) of judgments of other courts	3	1
(*c*) on recognizances made in justiciar's court	20	12
(*d*) on recognizances made in other courts	4	1
ENROLMENTS		
Recognizances	17	5
Charters	3	2
English writs of general attorney	5	—
Commissions under the English seal	1	6
MISCELLANEOUS FINES, AMERCEMENTS, MAINPRISES, etc. (usually because omitted from appropriate rolls)	19	13
JURISDICTION IN REVIEW		
proceedings in justiciar's court itself	1	1
in Dublin bench	5	2
on eyre	2	2
before justices of assize	3	—
of county court	1	—
uncertain (known from attorneys only)	5	3
INTERVENTION IN OTHER COURTS		
amendment of estreat rolls of the bench	2	—
Supersedeas of execution	2	—
RECORDS SUMMONED TO ENGLAND		
from justiciar's court		
(*a*) by undifferentiated *certiorari*	1	—
(*b*) by writ of error	—	1
(*c*) by *procedendo ad judicium* (with clause *si difficultas*)	—	1
from eyre, by writ of error	1*	—
from justices assigned, by *procedendo ad judicium*	1	—

* later returned to justiciar's court.

	34 Edw. I	1 Edw. II
PROCEEDINGS ORDERED IN CONNECTION WITH CASES IN ENGLAND	7	3
CERTIFICATIONS BY IRISH OFFICIALS WHY LANDS OR CHATTELS IN THE KING'S HAND	8	1
GENERAL BUSINESS		
Pardons and protections	4	2
Inquisitions and proofs of age	4	3
Notifications that heir has done homage in England	2	2
Miscellaneous licences	7	2
Warrants for *liberate*	7	10
Arrangements for Scottish war	6	—
Miscellaneous	13	11
TOTAL ITEMS	326	156

APPENDIX VI

LIST OF ROLLS OF THE DUBLIN BENCH, EDWARD I-II

The following list is based on those in *Ir. rec. comm. rep. 1816-20*, pp. 79-90, 522-4, and *P.R.I. rep. D.K. 26*, Appendix III, pp. 64-7, together with examination of the surviving sources. References to rolls for which no calendar of any kind survives have been omitted. In referring to the calendars prepared by the Irish record commissioners, only the form 'RC. 7' or 'RC. 8', for *Cal. plea rolls* or *Cal. mem. rolls*, as the case may be, with item number and page reference, has been adopted here; the item number is also a volume number, except in the case of RC. 7/13, a bundle of loose papers.

Regnal year	Law term	Record commissioners' number	Number of membranes	Reference
		Edward I		
6	P?	[none]	11?	RC. 8/1, pp. 23-65; cf. p. 9, n. 5, above
8	[*Sancti Johannis Baptiste*]*	6	8	RC. 7/2, pp. 1-89
8-9	M?	[none]	13	RC. 8/1, pp. 107-55
9	[8 S.J.B. to Morrow of the Ascension]	7	8	RC. 7/2, pp. 95-130
10	[From Morrow of S.J.B.]	[none]	9	RC. 8/1, pp. 157-75; a better Latin calendar in R.I.A., MS. 12 D 12
18	P	11	12	Now B.M., Add. Roll 13598
19	H	16	19	RC. 7/3, pp. 1-82
	T	18	10	RC. 7/3, pp. 155-80

* So the heading of amercements on m. 8 (pp. 77-8); other headings run from 8 S.J.B. to a month from S.J.B.

Regnal year	Law term	Record commissioners' number	Number of membranes	Reference
		Edward I		
23–4	M	23	24	RC. 7/3, pp. 331–462
24	H	24	9	RC. 7/4, pp. 1–48
	P	25	18	RC. 7/4, pp. 53–156
	T	26	17	RC. 7/4, pp. 159–230
24–5	M	(a) 31	20	RC. 7/4, pp. 437–97
		(b) 22	16	RC. 7/3, pp. 267–326
25	H	32	18	RC. 7/5, pp. 1–35
	P	33	19	RC. 7/5, pp. 41–80
	T	(a) 34	18	RC. 7/5, pp. 85–213
		(b) 35	9	RC. 7/5, pp. 217–55
26	T	(a) 37	23	RC. 7/5, pp. 309–58
		(b) 36	12	RC. 7/5, pp. 259–304
26–7	M	38	41	RC. 7/5, pp. 363–426
27	H	(a) 39	37	RC. 7/5, pp. 431–97
		(b) 42	21	RC. 7/6, pp. 121–99
	P	(a) 40	18	RC. 7/6, pp. 1–55
		(b) 43	13	RC. 7/6, pp. 203–41
	T	(a) 41	28	RC. 7/6, pp. 59–118
		(b) 44	20	RC. 7/6, pp. 245–96
27–8	M	50	39	RC. 7/7, pp. 273–365
28	H	51	25	RC. 7/7, pp. 371–406
	H, P, part of M	47	35	RC. 7/7, pp. 1–126
	P	48	28	RC. 7/7, pp. 131–98
	T	49	27	RC. 7/7, pp. 203–64
28–9	M	(a) 46	43	RC. 7/6, pp. 431–584
		(b) 45	30	RC. 7/6, pp. 299–425
29	T	56	27	RC. 7/8, pp. 95–204
29–30	M	52	21	RC. 7/7, pp. 411–514
30	P	62	26	RC. 7/9, pp. 309–88
	T	(a) 64	21	RC. 7/9, pp. 433–77
		(b) 63	16	RC. 7/9, pp. 391–426
30–31	M	61	36	RC. 7/9, pp. 227–304
31	P	67	19	RC. 7/10, pp. 1–61
31–2	M	[none]	41	RC. 8/1, pp. 189–262; RC. 8/2, pp. 135–296
32	T	69	31	RC. 7/10, pp. 203–88
32–3	M	68	52	RC. 7/10, pp. 65–199
33	H	72	31	RC. 7/10, pp. 405–520
	P	73	39	RC. 7/10, pp. 523–631
	T	(a) 74	39	RC. 7/11, pp. 1–103
		(b) 75	19	RC. 7/11, pp. 109–66
33–4	M	71	40	RC. 7/10, pp. 297–400
34	H	79	25	RC. 7/11, pp. 387–446
	P	80	25	RC. 7/11, pp. 453–524
	T	81	28	RC. 7/11, pp. 529–95
34–5	M	78	44	RC. 7/11, pp. 221–381

APPENDIX VI

Regnal year	Law term	Record commissioners' number	Number of membranes	Reference
		Edward II		
1	M	84	20	RC. 7/13 (mm. 1–11 only)
	P	86	27	RC. 7/13
1–2	T	87	26	Surviving in P.R.O.I.; also calendar, RC. 7/13
2	M	91	52	RC. 7/13
	H	92	42	RC. 7/13
4	M	[none]	33	RC. 8/6, pp. 1–148; also RC. 8/23, pp. 777–822 (mm. 1–8 only)
5–6	T	[none]	44	RC. 8/6, pp. 333–493
9	M	[none]	31	RC. 8/10, pp. 281–402
10	M	[none]	43	RC. 8/11, pp. 453–865. There is a charred lump in P.R.O.I., thought to be one of the rolls of this year
10	H	[none]	30	RC. 8/11, pp. 1–216
	P	[none]	9	RC. 8/11, pp. 216–42
10–11	T	[none]	25	RC. 8/11, pp. 242–453
11	M	120	38	RC. 7/12, pp. 283–369
	H	121	22	RC. 7/12, pp. 375–438
	P	122	26	RC. 7/12, pp. 441–504

APPENDIX VII

ANALYSES OF ROLLS OF THE BENCH

THE surviving rolls, Easter 18 Edward I and Trinity 1-2 Edward II, have been used for this purpose. The later roll has been supplemented, in view of its present condition, by reference to the calendar in P.R.O.I., RC. 7/13 (bundle of papers from the Irish record commission). Easter 1 Edward II has also been added from this source, so that comparison is possible with one of the justiciary rolls analysed in Appendix v, above. But the figures which result for the combined terms Easter-Trinity 1-2 Edward II are definitely incomplete.

Actions have been arranged in an order influenced largely by the third volume of Holdsworth, and, in the case of the real actions, the analysis in *Bracton's Note Book* (ed. Maitland, 1, 177-87); for the subdivisions of trespass reference has been made to Professor Milsom's article mentioned in the introductory remarks to Appendix v, above. Dower has not been subdivided: all the entries are consistent with the form *unde nichil habet*, although the phrase is not found (cf. Turner, *Brevia placitata*, p. xcii). The actions classified as 'uncertain' are known only from essoins or attorneys or are in essentials illegible. With one exception (indicated by asterisk) cases have been counted once only, but there are probably quite a few unobserved duplications in the larger and 'uncertain' categories.

	P. 18 Edw. I	P.-T. 1-2 Edw. II
A. REAL ACTIONS		
WRITS OF RIGHT		
of land	5	3
of advowson	1	2
DOWER	38	97
WRITS OF ENTRY		
sur disseisin	9	6
ad terminum qui praeteriit	3	3
cui in vita	9	12
dum fuit infra etatem	1	—
dum non fuit compos mentis	1	1
unspecified variety	1	1

APPENDIX VII

	P. 18 Edw. I	P.–T. 1–2 Edw. II
A. REAL ACTIONS (*cont.*)		
ASSIZES OF NOVEL DISSEISIN	10	6
ASSIZES: MORT D'ANCESTOR GROUP		
Mort d'ancestor	11	5
Aiel	9	3
Cosinage	1	1
ASSIZE UTRUM	2	—
DARREIN PRESENTMENT, etc.		
Darrein presentment	1	1
Quare impedit	3	3
Plea of advowson unspecified	1	1
MISCELLANEOUS		
Warrantia carte	7	7
Escheat by bastardy	1	—
Formedon	2	6
Placitum maritagii	1	—
Placita custodie	—	3
Quod reddat custodiam	—	1
Action against heiress for refusing proffered match (Stat. Westminster I, c. 22)	—	1
Placitum homagii et relevii	1	—
Mesne	4	1
Suit of county court	1	—
Suit of mill	1	—
Cessavit per biennium	2	1
Contra formam feoffamenti	1	—
Replevin	7	1
Waste	1	1
Placitum housebote et haybote	1	—
Receit of persons claiming rights in land subject to intended fine	—	4
Jury according to Stat. Westminster II, c. 32	—	1
UNCERTAIN (*placita terre, placita warrantie*)	61	56
TOTAL REAL ACTIONS	197	228
B. APPEALS AND TRESPASSES		
APPEALS		
Robbery	1*	—
TRESPASSES		
Assault and battery	3	4
Similar, *in contemptu protectionis*, etc.	3	—
False imprisonment	1	—
De bonis asportatis	2	5

	P. 18 Edw. I	P.–T. 1–2 Edw. II
TRESPASSES (*cont.*) B. APPEALS AND TRESPASSES (*cont.*)		
Quare cum communi consilio regni statuerit dominus rex etc. (distress contrary to *Districciones scaccarii*)	1	1
Ejectment from wardship, etc.	—	2
Rescue of cattle	1	1
Placitum conspiracionis et transgressionis	—	1
Uncertain (*placita transgressionis*)	2	10
TOTAL APPEALS AND TRESPASSES	14	24
C. CONTRACT		
Debt and detinue	5	37
Account	1	6
Covenant	1	6
TOTAL CONTRACT	7	49
D. JURISDICTION IN REVIEW AND BY TRANSFER		
Attaint of jury	4	—
False judgment: (*a*) county court	—	2
(*b*) seignorial court	1	2
Record of assizes: (*a*) eyre	—	1
(*b*) justices assigned	3	—
(*c*) uncertain	1	—
Placitum terre unde recordum	1	2
TOTAL JURISDICTION IN REVIEW, etc.	10	7
E. MISCELLANEOUS		
Prohibition	2	—
Uncertain cases	11	9
Process on recognizances and judgments	6	30
Enrolments of recognizances and charters	7	10
Note of cases sent to England	1	—
Note of cases sent to justiciar	1*	—
Writs of general attorney noted	2	3
Miscellaneous enrolments of writs, certifications, etc.	5	5
TOTAL MISCELLANEOUS	35	57
GRAND TOTAL	263	365

* Same case.

APPENDIX VIII

LIST OF ITINERANT JUSTICES' ROLLS, HENRY III–EDWARD I

THE following list is based on those in *Ir. rec. comm. rep. 1816–20*, pp. 79–90, and *P.R.I. rep. D.K. 26*, Appendix III, p. 63, together with examination of the surviving sources. References to rolls for which no calendar of any kind survives have been omitted. In referring to the calendars prepared by the Irish record commissioners, only the form 'RC. 7' for *Cal. plea rolls*, with item number and page reference has been adopted here: the item number is also a volume number. With regard to the rolls of the reign of Henry III reference should be made to p. 10 and Appendix I, above.

Regnal year	Proceedings recorded	Record commissioners' number	Number of membranes	Source
		Henry III		
36	Justices itinerant at Limerick, T. 1253	1	6	RC. 7/1, pp. 119–221
44	Same at Cork, H. 1260	2	26	RC. 7/1, pp. 225–309
45	Same at Limerick, T. 1261	4	16	RC. 7/1, pp. 339–412
45–6	Same at Dublin, M. 1261	3	7	RC. 7/1, pp. 313–35
53–4	Same at Dublin, M. 1269	5	18	RC. 7/1, pp. 415–89
		Edward I		
18	Eyre of Limerick (crown and common pleas)	13	46	RC. 7/2, pp. 139–283
	Same eyre (common pleas only)	14	30	RC. 7/2, pp. 289–443
25	Various assize membranes	27	9	RC. 7/4, pp. 233–48

Regnal year	Proceedings recorded	Record commissioners' number	Number of membranes	Source
	Edward I (*cont.*)			
25–6	Eyre of Kildare before the justiciar (crown pleas)	30	19	*C.J.R. 1295–1303*, pp. 167–208; RC. 7/4, pp. 405–34
29	Eyre of Louth (crown pleas)	53	14	RC. 7/8, pp. 1–16
	Similar	54	23	RC. 7/8, pp. 19–44
	Same eyre (common pleas)	57	10	RC. 7/8, pp. 207–68
29	Eyre of Cork (crown pleas)	55	57	RC. 7/8, pp. 47–91
	Similar	58	51	RC. 7/8, pp. 271–505
	Same eyre (Robert of Littlebury's roll, crown and common pleas)	59	55	RC. 7/9, pp. 1–217
33–4	Eyre of Tipperary (crown and common pleas)	76	92	RC. 7/11, pp. 175–213; P.R.O.I. has full text of mm. 1–4 and English calendar of mm. 39–69

APPENDIX IX

ANALYSIS OF PLEAS OF THE CROWN AND GAOL DELIVERY, EYRE OF KILDARE, 1297–8

THE analysis is of the judicial business found on the following membranes of the roll: mm. 4, 6, part of 9d, 10, 12, 13, 15, and 18 (beginning in *C.J.R. 1295–1303*, at pp. 200, 196, 175, 202, 193, 207, 191, and 205, respectively). Reference should be made to the pleas of the crown section of Appendix v, above.

HOMICIDE
    Made fine   6
    To be hanged   1
    Acquitted   2
                               TOTAL   9

RAPE
    Made fine   1
    To be outlawed as fugitive   1
                               TOTAL   2

ROBBERY AND BURGLARY
    Benefit of clergy (delivered as acquitted)   1
    Made fine   38
    To be hanged   2
    Acquitted   21
    To be outlawed as fugitive   1
    Doubtful   2
                               TOTAL   65

LARCENY
    Made fine   17
    Acquitted   13
                               TOTAL   30

RECEIVING STOLEN CHATTELS
    Pardoned   1
    Made fine   7
    Acquitted   1
    To be outlawed as fugitive   1
    To be 'punished by imprisonment' (poor, and principal not yet convicted)   1
                               TOTAL   11

HARBOURING FELONS

Produced letters of pardon	1
Benefit of clergy (delivered as convicted)	1
Made fine	29
Acquitted	6
Incomplete	1
Total	38

MISCELLANEOUS

Breach of sanctuary: acquitted	1
Sold ale contrary to the assize: amerced	1

Misdoings of local officials:
   Made fine 2
   Acquitted 1
   Guilty, punishment not recorded 2
	5

Escape
   Made fine 1
   Acquitted 1
	2

Wrongful imprisonment: made fine	1
Sued plea in court christian: made fine	1
Failure to raise hue and cry: amerced	1
Took fine from robber without licence: made fine	1
Pound-breach: acquitted	1
Prisoner's head tonsured (in order to secure benefit of clergy): acquitted	1

Serjeant deforced of goods seized:
   Made fine 1
   Acquitted 1
	2

Total	17
Grand Total	172

BIBLIOGRAPHY

I. MANUSCRIPT SOURCES

Cambridge: University Library
Additional 3104. Irish legal abstracts (seventeenth century).

Dublin: Muniments of the Dean and Chapter of Christ Church Cathedral
Novum registrum. Eighteenth-century compilation from deeds destroyed in the Public Record Office of Ireland, 1922.

Dublin: Muniments of the Lord Mayor and Corporation
White Book of the City of Dublin.

Dublin: Public Record Office of Ireland
1. Surviving original records:
   Justiciary roll (common pleas), 6–7 Edw. II.
   Common bench rolls, Trinity, 1–2 Edw. II and (uncertain term) 10 Edw. II.
   Memoranda rolls, 3 Edw. II and 13–14 Edw. II.
2. Calendars prepared for the Irish Record Commission:
   Calendar of plea rolls. 13 vols. (RC. 7).
   Calendar of memoranda rolls. 43 vols. (RC. 8).
3. Other modern transcripts and calendars:
   Transcript of justiciary roll (common pleas), 6–7 Edw. II.
   English calendar of justiciary rolls (in course of publication). Two rolls of 7 Edw. II, two of 11 Edw. II, one of 11–12 Edw. II (common pleas); rolls of 8–9, 9–11, and 11 Edw. II (pleas of the crown).
   Partial transcript and partial English calendar (both incomplete) of roll of the eyre of Tipperary, 33–4 Edw. I.
   English calendar of memoranda rolls. 22–3 and 31–5 Edw. I; 1 and 3 Edw. II. With index to calendar of rolls of Edward I.

Dublin: Royal Irish Academy
12D 9. Transcript of Irish pipe roll, 45 Henry III.
12D 12. Latin calendar of Dublin bench roll, 10 Edw. I.

London: British Museum
Cotton Augustus II, no. 104. Irish ecclesiastical *gravamina*.
Cotton Titus B XI, f. 1. Petition of the earl of Ulster.
Harleian 240. *Liber Niger de Wigmor.*

[251]

Harleian 712. Chronicle of Fordun.
Lansdowne 652. Fourteenth-century legal miscellanea.
Royal 13E x. Chronicle of Fordun.
Additional 4525. Collections of Thomas Madox, vol. xlvii.
Additional Charter 13598. Roll of the Dublin bench, Easter 18 Edw. I.
Additional Charter 13599. Justiciary roll (common pleas), 4 Edw. III.

London: Lambeth Palace Library
619, f. 206. Irish ecclesiastical petition.

London: Library of Lincoln's Inn
Hale 140, ff. 91–106v. Register of writs *secundum usum Ricardi de Bereford*.

London: Public Record Office
A list of classes will be found at pp. ix–x, above.

Oxford: Bodleian Library
Laud. Misc. 613. Carew Miscellanea (extracts from public records concerning Ireland).

II. PRINTED SOURCES

The following have been omitted from this list: (*a*) publications of the English record commission; (*b*) the standard modern series of record publications published by H.M. Stationery Office; (*c*) standard editions of the *Statutes*, whether Irish, English, British or United Kingdom. Irish record publications have, however, been included.

Ancient laws and institutions of Ireland. 6 vols. Dublin, 1865–1901.
Annals of Ireland by Friar John Clyn. Ed. R. Butler. Irish archaeological society, 1849.
Annals of Loch Cé. Ed. W. A. Hennessy. 2 vols. Rolls ser. 1871.
Black Book of Limerick. Ed. J. McCaffrey. Dublin, 1907.
Borough Customs. Ed. M. Bateson. 2 vols. S.S. 18, 21 (1904–6).
Bracton de legibus et consuetudinibus Angliae. All quotations are from the edition of G. E. Woodbine (4 vols. New Haven, 1915–42).
Bracton's Note-book. Ed. F. W. Maitland. 3 vols. London, 1887.
Brevia placitata. Ed. G. J. Turner. S.S. 66 (1951).
Britton. Ed. F. M. Nichols. 2 vols. Oxford, 1865.
Caithréim Thoirdhealbhaigh le Seán Mac Ruaidhrí mac Craith. Ed. S. H. O'Grady, with introduction by R. Flower. 2 vols. Irish Texts Soc. 26, 27 (1929).
Calendar of Archbishop Alen's register. Ed. C. McNeill. R.S.A.I. 1949.

BIBLIOGRAPHY

'Calendar of Christ Church deeds'. In *P.R.I. rep. D.K. 20, 23, 24* and *27* (Appendices).
Calendar of Ormond deeds. Ed. E. Curtis. 6 vols. Irish MSS. Comm. 1932–43.
Calendar of the ancient records of Dublin. Ed. J. T. Gilbert. 18 vols. Dublin, 1889–1922.
Calendar of the Gormanston register. Ed. J. Mills and M. J. McEnery. R.S.A.I. 1916.
Calendar of the justiciary rolls or proceedings in the court of the justiciar of Ireland. 3 vols. In progress. P.R.O.I. 1905–.
'Catalogue of great rolls of the pipe of the Irish exchequer.' In *P.R.I. rep. D.K. 35, 36, 37, 38, 39, 42, 43, 44, 45, 47, 53* and *54* (Appendices).
Chartae, privilegia et immunitates: being transcripts of charters and privileges to bodies corporate, 1171 to 1395. Ir. rec. comm. 1829.
'Charters of the Cistercian abbey of Duiske.' Ed. J. H. Bernard and M. C. Butler. *R.I.A. Proc.* xxxv (1918), 1–188.
Chartularies of St Mary's abbey, Dublin; with the register of its house at Dunbrody, and annals of Ireland. Ed. J. T. Gilbert. 2 vols. Rolls ser. 1884.
'Chronicle of Pembridge.' In *Chartul. St Mary's, Dublin,* II, 293–398.
Cole, H. (editor). *Documents illustrative of English history in the thirteenth and fourteenth centuries.* Rec. comm. 1844.
Court book of the liberty of St Sepulchre. Ed. H. Wood. R.S.A.I. 1930.
Críth Gablach. Ed. D. A. Binchy. Dublin, 1941.
Curtis, E. and McDowell, R. B. *Irish historical documents, 1172–1922.* London, 1943.
Davies, Sir John. 'A discoverie of the true causes why Ireland was never entirely subdued.' *Works,* II, 1–168; also in *Ireland under Elizabeth and James I,* ed. H. Morley (London, 1890), pp. 213–342.
  Les reports des cases et matters en ley resolves et adjudges en les courts del roy en Ireland. London, 1674. *Works of Sir John Davies.* Ed. A. B. Grosart. Privately printed, 1869–76.
Ehrle, R. 'Ein Bruchstück der Acten des Konzils von Vienne.' *Archiv für Literatur und Kirchengeschichte des Mittel-Alters,* IV (1888), 361–470.
Facsimiles of the national manuscripts of Ireland. 4 parts. H.M.S.O. 1874–84.
Fitzherbert, Sir Anthony. *Nouvelle Natura Brevium.* References are to the uniform foliation of the sixteenth-century editions.
Fleta. (*a*) Ed. J. Selden. London, 1647. (*b*) Ed. H. G. Richardson and G. O. Sayles. In progress; vol. II alone published. S.S. 72 (1953).
Fordun, John. *Scotichronicon.* (*a*) Ed. T. Hearne. 5 vols. Oxford, 1722. (*b*) Ed. W. Goodall. 2 vols. Edinburgh, 1759.

His Maiesties directions for the ordering and setling of the courts and course of justice within his kingdome of Ireland. Dublin, 1622. Also: ed. G. J. Hand and V. W. Treadwell, *Anal. hib.* (forthcoming).

Irish cartularies of Llanthony Prima and Secunda. Ed. E. St John Brooks. Irish MSS. Comm. 1955.

'Irish pipe roll of 14 John, 1211–12.' Ed. O. Davies and D. B. Quinn. Supplement to *Ulster journal of archaeology*, IV (1941).

Jacobi Grace Kilkenniensis annales Hiberniae. Ed. R. Butler. Irish arch. soc. 1842.

Liber primus Kilkenniensis. Ed. C. McNeill. Irish MSS. Comm. 1931.

'Lord Chancellor Gerrard's notes of his report on Ireland.' Ed. C. McNeill. *Anal. hib.* II, 93–291.

McNeill, C. 'Reports on manuscripts in the Bodleian Library, Oxford.' *Anal. hib.* I, 1–178.

MacNeill, E. 'Ancient Irish law; the law of status or franchise.' *R.I.A. Proc.* XXXVI (1923), 265–316.

Meekings, C. A. F. *Crown pleas of the Wiltshire eyre, 1249.* Wilts. Archaeological society, Records branch, vol. xvi. Devizes, 1961.

'Muniments of Edmund de Mortimer, third earl of March, concerning his liberty of Trim.' Ed. H. Wood, *R.I.A. Proc.* XL (1932), 312–55.

Proceedings against Dame Alice Kyteler, prosecuted for sorcery in 1324 by Richard de Ledrede, bishop of Ossory. Ed. T. Wright. Camden Soc. (old ser.), XXIV (1843).

Prynne, W. *Exact chronological vindication of our kings' supreme jurisdiction.* (Commonly called 'Prynne, *Records*'.) 3 vols. London, 1665–8.

Red book of the earls of Kildare. Ed. G. Mac Niocaill. Irish MSS. Comm. 1964.

Red book of Ormond. Ed. N. B. White. Irish MSS. Comm. 1932.

Register of the abbey of St Thomas the Martyr, Dublin. Ed. J. T. Gilbert. Rolls ser. 1889.

Register of the hospital of St John the Baptist without the New Gate, Dublin. Ed. E. St John Brooks. Irish MSS. Comm. 1936.

Register of the priory of the blessed virgin Mary of Tristernagh. Ed. M. V. Clarke. Irish MSS. Comm. 1941.

Registrum omnium brevium tam originalium quam iudicialium. 2nd ed. London, 1595.

'Rental of the manor of Lisronagh, 1333, with notes on betagh tenure.' Ed. E. Curtis. *R.I.A. Proc.* XLIII (1936), 41–76.

Reports of the commissioners appointed to execute the measures recommended in an address of the House of Commons respecting the public records of Ireland. 3 vols. London, 1815–25.

Reports of the Deputy Keeper of the Public Records of Ireland. In progress. Dublin, 1869–.

Rôles Gascons. Ed. F. Michel and C. Bémont. Documents inédits sur l'histoire de France: Paris, 1885–1906.
'Rôle Gascon de lettres closes, 1254–5.' Ed. C. Bémont. *Bulletin philologique et historique du comité des travaux historiques et scientifiques, 1915* (Paris, 1916), pp. 92–139.
Rotuli parliamentorum Anglie hactenus inediti, MCCLXXIX–MCCCLXXIII. Ed. H. G. Richardson and G. O. Sayles. Royal Hist. Soc., Camden 3rd ser. LI (1935).
Rotulorum patentium et clausorum cancellariae Hiberniae calendarium. Ir. rec. comm. 1828.
Select cases concerning the law merchant. Ed. C. Gross and H. Hall. 3 vols. S.S. 23, 46, 49 (1908–32).
Select cases in the exchequer of pleas. Ed. H. Jenkinson and B. E. R. Fermoy. S.S. 48 (1932).
Select cases in the court of king's bench. Ed. G. O. Sayles. In progress. S.S. 55, 57, 58, 74, 76, 82 (1936–   ).
Select cases of procedure without writ under Henry III. Ed. H. G. Richardson and G. O. Sayles. S.S. 60 (1941).
Sheehy, M. P. 'English law in medieval Ireland: two illustrative documents.' *Arch. hib.* XXIII (1960), 166–75.
Pontificia hibernica. 2 vols. Dublin, 1962–5.
'Sheriff's accounts of the honor of Dungarvan, of Tweskard in Ulster, and of county Waterford, 1261–63.' Ed. E. Curtis. *R.I.A. Proc.* XXXIX (1929), 1–17.
'Sheriff's accounts for county Tipperary, 1275–6.' Ed. E. Curtis. *R.I.A. Proc.* XLII (1934), 65–95.
State trials of the reign of Edward I, 1289–1293. Ed. T. F. Tout and H. Johnstone. Royal Hist. Soc., Camden 3rd ser. IX (1906).
Statutes and ordinances and acts of the parliament of Ireland, King John to Henry V. Ed. H. F. Berry. Dublin, 1907.
Song of Dermot and the Earl. Ed. G. H. Orpen. Oxford, 1892.
Year Books of the reign of King Edward the First. Ed. A. J. Horwood. 5 vols. Rolls ser. 1863–79.
Year Books of Edward II: 5 Edward II, 1311–1312. Ed. W. C. Bolland. 2 vols. S.S. 31, 33 (1915–16).
Year Books of the Eyre of Kent, 6 & 7 Edward II (1313–1314). Ed. F. W. Maitland, L. Harcourt, and W. C. Bolland. 3 vols. S.S. 24, 27, 29 (1909–13).

III. SECONDARY WRITING

Anon. (attributed, variously, to Richard Bolton and Patrick Darcy). 'A declaration setting forth how, and by what means, the laws and statutes of England, from time to time came to be in force in Ireland.' Ed. W. Harris, *Hibernica*, pt 2, pp. 9–45.

Armstrong, O. *Edward Bruce's invasion of Ireland*. London, 1923.

Bailey, S. J. 'Warranties of land in the thirteenth century.' 8 *Cambridge Law Journal*, pp. 274–99, and 9 *C.L.J.* pp. 82–106.

Ball, F. E. *The judges in Ireland*. 2 vols. London, 1926.

Binchy, D. A. 'The linguistic and historical value of the Irish law tracts.' *Brit. Acad. Proc.* XXIX (1943), 195–227.

Blackstone, Sir William. *Commentaries on the laws of England*. 1st ed., London, 1765.

Brooks, E. St John. 'The early Irish Comyns.' *R.S.A.I. Jn.* LXXXVI (1956), 170–86.

Bugge, A. 'Nordisk Sprog og Nordisk Nationalitet i Irland.' *Aarbogr for Nordisk Oldkyndighed og Historie*, 2nd ser. XV (1900), 219–32.

Butler, W. F. T. *Gleanings from Irish history*. London, 1925.

Cam, H. M. *Studies in the hundred rolls: some aspects of thirteenth-century administration*. Oxford studies in social and legal history, VI. Oxford, 1921.

Chaplais, P. F. 'The chancery of Guyenne, 1289–1453.' In *Studies presented to Sir Hilary Jenkinson*, pp. 61–96.

Clarke, M. V. *Fourteenth-century studies*. Oxford, 1937.

Connolly, J. *Labour, nationality, and religion*. 1st ed., Dublin, 1910.

Conway, C. (*see also* Ó Conbhuí). *The story of Mellifont*. Dublin, 1958.

Curtis, E. 'The English and Ostmen in Ireland.' *E.H.R.*, XXIII (1908), 209–19.

Medieval Ireland. 1st ed., Dublin, 1923. 2nd ed., London, 1938.

D'Arcy, R. F. *The life of John Darcy, first baron Darcy of Knayth, 1280–1347*. London, 1933.

Davies, R. R. 'The twilight of Welsh law, 1284–1536.' *History*, LI (1966), 143–64.

Delany, V. T. H. *The law relating to charities in Ireland*. Dublin, n.d. [1956?].

Denholm-Young, N. *Seignorial administration in England*. Oxford, 1937.

Dicey, A. V. *A fool's paradise*. London, 1913.

Dickinson, W. C. *Scotland from the earliest times to 1603*. (New history of Scotland, I.) 2nd ed. Edinburgh, 1965.

Dictionary of Welsh biography. English edition. Oxford, 1959.

BIBLIOGRAPHY

Donaldson, A. G. 'The application in Ireland of English and British legislation made before 1801.' Unpublished Ph.D. thesis, Queen's University of Belfast, 1952.
    Some comparative aspects of Irish law. Durham, N. C., and Cambridge, England, 1957.
English government at work, 1327–36. Ed. J. F. Willard, W. A. Morris, J. R. Strayer, and W. H. Dunham. 3 vols. Medieval Academy of America, 1940–50.
Féil-Sgríbhinn Eóin Mhic Néill. Ed. S. Ó Riain. Dublin, 1940.
Gabel, L. C. *Benefit of clergy in England in the later middle ages.* Smith College studies in history, XIV. Northampton, Mass. 1929.
Gilbert, J. T. *History of the viceroys of Ireland.* Dublin, 1865.
Green, A. S. *The making of Ireland and its undoing.* 2nd ed., London, 1909.
Green, F. 'The Wogans of Pembrokeshire.' *West Wales historical records,* VI (1916), 169–232.
Griffith, M. C. 'The Irish record commission, 1810–30.' *I.H.S.* VII (1950), 17–38.
Griffiths, R. A. 'Royal government in the southern counties of Wales, 1422–1485.' Unpublished Ph.D. thesis, University of Bristol, 1962.
Gwynn, A. 'Edward I and the proposed purchase of English law for the Irish, c.1276–80.' *R. Hist. Soc. Trans.* 5th ser. X (1960), 111–27.
    'Nicholas Mac Maol Íosa, archbishop of Armagh.' In *Féilsgríbhinn Eóin Mhic Néill,* pp. 394–405.
Hand, G. J. 'The Church and English law in medieval Ireland.' *Proceedings of the Irish Catholic historical committee, 1959,* pp. 10–18.
    'The dating of the early fourteenth-century ecclesiastical valuations of Ireland.' *Irish theological quarterly,* XXIV (1957), 271–4.
    'English law and its administration in Ireland, c.1290–c.1324, with special reference to the court of the justiciar.' D.Phil. thesis, University of Oxford, 1960.
    'The two cathedrals of Dublin.' Unpublished M.A. thesis, National University of Ireland, 1954.
Harris, W. *Hibernica: or some ancient pieces relating to Ireland.* 2nd ed., Dublin, 1770.
Hunnisett, R. F. *The medieval coroner.* Cambridge, 1961.
Jenkinson, H. 'The great seal of England: deputed or departmental seals.' *Archaeologia,* LXXXV (1936), 293–340.
Johnston, W. K. 'The first adventure of the common law.' 36 *L.Q.R.* (1920), 9–30.
Jones Pierce, T. 'Social and historical aspects of the Welsh laws.' *Welsh history review* (Special number, 1963), pp. 33–49.
King, R. *Primer of the church history of Ireland.* 3 vols. 3rd ed., Dublin, 1845–51.

Kohn, L. *The constitution of the Irish Free State*. London, 1932.

Lawlor, H. J. *Fasti of St Patrick's, Dublin*. Dundalk, 1930.

Le Patourel, J. 'The Plantagenet dominions.' *History*, L (1965), 289–308.

Lydon, J. F. 'Ireland's participation in the military activities of English kings in the thirteenth and early fourteenth centuries.' Unpublished Ph.D. thesis, University of London, 1955.

— 'The Bruce invasion of Ireland.' *Historical studies*, IV (Dublin, 1963), pp. 111–25.

— 'Edward II and the revenues of Ireland in 1311–12.' *I.H.S.* XIV (1964), 39–57.

— 'The Irish exchequer in the thirteenth century.' *Bulletin of the Irish committee of historical sciences*, no. 81, pp. 1–2.

— 'Three exchequer documents from the reign of Henry the Third.' *R.I.A. Proc.* LXV (1966), 1–27.

Lynch, W. *A view of legal institutions, honorary hereditary offices, and feudal baronies, established in Ireland during the reign of Henry II*. London, 1830.

MacInerny, M. H. *A history of the Irish Dominicans*. Dublin, 1916.

McNamara, L. F. 'An examination of the medieval Irish text *Caithréim Thoirdhealbhaigh*.' *North Munster antiquarian journal*, VIII (1961), 182–92.

McNeill, C. 'The secular jurisdiction of the early archbishops of Dublin.' *R.S.A.I. Jn.* XLV (1915), 81–108.

MacNeill, E. *Early Irish laws and institutions*. Dublin, n.d. [1935].

— *Phases of Irish history*. Dublin, 1919.

Maitland, F. W. 'The history of the register of original writs.' 3 *Harvard Law Review*, 97–115, 167–79, 212–25. Reprinted in *Select essays in Anglo-American legal history* (3 vols; Boston, 1907–9), II, 549–96, and in *Collected papers*, ed. H. A. L. Fisher (3 vols; Cambridge, 1911), II, 110–73.

— 'The introduction of English law into Ireland.' *E.H.R.* IV (1889), 516–17. Reprinted in *Collected papers*, II, 81–3.

Mason, H. J. M. *An essay on the antiquity and constitution of parliaments in Ireland*. 1st ed., Dublin, 1820; new edition, ed. J. O'Hanlon, Dublin, 1891.

Mayart, Sir Samuel. 'The answer of Sir Samuel Mayart, serjeant-at-law and second judge of the common-pleas in Ireland, to a book entitled, *A declaration setting forth how ... the laws ... of England ... came to be of force in Ireland*.' Ed. W. Harris, *Hibernica*, pt 2, pp. 47–231.

Medieval studies presented to Aubrey Gwynn, S.J. Ed. J. A. Watt, J. B. Morrall, and F. X. Martin, O.S.A. Dublin, 1961.

Mills, J. 'Tenants and agriculture near Dublin in the fourteenth century.' *R.S.A.I. Jn.* XX (1890), 54–63.

BIBLIOGRAPHY

Milsom, S. F. C. 'Trespass from Henry III to Edward III.' 74 *L.Q.R.* (1958), 195–224, 407–36, 561–90.
Moody, T. W. 'The writings of Edmund Curtis.' *I.H.S.* III (1942–3), 393–400.
Moran, F. E. 'The migration of the common law: 7: The Republic of Ireland.' 76 *L.Q.R.* (1960), 69–73.
Neilson, N. 'The court of common pleas.' In *English government at work, 1327–36*, III, 259–85.
Newark, F. H. 'The case of Tanistry.' 9 *N.I.L.Q.* (1952), 215–21.
 Notes on Irish legal history. Belfast, 1960. (Originally published in 7 *N.I.L.Q.* (1946), 121–39.)
Nicholson, R. G. 'Magna Carta and the Declaration of Arbroath.' *University of Edinburgh journal* (Autumn 1965), pp. 140–4.
Nugent, W. F. 'Carlow in the middle ages.' *R.S.A.I. Jn.* LXXXV (1955), 62–76.
Ó Conbhuí, C. (*see also* Conway). 'The lands of St Mary's abbey, Dublin.' *R.I.A. Proc.* LXII (1962), 21–84.
Orpen, G. H. *Ireland under the Normans.* 4 vols. Oxford, 1911–20.
O'Sullivan, M. D. *Italian merchant bankers in Ireland in the thirteenth century.* Dublin, 1962.
Otway-Ruthven, J. 'Anglo-Irish shire government in the thirteenth century.' *I.H.S.* V (1946–7), 1–28.
 'The chief governors of medieval Ireland.' *R.S.A.I. Jn.* XCV (1965), 227–36.
 'The constitutional position of the great lordships of South Wales.' *R. Hist. Soc. Trans.* 5th ser. VIII (1958), 1–20.
 'Knight-service in Ireland.' *R.S.A.I. Jn.* LXXXIX (1959), 1–15.
 'The medieval county of Kildare.' *I.H.S.* XI (1958–9), 181–99.
 'The medieval Irish chancery.' *Album H.M. Cam* (Louvain, 1961), I, 119–38.
 'The native Irish and English law in medieval Ireland.' *I.H.S.* VII (1950–1), 1–16.
 'The request of the Irish for English law, 1277–80.' *I.H.S.* VI (1948–9), 261–70.
Painter, S. *William Marshal.* Baltimore, 1933.
Pegues, F. 'The *clericus* in the legal administration of thirteenth-century England.' *E.H.R.* LXXI (1956), 529–59.
Plucknett, T. F. T. *Concise history of the common law.* 5th ed., London, 1956.
 Legislation of Edward I. Oxford, 1949.
 Statutes and their interpretation in the fourteenth century. Cambridge, 1922.
Pocock, J. G. A. *The ancient constitution and the feudal law.* Cambridge, 1957.

Pollock, F. and Maitland, F. W. *A history of English law before the time of Edward I.* 2nd ed., Cambridge, 1898.
Powicke, F. M. *The thirteenth century, 1216–1307.* Oxford, 1953.
Price, L. 'The origin of the word *betagius*.' *Ériu*, XX (1966), 185–90.
Quinn, D. B. 'Anglo-Irish local government, 1485–1534.' *I.H.S.* I (1938–9), 354–81.
Redford, A. 'The climax of medieval Ireland: the administration of Ireland under Edward II.' Unpublished B.A. thesis, University of Manchester, 1915.
Reville, A. '*L'abjuracio regni:* histoire d'une institution anglaise'. *Revue historique* L (1892), 1–42.
Richardson, H. G. 'The English coronation oath.' *Speculum*, XXIV (1949), 44–75.
— 'English institutions in medieval Ireland.' *I.H.S.* I (1938–9), 382–92.
— *The English Jewry under Angevin kings.* Jewish hist. soc. 1960.
— 'Magna Carta Hiberniae.' *I.H.S.* III (1942–3), 31–3.
— 'Norman Ireland in 1212.' *I.H.S.* III (1942–3), 144–58.
— Review of M. D. O'Sullivan, *Old Galway* (Cambridge, 1942). *I.H.S.* IV (1944–5), 361–7.
Richardson, H. G. and Sayles, G. O. *The administration of medieval Ireland.* Irish MSS. Comm. 1963.
— 'The early statutes.' 50 *L.Q.R.* (1934), 201–23, 540–71.
— *The Irish parliament in the middle ages.* 1st ed., Philadelphia, 1952.
— 'The Irish parliaments of Edward I.' *R.I.A. Proc.* XXXVIII (1929), 128–47.
— 'Irish revenue, 1278–1384.' *R.I.A. Proc.* LXII (1962), 86–100.
— *Parliaments and great councils in medieval England.* London, 1961. (Originally published in 77 *L.Q.R.* (1961), 213–36, 401–26.)
Richey, A. G. *Lectures on the history of Ireland down to 1534.* Dublin, 1869.
— *Short history of the Irish people.* Ed. R. R. Kane. Dublin, 1887.
Rothwell, H. 'The confirmation of the charters, 1297.' *E.H.R.* LX (1945), 16–35, 177–91, 300–15.
— 'Edward I and the struggle for the charters, 1297–1305.' In *Studies in medieval history presented to F. M. Powicke*, pp. 319–32.
Sayles, G. O. (*see also* Richardson). 'The siege of Carrickfergus Castle, 1315–16.' *I.H.S.* X (1956–7), 94–100.
— Review of *Calendar of justiciary rolls, 1308–14*. *E.H.R.* LXXIII (1958), 101–5.
Schuyler, R. L. *Parliament and the British empire.* New York, 1929.
Stewart-Brown, R. 'The advowries of Chester.' *E.H.R.* XXIX (1914), 41–55.

Stubbs, W. *Constitutional history of England.* 5th ed., Oxford, 1891.
Studies in medieval history presented to F. M. Powicke. Ed. R. W. Hunt, W. A. Pantin, and R. W. Southern. Oxford, 1948.
Studies presented to Sir Hilary Jenkinson. Ed. J. C. Davies. London, 1957.
Sutherland, D. W. Quo warranto *proceedings in the reign of Edward I.* Oxford, 1963.
Van Caeneghem, R. C. *Royal writs in England from the conquest to Glanvill.* S.S. 77 (1959).
Watt, J. A. 'English law and the Irish church: the reign of Edward I.' In *Medieval studies presented to Aubrey Gwynn,* pp. 133-67.
'Negotiations between Edward II and John XXII concerning Ireland.' *I.H.S.* x (1956-7), 1-20.
Young, J. I. 'A note on the Norse occupation of Ireland.' *History,* xxxv (1950), 11-33.

ADDENDA TO BIBLIOGRAPHY

II. *Printed Sources*

Mac Niocaill, G. (ed.). *Na Buirgéisí* xii-xiv *aois.* 2 vols. Dublin, 1964.

III. *Secondary Writing*

Hand, G. J. 'Christ Church, Dublin, and the common law, 1277-1382.' *R.S.A.I. Jn,* xcvii (1967) (forthcoming).
'The case of Nicholas John.' *County Louth archaeological society journal,* xv (1963), 273-6.
Mac Niocaill, G. 'The origins of the Betagh.' 1 *Ir. Jur.* (N.S.) (1966) 292-8.

TABLE OF STATUTES

Irish statutes are distinguished by the abbreviation (Ir.)

1225	9 Henry III: Magna Carta	
	c. 4 (waste by guardians)	page 163–4
	c. 11 (common pleas)	78
	c. 12 (assizes)	124
	c. 24 (precipe)	91
1236	20 Henry III: Statute of Merton	3, 161
	c. 6 (marriage)	62 n. 2
1267	52 Henry III: Statute of Marlborough	5, 161
	c. 2 (distress)	109
	c. 3 (replevin)	160
	c. 23 (*monstravit de compoto*)	5 n. 6
	c. 29 (entry)	5
1275	3 Edward I: Westminster I	5, 161
	c. 17 (distress)	160
	c. 22 (wardship)	245
	3 Edward I: *Districciones scaccarii*	162, 246
1278	6 Edward I: Statute of Gloucester	4, 5, 161
	c. 4 (*cessavit*)	167 n. 1
	c. 5 (waste)	150, 163–4, 169
	c. 8 (jurisdiction, trespass)	68, 71
	6 Edward I (Ir.)	
	c. 3 (English statutes)	4
	c. 5 (*kynkonges*)	172, 193, 203
	c. 7 (replevin)	160, 215
	c. 8 (escape)	204 n. 4
1279	7 Edward I: Statute of Mortmain	5, 108, 163, 164–6
1284	12 Edward I: Statute of Money	5
	12 Edward I: Statute of Rhuddlan	5
	12 Edward I: Statute of Wales	68, 187–8
1285	13 Edward I: Westminster II	5, 161, 163, 166–71
	Preamble	4
	c. 3 (receit)	167

TABLE OF STATUTES

1285	c. 5 (damages in *quare impedit*)	page 167
	c. 10 (eyre)	107, 168
	c. 11 (account)	167
	c. 12 (malicious appeals)	167
	c. 13 (false imprisonment)	167
	c. 14 (waste)	169
	c. 16 (wardship)	167, 180
	c. 18 (*elegit*)	167
	c. 21 (*cessavit*)	167
	c. 25 (novel disseisin)	169–70
	c. 30 (assizes)	148, 152, 153, 168
	c. 32 (mortmain)	91, 164–5, 168, 245
	c. 34 (rape; abduction)	168
	c. 36 (malicious distress)	167–8
	c. 38 (jurors' qualification)	168
	c. 40 (*cui in vita*)	170–1
	c. 41 (frankalmoin)	168
	c. 50 (commencement)	171
	13 Edward I: Statute of Winchester	161
	13 Edward I: Statute of Merchants	4, 5, 84, 161
	13 Edward I: *Circumspecte Agatis*	72
1290	18 Edward I: *Quia Emptores*	51, 162
	18 Edward I: *Quo Warranto*	114
	18 Edward I: *De consultatione*	162
1293	21 Edward I: *De illis qui ponendi sunt in assisa*	161
	21 Edward I: Ordinances for Ireland	162
1297	25 Edward I: *Confirmatio cartarum*	76
	25 Edward I (Ir.)	
	c. 4 (robbery)	159
	c. 11 (English dress)	201–2
1299	27 Edward I: *De Finibus Levatis*	162
	27 Edward I: Statute of False Money	161
	27 Edward I (Ir.): Servants	161
1300	28 Edward I: *Articuli super cartas*	
	c. 4 (common pleas)	76
	c. 11 (champerty)	162
	28 Edward I (Ir.): False money	161
1307	35 Edward I: Carlisle	161

1310	3 Edward II (Ir.) (unnumbered) (liability of kin) c. 5 (assizes)	*page* 203–4 111
1316	9 Edward II, stat. I.: *Articuli cleri* c. 15 (privilege of sanctuary) 9 Edward II, stat. 2: Statute of Lincoln	 63 n.1 161
1318	12 Edward II: Statute of York	161
1320	13 Edward II (Ir.) c. 2 (English statutes) c. 5 (assizes) c. 11 (cross-lands)	 161 112 114
1327	1 Edward III, stat. I c. 6 (attaint)	 69 n.2
1328	2 Edward III c. 2 (pardons)	 29 n.6
1331	5 Edward III c. 7 (attaint)	 69 n.2
1340	14 Edward III, stat. 1 c. 15 (pardons)	 29 n.6
1351	25 Edward III (Ir.): Ordinances of Kilkenny c. 16 (common law)	 210
1354	28 Edward III c. 8 (attaint)	 69 n.2
1366	40 Edward III (Ir.): Statutes of Kilkenny c. 4 (common law)	 210 n.5
1390	13 Richard II, stat. 2 c. 1 (pardons)	 29 n.6
1495	10 Henry VII (Ir.): Poynings' Law c. 22 (English statutes)	 161, 165
1954	Mortmain (Repeal of Enactments) Act, 1954 (Ir.) (no. 32 of 1954) Schedule, part I	 165 n.8

INDEX

Legal matters occurring only in Appendixes V, VII and IX are not individually indexed. Year Book and modern cases are listed under 'cases'. Persons who held judicial office in the Irish justiciar's court and common bench are distinguished by the added initials 'J.J.B.', 'C.J.C.P.', 'J.C.P.'; Irish justices itinerant and justices in eyre by 'J.I.'. The names of modern authors are italicized.

abjuration of the land, 61, 62, 137, 236
accedas ad curiam, writ of, 98, 118–19
account, action of, 81, 97, 142, 157–8, 167, 246
Ace, Thomas, J.J.B., 46
acquittals, 62, 63, 110–11; Appendixes V and IX
actions, *see under names of individual actions and* procedure without writ
Adare (Limerick), 165 n. 7
advowson, pleas of, 3, 10, 17, 122, 138, 150, 244–5; *see also* assizes: darrein presentment; *quare impedit*; right
affray, 144
Aghmacart (Athmakart) (Leix), 64 n.4
Alexander, William, J.I., J.J.B., deputy justiciar, 33, 44 n. 5, 46, 185
allocate, writ of, 158
Alta Ripa, Maurice de, 64 n. 3
amercements, 63, 71, 109, 124, 127, 129–30, 138, 154, 200
Amory, Roger, 121
Annaghdown (Galway), see of, 144
Any(Knockaney)(Limerick), fair of,134
appeals, 10, 19, 62, 113, 167, 245
Appleby, John of, 48
Aquitaine, 27
arbitrators, 73, 239
Arbroath, abbot of, *see* Linton Declaration of, 198
Ardee (Louth), 34
Ardfert (Kerry), 34, 53 n. 1, 214, 217 bishop of 203
Ardmayle (Tipperary), 32, 57, 58 n.4
Armagh, archbishop of, 151, 176, 204–5; *see also* Mac Maoil Iosa
Armstrong, O., 191
arson, 204; *see also* Ireland: liberties: pleas reserved to the crown
assault and battery, *see* trespass

assizes
of darrein presentment, 97, 245
the grand, 98, 148, 174, 176
justices of, *see* Ireland: courts
of measures, 134
of mort d'ancestor, 1, 2, 10, 65, 136, 180 n. 4, 184–5, 200, 224–5, 238, 245
of novel disseisin, 1, 10, 17, 65–6, 124, 127, 149, 152–6, 166, 169–70, 185, 200, 211, 223, 238, 245
summons of, to justiciar's court, 54–5
to be kept as in England, 2
other references, 32, 57, 65–6, 84, 97, 98, 118, 138, 168, 199–200, 201 n. 1, 246
Athmakart, *see* Aghmacart
Athy (Kildare), 33 n. 2
attaint of jury, *see* jury
attorneys, 20 n. 5, 22, 49, 87, 95, 96, 102, 127–9, 137, 142, 153, 170
king's, 48–9
letters of attorney, 20, 28, 137, 239, 246
Audley, Hugh (*d.* 1347), 121
Auney, John del, 87–8
autrefois acquit, 144
avowries, 197, 199

Bacon, Nicholas, 18 n. 1, 125
Bacquepuis, William of, J.I., Appendix I
Bagod, Robert (I), C.J.C.P., 8–9, 92, 96, 148, 158, 224
Robert (II), J.C.P., J.J.B., 40 n. 2, 45–6, 94, 95
Thomas, J.C.P., 49 n. 9
bail and mainprise, 53, 61, 63, 64, 136, 157–8; Appendix V
mainpernors to blind principals, 31 n. 3, 177–8

18   [265]   HEL

bail and mainprise (*cont.*)
  persons mainprised summoned before justiciar, 54–5
Ballygaveran, *see* Gowran
Ballygorman, William of, 152–6
Ballylynan (Leix), *see* Clonleynan
Ballymakelly (Ballynakelly, Dublin), 225
Bannockburn, battle of, 121
Bardfield, William of, J.C.P., 93, 95, 99
Barford (Bereford), Richard of, treasurer and chancellor of Ireland, 27 n. 4, 130, 152, 156, 158
Barry, John, 101
  William, J.I., 105
bastardy, escheat by, 3, 245
  exception of, 17
battle, trial by, 134, 174
Bellofago, Almaric de, 48, 56
  James de, 48
Belvoir, Robert of, J.I., Appendix I
bench, Dublin (Irish common bench), *see* Ireland, courts
benefit of clergy, 60–3, 174, 236; Appendix IX
Benet, William, 77 n. 2
Benger, John, J.C.P., 95
Berkeley, Arnold of, J.I., Appendix I
Bermingham, John de, earl of Louth, justiciar, 28–9, 36, 83, 93, 95, 132, 209
  Peter de, 27, 133
Berwick, John of, J.I. (England), 136
'betaghs', 190–1, 194–8, 206–7, 209–10, 213; see also *biatach*; *bothach*; *hibernicus*
biatach, 195, 213
biathad, 172 n. 4
Bicknor, Alexander of, archbishop of Dublin, J.I., justiciar, 105, 106, 131
Bigod, liberty, *see* Carlow
  Roger, earl of Norfolk (*d.* 1306) 120, 121
bills, justiciar's (warrants), 30, 39, 70
  modern civil bill, 79
  procedure by, *see* procedure without writ
Binchy, D. A., 193, 195
Birthorpe, Roger of, J.J.B., J.C.P., 45 n. 2, 46, 94
Blond (Blound), Adam le, 63 n. 5
  Master David le, J.J.B., 40 n. 2, 44 n. 5, 46, 47, 96, 111, 139
  Richard le, J.I., J.C.P., 49, 95, 128, 129, 131
Bodenham, John, 202 n. 5
  Walter of, 143
Bonevill, Robert of, 56
bothach, 193–5, 213
Bother, Richard de, 61 n. 2
Boun, Joan de, 17 n. 6
bounds, writ of, 3, 173–4; see also *de divisis faciendis*; *de rationabilibus divisis*
Bourne (Burne), William de, 44 n. 5, 47, 77 n. 2; Nicholas, his assistant, 47
Brabazon, Roger, C.J.K.B. (England), 126, 142
Bracton, Henry of, 136–7, 178–9
Brehon law, 172–3, 188, 192–5, 210, 214, 215
Breton, Adam le, 111–12
Brevia placitata, 3
Bristol, Robert of, J.C.P., 95
Brittas (Dublin), 231
Britton, 40, 68, 69–70, 137, 199–200
Brotherton, Thomas of, 121
Brown, Richard, J.J.B., J.C.P., 46
Bruce, Edward, invasion of Ireland by, 24, 25, 28, 29, 35–7, 52, 82, 91, 92, 93, 121, 123, 132, 141, 189, 191, 198, 216, 218
Bruges, merchants of, 15
Brun, Gilbert, son of John, 71 n. 2
  Neil le, escheator, 73 n. 7, 152, 153–6
  Reginald, 56 n. 2
Bunratty (Clare), liberty of, 131–2
Burgh, Richard de, justiciar (1228–32), 3
  Richard de, earl of Ulster, lord of Connaught, deputy justiciar (1299–1300), 23, 27, 44 n. 5, 87, 93, 112, 123, 142, 176 n. 2, 227; and the native Irish, 23, 87–8, 197–8
  Walter de, earl of Ulster, 207
  William de, deputy justiciar, 23, 24 n. 1, 227
burglary, 110, 203, 249
Burnell, Robert, chancellor of England, 17, 101, 182–3
Butler family, 85
  Edmund, justiciar, 24, 26, 27, 28, 32–3, 35, 40, 56, 82, 132,

INDEX

Butler *(cont.)*
    141–2, 151, 156, 185, 227–8;
    Appendix IV
    Theobald (II?), 141
    Theobald (V) (*d.* 1299), 23
Buttevant (Cork), 34

Caister, William of, J.I., Appendix I
Caithréim Thoirdhealbhaigh, 36
Canon, Hugh, J.I., J.C.P., J.J.B., 46, 93, 95
canon law, 71 n. 4, 174–5: see also Church
Cantok, *see* Quantock
cantreds, 64, 107–8, 132, 169 n. 2
Cardiff, Nicholas of, 49 n. 9
Carlow, liberty and county of, 11–12, 112 n. 1, 113 nn. 4 and 6, 116 n. 4, 120, 121
    cross-lands of, 73
    steward of, 116 n. 2, 117, 121
    town of, 33, 57, 58 n. 3, 65 n. 4
Carreu, Maurice de, 101
Carrick (Waterford), earldom of, 132
cases
    (i) Year Book cases
        Y.B. 21 & 22 Edw. I (Rolls) 309: 136
        Y.B. 33–5 Edw. I (Rolls) 242: 171 n. 2
        Y.B. 5 Edw. II (S.S.) 152: 142, 147
    (ii) Modern cases
        Little *v.* Cooper (1937), I.R. 1: 2 n. 4
        Maguire *v.* A.-G. (1943) I.R. 238: 218
        O'Hanlon *v.* Logue (1906) I.R. 247: 218
        Tanistry, Case of (1608) Dav. Rep. 28: 173
        R. *v.* Bailey (1956) N.I.L.R. 15: 218
Cashel (Tipperary), 8 n. 5, 32, 33, 56 n. 2, 57, 65 n. 2, 218, 231–2
    archbishop of, 138, 201; *see also* fitz John; MacCarwell
Castledermot (Kildare), 33, 52 n. 5, 57, 73, 231
Castle Kevin (Wicklow), 23
casus regis, 3
cattle-driving, 34–5
Caunteton, family, 172, 212 n. 2
célsine, 194, 197

dóer-chéle (*céle giallnai*), 194
sóer-rath, 194
sóer-chéle, 194
certiorari, writ of, 16, 17, 97, 117, 145, 147, 148, 150, 239
Chamberlain, Alexander, 224–5
champerty, 47, 162
charities, religious, modern Irish law of, 218
Charleville (Cork), 34
Charter, the Great, 2, 76, 78–9, 163–4; *see also* Table of Statutes
    charters, interpretation of general words in, 114
    royal, voucher of, etc., 13, 18, 84, 147
chattels, felons', 109, 133–4; *see also* licences
Chaumflour, William, 49 n. 9
Chedworth, Thomas of, J.C.P., 92 n. 1, 94–5, 101
Chester, 20, 197
Church, the
    bishops
        assent of chapter required for legal transactions, 115
        certificate from bishop as to bastardy, 17
        royal rights, *sede vacante*, and in elections, 18, 39, 81, 144, 176, 179–80, 239
    courts
        jurisdiction, 11 n. 2, 71, 72, 74, 174–5, 205, 239, 250
        and prohibitions, 28, 162, 239
        see also benefit of clergy; wills
    effects of Norman invasion upon, 3–4, 174–6, 206
    and of Bruce invasion, 36–7
    tithes, 72, 74–5
    see also cross-lands; sanctuary; *and under names of sees*, etc.
cin comfocuis (*kynkonges*), 172, 193, 203
Clare
    Gilbert de, earl of Gloucester (*d.* 1307), 145 n. 2
    Gilbert de, earl of Gloucester (*d.* 1314), 121
    liberties, *see* Bunratty; Kilkenny
    Thomas de, 16, 131
Clonard (Meath), abbey of, 114, 144
Clonleynan (? Ballylynan, Leix), 33, 57, 58 n. 3
Clonmel (Tipperary), 91, 232
cóe, 172 n. 4

INDEX

Cogan, John, 35, 139, 224–5
  Henry, 111–12
coinage, *see* false money
Colp (Meath), prior of, 72 n. 3
compurgation, 134, 201
Comyn, John (*d.* 1277), 179–85 *passim*
  Mabel, 179–85 *passim*
Conktilin (? Louth), 224
Connaught, 92, 114, 115, 123, 176, 220
  lord of, *see* Burgh
conspiracy, 47, 86, 156, 238, 246
consultation, writ of, 28
contempt, committal for, 146
contract, *see* account; covenant; debt; detinue; trespass
Coolock (Dublin), David and John, sons of Emma the nurse of, 208 n. 6
Cork, city, 28, 33, 34, 52 n. 5, 56 n. 2, 57, 73, 134 n. 7, 221, 232, 247
  county, 73, 111, 139
  eyre of: (*1260*) 8; (*1301*) 104, 105 n. 2, 109, 248
Corner, Richard de la, bishop of Meath, 152
  William de la, bishop of Salisbury, 152–6
coroners, 60, 108, 169, 202
count (upon a writ), 74
covenant, 72, 76, 81, 97, 246
Críth Gablach, 193–4
Crombe, Alice of, 224
  Philip of, 224
cross-lands, 12, 17, 108, 113–14, 115, 117, 122, 123, 125, 130
Crus, Milo de, 18
  Robert, son of Richard de, 18 n. 1
Cumberland, 184
curtesy, 2, 163, 177
Curtis, Edmund, 25, 191–2, 212, 216, 217
Cusack, Walter, J.I., 57 n. 1, 105
customs and services, writ of, 101

damages assigned to pleaders, 49
damages-cleer, 47–8, 96
Darcy, John, justiciar, vii, 25, 94, 210, 215
darrein presentment: *see* assizes
Davies, Sir John, 37, 189–91, 215
de bonis asportatis, *see* trespass
de divisis faciendis, writ, 1, 2, 173–4; *see also* bounds

de fugitivis et nativis, writ, 1; *see also de nativo habendo*
de libertate probanda, writ, 196
de nativo habendo, writ, 2 n. 1, 196
de rationabilibus divisis, writ, 2 n. 1, 173–4; *see also* bounds
de tallagio non concedendo, 76
debt
  in common bench, 10, 97, 246
  in exchequer, 101–2, 147
  in fair court, 134
  in justiciar's court, 81, 86, 238
  plaints of, 35, 68–70, 71, 76, 86
  by statute merchant, 143, 238
dedimus potestatem, writ, 137
defamation, 87–8, 144, 146, 188, 239
demonstratio, 71, 74
deodands, 110
Dermothyr (? Louth), 224
Derry, 123
  bishop of, *see* Mac Lachlainn
Desmond, earldom and liberty of, 132, 215
  lord of, *see* fitz Gerald
Despenser, Hugh the younger, 121, 131
  liberty, *see* Kilkenny
detinue, 71, 81, 86, 97, 238, 246
  of charters, 102
Deveneis (Deveneys), Grathagh le, *see* Uí Tuathail
  William le, J.I., J.C.P., 94–5
Devon, 22
Dieppe, 103 n. 1
Dies communes in banco (pseudo-statute), 96, 163
Dodingeseles, William, deputy justiciar and justiciar, 21, 43, 152, 157
Dodyng, John, 63 n. 2
Donaldson, A. G., 161
Dorset, 22
dower, 10, 122, 163, 164, 204–5, 244
Down, bishop and cathedral of, 115
Drogheda (Louth and Meath: *all references are to both or to Drogheda-in-Louth only unless Drogheda-in-Meath is specified*)
  borough court of, 103 n. 1, 134 nn. 7 and 8
  burgesses of (*-in-Meath*), 104
  citizens of, 28
  courts held at, 7 n. 8, 32, 33 n. 7, 57, 58 nn. 2 and 3, 65 n. 4, 73, 99, 152, 155, 231–2

INDEX

Drogheda (*cont.*)
  mayor and community of, 51
  steward of (*-in-Meath*), 62
  other references, 34, 49
drunkenness, 61
Dublin
  archbishop of, 141–2, 151, 176, 179–80, 196–7
  liberty of (St Sepulchre), 66, 132
  see also Bicknor; Havering; Sandford
  city
    bench at, *see* Ireland: courts
    borough court of, 16, 18, 19, 72, 134 nn. 7 and 8, 139, 150
    capture of (1170), 196
    castle of, 52; hall of pleas, outside, 52, 82
    cathedrals: Christ Church, 179–85 *passim*; St Patrick's, 38, 94, 101
    citizens of, 28, 29
    common seal of, 144
    council held in, 2
    courts held in, 6–9, 32–3, 57, 65, 72–3, 81–3; Appendixes I, IV and VIII
    mayor and community of, 36, 52 n. 4
    St John without the New Gate, hospital of, 110
    St Mary, abbey of, 179
    St Thomas, abbey of, 114, 122, 125, 130, 144, 148, 151, 224–5
  county
    customs that justiciar did not take assizes in, 57, 65–6
    eyre of: (*1291–2*) 104, 105, 152, 224; (*1310–11*) 93, 99, 104, 105
    sheriff of, 57, 65, 136 n. 3; and adjacent liberties, 12, 117, 119, 123, 127, 129, 130
    see also fitz John (Rory)
Dufford, *see* Ufford
Duleek (Meath), abbot of, 72 n. 3
  prior of, 61–2, 63
Dungarvan (Waterford), 138
Dunquin (Kerry), 214
Dysert O'Dea (Clare), battle of, 29 n.2, 132

East Dean, William of, treasurer of Ireland, 225

Edward I, king
  accusation of cowardice against, 146
  as lord of Ireland before accession to the throne, 14, 15, 16, 17, 20, 207, 219
  as king, 15, 23, 79, 126, 172 n.2, 175, 186, 187
Edward II, king, 130, 131
  as prince of Wales, 112
ejectio firme, see trespass
Eleanor of Provence, queen, 157
elegit, writ of, 146, 167, 195
Ely, bishop of, *see* Hotham
Emly, bishop of, *see* Quantock
énech, 194
England
  chancellor, chancery, Great Seal of, etc., 10, 17, 19, 20, 26–8, 39, 50, 135–7, 139, 206, 207–8, 209 n. 2, 212, 239; *see also* Burnell; Langton
  council of the king in, 14, 15, 18–19, 27, 102, 120, 124, 129, 135, 141, 144, 146, 150–1, 157, 161, 182–3, 185, 214
  courts
    common bench, 8, 66, 80, 94, 96, 118, 157, 180–3, 214
    general eyre, 54, 67, 81, 107–8, 136, 214
    king's bench, 30, 40, 45, 50 n. 3, 66, 67, 74, 80–1, 83, 96, 118, 137, 214; Irish jurisdiction of, 12, 14–19, 22, 81, 83, 84, 119, 131, 139, 140–56, 164, 168–71, 178–85, 214, 215
    exchequer, 99–100; Irish cases in exchequer of pleas, 157–8; *see also* Ireland: courts: exchequer
    Irish cases brought to, ch. VII *passim;* 13–19, 22, 83, 87, 125, 128, 168–71, 178–85, 215, 239, 246; *see also* England: courts king's bench
  liberties, 113, 114, 124
  parliament, 14, 120, 126, 144
  individual parliaments: (*June 1258*) 14; (*Hilary 1290*) 42, 137; (*Easter 1290*) 41, 137, 211; (*Easter 1293*) 183; (*Michaelmas 1293*) 138, 144; (*Trinity 1294*) 125; (*Michaelmas 1295*) 208; (*Easter 1302*) 165; (*Michaelmas 1302*) 128, 138; (*Lent 1305*) 129,

270　INDEX

England (*cont.*)
　130 n. 1, 138, 139; (Michaelmas *1320*) 93, 138, 140
　petitions in, 137–40, 144, 147, 148, 151, 204–5, *see also under individual parliaments and* king: petitions
English, death of, 29, 133–4, 201–2, 204, 208, 209
entry, writs of, 140, 150, 244
　cui in vita, 170–1, 244
　dum non fuit compos mentis, 150, 244
　in the *post*, 5
equity, references to, *de equitate*, 86
exchequer a *placea equitatis*, 99–100
éraic, 202
error, writs of, and examination for, 16, 83, 84, 96, 97, 102, 113, 116–19, 142, 149, 152, 154, 155, 183, 184, 239
esdin, 172 n. 4
escape, 204, 236, 250
escheat, 141–2
　through bastardy, writ of, 3, 245
essoins, essoiners, 32, 49, 84, 154, 160, 231–2, 244
Estden, *see* East Dean
excommunication, 2, 74–5
ex officio procedure, 18, 154, 184, 200
Exeter, Richard of (senior), J.I., J.J.B. (?), deputy justiciar, 10, 41–3, 46, 139, 182; Appendix I
　Richard of (junior), C.J.C.P., 41, 92, 93

false imprisonment, *see* trespass
false judgment, writs of, 83–4, 113, 118–19, 246
false money, 128, 161
Faughart (Louth), battle of, 132
fealty, 153, 178
fees, for bills and writs, 70, 75–6
　of justices and clerks, etc., 9, 42–3, 45, 96, 106
　of pleaders, 49
felons, harbouring of, *see* harbouring
felons' chattels, *see* chattels
Ferns (Wexford), bishop of, 12; *see also* St John
Fersketh (Limerick), 194
fieri facias, 71
fines, final concords, feet of fines, 8, 51, 97, 142, 157 n. 1, 219 n. 1, 245
fines made for offences, 53, 61–3 *passim*, 65, 110, 133, 204, 208; Appendixes V and IX; *see also* pardons
Fingal (Dublin), coroners of, 169
fish, fisheries, royal rights in, 87, 177, 239
fitz Alan, Griffin, J.I., 222
fitz Geoffrey, John, justiciar, 3
fitz Gerald, Agnes, *see* Valence
　Maurice, baron of Offaly, justiciar (*d.* 1257), 3, 6
　Maurice, baron of Offaly (*d.* 1268), 141
　Thomas fitz Maurice, lord of Desmond and keeper of Ireland, 21, 77, 145 n. 2, 151, 227
fitz Henry, Meiler, justiciar, 6
fitz John, Rory, J.C.P., 95
　Thomas, earl of Kildare, justiciar, 28–9, 36, 48, 93, 123, 209
　William, archbishop of Cashel, chancellor and keeper of Ireland, 93, 228, 230
fitz Maurice, Emelina, 145 nn. 2 and 3
　Nicholas, 56 n. 2
　Thomas, *see* fitz Gerald
fitz Richard, Simon, C.J.C.P., 49 n.9
fitz Roger, William, J.I., keeper, 21, 105
fitz Thomas, John, baron of Naas, etc., earl of Kildare, 21, 23, 27, 35, 50 n. 1, 60 n. 5, 123, 133, 141, 146, 151, 157
fitz Warin, Robert, J.I., 221
'five bloods', 205–6
Flanders, countess of, 16
Fleta, 69
Florence, merchant of, 157
folog, 173
forestalling, 11, 61, 113, 236; *see also* Ireland: liberties: pleas reserved to the crown
Forester, Henry, 49 n. 9
Franceys, Adam, 71 n. 2
franchises, *see* Ireland: liberties and Franchises
frankalmoin, 175–6
frankmarriage, 177
fraud, 47, 71, 155
Fressingfield, John of, J.J.B., 45, 46–7, 96, 156

INDEX

fuidir, 194–5
Fulbourn, Stephen of, bishop of Waterford, justiciar, 26, 42, 82 n. 3, 182
Fwelewryght, Thomas son of William, 61 n. 3

Gaius, *Institutes* of, 71 n. 4
gallóglaich, 216–17
Gaveston, Piers, king's lieutenant of Ireland, 23–4, 26, 40, 93, 209
Gervas, John, 49 n. 9
Geynvill, *see* Joinville
Gilbarry (family name), 201
Gloucester, earl of, *see* Clare
Goules, Adam de, 77 n. 2
Gowran (Ballygaveran) (Kilkenny), 32, 57, 58 n. 1, 231
Granson, Otto of, 91, 151
Gwynn, A., 192

hanging, 60, 63, 204, 236, 249
harbouring of felons, 51, 62, 63, 236, 250
Hastings, John, 11
Hatch, John of, J.C.P., 94
Havering, Richard of, archbishop-elect of Dublin, 142
Haye, Walter de la, J.J.B., escheator, deputy justiciar and keeper, 21, 44, 45–6, 146
Hengham, Ralph, C.J.K.B. (England), 180, 181
Henry II, king, 1, 210–11, 212
Henry III, king, 2, 14, 131
Hereford, 22
Eva of, *see* Rochfort
hibernicus, 86, 88 n. 1, 190, 194–6, 206 n. 7, 238; *see also* Ireland: native Irish
highways and passes, obstruction of, 109–10
Hill, William de la, J.C.P., 95
Hilletoun, Peter of, 96 n. 5
Hollywood (Wicklow), 141
homage, 3, 178–86 *passim*, 240, 245
homicide, 60–1, 63, 109, 160, 236, 249; *see also* English, death of; Ireland: native Irish
'horses at arms' (*form of military service?*), 110
hospitality, obligations of, 172
hostages, 35

Hotham, John of, bishop of Ely, 28, 48 n. 1, 52 n. 4
Houghton, John of, J.I., J.J.B., 10 n.4, 45, 46
housebreaking, 108
hue and cry, 133, 250
Hughelot (*personal name*), 61 n. 4
Huscarl, Roger, 6 n. 7
Hynteberg, Philip de, J.I., 221

Idefucoboll (*family name*), 201
'idlemen', 160, 172
indictments, 51, 60, 64, 65, 136, 167, 203, 204
Innocent III, pope, 175
inquisitions, 168
 ad quod damnum, 30, 165
Ireland
 chancellor, chancery, great seal, etc., 3 n. 6, 10, 26–30, 32, 39, 42, 51, 52, 56, 70, 73–4, 76, 78, 87, 92, 93, 116–17, 126–8, 135, 141, 144, 149, 157, 165, 177, 188, 209, 211, 212; *see also* Barford; Quantock; Thornbury
 chief governors, *see* Ireland: justiciar; king's lieutenant; keeper; steward
 council (justiciar's council), 25, 28, 30, 32, 36, 42, 49, 50–1, 125, 142, 146, 147, 148, 149, 162, 177, 182–3, 237
 courts: common (Dublin) bench, ch. IV
  early history of, 7–10, 41
  jurisdiction of, 11, 57, 65–6, 81, 96–103, 118–19; Appendix VII
  justices, clerks and other personnel of, 7–9, 39, 41–2, 51, 62, 63, 81 n.5, 82, 87, 91–6, 116, 128, 130, 144, 148, 149, 163, 164, 168, 169, 185, 224; *see also* Bagod; Bardfield; Benger; le Blond; Bristol; Chedworth; Deveneis; Exeter; fitz John; Fressingfield; Hatch; Hill; Kenley; Littlebury; Ludgate; Ponz; Snitterby; Taff; Thrapston; Wellesley; Willoughby
 rolls of, vii, 9–10, 34, 35 n. 5, 50, 89–91, 101–2, 234, 239; Appendix VI
 transfer and review of cases from, 14, 16–19 *passim*, 83, 97, 124,

272

INDEX

Ireland (cont.)
139, 141–2, 144–5, 149 n. 1, 150, 151, 163–4, 169, 171, 239
other references, 35, 45, 52, 80, 84, 127, 148, 153, 155, 167, 200, 214, 223
courts: county courts, 11–12, 73, 83–4, 97–8, 116, 118, 160, 211, 239, 245, 246; see also under individual counties
courts: the general eyre, 104–11
articles of the eyre, 107–8
jurisdiction of, 65, 81, 98–9, 100–1, 106–11; Appendix IX
justices, clerks and other personnel, 10, 38, 50, 92, 95, 105–6, 116, 149; see also Barry; Bicknor; Canon; Cusack; Deveneis; Exeter; fitz Roger; Houghton; Lenfant; Littlebury; Pinxton; Ponz; Power; St Leger; Wogan (William); Yardley
rolls of, vii, 10, 82, 104–5, 108–10; Appendix VIII
summons to, 106–7
transfer and review of cases from, 16, 83, 97, 139, 144–51 *passim*, 171, 239, 246
other references, 8 n.2, 60
for individual eyres see under names of counties
courts: justices of assize, 47, 56 n.2, 65, 83, 84, 92, 97, 98, 111–12, 147, 151, 152, 168, 170, 239, 246, 247
courts: justices of gaol delivery, 10, 56 n.2, 111; see also general eyre
courts: justices itinerant (i.e. prior to full differentiation of common bench and eyre), 7–9, 14, 181–2
rolls of, Appendix VIII; see also common bench; eyre; *for individual justices see* Bacquepuis; Belvoir; Berkeley; Caister; Exeter; fitz Alan; fitz Warin; Hynteberg; Nottingham; Repentigny; St Albans; St John; Shardlow; Taghmon; Wellesley; Weyland
courts: justices with other special commissions, 10, 25, 36, 56–7, 73, 111–12, 144, 145

courts: the justiciar's bench or court, ch. III
early history and development of, vii, 6–7, 9, 40–5
itineration by, 31–4, 40, 64–6
jurisdiction of, 19, 50–88, 96, 97, 113, 118–19, 214; Appendix V
justices of, 40–7, 56, 92, 94, 96, 105–6; see also Alexander; Birthorpe; le Blond; Brown; Canon; Exeter; Fressingfield; Haye; Houghton; Lenfant; Malton; Wogan (Walter)
lesser personnel, 47–8, 56, 70; see also Appleby; Bellofago; Bourne; Patrick's Church, *and under* attorneys; pleaders; serjeant pleaders
procedure without writ in, 67–81, 102, 167, 238–9
rolls of, 29–33, 41, 44, 52–3, 57–8, 80, 82, 89; Appendix III
sessions of, 23–4, 51–9, Appendix IV
summons to, writ of, 53–7, 60 n.1, 64
transfer and review of cases from, 14, 143–56 *passim*, 164
other references, 94, 98, 163, 168, 169, 170, 177, 185, 204, 246; see also Ireland: justiciar
courts: king's bench (*later form of justiciar's court*), 6, 173
courts: local, borough and seignorial, 1, 13, 84, 98, 118, 133, 134, 204, 246
courts, see also Ireland: exchequer, liberties and franchises; *and* Church: courts
customs of, ch. IX; also 99, 110, 113, 142, 156, 162, 202, 214; see also bail and mainprise; bounds; Brehon law; succession; wardship; wreck
escheator of, 10, 39, 93, 101, 164, 166, 179–80, 184; see also le Brun; de la Haye
exchequer of
barons, chamberlains, chancellors, clerks, and marshal of, 17, 51, 147, 158; see also Brown; Kenley; Montpellier; Thrapston; Uffington
equity of, 99–100, 103

INDEX

Ireland (*cont.*)
jurisdiction of, 11, 28, 76, 97, 99–103, 143, 195; *see also* Ireland: courts: common bench transfer and review of cases from, 16, 127–9, 142, 146, 147, 149, 151, 162
treasurer of Ireland, 26–7, 32, 42, 51, 92, 93, 137, 145, 149, 158; *see also* Barford; East Dean; Islip
treasurer and barons of, 81 n. 5, 135–6, 146, 147, 149, 162
treasurer's deputy, *see* Chedworth
treasury, 41, 81–2, 89
other references, 5, 23, 41, 44, 50, 51, 52, 139, 158
justiciar of, chs II and III *passim*
commissioned to review judgments of justiciar's court, 72, 83
deputies of, 20, 23, 33, 40, 43–4; *see also* Alexander; Burgh (Richard, William); Dodingeseles; Exeter; de la Haye; Lenfant; Malton; Ross; Thornbury
powers conferred upon, 1–2, 26, 27, 29, 136, 196, 209
present in common bench and in exchequer, 91, 100, 127–8, 147
seal of, 70
other references, 138, 157, 174, 177, 180–2, 185, 208
see also Ireland: council *and* courts: justiciar's court
see also Bermingham; Bicknor; Burgh; Butler; Darcy; Dodingeseles; fitz Geoffrey; fitz Gerald; fitz Henry; fitz John; Fulbourn; Marsh; Mortimer; Rochelle; Sandford; Ufford; de Verdun; de Vescy; Wogan
keeper (custos) of, 44; *see also* fitz Gerald; fitz Roger; de la Haye; Sandford
king's lieutenant of, 23, 40; *see also* Gaveston; Mortimer
liberties and franchises in, ch. VI
administration of, 86–7, 115–16
claims to, 109; *see also quo warranto*
county courts in, 11–12, 116, 118
fish royal, franchise of, 177

hanging Irishmen, franchise of, 204
jurisdiction of, 12, 17, 55, 57, 71, 113–14, 133–4
jurors from, 64
pleas reserved to the crown from, 11, 60, 113, 124, 132
transfer and review of cases from, 83–4, 97–9, 113, 116–19, 147
writs, execution and return of, within liberties, 116–17, 130, 132; *see also* Bunratty; Carlow; Carrick; cross-lands; Desmond; Down; Dublin (archbishop of); Kildare; Kilkenny; Leinster; Louth; Meath; Ormonde; Tuam; Ulster; Wexford
marshalsea, 48; *see also* Marshal; *and under individual courts*
native Irish
and English law, ch. X; death of, no felony, 134, 190, 201–3, 212; dower refused to Irish widows, 204–5; grants of English law to, 2, 192, 200, 205–10, 213, 215; incapacity as litigants of, 198–201; testamentary incapacity of, 205
other references, 23, 33–5, 62, 73, 110, 115, 133, 159, 236, 237
see also betaghs; *hibernicus*; Ostmen; villeins; war
parliament
individual parliaments: (*1278*) 4, 172, 193, 203; (*1297*) 25–6, 117; (*1299*) 161; (*Hilary 1310*) 161
other references, 30, 123
Public Record Office of, 9, 89–90
Record Commission, Irish, 31, 89–90, 100, 105, 229, 241, 244, 247
steward of, *see* Rochelle
Islip, Walter of, treasurer, 36, 93

James, Brother, son of John, 61 n. 1
John, king, 1–3, 13, 176, 201, 214, 216
John XXII, pope, see *Remonstrance*
Joinville (Geynvill), Geoffrey de, lord of Trim, 13, 18, 27, 83, 102, 124–31 *passim*, 133, 138 n. 4, 151, 157, 202–3
Jean de, 124
Joan de, 130

Joinville (*cont.*)
  Matilda de (de Lacy), 13, 124–31 *passim*
  liberty, *see* east Meath
  juries, 32, 73, 74, 85, 91, 126, 169, 188, 200
    attaint of, 19, 97, 246
    coroner's, 202
    of presentment, 51, 54–5, 60, 63–4, 108–9
    petty, 61–4, 110, 236

Kegworth, William de, 77 n. 2
Kells (Meath), 73
Kenilworth, siege of, 146
Kenley, Walter of, J.C.P., 95
Kent, Emma of, 139 n. 5
Kerry, county of, 53 n. 1, 66 n. 4, 211 n. 3, 214
  sheriff of, 65 n. 3, 167
Kilculliheen (Waterford), 32, 57
Kildare
  bishop of, 34 n. 5
  city of, 73
    friars minor of, 110
  county and liberty of, 11, 12, 25, 65 nn. 2 and 4, 66 n. 4, 72, 117 n.2, 119, 120, 121–3, 126, 132, 215
    administration, 115
    co-parceners of, 122–3, 144
    coroners of, 108, 109
    court of liberty of, 113 n. 3, 122, 148
    cross-lands of, 108, 114, 144
    earl of, *see* fitz John; fitz Thomas
    eyre of (*1297*), 104, 105, 108–11, 133, 165, 168, 248; Appendix IX
    lord of, *see* de Vescy
    sheriff of, 122; *see also* Sutton
    steward of, 122; *see also* le Brun (Neil); Lenfant (Walter, senior); Malton
    Sir William of (bastard of William de Vescy, *q.v.*), 122
Kilkenny
  city of, 33 n. 7
  county and liberty of, 11, 12, 113 n. 6, 120–1
  court of liberty of, 14, 118–19, 121, 150
  justice in, *see* Sutton
  steward of, 116 nn. 3 and 6, 117, 118, 121; *see also* Power (Arnold)
  see also de Clare; Despenser

Kilmallock) (Kilmehallok) (Limerick), 56, 66 n. 4, 232
king, the (*general aspects of monarchy*)
  lord of Ireland, 135; *see also* Edward I; John
  matters specially touching, 18–19, 81, 125, 145, 147; *see also* charters
  pardons not to be granted without consulting, 28
  peace, the king's, 54–5, 64, 119–20
  petitions to, 137–40, 144, 146, 165, 185; *see also* England: council *and* parliament
  proprietary rights of, 109
Kingsbury, *see* St Albans
Kinsale (Cork), 211 n. 3
Kinsaley (Dublin), 179, 183
knight service, 128, 176, 178–81 *passim*
Knockaney, *see* Any
kynkonges, see cin comfocuis
Kyteler, Alice, 121

Lacy, Hugh de, earl of Meath, 133
  liberty, *see* Meath
  Matilda de, *see* Joinville
  Walter de, earl of Meath (*d.* 1241), 13, 130–1, 133
  Walter de, of Rathwire (*fl.* 1286), 151
  Walter de (*fl.* 1315), 92
Laghles (? Lawless), family, 35–6
Landre, Richard, 77 n. 2
Langton, John, chancellor of England, 126
Lanthony (-by-Gloucester), prior of, 152, 164
larceny, 61–3, 110, 146, 147, 204, 236, 249
law merchant, 18, 238
Ledred, Richard, bishop of Ossory, 121
legal memory, limit of, 115, 176
Leinster, cross-lands of, 112
  liberty of, 11, 15, 18, 117, 120–1; *see also* Carlow; Kildare; Kilkenny; Wexford
  mountains of, 88
  royal family of, *see* Mac Murchada
Lenfant, Walter (senior), J.J.B., deputy justiciar, steward of Kildare, 42–6 *passim*
  Walter (junior), J.I., J.J.B., 45–7, 57 n. 1, 105, 128, 157

INDEX

Leonn, Geoffrey de, 124 n. 4
Joan de, 124 n. 4
Thomas de, 124 n. 4
Lessayn, William, 49 n. 9
Lesse, Roger de, 77 n. 2
Leynz, Adam de, 77 n. 2
Leys (cantred of, Kildare), 108
liberate, writs of, 30, 240
liberum maritagium, *see* frankmarriage
licences, 240
  in mortmain, 165
  to deal in 'pollards', 127
  to heads of family to do justice on those of their name, 35–6
  to treat with felons, 34
  to recover chattels taken by felons, 63, 237
  to proceed without writ, *see* procedure without writ
Limerick, bishop of, 34 n. 5
  city of, 8, 32, 34, 57, 65 n. 2, 134 n. 7, 211; Appendices I, IV and VIII
  county of, 111, 211 n. 3
  eyre of (*1290*), 10, 104, 145, 170–1, 247
  sheriff of, 129
limitation, on assizes, 2; on writ of naifty, 196
Linton, Bernard of, abbot of Arbroath, 198
Lissebon, William, 62 n. 4
Littlebury, Robert of, J.I., J.C.P., 92, 94, 96, 105 n. 2, 248
Louth, county of, 73, 111
  disturbances in (*riota Urgalie*), 24
  earl of, *see* Bermingham
  eyre of (*1301*), 82 n. 4, 104, 139, 165, 248
  liberty of, 132
Loxeudy (Lough Sewdy), *see* Meath; de Verdun
Lucca, merchants of, 101, 158
Ludgate, Simon of, C.J.C.P., 92, 152, 154
Lydon, J. F., 217
Lyt, Richard de, 63 n. 1
Lyuet, Richard de, 61 n. 8

McArny (*family name*), 196
McBren (*family name*), 201 n. 5
MacCarwell, David, archbishop of Cashel, 164 n. 2, 192, 207, 215
McCody (*family name*), 201

McCotyr, Macotere (Cotter), Reginald, 201, n. 5; Maurice, 211
McCurryn, Gilbert, 202 n. 5
McGildowy (*family name*), 201
MacGillemory family, 211
  John, 212
  Reginald, 212
McGothmund, Philip, 211
Mac Lachlainn, Geoffrey, bishop of Derry, 174
McMahons, 63
Mac Maoil Íosa, Nicholas, archbishop of Armagh, 115
MacMurchada, family of, 206
  Muirchertach (Maurice Macmurrough), 32
MacNeill, Eoin, 190, 193, 216–17
Maigue (An Máig, de Magio, Monasternenagh) (Limerick), 31 n. 3
mainour, 134, 203
mainprise, *see* bail
maintenance, 86, 238
Maitland, F. W., 187
Mallow (Cork), 34
Malmesbury, abbey of, 179–83 *passim*
Malton, John of, J.J.B., deputy justiciar, steward of Kildare, 44, 45 n. 1, 46, 122
mandamus, writ of, 17
Manning, Richard, 49
marches, marchers, 29, 34, 36, 43, 62, 204, 209, 237
Marreys, Herbert de, 62 n. 8
marriage (feudal incident), 81, 113, 178–86 *passim*
Marsh, Christina, 157
  Geoffrey, justiciar, 2, 3, 141
Marshal (Mareschal), estates, coparceners of, 11, 15, 18
  John (nephew of Earl William) (I), 48
  John (d. 1316), 48
  Robert, 63 n. 3
  William, Earl (I), 11, 48, 206
  William (d. 1314), 48
mayhem, 69, 134
Maynooth (Kildare), 38
Meath, bishop of, *see* de la Corner; St Leger; Taghmon
  earl of, *see* de Lacy
  east, liberty of, 11, 18 n. 1, 113, 117, 120, 124–31 *passim*, 148, 149, 151, 202–3

INDEX

Meath (*cont.*)
   court, 83, 133
   sheriff, 129, 133
   steward, 83, 117, 124–30 *passim*
   see also Joinville
   liberty of (undivided), 12, 133
   marches of, 43
   royal county of, 72, 73, 172
   eyre of: (*1301–2*), 104, 130, 131; (*1321–4*) 104–7, 130–1
   sheriff of, 65, 95, 117, 126
   royal family, Irish, of, *see* Ua Maíl Shechnaill
   west, liberty of, 13, 117, 123–4; *see also* de Verdun
Mellifont (Louth), abbot of, 143, 152
merchants, 100, 103 n. 1; *see also* Bruges; Florence; Lucca
Merton, council at (1236), 218
Middlesex, 66, **136**
Mills, James, 189–90
misadventure, 109
Monasternenagh, *see* Maigue
Montpellier, Thomas de, 48 n. 1
mort d'ancestor, *see* assizes
Mortimer, Joan (de Joinville), *see* Joinville
   liberty, *see* Louth; Meath
   Roger (*d.* 1282), 16
   Roger (*d.* 1330), king's lieutenant and justiciar, 24, 25, 28, 39, 40, 45 nn. 3 and 5, 83, 92, 93, 95, 130–1, 208–9, 228; Appendix IV
mortmain, 164–6
Morton, Geoffrey of, 112, 144, 146, 151
   Philip of, 61 n. 6
Munster, 9, 111, 207
Murthy (*family name*), 201 n. 1
Muscegros, Robert de, 131

Naas (Kildare), 60 n. 5
   baron of, *see* fitz Thomas
naifty, writ of, 196
nativus, 194, 196
Nettervill, family of, 73
   Nicholas, 67 n. 1
Newcastle McKynegan (Wicklow), 35
New Ross (Wexford), 231
nisi prius, 99
Norfolk, earl of, *see* Bigod; Brotherton
Normandy, 61
Nottingham, Alexander of, J.I., 8 n.5;. Appendix I
   Hugh of, 87
Notton, Robert de, 77 n. 2
novel disseisin, *see* assizes

O'Brien, Obryn, *see* Ua Briain
Ocarran, John, 201 n. 5
Oconyl (*personal name*), 62 n. 6
O'Driscoll (*family name*), 212 n. 2
Offaly, baron of, *see* fitz Gerald; fitz Thomas
   cantred of (Kildare), 108, 109
Offelan, cantred of (Kildare), 109
Offyn (*family name*), 194
Ohalwy (*family name*), 201
Oharill (*family name*), 201
Okethy (Ikeathy) (Kildare), 173
Omurethy, cantred of (Kildare), 108
Onethe (*family name*), 201
Orailly (O'Reilly), Malys (Myles), 88
ordinances made in England for Ireland, 26–8, 101, 116, 161, 162, 185–6
Ormonde, earldom and liberty of, 132, 215
Orpen, G. H., 25, 190–1, 192, 212, 216
Ossory, bishop of, *see* Ledred
Ostmen, 191, 193, 207 n. 5, 210–12
Ototheles, *see* Uí Tuathail
othrus, 173
Otway-Ruthven, J., 192, 213
outlawry, 61, 113, 149, 204, 236, 249
Owen, Roger, 49
Oxfordshire, 22

Palmerston, Palmerstown, *see Villa Palmeri*
pardons, 12, 28–29, 30, 61–2, 63, 65, 166, 209, 236; Appendix IX
Paris, Adam of, 78–9
Patrick's Church, John of, 47
Pax Normannica, 37
peace, keepers of the (*custodes pacis*), 56 n. 2
Pembroke, 20, 22, 38; *see also* de Valence
Petit, Peter le, 77 n. 2, 88
Pevensey, Richard of, 119
Picot, William, 139
Picton (Pembroke), 21
   Joan, heiress of, 37
Pinxton, Thomas of, 47–8
plaints, *see procedure without writ*
pleaders (narratores), 49, 139
   king's, 48–9

INDEX

pleaders (*cont.*)
   see also serjeant pleaders; Fressingfield; McCotyr (Reginald)
pleas of the crown, 11, 54–5, 57–8, 60–5, 109, 113, Appendices v and ix
pledge, blinds principal, 31 n. 3
   principal fails to acquit, 86
   see also bail and mainprise
Plunket, John, 49 n. 9
'pollards' (coins), 127
Ponz, John de, J.I., J.C.P., 49, 92, 94, 95, 110, 111, 112, 115, 155
Power, Arnold, J.I., 36, 106, 131
   Eustace, J.I., 27, 105
precipe in capite, 91
prerogative, royal, 109, 135
prescription, 176
presentment, *see* juries
prisons, prisoners, 36, 48, 54–5, 138
   wrongful imprisonment, 36, 250
   see also trespass
privilegium fori, *see* benefit of clergy
procedendo ad judicium, writ of, 17, 18, 83, 84, 97, 145–50 *passim*, 154, 170, 171, 239
   examples of, Appendix II
procedure without writ (bills, plaints), 32, 50, 54–5, 57–8, 67–79, 84–8 *passim*, 97, 107, 113, 143–4, 149, 156, 159, 160 n.7 167, 188, 199, 200, 203, 218 Appendices IV and V
   licence to employ, 67–70, 77–8
   oral plaints, 67
   see also debt; detinue; trespass, *and* Ireland: courts: general eyre *and* justiciar's bench
prohibition, writ of, 28, 101, 122, 148, 162, 239, 246
proofs of age, 27, 30, 240
protections, 17, 28, 91, 93, 122, 137, 238, 240, 245
purveyance, 160

Quantock (Cantok), Thomas, bishop of Emly and chancellor, 27, 112, 152, 165, 225
quare impedit, 148, 245
quasi-felonia, 147
Quintyn, William, 62 n. 2
quo warranto, 81, 102, 107 n. 3, 109, 114–15, 128, 130–1, 132

rape, 11, 60–1, 113, 236, 238, 249
   plaint (?) of, 86
Rathwire, *see* Lacy
receiving stolen chattels, 110, 249
recognizances, 87, 239, 246
record, courts of, 81, 83–4, 97–8, 117–19
recordari facias loquelam, writ of, 97–8, 118
records, amendment of, 50
Remonstrance of the Irish to John XXII, 189, 193, 198, 201–6 *passim*, 213
Repentigny, Peter de, J.I., Appendix I
replevin, 133, 160, 161, 211–12, 245
Richard II, king, 6
Richard, son of Robert, son of John, 152–6, 168 n. 7
Richardson, H. G., 192, 202, 212–13
   and Sayles, G. O., 14, 48–9, 67, 193, 217
Richey, A. G., 189, 192, 216, 217
right, writs of, 1, 10, 148, 174, 200, 224, 244
robbery, 51, 61, 63, 108, 110, 113, 136, 159, 160, 203, 236, 245, 249
Roche, Stephen, 57 n. 1
Rochelle, Richard de la, steward and justiciar, 14
Rochfort family, 173
   Eva de (of Hereford), 173
   Henry, son of Henry de, 173
   Henry, son of Simon de, 173
   Maurice de, deputy justiciar, 227
   Walter de, 173
Roscommon, castle of, 38
   county of, 73
   town of, 34, 217
Ross (Wexford), 32, 231
   William of, deputy justiciar, 82
Ryvere, Master William de la, 34 n. 5, 67 n. 1, 73 n. 7, 148 n. 1, 150 n. 1, 151, 152–6, 168 n. 7

Sadelhackere, Christina la, 61 n. 10
St Albans, Hugh of, J.I., Appendix I
St David's (Pembroke), 22
St John, Geoffrey of, bishop of Ferns, J.I., Appendix I
St Leger, Thomas, bishop of Meath, J.I., 105
St Sepulchre, liberty of, *see* Dublin, archbishop of
Salisbury, bishop of *and* canon of, *see* de la Corner

Sampford, Nicholas of, 77 n. 2
sanctuary, 63, 236, 250
Sandford, John of, keeper and justiciar, archbishop of Dublin, 10, 21, 43
Sayles, G. O., see Richardson, H. G.
Scotland, 19, 23, 26, 34, 86, 112, 135, 154, 240; see also Bruce
scutage, 101
seisin, livery of, 154
Selioc (Dublin: *possibly* Silliothill, *in* parish of Moone, Kildare), 224
sen-cléithe, 193–5
serjeants (local officials), 84, 86, 87, 112, 114, 121, 123, 130, 160, 250
serjeant pleaders, king's serjeant, 48–9, 50–1
see also Bardfield; le Blond (Richard); Owen; Ponz
Serle, William, 64 n. 4
Shandon (Cork), 136
Shardlow, Robert of, J.I., Appendix I
sheriffs
   appointment of, 135–6
   'book', 60
   misconduct of, 51, 86, 101, 112, 169, 196, 199
   record pleas in courts not of record, 97–8, 118
   summons to, for sessions of justiciar's court, 54–5 and for general eyre, 107
   tourn, 13, 64, 134
   see also under individual counties and liberties
si difficultas clause, see *procedendo*
'Slefblame' (? Slieve Bloom, Offaly), 62
Snitterby, Thomas of, J.C.P., 93 n. 1, 94
socage, 178–86 *passim*
sóer-chéle, sóer-rath, see *célsine*
Somerset, 22
sorcery, 121
Spyne, John de la, 61 n. 1
Staghlogh (*personal name*), 62 n. 5
standard, the king's, 51
Staple, Ordinances of the, 161
statutes, ch. VIII
   English
      application in Ireland, 4–5, 96, 159, 161–71, 215
      interpretation, 98, 145, 151

   Irish, 159–61, 215
   see also Table of Statutes
stocks, 236
subsidy, 78, 200 n. 9
succession, to chattels, custom of, 177
   to chieftaincies, Irish law of, 173
Sugagh, Reymund, 63 n. 5
supersedeas, writ of, 91, 155, 239
Sutton, Gilbert of, 110

Taff, Nicholas, J.C.P., 41
Taghmon, Hugh of, bishop of Meath, J.I., Appendix I
Taloun, Richard, 62 n. 3
Tel, John (*a fictitious name* ?), 87
Telyng, William, 61 n. 9
tenants-in-chief, 18
Thomastown (Kilkenny), Appendix IV
Thomond, 132
   king of, see Ua Briain
Thornbury, Walter of, chancellor and deputy justiciar, 33, 44 n. 5, 185
Thrapston, Henry of, 47, 96
Tipperary, county, 8 n. 1, 57, 111, 132, 181
   eyre of: (*1289*) 10; (*1305–7*) 104, 105, 248
   town, 144, Appendix I (*references may be to county*)
toll, quit of, *see* trespass
Tralee (Kerry), 34, 53 n. 1, 71
treasure-trove, pleas of, reserved to the crown from greater liberties, 11, 113
trespass
   (i) in general
      in common bench, 10, 97, Appendix VII
      in justiciar's court, Appendix V; by writ, 81, 86; by plaint, 68–73, 76, 81, 85–6, 156
      writs of, to be purchased in Ireland, 27, 51, 141
   (ii) subject-matter, 234–5, 238, 245–6
      abduction of wife and chattels, 86, 238
      assault and battery, 68–73 *passim*, 85, 86, 113, 200, 238, 245
      de bonis asportatis, 68–71 *passim*, 85, 86, 238, 245
      contracts, obligations and agreements, 86, 238

INDEX

trespass (*cont.*)
  ejectio firme, 85–6, 238
  false imprisonment, 69, 84, 149, 167, 238, 245
  quit of toll, 86, 238
  rape, 86, 238
  wrongs to plaintiff's Irishman, 86, 199, 238
  other forms, 86, 238, 239, 245–6
Trim, 125
  liberty of, *see* east Meath
  lord of, *see* Joinville
Tuam, archbishop of, 115, 144, 151, 176, 200, 205
Tullow (Carlow), 33
Turner, G. J., 3

Ua Briain, family of, 206
  Conchobar, king of Thomond, 20
  Muirchertach mac Tairdelbaigh, 29 n. 2
Ua Broin, family of, 29 n. 2
Ua Conchobuir, family of, 206
Ua Maíl Shechnaill, family of, 206
Ua Néill, family of, 206
  Domnall, 189, 198
Uffington, David of, 111
Ufford (Dofford), Robert of, justiciar, 6, 19
Uí Tuathail (Ototheles, O'Tooles), 61
  Grathagh le Deveneys, one of the, 34
Ulster, 114, 115, 206
  earl of, *see* Burgh
  liberty of, 12, 33, 84 n. 7, 115–16, 117, 118, 123
Urgalia (Oriel; Louth) *see* Louth

Valence, Agnes de, 141, 146, 151, 157–8
  Aylmer de, 38, 95, 120
  house of, 25
  Joan de, 119, 120
  liberty, *see* Wexford
  William de, 12, 16, 20, 22, 120
Valle, John de, 157–8
  Robert de, 37
venire facias omnes assisas (writ of summons to justiciar's court), 53–7, 60 n. 1, 64, 65, 67, 68, 79
Verdun family, 63, 130–1
  John de, 13
  junior branches, 24, 51
  Nicholas de, 87–8

Theobald (I) de, 139
Theobald (II) de, justiciar, 24, 123, 151, 228
Vescy, Agnes de, 120, 122–3
  William de, lord of Kildare, justiciar, vii, 21, 26, 44 n. 2, 108, 120, 121–3, 138, 144, 146, 148, 151; widow of, 122
vetitum namium, *see* replevin
Vienne, Council of, 205 n. 4
Villa Palmeri (Palmerston or Palmerstown, Dublin), 224
villeins, villeinage, 188, 190, 193, 194, 210
  exception of villeinage and exception of Irishry, 199–200, 205, 206, 207, 211
  see also betaghs; *hibernicus*
voucher of rolls, 170; *see also* warranty

wager of law, *see* compurgation
waifs, *see* chattels
Wales, 19, 22, 45, 113, 125, 130, 187–8, 195 n. 4, 197, 205
war, within Ireland, 23, 24, 26, 30, 35, 43, 51, 52, 62, 236; land of, 34
  elsewhere, 23, 26, 125, 216, 217, 240
  see also Bruce; Scotland
wards, wardship, 163, 167, 245, 246
  Irish customs of wardship, 18 n. 3, 178–86, 214–15
  prerogative wardship, 113
  ravishment of ward, 62, 63, 236
  royal wards, 16, 17, 18, 87, 238
warranty, voucher to, 14, 16, 17, 84, 98, 99, 119, 136–7, 145, 150, 170–1, 199, 225
Warwickshire, 180 n. 4, 183
waste, 150, 163–4, 245
Waterford, bishop of, *see* Fulbourn
  city of, 32, 33 n. 7, 57, 220, 231; priory of St Catharine at, 110
  county of, 65 n. 2, 111; eyre of (*1228*) 7; (*1290*) 104
  Ostmen of, 210–12
Wellesley, Walrand of, J.I., J.C.P., 8 n. 1, 14, 41; Appendix 1
Wendover, Roger of, chronicler, 2
Wentworth, Thomas, earl of Strafford, 165 n. 8
wergild, 190, 202
Westminster, bench at: *see* England: courts: common bench
Westmorland, 184

Wexford, county and liberty of, 11, 12, 17, 22, 34, 113 nn. 4 and 6, 119, 120
  steward of, 22, 32, 117 n. 2, 120
  see also Pevensey; Wogan (John I, Walter II); Sutton
Weyland, William of, J.I., Appendix 1
Wicklow, county of (*not a separate shire in medieval period*), 23, 24, 29 n. 2, 32, 33, 34, 52
  town of, 35
Willoughby, Richard of, C.J.C.P., 92
  Robert of, 52 n. 4
wills, testamentary matters, etc., 74, 174, 177, 205; see also succession
Wiltshire, 180, 183
Winchester, bishopric of (*or* barony of the bishop of), 179, 184
Wiston (Pembroke), 38
Wodeloc, Robert, 64 n. 5
Wogan, Amicia *or* Avicia, 37–8
  Isabella, 37–8
  John (I), justiciar
    career of, 21–6
    family of, 37–8
    historical significance of, 25–6, 217
    and application of English statutes, 96, 163
    and English jurisdiction in Irish cases, 141, 145
    and form of justiciary rolls, 30, 53
    and liberties, 114–15, 117, 126–30 *passim*
    and native Irish, 208, 215
    and procedure without writ, 75–9
    other references to, 34, 36, 40, 44 n. 5, 46, 49, 56, 64, 72, 82, 91, 92, 93, 99, 104, 105, 110, 112, 147, 149, 153, 185, 186, 214, 218, 227–8
  John (II), son of John (I) (?), 37–8
  John, J.J.B. (*person created by the historical imagination*), 25 n. 4
  Margaret, 37
  Thomas, son of John (II) (?), 38

Walter (I), brother of John (I), 38
Walter (II), son of John (I) (?), J.J.B., steward of Wexford, 25 n. 4, 38, 40 n. 2, 45–6
Walter (? III), 38
William, 38
wreck of the sea, 177
writs
  English, as warrants to the Irish chancery, 39
  English, not to be pleaded in Ireland, 27, 51, 141
  judicial, 50, 70 n. 3
  necessity for, if more than forty shillings, or freehold, at issue, 68–72, 76–8
  original, justiciar authorized to issue, 1
  procedure by, enjoined, 75
  registers of, sent to Ireland, 2–3, 174
  sine and *pro dono*, 68
  to be the same in Ireland as in England, 3–4
  see also *accedas ad curiam*; *advowson*; *allocate*; assizes; bounds; *certiorari*; consultation; customs and services; *de divisis faciendis*; *de fugitivis et nativis*; *de libertate probanda*; *de nativo habendo*; *de rationabilibus divisis*; *dedimus potestatem*; *elegit*; entry; error; escheat; false judgment; *fieri facias*; *liberate*; *mandamus*; naifty; *precipe in capite*; *procedendo ad judicium*; protection; *quo warranto*; *recordari facias loquelam*; right; *supersedeas*; trespass; *venire facias omnes assisas*
  see also England: chancellor *and* Ireland: chancellor
'World's End' (*place-name*) (Cork), 211 n. 3

Yardley, Master Philip of, J.I., 106
York, 22

Date

DE PAUL UNIVERSITY LIBRARY
30511000078445
340.09415H236E C001
LPX ENGLISH LAW IN IRELAND, 1290-1324